Justice and International Order:
East and West

Justice and International Order: East and West

RICHARD NED LEBOW
and
FENG ZHANG

OXFORD
UNIVERSITY PRESS

Oxford University Press is a department of the University of Oxford. It furthers
the University's objective of excellence in research, scholarship, and education
by publishing worldwide. Oxford is a registered trade mark of Oxford University
Press in the UK and certain other countries.

Published in the United States of America by Oxford University Press
198 Madison Avenue, New York, NY 10016, United States of America.

Library of Congress Cataloging-in-Publication Data
Names: Lebow, Richard Ned, author.
Title: Justice and International Order: East and West / Richard Ned Lebow, Feng Zhang.
Description: First Edition. | New York : Oxford University Press, [2022] |
Includes bibliographical references and index.
Identifiers: LCCN 2022000228 (print) | LCCN 2022000229 (ebook) |
ISBN 9780197598405 (Paperback) | ISBN 9780197598399 (Hardback) |
ISBN 9780197598412 (ePub)
Subjects: LCSH: Justice—Cross-cultural studies. | Hegemony—United States. |
Confucianism and state—China. | United States—Foreign relations—China. |
China—Foreign relations—United States.
Classification: LCC JC578 .L436 2022 (print) | LCC JC578 (ebook) |
DDC 320.01/1—dc23/eng/20220401
LC record available at https://lccn.loc.gov/2022000228
LC ebook record available at https://lccn.loc.gov/2022000229

DOI: 10.1093/oso/9780197598399.001.0001

1 3 5 7 9 8 6 4 2

Paperback printed by Lakeside Book Company, United States of America
Hardback printed by Bridgeport National Bindery, Inc., United States of America

To all my primary and secondary school teachers,
who would find it hilarious that I coauthored a book about order.
Ned Lebow

To my wife Shu Man and two daughters Han and Yi,
who bring meaning and joy to my life.
Feng Zhang

CONTENTS

PREFACE

This book is a follow-on project to our *Taming Sino-American Rivalry*, published by Oxford University Press in 2020. That volume addressed relations between these behemoths in terms of a conceptual scheme that Ned had developed in an earlier book.[1] It was motivated by our shared beliefs that there are no unresolvable clashes of interest between China and the United States and that there are many shared interests that could best be served by a meaningful accommodation. We reject outright the determinist notion that war between them is the "natural" and "most likely" product of China's recent and phenomenal growth in power.[2]

This book explores some of the most fundamental underlying reasons for common interests: shared values and understandings of justice. In sharp contrast to Samuel Huntington and others who characterize Sino-American conflict as a clash of civilizations, we show just how much the two cultures have in common in their understandings of justice.[3] Fairness and equality are central to both countries, and equality has become the more important of the two in the modern era. These conceptions of justice are packaged differently in the two countries, and in Western and Eastern cultures more generally, but this should not obscure their fundamental similarities. We believe that shared commitments of justice could provide a firm foundation for better understandings, not only between China and the United States, but among other countries as well.

---

[1] Richard Ned Lebow, *Avoiding War, Making Peace* (New York: Palgrave Macmillan, 2017).

[2] See Graham Allison, *Destined for War: Can America and China Escape Thucydides's Trap?* (New York: Barnes & Noble, 2017), for the most historically ill-informed and sloppiest presentation of this argument.

[3] Samuel Huntington, *The Clash of Civilizations and the Remaking of World Order* (New York: Simon & Schuster, 1996).

In this connection we describe the sharp contradictions that currently exist between the principles of fairness and equality and the structure and practice of international relations. We suggest that if both were brought more in line with these principles then everyone would benefit. This would involve important trade-offs between fairness and equality, which are matters of contention in domestic as well as international society. More important, it requires recognition that an international community with some degree of solidarity and legitimacy is not only an important goal but essential to the long-term interests of China and the United States. Americans embraced this truth in the early postwar era but seem to have lost sight of it in recent decades as so many citizens and leaders alike have narrowed their understandings of interest. There is arguably a parallel development in China. Our goal of narrowing the discrepancies between values and practice must be a long-term one, but it is not an impossible or unrealistic objective. We describe some pathways by which changes could come about to stimulate thinking and commitment toward a more harmonious and successful international order.

We were in the process of giving a final read to page proofs when Russia invaded Ukraine in February 2022. It came as a shock to us, as it did to almost everyone else. We were not surprised that the media were filled with "we told you so "assertions by realists and Realpolitikers. Not that they had predicted the invasion but rather that they had a jaundiced view of international relations, which they regard as unchanging in its insecurity, reliance on military force, and periodic acts of aggression by dissatisfied or ambitious leaders and peoples. These commentators maintain that Europeans especially were naïve in thinking that war on their continent was no longer likely, even inconceivable. In their view, international relations has once again revealed its true face, pulling the rug out from underneath liberals who put their faith in institutions and constructivists who trust in common identities.

We reject these critiques. The Russian invasion does indeed indicate that there are leaders who are willing to use force to advance their ends, and to kill without qualms many innocent civilians in the process. Such behavior was once routine and accepted as normal. No longer. The Russian invasion has been nearly universally condemned, support for Ukraine is widespread, and Russia and its leader are increasingly isolated—as are Belarus and its leader. NATO has not responded militarily but economically and diplomatically. Some see this as a sign of weakness but it can also be interpreted as a strength. War is unacceptable to European publics and governments short of defense of a member state attacked from the outside. However, there is nearly universal support for Ukraine and condemnation of Russia. The only dissenters are relatively isolated voices on the far right and left. Europe—the West as a whole—has united in a way never expected by foreign policy analysts, or presumably, Vladimir Putin. Military aid was quickly dispatched to Ukraine and crushing economic sanctions were imposed on Russia.

It is too early to predict what will happen; narratives leading to quite different outcomes are eminently plausible. The worst scenario involves Russian occupation of Ukraine, continuing opposition from Ukrainians in the form of guerrilla warfare, and escalating Russian reprisals, making the country resemble Syria. Such a grim situation would bring about untold suffering, but continuing economic isolation would also severely punish Russia and its leader. It has the potential to lead to his overthrow. More optimistic scenarios lead to a similar outcome with a less prolonged occupation and less suffering. If economic sanctions, local resistance, political isolation, and growing internal opposition to the war and Putin in Russia ultimately compel a Russian military withdrawal, it will be a signal—if costly—victory for all the forces that crude realists dismiss as indeterminate in international relations. It will send powerful signals to other leaders contemplating conquest.

Regardless of the outcome Russia has lost standing, as did the United States in the aftermath of its invasions of Afghanistan and Iraq. To the extent that status and influence are key goals of foreign policy, the Ukrainian invasion will again demonstrate that flexing military muscle in the absence of international authorization is counterproductive. Public opinion establishes the markers of status. In the eighteenth century, conquest conferred status; now it does the reverse. Today, nations gain standing by their wealth and well-being of their citizens, foreign aid programs, cultural and scientific achievements, and service of various kinds to international society. Status increases a state's influence and losing it correspondingly diminishes it.[4]

This political truth points to a deeper flaw in realist reasoning. Realists assume that material capability is the basis for power, and power for influence. These relationships are not so straightforward. Material capability can take many forms and is only one source of power. More important, it does not translate directly into influence. Influence is the ability to convince others to do as you wish. Threats based on military power and bribes based on economic power are sometimes successful but often not. They can also be costly. More successful persuasion relies on convincing people that what you want them to do is in their interest. Success here relies on shared interests and benefits from common identities, rhetorical skills, and a history of prior cooperation. Persuasion of this kind is undercut by threats and bribes, by what can be considered the use of raw power.[5]

[4] For evidence, Richard Ned Lebow, *Why Nations Fight: The Past and Future of War* (Cambridge: Cambridge University Press, 2010), and *Ethics and International Relations: A Tragic Perspective* (Cambridge: Cambridge University Press, 2021).

[5] Richard Ned Lebow and Simon Reich, *Good-Bye Hegemony! Power and Influence in the Global System* (Princeton, NJ: Princeton University Press, 2014); Lebow, *Ethics and International Relations*.

International cooperation in opposing Russia and Belarus in Ukraine is likely to strengthen the common identity of those states and peoples participating and to heighten awareness of their common interests. Depending on the outcome, it has the potential to reinforce the taboo against territorial conquest and the unilateral use of force, strengthen multilateral institutions, and enhance democracy. No verdict can be rendered at this time, and we need to keep an open mind and avoid drawing conclusions that support realism or any other paradigm of international relations.

The Problem of Order

Cranks, hacks, poverty-stricken scholars . . .
Hanging like bats in a world of inverted values,
Folded up in themselves in a world which is
safe and silent:

This is the British Museum Reading Room.
And under the totem poles—the ancient terror—
Between the enormous fluted ionic columns
There seeps from heavily jowled or hawk-like foreign faces
The guttural sorrow of the refugees.
                                                                    —Louis MacNeice[1]

MacNeice's poem, written in the shadow of World War II, describes two disconnected worlds: a largely hidden one of sheltered scholars, and a more visible one of the poor, homeless, and neglected. Scholars today are arguably more engaged than they were in MacNeice's day, and the numbers of refugees and others exposed to violence and exploitation has increased, as has inequality among people and states. Domestic and international order is threatened for a wide range of reasons, and at least some of the leaders and states that have the resources to address these problems turn a blind eye or are committed to self-serving understandings of order that stand in the way of reforms.

International relations scholars have taken diverse positions on order. Some deny the possibility of meaningful change. Others are keen to defend what they describe as the American liberal order. Still others offer thoughtful proposals for change or even transformation. We put ourselves in the last camp. We nevertheless acknowledge how difficult it is to create or reform order at any level of social aggregation, but especially at the international level where society is at its thinnest. At the same time, we recognize the imperative to make the attempt.

This is an unusually ambitious, even foolhardy, book that tackles head on the problem of international order. We define what we mean by order, consider its fundamental requirements, evaluate what passes for the current international

---

[1] Louis MacNeice, "The British Reading Room," *Poetry* 56, no. 11 (May 1940), pp. 66–67.

Justice and International Order: East and West. Richard Ned Lebow and Feng Zhang, Oxford University Press.
© Oxford University Press 2022. DOI: 10.1093/oso/9780197598399.003.0001

order, and suggest how it might be improved. We do not construct a utopia, but offer some alternatives that we think are feasible in the long term. They are admittedly difficult, but not impossible, to achieve for multiple reasons. By describing a workable and largely consensual order and how it would function, we create a goal toward which people can strive. We go further and identify some of the pathways that would lead to a more ordered, peaceful world, one in which the weak and poor as well as the rich and powerful would feel included and rewarded.

Our project rests on four substantive assumptions. First is our belief, widely shared in the international relations literature, that there is something seriously wrong with the current ordering of international order. It is frequently described as an American-dominated, liberal economic and political hierarchy that binds together most developed countries and attempts to compel others to join on terms it dictates. Alternatively, international order has been characterized as a loose great power condominium in which the powerful act as they see fit to advance their material and psychological needs at the expense of everyone else. Either form of hierarchy is based on inequalities and structured to maintain them. To have any prospect of gaining legitimacy hierarchies must to a reasonable degree be justified in the eyes of most participants. This condition is not met at present. Achieving this goal is exceedingly difficult. Ayşe Zarakol astutely observes that "hierarchy does not just shape the behaviours of actors in world politics but rather produces both the actors (or at least their worldview) and the space of world politics in which they act."[2] Asking actors to free themselves of them or transform their structures is not unlike asking leopards to change their spots.

Second is our expectation that neither kind of arrangement can endure in the long term because of the opposition in engenders. To sustain these forms of order, even in the short term, the great powers will increasingly have to rely increasingly on coercion. The three most powerful states, the United States, China, and Russia, already show an increased willingness to use force, threats, and economic pressure to gain desired ends. The goals they seek are often unreasonable and counterproductive, as were the American invasions of Afghanistan and the Russian invasion of Ukraine, as are Chinese efforts to enforce its nine-dash line in the South China Sea. Even when coercion succeeds, it may backfire in the longer term. The George W. Bush administration succeeded in keeping the Taliban from power in Afghanistan and overthrowing Saddam Hussein in Iraq. However, both "victories" were hollow. The United States finally

---

[2] Ayşe Zarakol, "Theorising Hierarchies: An Introduction," in Zarakol, ed., *Hierarchies in World Politics* (Cambridge: Cambridge University Press, 2017), pp. 1–14.

withdrew from Afghanistan, but it and Iraq were the longest—and some would say, least necessary—wars in American history. They seriously affected those who served, leading to large numbers of veterans unable to readjust to civilian life, a significant uptick in suicides, and a radicalization of American life. Veterans were prominent among right-wing militias and among those who occupied the Capitol building in January 2021.[3] It is too early to predict the longer-term costs to Russia of its invasion and occupation of Ukraine.

Third is our recognition that the status quo is never engraved in stone. Contrary to what some realists contend, Hobbesian worlds are neither inevitable nor inescapable. International relations takes place in a society—admittedly a thin one—not in an anarchical world. There is a growing potential to enlarge and deepen global society and by this means create a denser network of institutions to create stronger norms and greater incentives to conform to them. Interestingly, some of the most sophisticated realists, from Machiavelli to E. H. Carr, Hans Morgenthau, and John Herz, believed in and were committed to transforming relations among political units.[4] In an earlier book, Ned Lebow documented how foreign policies in accord with widely accepted norms are more likely to succeed than policies that violate them.[5]

Fourth is our belief that it is wrong to speak of "an international order." International society is only in part ordered, and this order takes multiple forms. There are a plurality of orders, some of them regional, and some of them more global in reach. They cut across national boundaries but often in different domains and to different degrees.[6] Some orders are closely connected with others and some are sharply at odds. All have different degrees of robustness and legitimacy in the eyes of those whom they affect. Their governance is most often multilayered.[7] All to some degree are hierarchical and confer different

---

[3] All Things Considered, "Nearly 1 in 5 Defendants in Capitol Riot Cases Served in the Military," *National Public Radio*, 21 January 2012, https://www.npr.org/2021/01/21/958915267/nearly-one-in-five-defendants-in-capitol-riot-cases-served-in-the-military (accessed 13 March 2021).

[4] Seán P. Molloy, "Pragmatism, Realism and the Ethics of Crisis and Transformation in International Relations," *International Theory* 6, no. 3 (2014), pp. 454–89, and "Machiavelli, Carr and the Impure Ethics of Realism in *The Twenty Years' Crisis*," forthcoming; William E. Scheuermann, *Hans Morgenthau: Realism and Beyond* (Cambridge: Polity, 2009), and *The Realist Case for Global Reform* (Cambridge: Polity, 2011); Richard Ned Lebow, "Machiavelli and Realism," in David Ragazzoni, ed., *Machiavelli's International Thought*, forthcoming.

[5] Richard Ned Lebow, *Ethics and International Relations: A Tragic Perspective* (Cambridge: Cambridge University Press, 2020).

[6] Andrew Hurrell, *On Global Order: Power, Values, and the Constitution of International Society* (Oxford: Oxford University Press, 2007); Chris Reus-Smit, *The Moral Purpose of the State, Culture, Identity, and International Rationality in International Relations* (Princeton, NJ: Princeton University Press, 1999).

[7] Hurrell, *On Global Order*; Michael Zürn, "Global Governance as Multi-Level Governance," in David Levi-Faur, ed., *The Oxford Handbook on Governance*, https://www.oxfordhandbooks.com/

degrees of status on participants. Vincent Pouliot describes them as "international pecking orders."[8]

The biggest barrier to positive change is disbelief in its possibility. Hardcore realists assert that efforts toward this end will only make matters worse.[9] There is little historical evidence in support of this assertion and much to suggest that learning has brought about positive changes in international relations. Consider domestic society, where it was long the conventional wisdom that democracies would inevitably result in the appropriation of the wealth of the rich, that public relief for the poor would discourage people from seeking employment, and that women were biologically incapable of scientific research, corporate management, or political leadership. Most damaging of all, laissez-faire economists pigheadedly insisted that governmental efforts to alleviate famines and poverty would impoverish everyone by interfering with the market. Changes in beliefs made democracy possible, and later, safety nets for the poor, and equal opportunities for women and minorities.

There is a similar pattern in international relations. The frequency of interstate war has steadily declined over the last 400 years.[10] There are multiple causes for this phenomenon but one of the most important has to do with learning. When political elites understood that total wealth was not finite but could be augmented by the division of labor, mechanical sources of energy, and economies of scale, cross-border economic cooperation was seen as beneficial and increasingly important. This insight all but put an end to mercantilism and wars of material aggrandizement; none of the great powers has gone to war against others for material gain since the late eighteenth century. A second wave of learning began in the nineteenth century and concerned the relative merits of collective versus autarkic approaches of security. After fitful starts, collective security has become well-entrenched, most effectively

view/10.1093/oxfordhb/9780199560530.001.0001/oxfordhb-9780199560530-e-51?rskey=TZJ WEo&result=1 (accessed 13 July 2021).

[8] Vincent Pouliot, *Pecking Orders* (Princeton, NJ: Princeton University Press, 2016).

[9] John J. Mearsheimer, *Tragedy of Great Power Politics* and *The Great Delusion: Liberal Dreams and International Realities* (New Haven: Yale University Press, 2019); Barry Posen, *Restraint: A New Foundation for U.S. Grand Strategy* (Ithaca, NY: Cornell University Press, 2015); Stephen M. Walt, *The Hell of Good Intentions: America's Foreign Policy Elite and the Decline of U.S. Primacy* (New York: Farrar, Straus & Giroux, 2018); Charles L. Glaser, "A Flawed Framework: Why the Liberal International Order Framework Is Misguided," *International Security* 43, no. 4 (2019), pp. 51–87.

[10] Quincy Wright, *A Study of War*, rev. ed. (Chicago: University of Chicago Press, 1965 [1942]), vol. 1, pp. 121, 237, 242, 248, 638; Jack S. Levy, *War in the Modern Great Power System, 1495–1975* (Lexington: University Press of Kentucky, 1983), pp. 139–40; Kalevi J. Holsti, *Peace and War: Armed Conflicts and International Order, 1648–1989* (Cambridge: Cambridge University Press, 1991); Kristian Gleditsch, "A Revised List of Wars between and within Independent States, 1816–2002," *International Interactions* 30 (2004), pp. 232–62.

institutionalized in NATO, and an important source of regional and international stability. A third wave of learning, still in its infancy, is bringing about a shift in how states achieve status. Historically, military success was the principal means of gaining standing and recognition as a great power. War is now frowned upon, and states that initiate wars unauthorized by appropriate international organizations lose standing, as the United States did in Iraq and Russia in Ukraine. In its place, alternative, peaceful means of achieving status have emerged (e.g., wealth, technological and cultural achievement, foreign aid and humanitarian assistance, sponsorship of practices regarded as in the common interest). In effect, the three principal motives for war—wealth, security, and status—have increasingly become disengaged from it and recognition is becoming more widespread that war is likely to stand in the way of their attainment.[11]

We are to a great extent prisoners of our beliefs and can sometimes make them into realities. This process is well-documented with regard to educational expectations and ethnic and racial stereotypes.[12] The self-fulling prophecy is a danger we also face in international relations. Advocates of *Realpolitik* constantly warn us that it is naïve and dangerous to put trust in any form of security other than military might. Some realists and power transition theorists insist that war between the United States and China is all but inevitable, or if not, very difficult to avoid. Such a belief encourages policies by both powers that raise the risk of war.[13] Our beliefs and hopes also have the potential to help us transcend limitations thought to be determinative and to transform our world in ways inconceivable to our predecessors. This kind of change has become routine in the modern era but admittedly less evident in international relations. However, as the example of war shows, it is not impossible. Proponents of dramatic change often spit in the wind, but sometimes—for better and worse—the direction of the wind changes and their visions are realized, at least in part. They are then hailed—or reviled—as prophets.

---

[11] Richard Ned Lebow, *Why Nations Fight: The Past and Future of War* (Cambridge: Cambridge University Press, 2010).

[12] Robert K. Merton, "The Self-Fulfilling Prophecy," *Antioch Review* 8, no. 2 (1948), pp. 193–210, and *Social Theory and Social Structure* (New York: Free Press, 1949); Samuel S. Wineburg, "The Self-Fulfillment of the Self-Fulfilling Prophecy," *Educational Researcher* 16, no. 9 (1987), pp. 28–37; William E. Wilkins, "The Concept of a Self-Fulfilling Prophecy," *Sociology of Education* 49, no. 2 (1976), pp. 175–83; James L. Hilton and William von Hippel, "Stereotypes," *Annual Review of Psychology* 47, no. 1 (1996), pp. 237–71; Richard Ned Lebow, *White Britain and Black Ireland: Social Stereotypes and Colonial Policy* (Philadelphia: Institute for the Study of Human Issues, 1976).

[13] For the most egregious and historically inaccurate of these Cassandras, see Graham Allison, *Destined for War: Can America and China Escape Thucydides's Trap?* (Boston: Houghton Mifflin Harcourt, 2017).

We eschew any claim to prophecy and are hardly original in imagining a more cooperative and peaceful world. There is a long tradition of such speculation by such prominent thinkers and politicians as Immanuel Kant, John Cobden, Woodrow Wilson, Jean Monnet, and Mikhail Gorbachev. In China, Kongzi (conventionally known as Confucius, 551–479 BCE), after whom Confucianism is named, imagined a harmonious world five centuries before the Common Era. While none of their visions have been fully realized, these figures and others like them have had a profound effect on the practice of foreign policy and the ordering of international relations. We have avoided great power war since the end of World War II, the longest hiatus in modern history. Until Russia's invasion of Ukraine, we thought Europe has been transformed from the principal source of civil and interstate war into a largely peaceful region. We thought most of its constituted what Karl Deutsch called a "pluralistic security community."[14] Nuclear weapons have, alas, proliferated, but they have not been used since 1945. Regional conflicts have been frequent and sometimes made worse or prolonged by great power backing of one or both sides. Other regional conflicts have been managed to prevent or stop wars. Relations between Russia and the West are tense, as they are between China and the United States. There is reason for concern in light of recent developments, and we can envisage starkly different futures for Europe and the world. Russia and China might draw closer and support each other's territorial designs, making military force once again the arbiter of disputes and raising the prospect of great power war. A more optimistic scenario involves the isolation of Russia and growing opposition at home and in Ukraine to the Russian occupation, undermining Putin's grip on power. His replacement by a more moderate leadership could significantly reduce international tensions. We must bear in mind that progress of any kind, but especially political, is rarely linear in nature.

Our enterprise sits squarely within the tradition of twentieth-century international relations theory. Hardheaded realists like Hans Morgenthau and John Herz did their best to conceptualize the world as it was, but their theories were motivated by visions of transformation. Herz considered the postwar order fragile, like all preceding orders, but thought improvement a realistic goal. Toward this end, he sought to create a synthesis of realism and liberalism anchored in international law.[15] In his mature years, Morgenthau wrote about the

---

[14] Karl W. Deutsch et al., *Political Community and the North Atlantic Area* (Princeton, NJ: Princeton University Press, 1957).

[15] John H. Herz, *Political Realism and Political Idealism* (Chicago: University of Chicago Press, 1951); Peter Stirk, "John H. Herz: Realism and the Fragility of the International Order," *Review of International Studies* 31, no. 2 (2005), pp. 285–306; Casper Sylvest, "John H. Herz and the Resurrection of Classical Realism," *International Relations* 22, no. 4 (2008), pp. 441–55, and "Realism and International Law: The Challenge of John H. Herz," *International Theory* 2, no. 3 (2010), pp. 410–45. William E. Scheuerman, *The Realist Case for Global Reform* (Cambridge: Polity Press, 2011) for a continuation of this tradition.

need to supersede national sovereignty to deal effectively with the twin threats to human survival posed by nuclear weapons and environmental degradation.[16] David Mitrany's conception of functionalism provided one of the intellectual inspirations and pillars of the European project.[17] Karl Deutsch conceived of pluralistic security communities in the mid-1950s, at a time, he thought, that there were only two: Scandinavia and the United States/Canada.[18] Today, almost all of Europe, North America, and the South Pacific qualify, and progress toward it has been made in parts of the Pacific Rim.[19]

International relations theory has encouraged change and ways of achieving it. Even projects that have not succeeded have provided templates for possible change. Alternatively, as in the case of World Federalists, they have provoked critiques that identified more feasible pathways to the same ends.[20] Functionalism and security communities might both be understood in this light, conceived of by Mitrany and Deutsch respectively as more limited, more bottom-up, and more practical pathways to international peace.

[16] Richard Ned Lebow, *The Tragic Vision of Politics: Ethics, Interests, and Orders* (Cambridge: Cambridge University Press, 2003), ch. 5; Seán Molloy, "Truth, Power, Theory: Hans Morgenthau's Formulation of Realism," *Diplomacy and Statecraft* 15, no. 1 (2010), pp. 1–34; William E. Scheuerman, *The Realist Case for Global Reform* (New York: Polity, 2011); Alexander Reichwein, *Hans J. Morgenthau und die Twenty Years' Crisis: Eine kontextualisierte Interpretation des realistischen Denkens in den IB* (London: Palgrave, 2020).

[17] David Mitrany, *A Working Peace System: An Argument for the Functional Development of International Organization* (London: Royal Institute of International Affairs, 1943), and "The Prospect of Integration: Federal or Functional," *Journal of Common Market Studies* 4, no. 2 (1965), pp. 119–49; Cornelia Navari, "David Mitrany and International Functionalism," in David Long and Peter Wilson, eds., *Thinkers of the Twenty Years Crisis: Inter-War Idealism Reassessed* (Oxford: Oxford University Press, 1995), pp. 214–46; Jens Steffek, "The Cosmopolitanism of David Mitrany: Equality, Devolution and Functional Democracy Beyond the State," *International Relations* 29, no. 1 (2014), pp. 23–44; Scheuerman, *Realist Case for Global Reform*, ch. 3.

[18] Deutsch et al., *Political Community and the North Atlantic Area.*

[19] Emanuel Adler and Michael Barnett, eds., *Security Communities* (Cambridge: Cambridge University Press, 1998). For a critique of the concept, Ondrej Ditrych, "Security Community: A Future for a Troubled Concept?" *International Relations* 28, no. 3 (2014), pp. 350–66.

[20] Joseph Preston Baratta, *The Politics of World Federation: United Nations, UN Reform, Atomic Control,* 2 vols. (Westport, CT: Praeger, 2004); Or Rosenboim, *The Emergence of Globalism: Visions of World Order in Britain and the United States, 1939–1950* (Princeton, NJ: Princeton University Press, 2017). For subsequent work in this tradition, Daniele Archibugi, *The Global Commonwealth of Citizens: Toward Cosmopolitan Democracy* (Princeton, NJ: Princeton University Press, 2008); Luis Cabrera, *Political Theory of Global Justice: A Cosmopolitan Case for the World State* (New York: Routledge, 2004), and "Review Article: World Government: Renewed Debate, Persistent Challenges," *European Journal of International Relations* 16, no. 3 (2010), pp. 511–30; Mathias Albert, Gorm Harste, Heikki Patomäki, and Knud Erik Jørgensen, "Introduction: World State Futures," *Cooperation and Conflict* 47, no. 2 (2012), pp. 145–56; Michael Zürn, *A Theory of Global Governance: Authority, Legitimacy, and Contestation* (Oxford: Oxford University Press, 2018).

We offer our book in this progressive spirit. In doing so, we hope to honor our predecessors, keep their tradition alive, and give encouragement to transformative projects. Like them, we offer our bright, forward-looking vision at a very dark and backward moment of history.

Our starting point is order. We maintain that social order consists of legible, predictable behavior in accord with recognized norms.[21] Behavior of this kind has the potential to build solidarity and encourage cooperation, which can construct some degree of common identity. They in turn foster solidarity that helps to cushion shocks and sustain order. The absence of solidarity, meaningful norms, and predictable behavior are the outward signs of disorder. Predictable behavior is possible without solidarity, as in the *favelas* of Rio de Janeiro or the streets of Mogadishu. But it is certain to involve a significant degree of force and predation.[22] An alternative definition of order defines it in terms of arrangements that lead to particular, desired results. Aristotle had this normative conception very much in mind when he described the polis.

In *The Rise and Fall of Political Orders*, Ned Lebow distinguishes top-down from bottom-up orders. Top-down orders rely on rules and procedures that have originated with or are sanctioned and enforced by central authorities. Bottom-up orders are the product of iterative and self-correcting process of trial and error with multiple feedback loops and branches in logic. They are emergent rather than stipulated.[23] These two kinds of orders roughly coincide with state and society. Governments and their associated bureaucracies are unambiguously top-down. Civil society is best characterized as bottom-up. The two kinds of order invariably penetrate the other to some degree. Local governments often combine elements of both top-down and bottom-up orders. Societies of any size and complexity rely on both kinds of order, although totalitarian governments do their best to eliminate bottom-up orders. The coexistence of top-down and bottom-up orders, even when welcomed by governments and people, is never unproblematic.

---

[21] Richard Ned Lebow, *The Rise and Fall of Political Orders* (Cambridge: Cambridge University Press, 2019), pp. 20–21. Also, Jon Elster, *Cement of Society* (New York: Cambridge University Press, 2010); Friedrich V. Kratochwil, *International Order and Foreign Policy: A Theoretical Sketch of Post-War International Politics* (Boulder, CO: Westview, 1978); Bull, *Anarchical Society*, pp. 3–21; Hurrell, *On Global Order*, pp. 2–3.

[22] Ben Pengalese, "The Bastard Child of the Dictatorship: The Comando Vermelho and the Birth of 'Narco-Culture' in Rio de Janeiro," *Luso-Brazilian Review* 45, no. 1 (2008), pp. 118–45; Enrique Desmond Arias and Corinne Davis Rodrigues, "The Myth of Personal Security: Criminal Gangs, Dispute Resolution, and Identity in Rio de Janeiro's Favelas," *Latin American Politics & Society* 48, no. 4 (2006), pp. 53–81; Michael Hechter and Nika Kabiri, "Attaining Social Order in Iraq," in Stathis N. Kalyvas, Ian Shapiro, and Tarek Masoud, eds., *Order, Conflict, and Violence* (Cambridge: Cambridge University Press, 2008), pp. 43–74.

[23] Lebow, *Rise and Fall of Political Orders*, pp. 21–30.

In domestic societies, the top-down/bottom-up distinction maps very roughly on that between state and society. As a general rule, both kinds of order are present and essential in all but the most totalitarian societies. They perform largely separate functions, but functions that are equally necessary. Bottom-up orders become more important when top-down orders are thin or seriously contested, and vice versa. Top-down orders can have multiple layers, as they do in federal states. They can be intrusive or restrictive, a distinction roughly coinciding with the long-standing one between strong and weak states. So too can societies be classified as strong or weak depending on their relative authority vis-à-vis their top-down counterparts.

To become robust, orders must attain some degree of legitimacy. They do so by addressing actor needs, developing and enforcing accepted norms, and building solidarity through collaboration. They must instantiate to some degree the principles of justice on which they are based. It also helps to foster discourses that explain away violations of these principles. Orders decline for the same reasons in reverse: they fail to meet actor needs, the gap between theory and practice becomes more evident and less acceptable, solidarity breaks down, and they lose legitimacy. Particularly damming in this regard are blatant violations of rules and norms by those at the apex of their hierarchies, who are already rewarded disproportionately.[24] At a deeper level, orders become fragile when their justifying discourses lose traction or the principles of justice on which an order is based lose their appeal relative to other principles or formulations of them.[25] The first set of conditions are short-term and very much attributable to agency. The latter are longer-term and more difficult for individual actors to influence. They do so collectively, in largely uncoordinated ways, and with unpredictable consequences.[26]

There is an interactive process between discourses and legitimacy, and between discourses and principles of justice. All historical orders have ultimately collapsed, often from internal revolts or high levels of dissatisfaction that led to politically negotiated transformations. In the modern era, high levels of dissatisfaction are the product of poor performance, but also of discourses that highlight

---

[24] We write during the COVID pandemic when nothing seems to enrage publics as much as violations of lockdown orders by privileged elites. Daisy Fancourt, "People Started Breaking Covid Rules When They Saw Those with Privilege Ignore Them," *Guardian*, 2 January 2021, https://www.theguardian.com/commentisfree/2021/jan/02/follow-covid-restrictions-break-rules-compliance; Leyland Cecco, "Covid Livid: Canadian Fury at Leaders' Holidays amid Other People's Misery," *Guardian*, 8 January 2010, https://www.theguardian.com/world/2021/jan/08/canada-coronavirus-travel-holiday-travel-scandals (both accessed 8 January 2021).

[25] Lebow, *Rise and Fall of Political Orders*; Richard Ned Lebow and Ludvig Norman, eds., *Regime Fragility and Robustness* (Cambridge: Cambridge University Press, 2022) for elaboration.

[26] Lebow, *Rise and Fall of Political Orders*.

these failures and mobilize support for alternatives. Our narrative indicates that the so-called American liberal order is encountering problems of both kinds.

The most robust orders are those where the two kinds of orders are largely compatible in their values and reinforcing in their practices. What works on the street, in everyday life, or in face-to-face encounters in different domains is often the product of trial and error, implicit and explicit communication among actors, and common attempts to maximize certain shared values or goals. To the extent that these values and goals are widely shared, top-down orders that adopt, implement, and enforce them can win wide popular support, demonstrate efficiency, and build solidarity, and legitimacy. This condition is rarely, if ever met. Top-down orders develop a set of values and practices generally determined by what it takes to run a government and bureaucracy. They are invariably at odds in important ways with those of bottom-up orders. Ned Lebow has described such conflicts in healthcare, education, and government. They are most likely to find expression in liminal areas where the authority of the two kinds of orders encounter one another and possibly overlap.[27]

All but the smallest of orders (e.g., hunter-gatherers, kibbutzim) are hierarchical in the sense that some people receive more rewards than others. Any definition of order must accordingly incorporate social rank as one of its the organizing principles. Hierarchy can be another source of norms and solidarity when those toward the top assume responsibilities for helping those beneath them. It can just as easily become a source of conflict, especially if the hierarchy is based on claims not regarded as legitimate by much or most of the population. A good definition of a robust, as opposed to minimal, order would describe it as a hierarchical arrangement, supported by most of its members, that fosters security, self-esteem, and social contact, encourages solidarity, and results in legible, predictable behavior.

International order presents a much greater challenge than do its domestic counterparts. International society is thinner, there is no consensus about principles of justice, there is less solidarity among its peoples and states, it has a long history of disorder and violence, and it lacks social glue. In addition, nationalism is rife and *Realpolitik* is accepted by many powerful political actors as a legitimate way to behave. Domestic orders often benefit from synergy between their top-down and bottom-up components. This too, for reasons we will make clear, is more difficult at the international level.

The differences between international and domestic orders are not absolute, as many commentators assume. For a start, students of international relations routinely exaggerate the homogeneity of culture at the domestic level and its

---

[27] Ibid.

heterogeneity at the international one.[28] Christian Reus-Smit rightly objects to the general treatment of culture as unitary in values and practices and geographically bounded.[29] He properly describes domestic and international societies as "polyvalent, multilayered, riven with fissures, often contradictory, and far from coherently integrated or bounded."[30] There is often as much cultural heterogeneity in domestic as in international society and what homogeneity exists is rarely coterminous with national borders. At the same time, many commentators downplay the many things diverse cultures share in common. The principal goal of the first part of our book, comprising chapters 2–5, is to demonstrate these truths, in the context of China and the West. We show the enormous diversity in understandings of justice in both cultures, but also just how much they share in common.

Another difference to consider is the origin and evolution of orders. Most orders were imposed by force, but many at the domestic level have over time become legitimate and consensual, most often through a process of democratization. China is perhaps a notable exception, as there has been little democratization but government practices have still responded to a significant degree to the desires of its people. All successful domestic orders have to some degree become negotiated, and a few, like the United States, began life this way. This is much less true internationally. Throughout history most orders at the regional level have been imposed and took the form of empires. John Ikenberry famously argued that the postwar American liberal order represented a sharp break with the past because it was negotiated, not imposed. American leaders embedded themselves in economic, political, and military institutions where their country was at best primus inter pares, requiring majority approval for its preferred initiatives.[31]

There is some truth to Ikenberry's claim but his thesis in our view is overstated. The United States has not been nearly as constrained as Ikenberry

[28] For example, Martin Wight, *System of States* (Leicester: Leicester University Press, 1977); Hedley Bull, *The Anarchical Society: A Study of Order in World Politics* (New York: Columbia University Press, 1977); Henry Kissinger, *World Order: Reflections on the Character of Nations and the Course of History* (London: Allen Lane, 2014); Michael Barnett and Martha Finnemore, *Rules for the World: International Organizations is Global Politics* (Ithaca, NY: Cornell University Press, 2001). An exception is Robert Jackson, *Quasi-States: Sovereignty, International Relations, and the Third World* (Cambridge: Cambridge University Press, 1990), and *The Global Covenant: Human Conduct in a World of States* (Oxford: Oxford University Press, 2000).

[29] Christian Reus-Smit, *On Cultural Diversity: International Theory in a World of Difference* (Cambridge: Cambridge University Press, 2018), esp. ch. 3.

[30] Ibid., p. 12.

[31] G. John Ikenberry, *After Victory: Institutions, Strategic Restraint, and the Rebuilding of Order after Major War* (Princeton, NJ: Princeton University Press, 2001).

claimed and has been much less so in the aftermath of the Cold War. Nor were all prior attempts at constructing postwar order hegemonic in origin. The Treaties of Westphalia, the Congress of Vienna, and peacemaking at Versailles were the result of considerable horse-trading among the great powers and also negotiation with lesser powers.[32] The orders they brought into being required considerable further negotiation, and did not last when there was no longer a consensus among the great powers.

All of these orders were nevertheless top-down. They were designed, imposed, or negotiated by a small number of great powers and intended to serve their interests. The American liberal order is no different. What distinguishes Westphalia, the Congress of Vienna, Versailles, and Bretton Woods is that postwar orders were not imposed by a single power but negotiated at multinational conferences. This was not true of empires, imposed by force, whose rules were largely non-negotiable, and whose goals were almost entirely self-centered. But here too we must be careful not to overdraw the distinction. In his study of Chinese, Islamic, and Southeast Asian political orders—most of them empires—Hendryk Spruyt argues that they claimed to be universal in their rule. This created a problem when they had to acknowledge the existence of other authorities without threatening their internal legitimacy. To incorporate other political units into their empires, their legitimation, ordering, and practices had to become "multivocal."[33] Even in empires, therefore, there was some recognition of bottom-up order and the need to incorporate and benefit from it.

Bottom-up order is more important than ever before. There are two primary reasons for this claim. The first, spelled out in detail in the initial part of the book, is the emergence of equality as the primary principle of justice. First evident in the West, but now a global phenomenon, it is one of the significant defining features of the modern era. Top-down orders can only achieve legitimacy by representing, or appearing to represent, the interests and desires of the populace, no longer characterized as "subjects" but as "citizens." This principle and practice, we contend, is also becoming more evident in relations among states.

The second reason is growing interdependence. To the extent to which we can speak of an international order it is not merely a composite or reflection of diverse

---

[32] Derek Croxton, *Peacemaking in Early Modern Europe: Cardinal Mazarin and the Congress of Westphalia, 1643–1648* (Selinsgrove, PA: Susquehanna University Press, 1999), and *Westphalia: The Last Christian Peace* (New York: Palgrave-Macmillan, 2015); Adam Zamyski, *Rites of Peace: The Fall of Napoleon and the Congress of Vienna* (New York: Harper, 2008); Brian E. Vick, *The Congress of Vienna: Power and Politics after Napoleon* (Cambridge, MA: Harvard University Press, 2014); Margaret MacMillan, *Paris 1919: Six Months That Changed the World* (London: John Murray, 2019).

[33] Hendryk Spruyt, *The World Imagined: Collective Beliefs and Political Order in the Sinocentric, Islamic and Southeast Asian International Societies* (Cambridge: Cambridge University Press, 2020). Quote on p. 8.

regional orders, or as the English School described it, a thin veneer of practices based on the Western institution of sovereignty. Political units are connected in ways not envisaged by early postwar theorists. Their economic, political, social, and demographic relationships have become sufficiently intertwined that a country like North Korea—a striking anomaly in this regard—pays a huge price for its relative isolation. Global pandemics, refugees from violent or economically unsuccessful countries, and the climate crisis further intensify the growing sense that we are all in this together and need to find and coordinate common responses to the most pressing problems and threats.

The world requires an order that bridges diverse cultures and practices, accepts the existence and authority of multiple regional orders, and operates more by consensus than great power diktats. It must value bottom-up contributions as much as it does top-down ones and undergo a shift in political gravity in the direction of the former. Its structure and practices must be negotiated, not imposed, and leave ample wiggle room for leaders and states to diverge in at least some of their practices. It must build on shared, or at least negotiated, understandings of justice, and its most powerful units must exercise at least as much self-restraint as they do leadership. Neither condition appears likely in the near future.

To compound these difficulties, there is no consensus about the nature of justice. From time immemorial philosophers have debated its meaning and how it should be applied. We do not engage this controversy. We are less concerned with how people ought to act and more with understanding the ways in which justice is essential to order and might be mobilized toward this end. We want to know something about the development and evolution of diverse conceptions of justice, their implications for political orders, and how similar and different this has been around the globe. As our knowledge is culturally limited, we focus on conceptions of justice that have emerged in China and the West. We use our analysis to consider the character of regional and international orders that might receive the widest support.

We acknowledge that we would benefit by including, say, South Asian, Middle Eastern, and African conceptions of justice. We believe there are differences but also fundamental similarities across almost all cultures so that focusing on China and the West is as good a starting point as any. It also has the advantage of building on conceptions native to North America, Europe, and East Asia, which contain actors absolutely central to any kind of international order. We hope in due course that other scholars will explore conceptions of justice in other cultures and augment, build on, and critique our project.

There are many ways we could structure our comparison of justice discourses. As our ultimate interest is a peaceful and collaborative international order, we focus on categories that seem the most germane to this end. Ours is a purely intellectual exercise, although with an avowedly political goal. We must

accordingly consider the relative appeal and political acceptability of the intellectual traditions we investigate. If we are to build on local understandings
of justice, they must be ones that find wide resonance and political acceptance. At first sight this seems a particular problem for Sino-Western relations
given the striking cultural, intellectual, and historical differences between these
civilizations. We contend that the gulf is not as wide as it appears. Philosophical
traditions in China and the West uphold equality and fairness as central principles of justice, albeit in different expressions and forms, and this is only the most
important of their many similarities or parallels. We believe something like this
holds true for most other cultures, including the Indian subcontinent and the
Middle East. We are not suggesting that competing ideologies, philosophies, or
religions are reconcilable or compatible, only that they build on a common set of
fundamental principles and address a common core of concerns.

Our comparisons within and across cultures are accordingly conducted
with the purpose of finding common ethical ground between East and West.
As principles of justice must provide the foundation for regional and international orders, we want to anchor them in principles that resonate in Eastern and
Western cultures, if not globally. The first part of our book is devoted to this set
of concerns.

Chapter 2 focuses on Western conceptions of justice. This is admittedly a vast
and daunting subject. There is no way a chapter can identify, let alone elaborate, the variety of approaches to this subject. Instead, we make a reductive argument, one that takes the form of a radical claim certain to encounter objections
from those who revel in the diversity of the Western philosophical tradition. We
maintain that all forms of justice build on two underlying principles: fairness
and equality. Fairness stipulates that those who contribute the most should receive the most in return. Equality demands an equal distribution of whatever is
valued. Fairness and equality are constitutive of social harmony and accordingly
universal across human societies. More evidence for their importance derives
from the efforts of all utopias from Plato to Rawls to combine in some way these
two principles of justice.[34]

Fairness and equality are often at odds, although they can sometimes be
reconciled to the general satisfaction of most people. Their formulation, relative
importance, and synergy vary across societies and epochs. In the West—and
also in the East—we observe an historical progression from equality to fairness
and then back to equality. Each stage of development is brought about in part

[34] Plato, Republic and Laws, in Edith Hamilton and Huntington Cairns, eds., Plato: Collected
Dialogues (Princeton, NJ: Princeton University Press, 1989); Thomas More, *Utopia*, ed. George M.
Logan and Robert M. Adams, rev. ed. (Cambridge: Cambridge University Press, 2002); John Rawls,
A Theory of Justice, rev. ed. (Cambridge, MA: Harvard University Press, 1999).

by tensions inherent in the preceding principle. Later in the book we identify the principal tensions and the immanent critiques that both principles readily generate. We describe some of the pathways by which material and ideological changes bring about unanticipated pressures for change. This dialectical progression constitutes a long-term serious threat to order at every level of social aggregation. Regardless of which principle is dominant in any era, the other is invariably present too and may have considerable support. In today's world, not everyone prefers equality to fairness; many people think both appropriate in different, or sometimes, in the same, domains. In the Anglosphere, neoliberalism has reinvigorated the principle of fairness. Different preferences for these principles, often pronounced within societies, greatly exacerbate conflict. They can also serve as a positive source of change to the extent that they encourage compromise, reform, or restructuring and redistribution. Conflicts of this kind have the potential to undercut or strengthen orders. We will argue that conflict over principles is particularly acute in international relations, a major source of conflict, and something that needs to be addressed and muted as a precondition for any kind of consensual order.

Like almost all orders, domestic, regional, and international societies are hierarchical. The minority at the apex receives more in the way of rewards than the rest. The shifting preferences in principles of justice and the tighter connections between material possessions, status, and self-esteem have important implications for how people respond to these inequalities. We argue that the degree of inequality is less important than what the disadvantaged think about it. When equality is the dominant principle, people become correspondingly hostile to hierarchies and more likely to demand that they be flatter, nondiscriminatory, or even negated. To legitimize hierarchies in an age of equality, elites must convince others that their greater material rewards and status are based on achievement and well deserved for the benefits they confer the society as a whole. Liberals have propagated this kind of discourse with mixed results.

Throughout history, ordinary people have had few, if any, ways of redressing grievances. One of the key political features of the modern world is the greater political power of the majority. Democracy has given more people a voice in government, initially through elections, and now more informally through public opinion polls and social media. It is, of course, a matter of debate about whether people in Western democracies have real authority or merely the illusion of it. There is a large literature on the oppressed, given a big impetus by Marxism, and more recently by critical theory, feminist, poststructuralism, and postcolonialism. Writers in these several traditions have documented inequality and injustices and their pernicious effects.

Justice is intended to guide collective as well as individual behavior. In practice, it often functions as a cover for hypocrisy. People pretend to act justly, or claim to do so when they have done the reverse. Immanuel Kant saw an upside to hypocrisy. He observed that most people performed behavior mandated by society because they recognized that it was in their interest to be respected by others. Routinely acting in accord with accepted norms made good behavior habitual. By this means, the "crooked timber" of humanity was able to sustain societies that incorporated principles of justice and expected people to act in terms of them.[35] There is just as much reason to think that people look for ways of circumventing justice and avoiding its obligations when they judge them costly or in some other way disadvantageous. The tension between values and practice is arguably more pronounced in organizations and governments than it is in individuals. There is accordingly a complex, uncertain, and highly context dependent relationship between justice and order. They are only fully represented and reinforcing in utopias. In real worlds, they are more often in conflict, even though all successful orders rest on principles of justice.

Chapter 3 is the first of two chapters on Chinese conceptions of justice. The Chinese understanding that bears the closest resemblance to justice in Western intellectual history is *yi* (義). We accordingly begin with an exploration of Confucian thought on *yi* as justice. *Yi* denotes an achieved sense of appropriateness that enables one to act in a proper manner. Confucians understand *yi* either as a personal virtue, in which case it may be translated as righteousness, or as social standards by which personal conduct is evaluated, in which case it is best rendered as appropriateness. In both cases, Confucians take *yi* to be a moral constraint on the pursuit of material interests. It is a nonutilitarian idea.

Confucians build an elaborate theory of justice with two additional concepts: *ren* (仁, humaneness) and *li* (禮, ritual propriety). They ground justice internally in the emotional foundation of *ren* practiced through the principle of universal but differential care, and identify its external realization in the rules, norms, and institutions of *li*. Justice, in this account, is founded on humaneness and manifested in ritual practices. Confucian justice is based on an elastic ethic of universal but differential care, so it has none of the connotation of an absolute moral standard found in some Western conceptions of justice. As Confucianism takes harmony to be the ultimate goal of social and political order, harmony can be seen as the goal of Confucian justice.

---

[35] Immanuel Kant, "Idea for a Universal History with a Cosmopolitan Purpose," Hans Reiss, ed., H. B. Nisbet, trans., in *Kant's Political Writings*, 2nd ed. (Cambridge: Cambridge University Press, 1991), pp. 41–53, and *Anthropology from a Pragmatic Point of View*, Robert Louden, ed. (Cambridge: Cambridge University Press, 2006); Seán Molloy, *Kant's International Relations: The Political Theology of Perpetual Peace* (Ann Arbor: University of Michigan Press, 2017), pp. 94–96, 100–11.

Confucian justice espouses a strong principle of fairness and a subdued principle of equality. It conceives of fairness in two ways, fairness based on merit, virtue, or status, and fairness based on the reciprocity of obligations. It suggests four senses of equality, equality of human dignity and respect, equality of human nature and especially moral potential, political equality, and equality in friendships. Political equality and the equality of moral potential are largely ideals. In practice, fairness—and the inequality associated with it—is held to be the dominant principle of justice in a hierarchical society dominated by absolute rulers and the educated elite. There is an inescapable tension between fairness and equality in Confucian thought, with fairness nearly always trumping equality.

Chapter 4, our second look at Chinese conceptions of justice, addresses Mohist, Legalist, and Daoist thought. After Confucianism, Mohism offers ancient China's second most elaborate theory of justice. The Mohist theory, however, is an inversion of the Confucian theory. While Confucianism is nonutilitarian, Mohism is the first major theory of consequentialism in Chinese history. It takes justice to be only a means for achieving the utilitarian ends of benefit, especially that of economic wealth and political order. Mohism's most distinctive doctrine is impartial care, within which four conceptions of equality are embedded. These are the moral equality of human beings, equality of reciprocity, corrective equality, and political equality. But, in practice, Mohists are as much in favor of a hierarchical order as are Confucians. Moreover, they exalt a divinely sanctioned fairness based on the will of Heaven, a religious conception alien to Confucianism. As in Confucianism, equality and fairness exist in an uneasy tension in Mohism.

No such tension is apparent in Legalism, for this is a doctrine unconcerned with fairness. Equality it supports with the doctrine that everyone, with the notable exception of the ruler, must be subject to the law of punishments and rewards. If this notion of equality reflects retributive justice, it is a very narrow one because it exempts the ruler from the jurisdiction of law. The ruler is in fact extolled as the sole source of law, and being the lawgiver he sits above law. Indeed, Legalism is infamous for its glorification of the accumulation of state power, the subjugation of the individual to the ruler, the uniformity of thought, and the use of force.

Daoism, like Legalism, contains no tension between equality and fairness, but for a different reason: its defense of equality is so thorough that fairness can find no place. Daoism's radical doctrine of the natural equality of all things derives from its assumption that Dao, a metaphysical entity whose essence is Nature itself, is at once the beginning of all things and the way in which all things pursue their course. Daoism manifests five conceptions of equality, two individualist and three social. The individualist conceptions are equality between Heaven and humans and equality of human beings. The social conceptions are political equality, economic equality, and the equality of thought and expression. Of all the intellectual traditions in Chinese history, Daoism is the most thoroughgoing advocate of equality, and its doctrine of justice is but a doctrine of equality.

Chapter 5 compares Western and Eastern conceptions of justice. There are many ways we could structure this comparison. As our ultimate interest is a peaceful and collaborative international order, we select categories that seem the most germane to this goal. Key here is the shared belief among Chinese and Western philosophers that people everywhere have the same needs and emotions and want to live in just and ordered societies. China and the West both theorize equality and fairness as central principles of order and justice, albeit in different expressions and forms. In China, as in the West, equality has increasingly made inroads vis-à-vis fairness as the dominant principle of justice.

Chinese and Western discourses also recognize the gap that exists between principles of justice and how political and social orders actually function. They devote almost as much effort to urging compliance on people and rulers as they do elaborating the principles that should govern behavior and the domains to which they should be applied. Chinese and Western discourses pursue a parallel line of argument in this connection. Beginning with Kongzi and Plato, they argue that it is in the true self-interest of people to adhere to norms and for elites to conform to their rule packages. Another common feature is the creation by philosophers of better or ideal worlds to which justice principles could lead. They encourage emulation but also stimulate people to view their present world in a more negative light.

There is enormous diversity in the justice discourses of these two regions. In China and the West, competition among rival philosophies and religions has generally been an impediment to solidarity and order. Pluralism and the conflict it engenders nevertheless has its advantages. Chinese and Westerners have learned to some degree how to live with multiple philosophies and value systems. Deep divides remain within both cultures over core values and understandings of justice. These divisions exist in regional and international societies and will, without doubt, continue to characterize them for the foreseeable future. By comparing conceptions of justice within and across cultures, we can gain a better understandings of these conflicts at every level of society. We might also learn something about how the negative consequences of these differences might be muted.

We also stress the similarities across cultures, not in justice discourse, but in the principles that are foundational to them. China and the West build on a shared set of insights into human nature and what is necessary to a happy, successful, and ordered society. We show that the most intense disputes over the meaning of justice is within not between cultures. Our inquiry is more evidence of the absurdity of Samuel Huntington's infamous claim about the "clash of civilizations."[36]

Philosophical traditions reveal varying degrees of malleability. Chinese philosophies appear on the whole less adaptable than their Western counterparts. Confucianism has survived for more than two millennia with a core vocabulary handed down by Kongzi. Since the rise of classical Confucianism, it underwent only two periods of further significant evolution: during the Song-Ming dynasties (960–1644) that gave rise to Neo-Confucianism, and a further reformulation that began in the twentieth century.[37] Daoism gained sophistication over the centuries and spawned a popular religious movement, but no major doctrinal shift occurred. Mohism disappeared from the scene in the last century before the Common Era. Nobody ventured to take Legalism further because its doctrines are too amoral for anyone to uphold publicly, even though in practice many ambitious men followed them with glee.

In the West, deity-anchored philosophies are the most rigid, as is evident with conservative, evangelical sects. Another critical factor is the degree of institutionalization. Highly bureaucratic and top-heavy Roman Catholicism has proven less flexible with regard to ethics than many of its Protestant counterparts. Secular philosophical traditions have evolved more rapidly, as have liberalism, political conservatism, and Marxism. Liberalism—based on equality—and conservatism—rooted in fairness—have evolved considerably in the last 150 years. There are now many competing understandings of these philosophical traditions. The biggest difference between East and West in this regard is the tight control over philosophy in the East in comparison to its openness in the West—countries like Russia aside.

Both sets of religious and philosophical traditions acknowledge human frailty. Confucians understand that their ideals are too lofty for most people to live up to. Kongzi developed those ideals out of a deep concern about the political and moral decay of the Spring and Autumn period (770–475 BCE). In the end, he turned inward and focused on cultivating personal virtues, especially humaneness (*ren*). The Confucian moral vision nevertheless provided a critical inspiration for generations of Chinese literati, contributing to the making of a more humane and just society in spite of ethical violations.[38]

---

[36] Samuel Huntington, *The Clash of Civilizations and the Remaking of World Order* (New York: Simon & Schuster, 1996).

[37] Liu Shu-hsien [劉述先], *Lun rujia zhexue de sange dashidai* [論儒家哲學的三個大時代, The Three Epochs of Confucian Philosophy] (Hong Kong: The Chinese University of Hong Kong Press, 2015).

[38] Feng Zhang, *Chinese Hegemony: Grand Strategy and International Institutions in East Asian History* (Stanford, CA: Stanford University Press, 2015), p. 179.

The Daoist conception of ethical violations is very different. In contrast to Kongzi, Zhuangzi does not advocate a particular way of life as an ethical model to emulate. His ethics of difference holds that a truly moral person "is one who can naturally, spontaneously, and effortlessly recognize and respect the equal value of diverse ways of life."[39] Imposing one's own values and ways of life on others is immoral. Ethical violations take place when people do not regard other ways of life as having equal worth; correspondingly these people can no longer deserve the respect from others. Zhuangzi is not a relativist for whom ethical violations do not occur; he is a virtue ethicist who urges us to respect the difference of others.[40]

Jews and Christians do not expect people to live up to their moral codes. Roman Catholics require confession and allow penance for most sins. Jews have a yearly reckoning with god on Yom Kippur where individuals, acting in conjunction with other members of the community, ask forgiveness for vows they have not honored. The conception of sin and cleansing has spilled over into politics. In Germany, *Vergangenheitsbewältigung* (coming to terms with the past) involves public acceptance of responsibility for Nazi crimes, educational programs, and diverse forms of commemoration.[41] Forgiveness and reconciliation tribunals are an increasing common practice in international relations.[42]

Our analysis of justice discourses indicates that there is more diversity within China and the West than there is between them. We find numerous similarities in individual philosophies in both regions with respect to foundational principles, recognition of the difficulties of putting ethical codes into practice, and responses to violations of them. There is accordingly ample ground on which common action, rooted in common ethical principles, could be based.

Part II begins with chapter 6, which examines the current international order. We open with a discussion of order and different ways of defining it. We

---

[39] Yong Huang, "Respecting Different Ways of Life: A Daoist Ethics of Virtue in the *Zhuangzi*," *Journal of Asian Studies* 69, no. 4 (2020), pp. 1049–69, at p. 1059.

[40] Ibid.

[41] Norbert Frei, *Vergangenheitspolitik. Die Anfänge der Bundesrepublik und die NS-Vergangenheit* (Munich: Beck, 1996); Jeffrey Herf, *Divided Memory: The Nazi Past in the Two Germanys* (Cambridge, MA: Harvard University Press, 1997); Wulf Kansteiner, *In Pursuit of German Memory: History, Television, and Politics after Auschwitz* (Athens: University of Ohio Press, 2006).

[42] Priscilla Hayner, *Unspeakable Truths: Transitional Justice and the Challenge of Truth Commissions*, 2nd ed. (London: Routledge, 2010); Rachel Kerr and Eirin Mobekk, *Peace and Justice: Seeking Accountability after War* (London: Polity, 2007); Naomi Roht-Arriaza and Javier Mariezcurrena, *Transitional Justice in the Twenty-First Century: Beyond Truth versus Justice* (Cambridge: Cambridge University Press, 2007); Richard A. Wilson, *The Politics of Truth and Reconciliation in South Africa: Legitimizing the Post-Apartheid State* (Cambridge: Cambridge University Press, 2001); Rebekka Friedman, *Competing Memories: Truth and Reconciliation in Sierra Leone and Peru* (Cambridge: Cambridge University Press, 2017).

then turn to the question of international order and the extent to which diverse analysts think there is one. Many find it in something they call the "liberal international order" centered on the United States. Others describe a hierarchy in which the great powers establish rules they attempt to enforce but violate at will. Still others highlight a nascent global society, whose institutions have assumed an increasingly important role in global governance.

A review of the relevant literature indicates that orders are defended or criticized on the basis of their goals, how well they achieve them, at what cost, and to whom. These judgments draw on beliefs about what is politically possible and desirable, and this latter judgment ultimately rests on conceptions of what theorists and other analysts think is just. Those supportive of the liberal order describe it as fair in the sense that the more rewards go to those who contribute the most to development and order. Those opposed condemn it for its exploitation and the inequalities. International relations mirrors domestic politics in that the principles of fairness and equality are often at odds. The more powerful an actor, the more likely it is to seek special privileges or advantages and defend them on the basis of fairness. Those who are less powerful mobilize the principle of equality in an effort to restrain the powerful and protect and advance their interests.

There has been a long-term shift away from fairness and toward equality as the preferred principle of justice. It has been a primary cause of domestic and international unrest since the eighteenth century. As early as the first half of the nineteenth century, perceptive aristocrats like Metternich, Talleyrand, and Tocqueville recognized that regimes would henceforth have to be justified in terms of equality.[43] The transition to equality is still under way and a major cause of political conflict on almost every continent. Historically, changes in international society lag behind those in many member states, so the international order has only become subject to growing demands for changes on the basis of equality in the postwar era.[44] This is evident in demands for expanding membership in the Security Council, "G" organizations, and rising opposition to alliances between developed countries and multinational organizations to develop natural resources, whether land- or sea-based, in ways that disadvantage poorer countries.

---

[43] Maurice de Talleyrand-Périgord, *The Correspondence of Charles Maurice de Talleyrand-Périgord and King Louis XVIII during the Congress of Vienna* (New York: Harper & Brothers, 1881), p. 289; Alexis de Tocqueville, *Democracy in America*, trans. and ed. Harvey C. Mansfield and Debra Winthrop (Chicago: University of Chicago Press, 2000), I. 2.9 and II.2.1, pp. 301 and 482.

[44] Some scholars argue the reverse. See Paul Keal, *European Conquest and the Rights of Indigenous Peoples: The Moral Backwardness of International Society* (Cambridge: Cambridge University Press, 2003); Anthony Pagden, *Lord of All the World: Ideologies of Empire in Spain, Britain and France, c. 1500–c. 1800* (New Haven, CT: Yale University Press, 1995).

Hegemony and hierarchies are rooted in the principle of fairness. The current order, whether we describe it as the US-dominated liberal order, or also as a kind of minimal great power condominium, satisfies only one condition of a fairness-based order. It provides special privileges to the powerful, and does so at expense of weaker actors. The United States, its Western European allies, Russia, and China claim privileges on the basis of fairness and abuse their power in blatant ways. Enough of the benefits flow in one direction that they have generated considerable hostility. Much of it is directed against the United States as it is perceived as "top dog" and thus a natural target for the disenfranchised, disgruntled, and humiliated.

Many American liberals claim that the United States lives up to the expectations of a fairness-based order. They assert that by providing security and the conditions for successful development, the Western order has enabled the kind of absolute improvement in security and material well-being that justifies its privileges and rewards. There are undoubtedly countries and populations where this argument resonates (e.g., some parts of Europe, Israel, South Korea, Taiwan) but many others where it does not. Public opinion polls indicate that publics in America's closest allies have significantly revised their opinion of its role in world affairs. It is no longer seen by majorities as an upholder of a system from which they benefit but a principal cause of insecurity and conflict. Liberal American academics do not determine the justness of the liberal order. States and peoples do, and the majority have found the United States and its order wanting. China too is encountering increased criticism as it begins to throw its weight around in the world.

Fairness and equality are both valued, but equality is increasingly seen as the more important of the two and the domains in which it is thought applicable have been extended. Almost everywhere, monarchies and aristocracies gave way to democracies. Not all of these democracies survived, but it is fair to say that everywhere in the West—and now in much of the rest of the world—democracy is perceived as the only legitimate form of government. The application of the principle of equality to regional and international relations was a more recent development. Fairness predominated, and still does to a large degree even though equality has increasingly become the norm. We note as evidence the perceived need for those demanding special status and privileges (e.g., India, Brazil, South Africa) to couch their demands in the language of equality. Hierarchies seen as exploitative are that much less acceptable where equality has become the dominant principle of justice. In such a world, *relative* wealth, status, longevity, and physical well-being assume a much greater importance.

We review critiques of the liberal order and tacit great power concert. Not surprisingly, they boil down to charges that the liberal order does not live up to its principles. Critics further contend that fairness must be balanced by, or give way to, equality. Some emphasize the anger the current order provokes and how efforts by the United States and its allies to police it have produced greater disorder and backlashes inimical to everybody's economic interests and security. Critiques spawn proposals for change and we examine diverse suggestions for reforming the liberal order and for restructuring international relations more generally. We conclude with our own assessment of what would have to be done to reorder international relations in ways to promote more effectively peace and development and reduce current sources of tension and conflict, or at least mitigate their effects. This analysis forms the basis for the next two chapters that explore different possible orders.

There is much talk among reformers about regional order. However, there is no reason to think that a world organized around such orders would be any less coercive than their top-down counterparts. Perhaps the best way to achieve a more peaceful and consensual order is to create incentives likely to reduce the use of violence and other forms of coercion. Such an arrangement would rely on bottom-up and top-down orders that are regional and international in scope, involve extensive negotiation at all levels, and rely more on carrots than sticks. Whatever arrangements come into place would attempt to address the security, material, and status needs of those who are currently most deprived, but also speak to the needs of regional and great powers that feel undervalued.

Putting such an order together from scratch is undeniably a utopian project. Rather, we must work with what is at hand, rely on bricolage more than de novo design, and move toward our objective in a piecemeal and drawn-out way. Progress of this kind would involve a number of bilateral as well as multilateral agreements put in place after the widest possible consultation. Above all, it requires a shift in thinking in many of the world's capitals. This is essential but, alas, the most difficult task of all.

Chapters 7 and 8 offer our thoughts about how more and better orders might function in international relations. Our suggestions explore several different pathways to order. They aspire to do more than reduce the likelihood of interstate war. Our goal is to create more substantial orders that incorporate bottom-up and top-down components and address needs not only for physical security and material well-being but also for status and self-esteem.

Andrew Hurrell distinguishes between pluralist and solidarist approaches to international relations.[45] Pluralists envisage a limited society of sovereign states that at best can mitigate the conflicts that arises from their clashes over interest and identity by means of hierarchy and the balance of power.[46] Such an order

[45] Hurrell, *On Global Order*, pp. 2–3.
[46] Ibid., ch. 2 for elaboration.

might be capable, in the words of Raymond Aron, of establishing the "minimum conditions of coexistence."[47] Solidarists stresses the importance of an international community capable of cooperating to achieve a wider range of goals. They emphasize the role of institutions and norms in rule-making and governance. Both kinds of order consider states the essential actors, although solidarists also envisage federal regional or international orders created by states. Both are top-down phenomena.[48]

In the postwar era, Hurrell notes, a third approach to global order emerged. Growing out of liberal solidarism, "complex governance" emphasizes what we describe as bottom-up order.[49] Its diverse proponents contend that the complexity of regional and global rule-making must involve private businesses, non-profit organizations, and movements comprising a global civil society in addition to states. This is because they articulate values and goals increasingly absorbed by international institutions that have steadily eroded the distinctions between international and domestic and public and private spheres of law, business, and government.[50]

All three formulations have their proponents. Their differences are political as well as intellectual. In the pluralist camp we find realists who deny or minimize the significance of non-state actors and warn against placing trust in international institutions versus armed forces and alliances. Neo-liberals can also be considered pluralists to the extent they embrace the regulatory state as a means of protecting and isolating markets from democratic intervention and governance at the national, regional, and international levels.[51] Liberal institutionalists should for the most part be considered solidarists, and most constructivists advocate complex governance.

Hurrell argues, correctly in our view, that any framing of order in pluralist terms is too narrow, impractical, and probably politically unworkable.[52] Equally impractical would be efforts to bypass states and build order solely on the basis of a still very thin global civil society. This is because it is deeply divided on issues of religion, political and social values, and, more broadly speaking, culture.[53]

[47] Raymond Aron, as reported by Stanley Hoffman, "Conference Report on the Conditions of World Order," *Daedalus* 9, no. 52 (1966), pp. 455–78.

[48] Hurrell, *On Global Order*, ch. 3 for elaboration.

[49] Ibid., ch. 4 for elaboration.

[50] Commission on Global Governance, *Our Global Neighborhood* (New York: Oxford University Press, 1995).

[51] Quinn Slobodian, *Globalists: The End of Empire and the Birth of Neoliberalism* (Cambridge, MA: Harvard University Press, 2018).

[52] Hurrell, *On Global Order*, p. 25.

[53] Amartya Sen, *Inequality Reexamined* (Oxford: Oxford University Press, 1992); Hurrell, *On Global Order*, p. 40.

As noted, pluralists insist that a weak order based on the balance of power is the best the world can hope for. They dismiss liberal attempts to build order as unworkable and dangerous. Their claims are buttressed by recent events but also represent scare tactics intended to make their predictions self-fulfilling. Equally questionable are claims by those in the complex interdependence camp that states would decline in authority relative to what we call bottom-up forms of order. Hurrell is probably right again in his expectation that states will continue to dominate international relations but that they and inter-state groups will be more responsive to and affected by a range of non-state actors.[54] This has long been evident when it comes to economic policy, and is increasingly apparent in other domains, including law, security, science, health, and the environment.[55]

Our designs for world order are rooted in solidarist and complex governance approaches. They seek to encourage a thicker international order and society that acknowledges states as still the most important actors but creates more representation for less powerful states and the institutions of global society. We start by discussion Sino-American relations and then expand our discussion to the widest range of state and non-state actors. Stitching together a better order together from scratch is a utopian project. Rather, we must work with what is at hand and seek to build on it or transform it, where necessary. Progress of this kind would involve a number of bilateral as well as multilateral agreements, only put in place after the widest possible consultation. Above all, it demands a shift in thinking on the part of political leaders and their recognition that changes that make order more acceptable to weaker and poorer peoples and states serve their longer-term interests.

In chapter 7 we develop a framework for Sino-American relations based on mutually acceptable formulations of the principles of fairness and equality. We begin by documenting how policies at odds with these principles have intensified mistrust and exacerbated conflict between the two countries. We argue for the importance of fairness and equality in managing disputes and show how this might work in six major areas of contention: status, ideology, security, economy, technology, and society. Key to our argument is a tragic understanding of politics, and its emphasis on the dangers of viewing the world entirely through the lenses of one's values and goals and of emphasizing the benefits of conflict over those of cooperation. Altering the trajectory of Sino-American relations, let alone transforming it, depends on process as much as it does on reframing of the goals each country seeks. Reciprocity in its several dimensions must be

---

[54] Hurrell, *On Global Order*, pp. 97–98.
[55] Commission on Global Governance, *Our Global Neighborhood*.

made a central feature of process, and we illustrate several ways in which this might be implemented. Rethinking how long-standing goals can be achieved in a less confrontational manner and restructuring dialogue and diplomacy have the potential to reduce tensions and mistrust. They might even transform an increasingly acute confrontation into a relationship of benign competition and sector-specific cooperation.

Chapter 8 moves from bilateral to multilateral relations and extends our discussion of order to the global level. Our analysis is based on the same principles of justice we used to restructure Sino-American relations, with some modifications. It describes minor and major pathways to orders that give greater emphasis to equality, but in a way that satisfies the interests and status of those committed to fairness. These two principles cannot be fully reconciled outside of utopias, but conflicts between them can be reduced or finessed and an order created that many diverse states and peoples would have a stronger interest in supporting. A more robust order in turn would enable many more practical and symbolic rewards.

Here, too, process is important. Less wealthy and less powerful political units, especially those of the Global South, must be made to feel like valued participants whose concerns are listened to and addressed in any attempt to reform or restructure order. Historically, multilateral negotiations, even when involving only a small number of parties, have usually been organized around the principle of fairness, with the more powerful actors making the most important decisions and often behind closed doors. Success requires addressing the interests and needs for recognition and self-esteem of large numbers of actors, and this can only be done through a process that is largely, although certainly not entirely, egalitarian and has a significant bottom-up component.

Working within these guidelines, we explore several kinds of possible orders and pathways to them. None of the orders and pathways are entirely distinct. We treat orders and pathways separately and sequentially. If any significant change ever comes about, we recognize that it is almost certain to be partial rather than total and achieved in the longer rather than short term. Our orders accordingly represent something akin to ideal types but are nevertheless useful, perhaps even necessary, to stimulate debate and serve as a catalyst for political action.

Chapter 9, our conclusion, briefly reviews our effort to explore principles of justice in the West and China and find common ground for a more productive and peaceful relationship. It is a relationship that would serve well the most important interests of both countries. The principal barrier in the way of such an accommodation is the deep-seated emotional commitment to cultural superiority that characterizes American and Chinese culture. It prompts leaders and citizens of both countries to view the other as a rival and their relationship as something close to a zero-sum game. A secondary impediment is their very different political systems. America's political and economic liberalism confronts China's authoritarianism and prompts leaders and opinion leaders in both countries to perceive the other as a threat. Each superpower, moreover, behaves in ways that appear to challenge the other's core values. Some of these differences, we suggest, can be designed around and other finessed. This requires self-restraint in policy and rhetoric.

Ironically, the mutual sense of superiority could in theory be exploited to bring about cooperation based on the idea of a condominium. This might ease Sino-American tensions but at the expense of heightening them with everyone else. A more constructive way of gaining status would be for both countries to take the lead in ordering the world in ways more beneficial to third parties, including middle powers and the presently disadvantaged countries of the Global South. The model here is the kind of clientalist relationship theorized and practiced by the ancient Greeks and imperial China. It needs some reformulation, as it foregrounds fairness over equality. It is nevertheless a useful starting point for our inquiry. Our goal in this chapter is to think about the "fit" and implications of improvements and accommodation in Sino-American relations for world order. We also consider the ways in which changes in global order might affect Sino-American relations.

We began our inquiry with a discussion of justice and its relevance to accommodation and global order. We examined Eastern and Western ethical traditions looking for similarities and differences with the aim of finding mutually acceptable principles that could provide the basis for Sino-American accommodation and perhaps a reordering of global relationships. We conclude by considering the problem of global versus national justice. Just how do the principles of fairness and equality, on which we have focused, relate and contribute to the existing literature on global justice? Drawing on conceptions derived from the Confucian classic *Great Learning*, we offer a new perspective on these relationships.

We want to close this chapter by drawing reader attention back to the fundamental philosophical move that we make. This is the claim that more or less all principles of justice can be reduced to those of fairness and equality. Each has ancient and modern definitions, and we offer not a full genealogy of fairness and equality in the West, but an account of how these two concepts were understood as quite distinct and directly antagonistic in ancient times, how each has acquired secondary definitions in modern times, and how utopians, from Plato to Rawls, have tried to combine them. We also discuss how the two principles of justice have been blurred, even made interchangeable, in contemporary parlance, especially in the Anglosphere. In China, we show how different schools of thought have addressed fairness and equality, sometimes treating them as underlying principles of order and at other times seeing them as the product of good order.

We make the case for the analytical utility of keeping the concepts of fairness and equality distinct. We cite numerous surveys and experiments that demonstrate the nearly global preference for equality in the modern era, but also the continuing relevance of fairness. People almost everywhere recognize the need to make trade-offs between these two principles but differ about the domains in which one or the other should be dominant. On the whole, however, there is overwhelming qualitative and quantitative evidence in support of the dominance of equality in most domains, but also for the continuing relevance of fairness.

Focusing on these two principles of justice reflects, or nicely captures, what people have believed over the ages and across cultures. It is also central to any analysis of what people think is the appropriate distribution of material goods and other rewards. Traditional and modern definitions of fairness and equality are largely but not only applied to distributive justice. We nevertheless discuss and incorporate concerns for status and acceptable treatment in our definitions and discussion. We use both concepts, not as descriptions of reality, but as Weberian ideal types to measure what people advocate and to assess distributions found in practice.

PART I

2

Justice in the West

All political systems, from tribal groupings to states, make authoritative decisions about the distribution of power, status, and wealth. Some small societies aside, these rewards are unequally distributed. Some people get more—often a lot more—than everyone else. To legitimize the resulting hierarchies societies must convince people that they are somehow justified. Toward this end they invent and propagate theodicies and principles of justice. The former invoke deities and past transgressions to justify present-day inequality and suffering. The latter rely on arguments, often claiming divine sanction, about the proper and necessary ordering of society. Principles of justice are equally important as guides for structuring relations among members of a society. They make behavior more predictable and channel it down pathways regarded as beneficial for the society as a whole.[1]

Principles of justice are universal to developed societies. They are just as evident, although not theorized, among hunter-gatherers.[2] Tyrannies aside, all governments claim to rest on principles of justice, and even some tyrannies make this claim. Principles of justice are enshrined in constitutions and inculcated and reinforced through education, official memory, and communal enactments. Principles of justice are double-edged swords. They justify hierarchies and sustain order by making behavior more predictable, but they also make demands on those at the apex of the hierarchy. They must live up to these principles of justice or arouse envy and dissatisfaction and possibly make their privileged positions

---

[1] Richard Ned Lebow, *The Rise and Fall of Political Orders* (Cambridge: Cambridge University Press, 2018), on justice as an ordering principle of society and how it is foundation to social and political orders.

[2] Colin M. Turnbull, *The Forest People* (New York: Simon & Schuster, 1964), pp. 110–14; Richard B. Lee, *The Dobe Ju/'hoansi*, 3rd ed. (Toronto: Wadsworth, 2003), pp. 109–24; Megan Biesele and Robert K. Hitchcock, *The Ju/'hoan San of Nyae Nyae and Namibian Independence* (New York: Berghahn, 2011), pp. 65–90.

Justice and International Order: East and West. Richard Ned Lebow and Feng Zhang, Oxford University Press.
© Oxford University Press 2022. DOI: 10.1093/oso/9780197598399.003.0002

untenable. Regardless of the principle or principles of justice on which a society rests, there is inevitably a large gap between theory and practice. To reduce or overcome whatever opposition this arouses, elites propagate discourses to justify or explain away these discrepancies.

Ceteris paribus, the survival of political orders depends upon widely accepted principles of justice, some degree of elite conformity to practices based on these principles, and discourses that justify the discrepancy between theory and practice. Failure to meet any of these conditions can make a political order fragile, and failure to meet any of them is almost certain to do so. Orders not based on justice are generally regarded as tyrannies, and Aristotle, Machiavelli, and Max Weber rightly describe them as the shortest-lived of all regime types. Depending on the circumstances, perceptions of even moderate fragility can encourage a cycle of opposition, repression, and rebellion.[3] Alternatively, as in East Germany, they can result in a mass outpouring of dissent if and when the government looks weak and indecisive.

Justice is a fundamental human concern but is not the only one. People crave security, intimacy, and material well-being. If justice is the foundation of order, it is generally a prerequisite for these other goals because they require a stable social and political order.[4] In an ideal world, justice and order would be mutually reinforcing, as they are in utopias. This is hardly ever the case in real worlds. They are invariably to some degree at odds, and often very much so. Justice is accordingly an ideal that societies may approach but never achieve. For much of history—East and West—people had low expectations of justice. At best, it was another elite benefit, leading many of the privileged to develop a strong sense of justice as a matter of self-interest.

Groups and individuals lower down the hierarchy would later invoke principles of justice and practices on the grounds that they should be universal in their application. Magna Carta is a case in point. In 1215, barons, invoking principles of justice, forced King John of England to promise to uphold church rights, refrain from their illegal imprisonment, and guarantee access to swift justice, and they imposed limitations on feudal payments to the Crown. Neither king nor barons honored their commitments. The charter was annulled by Pope Innocent III, leading to the First Barons' War.[5] There was renewed interest in

---

[3] Richard Ned Lebow and Ludwig Norman, eds., *Robustness and Fragility: Perceptions and Consequences* (Cambridge: Cambridge University Press, 2022), on the complex relationship between perceptions of robustness and fragility, their policy consequences, and the often unpredictable results of these policies.

[4] Lebow, *Rise and Fall of Political Orders*, ch. 1, on the distinction and relationship between social and political orders.

[5] James C. Holt, *Magna Carta*, 3rd ed. (Cambridge: Cambridge University Press, 2015); Thomas Garden Barnes, *Shaping the Common Law: From Glanvill to Hale, 1188–1688* (Stanford, CA: Stanford University Press, 2008).

Magna Carta in the sixteenth century, when lawyers and historians invented the myth of an ancient English constitution dating back to Anglo-Saxon times that guaranteed individual English freedoms. They claimed that they had been brushed aside by the Normans and that Magna Carta was a popular attempt to restore such rights as habeas corpus and the powers of parliament. In the seventeenth century, Edward Coke mobilized Magna Carta against the Stuarts' appeal to the divine right of kings. The political myth of Magna Carta and its protection of ancient personal liberties persisted after the Glorious Revolution of 1688. It influenced the early American colonists in the Thirteen Colonies and the formation of the US Constitution.[6] Each of these moves was motivated by attempts to justify political change and relied on fanciful readings of the past that made it appear that the liberties in question were traditional and that they were merely restoring the status quo.

Justice is accordingly a source of both solidarity and conflict. The former builds on widely shared conceptions of what is right and how it should be instantiated in practice. The latter arises from conflicts about interpretations of principles of justice or those between principles of justice, the domains in which they apply, and just how they should shape practice. Sometimes justice is mobilized as a rationalization for what people want to do for other reasons, but perhaps just as often it determines how people approach a problem. Disagreements about many issues can readily be settled by compromise; each side settles from something less than it wanted. This is more difficult to do when the problem has been framed as one of justice and presented in the language of justice as opposed to that of interest. Actors are much less willing to compromise in these circumstances. Aeschylus and Sophocles explore both kinds of situation, and their plays dramatize the dangers to individuals and their communities of rigid adherence to any principle of justice.[7]

Justice

Justice is a notoriously difficult concept to define, as Plato demonstrates in his *Republic*. Cephalus, a representative of the commercial class, confidently asserts

---

[6] Claire Breay and Julian Harrison, eds., *Magna Carta: Law, Liberty, Legacy* (London: The British Library, 2015); Charles Black, *A New Birth of Freedom: Human Rights, Named and Unnamed* (New Haven, CT: Yale University Press, 1999); Paulina Kewes, *The Uses of History in Early Modern England* (Berkeley: University of California Press, 2006).

[7] Richard Ned Lebow, *Ethics and International Relations: A Tragic Perspective* (Cambridge: Cambridge University Press, 2020), ch. 2.

that justice is speaking the truth and paying one's debts.[8] Polemarchus offers the traditional understanding of justice as "doing good to friends and harm to enemies."[9] Thrasymachus, speaking as a radical Sophist, insists that justice is nothing more than "the interest of the stronger."[10] Socrates challenges these accounts and the jaundiced claim of Glaucon that people only act justly for instrumental reasons. Socrates tries to persuade his interlocutors that justice is a quality of soul that leads people to act properly because it promotes their happiness. It encourages self-mastery over appetite and *thumos* (spirit), leading people to behave in ways that benefit, not only themselves, but the community at large. Socrates' conception of justice rests on the principle of fairness, which, he believes, enables the harmonious functioning of the polis. An ideal society has three classes of people: producers (craftsmen, farmers, artisans, etc.), auxiliaries (warriors), and guardians (rulers). Justice consists of ordered relations among three classes, which requires each group to perform its proper function.[11] The several definitions of justice that Socrates interrogates find contemporary resonance, as does his own account.[12]

Homer, the Greek playwrights, philosophers like Plato and Aristotle, and the Hebrew prophets are founders and early exemplars of a long-standing tradition in the West to discover, propagate, and defend principles of justice appropriate to individual and collective behavior. These principles are invariably put forward as universal, not local, in their import. Until the Enlightenment they were most often justified with reference to supra-human authority in the form of deities or a deity.[13]

There is no getting around the subjective nature of these efforts. They reflect the values of their societies—or reactions against them—and the personal

---

[8] Plato, *Republic*, 328e–31d, in Edith Hamilton and Huntington Cairns, eds., *The Collected Dialogues* (Princeton, NJ: Princeton University Press, 1961).

[9] Ibid., 332c.

[10] Ibid., 338c.

[11] Ibid., books II–IV.

[12] David Miller, *Principles of Social Justice* (Cambridge, MA: Harvard University Press, 1999), p. 21, characterizes justice as a social virtue that tells us how to order our relationships, what we must rightly do for one another; Stuart Hampshire, *Innocence and Experience Innocence and Experience* (London: Allen Lane, 1989), p. 63, writes that "from the earliest time to today, justice refers to an ordered and reasonable procedure of weighing claims." John Rawls, *A Theory of Justice*, rev. ed. (Cambridge, MA: Harvard University Press, 1999), equates it with fairness, which he describes as a society of free citizens holding equal basic rights and cooperating within an egalitarian economic system. Alasdair MacIntyre, *Whose Justice? Which Rationality?* (Notre Dame, IN: University of Notre Dame Press, 1988), p. 39, says, "Justice is a disposition to give to each person, including oneself, what that person deserves and to treat no one in a way incompatible with their deserts."

[13] Plato is an obvious exception.

beliefs and projects of those advancing or attacking these values.[14] Immanuel Kant offers a telling example. His elaborate, creative, and enormously influential turn to reason to construct an ethical code ended up producing a justification for the conventional Protestant morality of the late eighteenth century. A century later, Friedrich Nietzsche and Max Weber famously observed that the gods had departed from the skies.[15] In the absence of a belief in a cosmic order, it was no longer possible to find an acceptable foundation for ethics or justice. Competing understandings emerged—as they had in fifth-century Greece for much the same reason. They flourished in a way they never had before given the emergence of civil society, the rule of law, and the guarantees of freedom of speech and assembly, all central features of the liberal democratic tradition. As Weber rightly noted, there is no logical way of adjudicating among these competing conceptions.[16] More recently, the universality assumption has also come under fire, with communitarians insisting that conceptions of justice and ethical practices are local in nature.[17]

This inescapable pluralism has not put an end to the Kantian project, Christianity, or Marxism. They continue to have adherents, as do a host of other philosophical projects, humanistic ones, and, of course, religion. Nor has pluralism prevented moral philosophers and ethicists from asserting that they can resolve, or help resolve, value conflicts.[18] Their beliefs and judgments, no matter how well presented and defended, are inescapably personal. There are no objective grounds for preferring any one of them to others.

We maintain that there are nevertheless some shared foundational elements to many of these various ideologies, philosophies, and religions. They all rest on the principles of fairness or equality, or some combination of the two. This is a strong claim and bound to be controversial. We nevertheless believe there is ample evidence in its support and will present some of it in the next section of the chapter. Our finding does not mean that competing ideologies, philosophies, or religions are reconcilable or compatible, only that they respond to and build

---

[14] Herodotus, *The Histories*, trans. George Rawlinson (New York: Knopf, 1997), is among the first to voice this critique.

[15] Marianne Weber, *Max Weber: A Biography*, trans. Harry Zohn (New York: Wiley, 1974), p. 325.

[16] Richard Ned Lebow, "Weber's Search for Knowledge," in Richard Ned Lebow, ed., *Max Weber and International Relations* (Cambridge: Cambridge University Press, 2017), pp. 40–78.

[17] For an overview of the origins of this debate, David Rasmussen, *Universalism vs. Communitarianism: Contemporary Debates in Ethics* (Cambridge, MA: MIT Press, 1990).

[18] Miller, *Principles of Social Justice*, pp. 39–40, is a case in point. He attempts to adjudicate between solidaristic and instrumental relationships. He asserts that we give too much attention to individual choices and not enough "to demands stemming from citizenship." He criticizes Rawls and Dworkin for developing theories of justice based solely on citizenship and seeks "to correct distortions in everyday thinking about fairness."

on a common set of concerns. Almost every contemporary Western account of justice rests on the principle of equality. This near-consensus has not led to any broader agreement because philosophers do not agree among themselves what equality is, how it might be achieved, or to whom and how it ought to be applied.[19] This is equally true of fairness, which is the other foundational principle. Most philosophies and almost all utopias attempt to combine the two principles of justice, as do, for example, Plato, Thomas More, and John Rawls.[20] They do so in different ways and give different weight to these principles.

We observe something similar in China. Fairness and equality, or some combination of them, capture the core claims of justice from all the major intellectual schools in Chinese history, especially Confucianism, Mohism, Daoism, and Legalism. Confucianism is most notable for its justification of fairness, but it also espouses a subdued form of equality. Daoism is the most thorough advocate of equality and genuinely dislikes the kind of hierarchy that Confucianism supports. Between these two poles, Mohism promotes both equality and fairness. With no concern for fairness, Legalism advances a restrictive notion of equality. In the modern era, Western notions of equality have so engulfed Chinese thinking that part of modern China's discourse on justice can be read as an attempt to reconcile the traditional notion of justice as fairness with the modern understanding of justice as equality. This brief *tour d'horizon* indicates that the principles of fairness and equality are central across cultures.

Discourses about justice are unique to human beings. However, many primate societies appear to function on the basis of fairness and equality. Noted ethologist Frans de Waal reports that young chimpanzees learn rules of comportment and subsequently trust only those who follow them. One of the most important rules is to share food if, for whatever reason, you have more than others. Alpha males, who are generally allowed to eat first on what we would call the principle of fairness, nevertheless uphold the principle of equality by distributing most of what they are given to others. Reciprocal performance of these principles of justice behavior builds trust and solidarity and reduces social conflict.[21] Christopher Boehm reports that human foragers deal the same way with the meat problem. "They invariably treat a sizable carcass as being community rather than individual property, and they put its distribution in the hands

[19] Roemer, *Equality of Opportunity*, for an overview.

[20] Plato, *Republic* and *Laws*, in Hamilton and Cairns, *Collected Dialogues*; Thomas More, *Utopia*, ed. George M. Logan and Robert M. Adams, rev. ed. (Cambridge: Cambridge University Press, 2002); John Rawls, *A Theory of Justice*, rev. ed. (Cambridge, MA: Harvard University Press, 1999).

[21] Frans B. M. De Waal, "Natural Normativity: The 'Is' and 'Ought' of Animal Behavior," in Frans B. M. De Waal, Patricia Smith Churchland, Telmo Pievani, and Stefano Parmigiani, eds., *Evolved Morality: The Biology and Philosophy of Human Conscience* (Leiden: Brill, 2014), pp. 161–82.

of a neutral party who will not try to politicize the meat distribution and come out ahead."[22]

Reciprocity in the form of giving and receiving is a central feature of social life among chimpanzees and bonobos. There is little evidence of food stealing among these species; they respect possession and will punish and chase off thieves and freeloaders. Alpha males will not take food from others, but beg for it. Those who grab food lose support and encourage younger challengers to step forward. Sharing is nevertheless more frequent with grooming partners, which offers more evidence for reciprocity, and also for memory and gratitude.[23]

Many animals appear to possess a commitment to equality. Capuchin monkeys are particularly sensitive to what they and others receive. Frans de Waal and his students conducted experiments in which Capuchins were given two foods valued differently, like cucumbers and grapes. Offering one animal the preferred food and the other the less valued one prompts anger at the experimenter.[24] Additional evidence of the importance of equality among Capuchins is their refusal to work when they observe others who do not but still get food rewards. Experiments with dogs indicate that they can easily be taught to put their paw out for food but will do less often if they observe other dogs who receive food without having to put out their paws. Among cooperative mammals, individuals look to see what others get and become angry if they receive less.[25]

What accounts for our commitment to fairness and equality is an open question. These principles may be part of our evolutionary inheritance as primates. Alternatively, they are evidence of convergence. Fairness and equality in some form appear to be the foundations on which social orders are built and sustained. Only orders that incorporate them are likely to survive.[26]

Fairness and equality can be formulated and applied in different ways, a question we will soon address. They can be reinforcing and crosscutting, depending on context. Their formulation, relative importance, and synergy vary across societies and historical epochs. This variation can help us define the envelope in which robust orders are found. It also tells us something about the development of human societies. In the East and the West we observe an historical movement from equality to fairness and back to equality. It is a dialectical progression.

[22] Christopher Boehm, *Moral Origins: The Evolution of Virtue, Altruism, and Shame* (New York: Basic Books, 2012).

[23] Frans B. M. De Waal and Peter L. Tyack, *Animal Social Complexity: Intelligence, Culture, and Individualized Societies* (Cambridge, MA: Harvard University Press, 2003); Frans D. M. De Waal, *Bonobo: The Forgotten Ape* (Berkeley: University of California Press, 1997).

[24] Frans B. M. De Waal, "Monkey Cucumber Grape Experiment," *YouTube*, 9 July 2012, http://www.youtube.com/watch?v=OwR5l8wfXlU (accessed 28 April 2020).

[25] De Waal and Tyack, *Animal Social Complexity*.

[26] Lebow, *Rise and Fall of Social Orders*, chs. 1 and 8.

Each stage of development is brought about in part by tensions inherent in the preceding principle. Later in the book we will describe these tensions in the form of immanent critiques of fairness and equality and identify some of the pathways by which they bring about unanticipated pressures for change. This dialectical progression constitutes a serious threat to order at every level of social aggregation. It also offers opportunities for reforms and restructuring that has the potential to strengthen these orders. This is also a question to which we will return in the context of regional and international society.

Varieties of Justice

Equality and fairness—the latter often referred to as "equity" by psychologists— are commonly framed as principles of distributive justice.[27] This refers to possession or control over whatever people desire but is limited in its availability. It includes property, status, sexual partners, access to education, health care, and much of anything else that is valued. Competition for these rewards gives rise to conflicts, and this is where politics enters the picture. In the famous words of Harold Lasswell, it is all about "Who gets what when and how?"[28]

There is more to politics than authoritative decisions about rewards, and many of the decisions about rewards are not made by governments. This is especially true in liberal democratic societies where markets and other civil institutions are the source of most benefits, and, often, adjudication about their distribution. In ordered societies this process is rule-governed, whether it is governmental or civil, so procedural justice enters the picture.[29] Governments, markets, and other civil institutions make other important decisions. They constitute actors and establish rules for their behavior and for punishing violators. Constitutive

[27] Morton Deutsch, *Distributive Justice* (New Haven, CT: Yale University Press, 1985), p. 1. G. C. Homans, *Social Behavior: Its Elementary Forms*, rev. ed. (New York: Harcourt, Brace, Jovanovich, 1974), for the pioneering study of distributive justice.

[28] Harold Lasswell, *Politics: Who Gets What, When, How* (New York: McGraw-Hill, 1936 and 1952). Lasswell also offers broader definitions of politics in this book: as the conditions and justification of influence and control, and as deliberation and action toward the common good.

[29] For psychological studies on procedural justice, J. W. Thibaut and L. Walker, *Procedural Justice: A Psychological Analysis* (Hillsdale, N.J.: Erlbaum, 1975); George S. Leventhal, "Fairness in Social Relationships," in J. W. Thibault, J. T. Spence, and R. C. Carson, eds., *Contemporary Topics in Social Psychology* (Morristown, NJ: General Learning Press, 1976), pp. 211–39; E. A. Lind, R. Kanfer, and P. C. Earley, "Voice Control and Procedural Justice: Instrumental and Noninstrumental Concerns in Fairness Judgments," *Journal of Personality and Social Psychology* 59, no. 5 (1990), pp. 952–59; E. A. Lind and T. R. Tyler, *The Social Psychology of Procedural Justice* (New York: Plenum, 1988); J. Brockner and B. M. Wiesenfeld, "An Integrative Framework for Explaining Reactions to Decisions: Interactive Effects of Outcomes and Procedures," *Psychological Bulletin* 120, no. 2 (1996), pp. 189–208.

and commutative justice describes how actors should be recognized and how they ought to behave in commercial and other kinds of transactions. Retributive justice concerns the punishment of those who fail to honor laws or norms. There are other principles of justice, more limited in scope. William Barbieri makes the case for "constitutive justice," on the grounds that membership in a community is logically prior to distribution and subject to its own form of justice.[30] Another example is organizational justice. It addressed how employees judge productivity, their contribution to it, and their relationship to the organization.[31]

Justice can be framed in terms of rights. Robert Nozick, arguably the most extreme proponent of this approach, rejects equality as a principle. This move, he claims, "is justified by a fundamental moral insight." A just outcome is one in which no rights were abused in the trail of transactions leading up to it. His theory of justice is not what he calls a "patterned" one. A just outcome might be grossly unequal, but nevertheless be just because it is based on a trail of proper transactions between or among rights holders. What does matter is that the initial set of holdings is just. Here at the beginning of trading—when the market opens, as it were—fairness and equality find traction. Equality is present in another way for Nozick and liberal rights theorists who consider just outcomes that many others would consider unequal and therefore unjust. It resides in the equal sets of rights individuals are taken to possess.[32] In effect, Nozick is defending the status quo, and doing so by rejecting equality and fairness as principles. This may help to explain why it has found so little traction.

Michael Walzer categorizes types of benefits and burdens and looks for principles relevant to each. His theory of justice maintains that different principles should govern different spheres of activity.[33] The rules of friendship are accordingly different from those of market competition. Drawing on Aristotle's conceptualization of friendship, Walzer argues that friends do things for one another because they are friends—but they become close friends in part because they treat each other as equals and with fairness. In market transactions, equality is central; buyers and sellers should be treated the same way and have access to the same market mechanisms. Similar arguments are made by Jon Elster and

---

[30] William Barbieri Jr., *Constitutive Justice* (London: Palgrave-Macmillan, 2015), pp. 2–3.

[31] J. A Colquitt, J. Greenberg, and C. P. Zapata-Phelan, "What Is Organizational Justice? A Historical Overview," in Greenberg and Colquitt, eds., *Handbook of Organizational Justice* (Mahwah, NJ: Erlbaum, 2005), pp. 3–56; J. R. Crawshaw, R. Cropanzano, C. M. Bell, and T. Nadisic, "Organizational Justice: New Insights from Behavioural Ethics," *Human Relations* 66, no. 7 (2013), pp. 885–904.

[32] Robert Nozick, *Anarchy, State, and Utopia* (New York: Basic Books, 1974).

[33] Michael Walzer, *Spheres of Justice: A Defense of Pluralism and Equality* (New York: Basic Books, 1983).

H. P. Young, both of whom maintain that different principles of justice should apply in different spheres of life.[34]

John Rawls argues that justice is achieved through a proper balance of liberty and equality. He assumes a society of moderate scarcity populated by actors who are not entirely selfish, prefer cooperation to conflict, and are accordingly willing to advance their interests through compromises. He contends that people placed behind a "veil of ignorance"—deprived of their existing possessions and status in society—would find the two principles of justice he proposes the most acceptable. They would agree that everyone should "have an equal right to the most extensive basic liberty compatible with a similar liberty for others."[35] He enumerates a list of essential liberties, almost all drawn from the US Constitution's Bill of Rights. People would also insist on equal opportunity to acquire wealth and offices, but under conditions of "fair equality of opportunity" that are of the greatest benefit to the least-advantaged members of society.[36] This requires that offices and positions be distributed on the basis of merit, but that everyone has a reasonable opportunity to acquire the skills necessary to compete for them.

Rawls's liberal world attempts to blend the principles of fairness and equality, and to find a justification for making trade-offs between them. His principle of liberty is a constitutive one, as it describes a set of conditions (e.g., freedom of speech, assembly, religion) that enable a liberal political order and independent civil society. These conditions require or enable fairness or equality, but, he insists, cannot be reduced to them because they concern distribution only indirectly. Rawls's principle of liberty fails to meet the test of universality. It would be incomprehensible to anyone in ancient Europe and much of the contemporary world. It is liberal ideology masquerading as moral philosophy.

Rawls supposes universal, innate understandings of justice. To test his claim, he imagines an experiment that puts people in the original condition, that is, stripped of existing roles, possessions, and intellectual commitments. They must then construct what they consider to be an ideal society, or evaluate constitutive, procedural, and distributive principles presented to them. Rawls expects something of a consensus to emerge. We think it more likely that people from different cultures and epochs would respond quite differently. More problematic for Rawls is the assumption underlying his *Gedankenexperiment*. Rawls, Walzer, and Nozick are representatives of the liberal tradition and take for granted that

---

[34] Jon Elster, *Local Justice: How Institutions Allocate Scarce Goods and Necessary Burdens* (Cambridge: Cambridge University Press, 1992); H. P. Young, *Equity* (Princeton, NJ: Princeton University Press, 1994).

[35] Rawls, *Theory of Justice*, p. 52.

[36] Ibid.

the appropriate starting place for any understanding of justice is the autonomous individual. Such a being is pure fiction. The ancient Greeks and Thomas Hobbes understood that people removed from their affiliations, roles, and the constraints of society are largely deprived of their humanity and reduced to a bundle of raw appetites guided by short-term instrumental reason.[37] They would be like mythical wolf-children, or the odd historical feral child: without language, empathy, social skills, or cognitive capacity to grasp the meaning of justice. Traditional Chinese thinkers, notably Confucians, always situate the individual in familial and social relationships.[38]

Two centuries before Rawls, David Hume conducted an amusing but compelling thought experiment to demonstrate the impossibility of explaining the concept of justice to Adam and Eve. Justice must be internalized to work, a process beyond the ken of the inhabitants of the Garden of Eden, Hume believed, or of any small group of hunter-gatherers.[39] Rawls commits an error common to Romantics and many contemporary philosophers who assume that people have identities independent of their affiliations, roles, relationship to their bodies, and histories.[40] He too is peddling an ideology in the guise of objective inquiry.

There are social, as opposed to individual, understandings of justice. One of the oldest and most universal may be what the ancient Greek called *xenia* (guest friendship). It required travelers to offer food and shelter to needy travelers. They in turn were expected to honor their hosts and not overstay their welcome.[41] All forms of solidarity, of which guest friendship is only one, rest on "special obligations" or duties. These duties may be to one's family, fellow citizens, nation, humanity, or the planet.

All these principles of justice find expression in some combination of fairness and equality. We have already discussed distributive justice in this regard. Let us consider retributive justice, which pertains to punishment. Legal systems in democratic countries, whether based on common law, the Napoleonic Code, or some other set of constitutional principles, are expected to enforce laws impartially, treating people brought before juries or magistrates in the same way. These rules rest on the principle of equality. In common law systems, grand juries must be convinced that the evidence against the accused warrants a trial; people

---

[37] Thomas Hobbes, *Leviathan*, ed. Richard Tuck (Cambridge: Cambridge University Press, 1996), chs. 13–14.

[38] Roger T. Ames, *Confucian Role Ethics: A Vocabulary* (Honolulu: University of Hawai'i Press, 2011).

[39] David Hume, *A Treatise of Human Nature*, ed. P. H. Nidditch, 2nd ed. revised (Oxford: Oxford University Press, 1978), 3.2.2.10.

[40] Lebow, *Politics and Ethics of Identity*, ch. 1.

[41] Moses I. Finley, *The World of Odysseus* (New York: Viking, 1978), pp. 99–101, on guest friendship in the Homeric age.

arrested and charged must be informed of the charges they face. These rules rest on the principle of fairness. In petit juries that try criminal cases, the accused must be presented with the evidence against them, and their attorneys allowed to present their own evidence and to cross-examine witnesses. The accused must be tried by a petit jury of their peers, and if convicted, sentenced within pre-approved guidelines for the crime in question. Judges who preside over trials are required to follow accepted criminal procedure, and appeal against conviction is possible on the grounds that they did not. All the rules and procedures combine equality and fairness. In chapter 4 we shall examine a different conception of retributive justice held by China's Legalist school.

Constitutive justice concerns the recognition of actors. In democracies the core unit is the citizen, and all are considered equal in the sense of having one vote. The Declaration of Independence opens with the sentence: "We hold these truths to be self-evident, that all men are created equal." It foregrounds the principle of equality. So too does the motto of French Republic: *liberté, égalité, fraternité*. The US Constitution nevertheless sought to balance equality and fairness. The House of Representatives was to be elected from districts with roughly the same number of voters, in practice privileging the most populous states. In the Senate, every state has two senators, privileging the less populated states, as there were—and still are—more of them.

Attempts to balance equality and fairness can sometimes lead to seemingly bizarre compromises. A case in point, again from the US Constitution, concerns the status of African-Americans. The population of states was important for purposes of representation and taxation. The Three-Fifths Compromise, reached among state delegates to the 1787 US Constitutional Convention, counted three out of every five slaves as people for this purpose. It effectively gave Southern states a third more seats in Congress and a third more electoral votes in presidential elections than they would have if slaves were ignored, but fewer than if slaves and free people had been counted equally.[42] After the Civil War, the Constitution was amended, and the Fourteenth Amendment, adopted in 1868, recognized African Americans as full persons entitled to vote. In practice, Southern states disenfranchised Black voters during the Reconstruction era and it was not until the civil rights movement of the 1960s that they began to obtain de facto equality.

A similar tension exists in international relations. State actors are constituted—and de-constituted—by recognition of other actors and above all by their admission into the United Nations. The General Assembly is the organ responsible for

---

[42] Garry Wills, *"Negro President": Jefferson and the Slave Power* (Boston: Houghton Mifflin, 2003); Hanes Walton Jr., Robert C. Smith, and Sherri L. Wallace, *American Politics and the African American Quest for Universal Freedom*, 3rd ed. (New York: Pearson Longman, 2006), ch. 12.

admitting states and it is organized on the basis of equality, with each member state given one vote. The Security Council, as its name suggests, is responsible for overseeing security. It has five permanent members, all of them great powers, and each with the right of unit veto. It also has ten rotating members, none of whom are great powers, which do not have a veto. In accordance with the principle of fairness, the great powers are given special privileges because they are expected to assume special responsibilities. The United States has claimed even more privileges on the grounds of its alleged hegemony, and with it, primary responsibility for upholding global security and economic relations. Other states have not bought in to either claim.[43]

Commutative justice describes how actors ought to behave in commercial and other kinds of transactions. Here too, equality and fairness are paramount. Fairness requires purchasers to pay market rates for good and services. In many transactions it also demands treating customers or applicants on a first-come-first-served basis. Equality requires customers to be treated equally, a matter of tension and legal actions in jurisdictions where discrimination of any kind is practiced. Fairness and equality frequently come into conflict, as they do with conflicting claims over school admissions, graduated tax rates, and, most recently, precedence for COVID vaccinations until they became widely available.

To varying degrees, equality and fairness underlie the norms of family life in all cultures. They also justify civic duties such as paying taxes and military service. Perhaps the most convincing evidence for the importance and universality of these principles is provided by the arguments of those who oppose particular arrangements. They invariably invoke the principles of fairness or equality (e.g., it is unfair for the rich to pay less tax than the poor; military service, like all obligations, should be borne equally and not levied disproportionately on the poor or less educated; our pensions should not be reduced, as we will have less in retirement than those who preceded us; we have worked here longer so deserve preferences with regard to promotion and job security; I have more experience so should be paid more than co-workers with less).

Equality and Fairness

Equality may be the older of the two principles. It is central to surviving hunter-gather groups. In the pre-classical Greece, *nomos* was associated with leaders who distributed meat among their followers. Homer seems to have envisaged

---

[43] Simon Reich and Richard Ned Lebow, *Good-Bye Hegemony! Power and Influence in the Global System* (Princeton, NJ: Princeton University Press, 2014) for US claims and a critique.

fair food distribution as a core constituent of the political order. In classical Greece, nomos expanded to encompass laws, rules, procedures, and customs. It still retained a connotation of equality in the word *isonomia*, which was later gradually extended in scope to embrace political rights. Equality remained alive as a concept in Europe and not infrequently surfaced as a demand or practice of breakaway religious sects or peasant rebellions.

Equality demands a more or less even distribution of whatever it is that people value. Equality can also be applied to non-distributive issues. According to Aristotle, it requires that the victims of wrongdoings be compensated equally regardless of their wealth or status.[44] Equality before the law is a central tenet and test of modern democracy. In the late eighteenth century, David Hume and Adam Smith extended the principle of equality to property; both men considered it immoral—and against the interests of society—that the poor should suffer to provide luxuries for the rich and that the latter should own considerable property and the former little to none.[45] Many socialists would go a step further and abolish almost all private property. Equality also pertains to the law, and in the modern era the scope of law has been widely extended. In some domains—education, for example—the goal was to bring about equality.[46] The recent Black Lives Matter movement in the United States focused on equal treatment by police.[47]

In liberal theory, equality assumed a second meaning: equality of opportunity.[48] This framing is particularly pronounced in American political theory, where John Roemer suggests it finds expression in two distinct formulations.[49] The first maintains that competition for wealth and status should be judged only with respect to the performance of the duties in question. "Extraneous" attributes like race, gender, and family background and the advantages they

---

[44] Aristotle, *Nicomachean Ethics*, 1132a4–a5, in *The Complete Works of Aristotle*, 2 vols., ed. Jonathan Barnes (Princeton, NJ: Princeton University Press, 1984).

[45] Adam Smith, *An Inquiry into the Nature and Causes of Wealth of Nations*, in Edwin Canaan (Chicago: University of Chicago Press, 1976), I.viii.36; Hume, *Enquiry Concerning the Principles of Morals*, ed. P. H. Nidditch (Oxford: Oxford University Press, 1975). David Hume, *A Treatise of Human Nature*, ed. P. H. Nidditch, 2nd ed. revised (Oxford: Oxford University Press, 1978), 3.9–12.

[46] Ronnie Hjorth, *Equality in International Society: A Reappraisal* (London: Palgrave-Macmillan, 2014), p. 6; C. A. R. Crosland, *The Future of Socialism* (London: Cape, 1956), for an attack on public schools, inherited wealthy, and other privileges that sustain the British elite.

[47] Ta-Nehisi Coates, *Between the World and Me* (New York: One World, 2015); Wesley Lowery, *They Can't Kill Us All: The Story of the Struggle for Black Lives* (Boston: Back Bay Books, 2017); Isabel Wilkerson, *Caste: The Origins of Our Discontents* (New York: Random House, 2020).

[48] Rawls, *Theory of Justice*, for a justification of an unequal distribution if it was arrived fairly and benefits the society as a whole.

[49] John E. Roemer, *Equality of Opportunity* (Cambridge, MA: Harvard University Press, 1998), for a review and critique of the relevant literature.

confer should not be taken into account. The second insists that society should attempt to level the playing field, especially in the critical formative years of life, so people actually have equality of opportunity.

Either formulation is consistent with hierarchies and can be understood as an effort to justify them. If everyone is equal at the onset of a competition the outcome reflects the skill, virtue, diligence—and admittedly, sometimes the good luck—of the contestants. Liberal equality reintroduces the principle of fairness through the back door, and indeed was initially propagated by representatives of the commercial classes to justify their claim to power.[50] Contemporary neoliberals offer it as a justification for the growing disparity of wealth in the Western world.

The principle of fairness goes by many names. They include "virtue," "merit," "worthiness," and "deservingness." It is an ancient concept, but one associated with societies having a division of labor and hierarchy based on birth or achievement. It makes its earliest appearance in warrior-based honor societies. We have evidence of fairness in the *lex talonis* law systems that date back to ancient Babylonia. The code of Hammurabi and Hebrew law stress fairness, but only in the context of compensation for loss. By the fifth century BCE, the discourse of virtue provided secular justifications for Greek aristocratic and oligarchic hierarchies. Plato and Aristotle develop different versions of it in their writings. They sought to downgrade the principle of equality because it was the justification for democracy.[51]

Until quite recently, fairness was the dominant principle of regional and international orders. In Europe, and subsequently, worldwide, states gained honor, and often territory and wealth, by displaying military prowess. The resulting hierarchy of great and lesser powers was justified on the basis of the responsibility the former allegedly assumed for the maintenance of order and survival of international society and its members. This informal understanding was given official status by the Congress of Vienna.[52] As noted, it is also enshrined in the United Nations where the great powers have been given special privileges. The US claim for special privileges on the basis of its alleged hegemony is unambiguously based on the principle of fairness.

---

[50] Albert O. Hirschman, *The Passions and the Interests: Political Arguments for Capitalism before Its Triumph* (Princeton, NJ: Princeton University Press, 1977); Istvan Hont, *Jealousy of Trade: International Competition and the Nation-State in Historical Perspective* (Cambridge, MA: Harvard University Press, 2005); Lebow, *Cultural Theory of International Relations*, ch. 3.

[51] Plato, *Republic*, 560e5, 561a6–62a2, 561c6–d5, and 572b10–73b4.

[52] Richard Ned Lebow, *National Identities and International Relations* (Cambridge: Cambridge University Press, 2016), ch. 4.

Fairness offers "merit" as a countervailing principle to equality. It insists that some people are more deserving of wealth or status than others. It justifies the resulting hierarchies on the grounds that those who occupy higher rungs deserve more because of their greater contribution to the general welfare. Plato and Aristotle invoke the principle to justify the political authority of elites.[53] For Aristotle, an aristocrat and defender of aristocracy, only well-born people had leisure, and with it the possibility of attaining virtue and providing good government for the polis. Politics in ancient Greece and Rome was framed in terms of virtue. Individuals and groups vying for power claimed to possess qualities that made them more qualified to rule. In the eighteenth and nineteenth centuries, liberal thinkers contested the claim that some people possessed more moral worth than others because of their "noble" birth. They affirmed the natural equality of human beings.

A second and modern formulation of fairness stipulates that whatever is available should go to those who need it the most. Its most famous expression is Marx's dictum: "From each according to his abilities, to each according to his needs."[54] It is evident today in such practices as handicapped parking spaces, special education programs, scholarships based on need, and tax deductions for medical expenses. Although this was certainly not Marx's intention, fairness framed this way can be used to justify hierarchies, or at least make them more acceptable. It softens their consequences by looking after those who have lost out or are unable to compete.

Figure One

Fairness	Equality
Traditional Definition	*Traditional Definition*
More rewards to those who are more deserving because they contribute more	Equal distribution
Modern Definition	*Modern Definition*
More reward to those who need more (e.g., the disabled)	Equal opportunity to compete

---

[53] Aristotle, *Nicomachean* Ethics, 1131b29–30. Lebow, *Cultural Theory of International Relations*, chs. 3 and 4, for a discussion.

[54] Karl Marx, *Critique of the Gotha Program* (Rockville, MD: Wildside Press, 2008).

Contemporary analyses of distribution frequently fail to distinguish between fairness and equality. In an otherwise excellent policy text, Deborah Stone writes: "Keep in mind that in a distributive conflict, *all* sides seek equality; the conflict comes over how the sides envisage a fair distribution of whatever is at stake."[55] Fairness and equality are different principles and identify different criteria for distribution. Stone identifies nine criteria of equality: membership, merit, rank, group-based, need, value, competitions, lotteries, and elections.[56] But only membership and competition might qualify, depending on what percentage of the population is included. Merit, rank, need, and value are all forms of fairness. Lotteries and elections are forms of commutative justice, and can be reduced to equality or fairness.

The elision of fairness and equality is not a sign of intellectual sloppiness but rather reflective of efforts in the modern era to combine these principles. Consider the institution of the Electoral College and the American practice— continually challenged in the courts—of affirmative action. They are highly contentious, in large part because of how they try to combine fairness and equality. The Electoral College was set up to strike a balance between the more populous urbanized states and less populous rural ones, privileging fairness over equality, but also recognizing equality by awarding more electoral votes to populous states. Democrats, invoking the principle of equality, resent the advantage this gives to Republican states and the presidential victory it provided to Donald Trump in 2016, who trailed Hillary Clinton by three million votes.

Affirmative action was based on fairness—giving special privileges to African Americans, many of whom were otherwise disadvantaged in the university admission process. Its longer-term goal was racial equality that would make special privileges unnecessary. Proponents argued that it was redressing de facto affirmative action for well-to-do whites, many of whom attended better-funded and higher-quality primary and secondary schools. Some gained admission to private universities on the basis of being "legacies," that is, sons or daughters of graduates. Fairness was invoked to produce equality. Opponents of affirmative action argued that it was unfair because the same admission criteria were not applied across the board. They invoked equality to oppose fairness.

The controversy over affirmative action also involves different understandings of fairness and equality. Those in favor frame fairness as the requirement to give more to those who most need it, and equality as equal distribution (their longer-term goal being equalization of black and white incomes by means of education

---

[55] Deborah Stone, *Policy Paradox: The Art of Political Decision Making*, rev ed. (New York: Norton, 2001), p. 39.

[56] Ibid., pp. 39–60.

and the better career opportunities it provides). Those opposed define fairness as giving more to those who deserve it by virtue of their excellence. They are committed to equality in the liberal sense of the equal opportunity to compete. Beginning in the 1950s, many conservatives argued that African Americans had no claim to equal school funding because they did not produce enough tax revenue to support them.[57] As this example illustrates, framings can be selective and self-serving, but the ability of the two sides to appeal to what to them were obvious principles of justice made them more unyielding and their conflict accordingly more acute.[58]

When two principles of justice are combined, as they are in the Electoral College and affirmative action, it becomes difficult to keep them apart. In contemporary Western discourses, as noted, fairness and equality are increasingly used interchangeably. Equality is described as fairness, and fairness as equality.[59] This is promising in one respect because all best worlds combine the two principles in some form. But it is confusing and leads to misunderstandings and people talking at cross purposes. It also finesses hard choices. There are good normative and analytical reasons to differentiate the two principles. For millennia in the West they were considered not only distinct but competing conceptions of justice. It is analytically useful—indeed essential—to maintain their separation to understand different formulations of justice and the conflict to which they give rise.

Origins of Justice

David Hume was among the first modern thinkers to offer an account of justice and government that is historical and dispenses with the twin fictions of the state of nature and the social contract.[60] Early human societies, he contends, were little more than extended family groups—bottom-up orders in our language. They functioned on the basis of "natural justice," which derives from love of oneself and one's friends. People come to know and experience the feelings of others and develop sympathy for them.[61] Such sympathy grew fainter with physical and social distance.[62] "Artificial justice" developed at a later stage and

---

[57] Nancy MacLean, *Democracy in Chains: The Deep History of the Radical Rights Stealth Plan for America* (New York: Viking, 2017).

[58] On this point, Lebow, *Rise and Fall of Political Orders*, pp. 337–42.

[59] Walter Scott, *Heart of Midlothian* (Oxford: Oxford University Press, 2008), is based on this premise.

[60] Hume, *Treatise of Human Nature*, 3.2.2.15, on the state of nature.

[61] Ibid., 2.3.6.8, and *Enquiry Concerning the Principles of Morals*, section 3, appendix 3.

[62] Hume, *Enquiry Concerning the Principles of Morals*, 5.2.42.

consists of conventions intended to reduce conflict in conditions of scarcity. Hume theorizes that it is a response to problems people encounter as their societies become larger and more complex.[63]

As the size of communities increases, so do disputes over all kinds of possessions. People are motivated to reduce conflict and develop mechanisms to do this by trial and error. Their experiments take the form of interpersonal agreements that, if successful, prompt imitation. By this means, some conventions and practices become more general.[64] When society becomes larger still, some people can ignore or flout conventions and get away without being observed or punished.[65] The attractiveness of free-riding creates the need for some enforcement mechanism and, ultimately, for government.[66] People will only restrain themselves, Hume suggests, when they believe that others will do so as well. The expectation of reciprocity in self-restraint accordingly demands some authority that enforces rules.[67]

Hume was probably right in reasoning that equality was the dominant principle of justice among hunter-gathers and early agriculturalists. Anthropologists have documented this among formerly isolated hunter-gatherer societies. Groups like the Dobe Ju/'hoansi (previously described as the !Kung) in southern Africa, and the BaMbuti of the Ituri Forest in Zaire (formerly called Pygmies), had no government or even informal leadership. They created solidarity on the basis of kinship, friendship, and equality. They later learned the principle of fairness from outsiders and used it to govern their relations with them, but not among themselves.[68]

Elsewhere in the world, sedentary agriculture and economic development led to larger societies and more formal kinds of hierarchies. They often employ principles of fairness and equality, and struggle to reconcile them. This is certainly the case in many, if not most, present-day states. Generally speaking, everyone is liable to income tax, although many, mostly rich people, find ways of avoiding it. Many governments levy no tax on those they deem poor and impose proportionately higher rates on those with substantial incomes. As noted, in the US Congress, representation in the Senate is based on equality and in the House of Representatives on proportionality, the latter a form of fairness.[69]

---

[63] Hume, *Treatise of Human Nature*, 3.2.2.4.

[64] Ibid., 3.2.2.1–22.

[65] Ibid., 3.3.1.10; *Enquiry Concerning the Principles of Morals*, section 4.

[66] Hume, *Treatise of Human Nature*, 3.2.7.

[67] Ibid., 3.2.2.10.

[68] Turnbull, *Forest People*, pp. 110–14; Lee, *Dobe Ju/'hoansi*, pp. 109–24; Biesele and Hitchcock, *Ju/'hoan San of Nyae Nyae and Namibian Independence*, pp. 65–90.

[69] Madison, "Federalist 62," in Alexander Hamilton, James Madison, and John Jay, *The Federalist Papers* (Baltimore: Johns Hopkins University Press, 1981).

Utopias almost invariably incorporate both principles of justice. John Rawls, for one, prioritizes equality in wealth, but is willing to allow some actors to receive additional compensation if they demonstrably increase the overall wealth or well-being of the society.[70]

Plato was among the first Western philosophers to assert that orders depend on principles of justice, and his counterparts in China, especially Kongzi (551–479 BCE) and Mozi (c. 479–438 BCE), as we shall see in the next two chapters, made much the same argument. Plato's Protagoras recounts a founding myth of Greek society.[71] At the outset, humans fed, housed, and clothed themselves by relying on instinct. They lived isolated lives and were prey to wild animals. They banded together for self-protection, but treated one another so badly that they soon sought refuge again in their individual caves. Zeus took pity on them and sent Hermes to give them *aidōs* (respect, reverence) and *dikē* (justice) so they could live together harmoniously. *Dikē* is an ordering principle that requires people to treat others as equals, attempt to see things from their point of view, and empathize with them.

Justice in this understanding is closely related to trust. Trust is the expectation that others will honor their promises and conform to their rule packages. Political orders, like their economic and social counterparts, rely on a high degree of trust, as many critical actions are sequential rather than simultaneous. Actors are unlikely to commit themselves to any venture involving significant upfront costs if they do not believe that others live up to their part of the bargain.[72] Reciprocity, the principal mechanism of trust, builds on the principles of fairness and equality: tit-for-tat in obligations, and equal standing of actors in any bargain regardless of other inequalities between them.

Justice and Discourses

Legitimate orders are those supported by most of their population. Legitimacy is a daily referendum in which people decide to follow or defy norms and laws.[73] All legitimate orders rest on principles of justice, but no order fully lives up to them. As noted, elites are everywhere more privileged in practice than warranted by the principles of justice associated with their societies' hierarchies.

[70] Rawls, *Theory of Justice*.

[71] Plato, *Protagoras*, 322c8–323.

[72] Mark E. Warren, *Democracy and Trust* (Cambridge: Cambridge University Press, 1999), on the debate over trust and democracy.

[73] Juan Linz, *The Breakdown of Democratic Regime: Crises, Breakdown, and Requilibration: An Introduction* (Baltimore: Johns Hopkins University Press, 1978), pp. 15–17.

Elites invariably sponsor or support discourses to justify the inequalities from which they benefit and to explain away differences between what justice would demand and the realities of their society. Early efforts of this kind generally appealed to gods rather than principles of justice. In Western culture, these theodicies often took the form of golden ages. The two best known are Hesiod's *Works and Days* and the Garden of Eden story in the Book of Genesis. The former describes the successive degeneration of people from a "golden race" to the present, and from a society governed by justice to one ruled by force.[74] The Garden of Eden is a paradise from which people are expelled because of their violation of god's command not to eat from the tree of knowledge. In *Works and Days*, gods, not rulers, are responsible for the current state of affairs, and nothing can be done to improve it. In Genesis, it is the fault of our forebears. Hunger, death, pain in childbirth, and injustice—in Roman Catholic readings—are the price we must pay for Adam and Eve's transgression.[75]

In European culture, cosmic justifications of order were dominant in the Middle Ages and the basis for the divine right of kings. In China, the equivalent was the Mandate of Heaven, and other indigenous forms developed in South and Southeast Asia. Friedrich Engels and Antonio Gramsci made us more sensitive to the extent to which elite-sponsored discourses can create "false consciousness" that reconciles people to orders in which they are exploited.[76] President Trump and the Republicans played this game with notable success in the 2016 elections.

Discourses of this kind have enabled a wide range of societies to establish more legitimacy than they might otherwise have. Engels and Gramsci lament that one of the distinguishing features of their success is the degree to which respect for authority and the ideology on which it rests are internalized by the very people these orders disadvantage. For this reason, the European bourgeoisie, especially in central Europe, did not behave as Marx expected; its members often placed social over class interests, assimilated many aristocratic ambitions, and accepted their leadership of foreign policy. This novel and largely unexpected alignment, as Max Weber noted, allowed the aristocracy to maintain its privileges, and in some countries, its power, in the face of the twin political and economic challenges of working class democracy and finance capital allied to export-oriented industry.[77]

---

[74] Hesiod, *Work and Days*, in Hesiod, *Theogony and Works and Days*, trans. M. L. West (Oxford: Oxford University Press, 1988).

[75] Lebow, *Politics and Ethics of Identity*, ch. 2, for an analysis and comparison of these texts.

[76] Karl Marx and Friedrich Engels, *The German Ideology* (New York: Prometheus, 1998); Antonio Gramsci, *Letters from Prison*, 2 vols., trans. Raymond Rosenthal (New York: Columbia University Press, 1994).

[77] Max Weber, *Economy and Society*, eds. Guenther Roth and Claus Wittich (Berkeley: University of California Press, 1968), vol. II, p. 920–21.

Many Marxists and postmodernists largely ignore the potential of counter-discourses, even though they are active in creating them. Discourses of this kind may be successful in arousing opposition to orders, especially when disaffection within them mounts for whatever reason. Indeed, they can be important sources of disaffection in their own right because, we have argued, it is never so-called objective features of societies that determine support or opposition to them but rather subjective assessments. They are in turn the product of discourses that encourage people to frame their assessments in particular ways. One of the features of contemporary Western politics is the extent to which conspiracy theories based on misinformation have proliferated and become a powerful counter-discourse.[78]

A monopoly over discourses and communication channels enhances governmental authority. It stifles imagination and dissent, the former being the prerequisite of dissent. Combined with some kind of intrusive police apparatus—as control over discourses so often is—it can make it difficult for any opposition to develop. Many traditional orders benefited from near total elite control over discourses. In Medieval Europe, the Catholic Church prohibited translations of the Latin Bible into vulgate because churchmen correctly understood that they would lose control over the text that sustained their authority. The first English translation, by William Tyndale in 1525, was banned in England, and English clerics visiting the continent were instructed to buy and burn as many copies as they could.[79] Access to the Bible in English enabled the rise of the Puritans and other dissenting sects, and their rejection of religious and civil authority was an underlying cause of the English Civil War.

Monopolizing discourses is more difficult for modern governments, but not impossible. Czarist Russia tried and failed. Stalin's Soviet Union was reasonably effective. Contemporary dictatorships struggle to control discourses and communication channels, and North Korea is arguably the most successful. In *1984*, George Orwell explored the mechanisms that can be mobilized toward this end. They include control of the media, relentless propaganda, transformation and dumbing down of language to prevent independent thought, and a police apparatus that prevents the formation of civil society.[80]

---

[78] Nancy L. Rosenblum and Russell Muirhead, *A Lot of People Are Saying: The New Conspiracism and the Assault on Democracy* (Princeton, NJ: Princeton University Press, 2019); Anna Merlan, *Republic of Lies: American Conspiracy Theorists and Their Surprising Rise to Power* (New York: Metropolitan Books, 2019).

[79] Stephen Greenblatt, *Renaissance Self-Fashioning: From More to Shakespeare* (Chicago: University of Chicago Press, 1980).

[80] George Orwell, *1984* (New York: Harcourt, Brace, 1949).

Monopolization of discourses can be threatening to religions and governments in the longer term. China aspires to this level of control, and its recent tightening of censorship is part and parcel of this strategy.[81] The regime regards control of information as a source of stability. However, the fragmentation of society it brings about and the stifling or suppression of dissent discourage or impede creativity and productivity, possibly making China less rather than more competitive. So too does the central control over political, economic, and cultural life that monopolization requires. Liberals describe these features of the Soviet Union as an underlying cause of its collapse.[82] North Korea went from a rapidly developing economy to a basket case, with a population haunted by the prospect of famine and now, with some encouragement of the market, once again, a developing economy.[83]

In 1932, in a speech to the British House of Commons, Prime Minister Stanley Baldwin famously warned that in a future war "the bomber will always get through" and that Britain's cities would be destroyed.[84] He was wrong, of course. Discourses, by contrast, are much more likely to get through, as they did in the eras of Christian and Muslim proselytizing. Enlightenment assaults on the cosmic order, and especially the divine right of kings, and the espousal of the power of humans to understand and reshape their physical and social environments had wide appeal. According to Tocqueville, pre-revolutionary France was made ripe for revolution by the influence that elite anti-establishment narratives of this kind had on the masses.[85] *Anciens régimes* sought to suppress books that might lead people to question the authority of church or state, but this notoriety made such books more popular, and greater demand for them made them more available.[86]

---

[81] Peter Lorentzen, "China's Strategic Censorship," *American Journal of Political Science* 58, no. 2 (2014), pp. 402–14.

[82] George Breslauer, *The Rise and Demise of World Communism* (Oxford: Oxford University Press, 2021), for a general take on the rise and fall of communist regimes.

[83] Nicholas Eberstadt, *The North Korean Economy: Between Crisis and Catastrophe* (New Brunswick, NJ: Transaction, 2009); Victor Cha, *North Korea: The Impossible State* (London: Bodley Head, 2012).

[84] Stanley Baldwin, "Fear of the Future," 10 November 1932, House of Commons Debate, International Affairs, *Hansard*, 270, pp. 631–35, http://hansard.millbanksystems.com/comm ons/1932/nov/10/international-affairs#S5CV0270P0_19321110_HOC_284 (accessed 28 April 2020).

[85] Alexis de Tocqueville, *The Old Regime and the French Revolution*, trans. Stuart Gilbert (Garden City, NY: Doubleday Anchor, 1955), pp. 142–44; Jonathan I. Israel, *Revolutionary Ideas: An Intellectual History of the French Revolution* (Princeton, NJ: Princeton University Press, 2014), pp. 30–53.

[86] T. C. W. Blanning, *Joseph II and Enlightened Despotism* (New York: Harper & Row, 1970), pp. 136–44.

Discourses must be considered double-edged swords. They help sustain the nomos essential to any society. By nomos, we mean that norms, rules, laws, and accepted practices make behavior legible and more predictable by directing it down some channels and away from others. Nomos facilitates the legitimization of hierarchies, but unlike golden age narratives, also encourages people to hope, even expect, that their societies will live up to their ethical justifications and abide by their sanctioned practices. The more societies propagate and publicize discourses intended to justify them, the more they become vulnerable to immanent critiques that expose the gap between theory and practice. Modern history is replete with critical discourses of this kind and political movements that sponsor or build on them to promote change.[87] Political elites can often suppress these discourses and those who produce and distribute them, but help to validate them by these efforts.

The ability of critics to produce and publicize counter-discourses, the ease with which authorities can suppress or counter them, and the relative appeal of discourses and counter-discourses are always context-dependent.[88] Some generalizations are nevertheless possible. Theodicies do not lend themselves so readily to immanent or empirical critiques, although they are certainly possible. Nor does their legitimacy depend on elite behavior. Indeed, elite exploitation and mass suffering are perfectly consistent with them. Widespread suffering might even be offered as confirmation of the claims of such works as Hesiod's *Works and Days* and the Garden of Eden story in Genesis. By contrast, discourses that defend elite status privileges on the basis of the benefits elites provide to the society are open to challenge when elites fail to live up to their self-proclaimed rule packages. All modern governments and political orders rest on such claims, which can build legitimacy—or make them vulnerable—depending on public attitudes. This explains why political protest is more prevalent and more successful in the modern era.

The Book of Genesis and its Garden of Eden story are a quintessential theodicy. Augustine sought to strengthen this discourse by portraying Adam, Eve, and the serpent as real beings, not as allegory, as Jews and some early Christians like Origen maintained. Augustine was successful in imposing this view on Catholicism, and convinced it would help propagate the religion. By the Renaissance it had become a source of doubt and stimulus for disbelief. It

---

[87] Richard Ned Lebow, *Reason and Cause: Social Science in a Social World* (Cambridge: Cambridge University Press, 2020), makes the case that immanent critique begins with Homer's *Iliad*.

[88] Theda Skocpol, *State and Social Revolutions: A Comparative Analysis of France, Russia, and China* (Cambridge: Cambridge University Press, 1979); Jack A. Goldstone, *Revolutions in the Early Modern World* (Berkeley: University of California Press, 1991); Jack A. Goldstone, Ted Robert Gurr, and Farrokh Moshiri, eds., *Revolutions in the Late Twentieth Century* (Boulder, CO: Westview, 1991).

brought into sharper focus the ethical dilemmas associated with the story, especially the inexplicable transformation from innocence to wickedness. It also encouraged people to look for the real Garden of Eden, to compute how many generations had elapsed since creation, and to ponder where and how Cain would have found a wife once expelled from his family if his parents, Adam and Eve, were the first humans. The discovery of the New World and its peoples who felt no shame in nudity was the first of many empirical conundrums for true believers.[89] Geology's discovery of the age of the earth, and biology's of evolution, would only heighten these tensions and convince many to dismiss Genesis as a fable.[90]

Critics of Marxism and neoliberalism relied on the same kind of reasoning. They foregrounded internal contradictions in their respective logic as well as failed empirical claims. The stronger and more vivid the claims of a discourse, the more likely the possibility of an immanent critique, and the more powerful the discourse, the more effective the critique—in the absence of its suppression. But suppression can shift the grounds of the contest, and in the longer term in a way unfavorable to those attempting to uphold the discourse in question.

Discourses can generate misplaced trust in and respect for elites. The more the demos trust the elite, the more the elite can exploit them. This results in orders that deviate further from their proclaimed principles of justice. The less faith the demos have in elites, the more likely they are to hold them accountable to relevant principles of justice, unless their anger can be deflected elsewhere. Too much trust threatens justice and order, as does too much distrust. In practice, order and justice need to be balanced, and this requires a degree of distrust, but not so much as to cause high levels of alienation and violation of norms.[91] Order also requires some degree of tension between discourses and behavior that support existing values and practices and those that oppose them.

Justice in the Modern World

Throughout history, ordinary people have had to behave like grass in the wind—and still do in many parts of the world. They have had little power and few, if any ways, of redressing grievances. Aristotle observed that the powerless cannot

---

[89] Stephen Greenblatt, *The Rise and Fall of Adam and Eve: The Story That Created Us* (New York: Norton, 2018), pp. 241–61.

[90] Brenda Maddox, *Reading the Rocks: How Victorian Geologists Discovered the Secret of Life* (London: Bloomsbury, 2017).

[91] Richard Ned Lebow, in Benedict Wilkinson, ed., *The Art of Creating Power: Freedman on Strategy* (London and Oxford: Hurst and Oxford University Press, 2017), pp. 243–58.

afford to become angry because they have no effective means of seeking re-venge. Their anger would only eat away at them and make them unhappier still.[92] People can, however, engage in all kinds of passive resistance, of the kind James Scott documents and offers as evidence that oppressed peoples do not consent to their dominance.[93]

One of the key political features of the modern world is the greater polit-ical power of subalterns. Democracy has given ordinary people voice in gov-ernment, initially through elections, and now also through public opinion polls and social media. It is nevertheless a matter of debate among Western intellectuals whether people have real authority or the illusion of it. There is a large literature on the oppressed, given a big impetus by Marxism, and more recently by critical theory, feminist, poststructuralism, and post-colonialism. Writers in these several traditions have documented inequality and injustices and their pernicious effects.[94]

In the United States, inequality was high between the world wars and fell to all-time lows after 1945. It began growing again in about 1980. Today, the per-centage of income going to the richest 1 percent of the population has increased almost tenfold in the United States since 1945.[95] In 2012, the net worth of the 400 wealthiest Americans exceeded that of the bottom half of all Americans.[96] Research indicates that economic gains for the rich have resulted in losses for the middle class and that their financial problems are more acute because many spend beyond their means to imitate the life style of the wealthy.[97] Greater wealth carries across-the-board health benefits. Studies find that rich Americans live fifteen years longer on average than poorer peers in their age cohort.[98] Their

[92] Aristotle, *Rhetoric*, 387a31–33, 1370b13–14, and *Nicomachean Ethics*, 1117a6–15.

[93] James C. Scott, *Weapons of the Weak: Everyday Forms of Peasant Resistance* (New Haven, CT: Yale University Press, 1985).

[94] Thomas Piketty, *Capital in the Twenty-first Century*, trans. Arthur Goldhammer (Cambridge, MA: Harvard University Press, 2014), and *The Economics of Inequality* (Cambridge, MA: Harvard University Press, 2015).

[95] Anthony Atkinson, *Inequality: What Can Be Done?* (Cambridge, MA: Harvard University Press, 2015). Also, Robert H. Frank, *Falling Behind: How Rising Inequality Harms the Middle Class* (Berkeley: University of California Press, 2007); Marianne Bertrand and Adair Morse, "Trickle Down Consumption," National Bureau of Economic Research, Working Paper 1883, March 2013; Piketty, *Capital in the Twenty-first Century*.

[96] Jesse Bricker, Arthur Kennickell, Kevin Moore, and John Sabelhaus, "Changes in U.S. Family Finances from 2007 to 2010: Evidence from the Survey of Consumer Finances," *Federal Reserve Bulletin* 98, no. 2 (2012), pp. 1–80.

[97] Frank, *Falling Behind*; Bertrand and Morse, "Trickle Down Consumption."

[98] Jessica Glenza, "Rich Americans Live up to 15 Years Longer than Poor Peers: Studies Find," *The Guardian*, 7 April 2017, https://www.theguardian.com/us-news/2017/apr/06/us-healthcare-wealth-income-inequality-lifespan (accessed 7 April 2017).

consequences became tragically apparent during the recent COVID-19 pandemic; the wealthy had lower rates of infection, higher rates of survival, and more comfortable lockdowns.[99]

It is nevertheless true that people almost everywhere are wealthier and healthier than they were a century ago. This has led some economists to propagate a counter-discourse that maintains that inequality is inescapable and that we should not be dismayed by it. We should pay less attention to the Gini coefficient—the accepted measure of inequality among values of a frequency distribution. It is driven by how rich people are; if everyone's income doubled, the gap between the rich and poor would increase considerably. Deidre McCloskey accordingly argues that instead of making comparisons between rich and poor, we should ask if those at the bottom are better off than they were fifty and one hundred years ago.[100] What counts in her view is absolute, not relative, wealth.

There is abundant evidence that both kinds of wealth matter, and that relative wealth becomes increasingly salient when people leave poverty behind. People become more concerned with status once they achieve even a modest degree of material well-being.[101] They are correspondingly sensitive to threats to their status or reminders that others have higher status.

Air rage provides a compelling example. In the United States, it is four times likely to occur in the coach section of an aircraft with a first-class cabin than in a plane without one. It is twice as likely if economy passengers board at the front and have to walk through the first-class section to their smaller, cramped seats. First-class passengers in turn are several times more likely to succumb to air rage if they have to mix with economy passengers before or during the boarding process.[102]

---

[99] Max Fisher and Emma Bubola, "As Coronavirus Deepens Inequality, Inequality Worsens Its Spread," *New York Times*, 16 March 2020, https://www.nytimes.com/2020/03/15/world/eur ope/coronavirus-inequality.html; Nicholas Kristof, "This Pandemic Is Bringing Another with It," *New York Times*, 22 April 2020, https://www.nytimes.com/2020/04/22/opinion/coronavirus-pandemics.html (both accessed 29 April 2020); Caelainn Barrl, "Covid-19 Deaths Twice as High in Poorest Areas in England and Wales," *The Guardian*, 1 May 2020, https://www.theguardian.com/world/2020/may/01/covid-19-deaths-twice-as-high-in-poorest-areas-in-england-and-wales (accessed 1 May 2020).

[100] Dierdre McCluskey, *Bourgeois Inequality: How Ideas, Not Capital or Institutions, Enriched the World* (Chicago: University of Chicago Press, 2016), pp. 46–47.

[101] Ronald Inglehart, *The Silent Revolution: Changing Values and Political Styles among Western Publics* (Princeton, NJ: Princeton University Press, 1977), and *Culture Shift in Advanced Industrial Society* (Princeton, NJ: Princeton University Press, 1999); Avner Offer, *The Challenge of Affluence: Self-Control and Well-Being in the United States and Britain since 1950* (Oxford: Oxford University Press, 2006).

[102] K. A. DeCelles and M. I. Norton, "Physical and Situational Inequality on Airplanes Predicts Air Rage," *Proceedings of the National Academy of Sciences* 113 (2006), pp. 5588–91.

Wealth confers status in the eyes of most people, so it tends to be evaluated in relative versus absolute terms. In the ancient world the principles of fairness and equality were distinct. In the modern West they became more intertwined. Jean-Jacques Rousseau and Adam Smith noted how wealth and status had become increasingly indistinguishable. People often desired material goods not for themselves but for the increase in status that ownership would provide.[103] By the end of the nineteenth century, Thorstein Veblen maintained, wealth had not only become "the definitive basis of esteem," but "a conventional basis for reputability." It was now regarded as "intrinsically honorable and confers honor on its possessor."[104] More so than in the past, material possessions conferred status, and status, as always, was an important source of self-esteem.

The shift in principles of justice and the tighter connections between material possessions, status, and self-esteem have important implications for how people respond to perceived inequalities. Ever since settled agricultural societies emerged, there has been a striking gap between rich and poor, and in some eras, including the first century of the Industrial Revolution, the gap increased noticeably. The discrepancy between wealthy and poor is less important than what those who are disadvantaged think about it. This is affected in the first instance, we theorize, by the dominant principle of justice in the society. Fairness justifies hierarchies of status and wealth. Equality maintains that everyone is equal and should be treated equally. It is deeply suspicious of hierarchies and insists that those that exist be made flatter. It has become the dominant principle of justice in the modern era, in Asia as well as the West. To legitimize hierarchies in an era of equality, elites must convince others that their privileges are based on achievement and well deserved for the benefits they offer the society as a whole.[105]

This shift from fairness to equality is most evident in domestic societies but has penetrated regional and international societies as well. To legitimize orders at any level, we must take it into account. The problem of order is further complicated by the continuing existence of the principle of fairness. As noted, people value both principles of justice, want their societies to enact them, and also mobilize them instrumentally to advance their parochial goals. These principles are sometimes reinforcing but are probably just as often in conflict. When people advance different principles, framings of them, and weigh their relative importance differently in the same domains, the quest for justice becomes a source of

---

[103] Jean-Jacques Rousseau, *Du contrat social* (Paris: Editions Garnier Frères, 1962), ch. 3, pp. 252–53; Adam Smith, *The Theory of Moral Sentiments* (Cambridge: Cambridge University Press, 2002 [1759]), I.iii.2, p. 71.

[104] Thorstein Veblen, *The Theory of the Leisure Class: An Economic Study in the Evolution of Institutions* (New York: Modern Library, 1934), p. 29.

[105] Rawls, *Theory of Justice*, builds his argument on this recognition.

conflict rather than a means to its resolution. Instead of building solidarity, it fosters discord.

Justice is intended to guide individual and collective behavior. It is also a source of hypocrisy. People pretend to act justly, or claim to do so when they have done the opposite. There is just as much reason to think that people look for ways of circumventing justice and avoiding its obligations when they are seen as costly or in some other way disadvantageous. The tension between values and practice is more acute for most organizations, including governments. They invoke principles of justice, but instantiate them even less than individuals. This may be because they have more power to act this way and often a greater ability to keep what they do from the public eye. There is accordingly a complex, uncertain, and highly context-dependent relationship between justice and order. They are only fully supporting and reconcilable in utopias. In real worlds, they are more often in conflict, even though all successful orders rest on principles of justice. Sometimes this conflict is destructive of order, but on other occasions the tension between them is productive.

The long-term shift away from fairness and to equality has been a primary cause of domestic and international unrest since the eighteenth century. This transformation occurred not only in politics but in civil society as well. In Western Europe, but also in the Habsburg Empire, by the early nineteenth century many organizations formerly restricted to aristocrats were now open to anyone who could pay the fees. This created a space where classes interacted on the basis of equality.[106] The transition to equality is still under way and a major cause of political conflict on almost every continent. Historically, changes in international society lag behind those in many member states, so the international order has only become subject to growing demands for chances on the basis of equality in the postwar era.[107] This transformation is not linear in nature. Not everyone prefers equality to fairness; many people think both appropriate in different, or even the same, circumstances, and in the United States and United Kingdom, fairness has undergone something of a revival under the banner of neoliberalism. Different preferences for principles of justice, often pronounced within societies, greatly exacerbate conflict.

International relations scholars disagree about the extent to which changes in domestic values and practices influence those at the international level, or

---

[106] Pieter M. Judson, *The Habsburg Empire: A New History* (Cambridge, MA: Harvard University Press, 2016), p. 142.

[107] Some scholars argue the reverse. See Paul Keal, *European Conquest and the Rights of Indigenous Peoples: The Moral Backwardness of International Society* (Cambridge: Cambridge University Press, 2003); Anthony Pagden, *Lord of All the World: Ideologies of Empire in Spain, Britain and France, c. 1500–c. 1800* (New Haven, CT: Yale University Press, 1995).

whether changes in international values and practices penetrate domestic orders.[108] In *National Identifications and International Relations*, Ned Lebow attempts to document both kinds of change and how the principle of equality has been mutually reinforcing in domestic and international societies.[109] International society nevertheless differs from its domestic counterparts in important respects. There is much less of a consensus about fundamental values and practices.[110] Secular versus religious values are in conflict in addition to fairness and equality, all of which promote different practices and bases for status.

The principle of equality penetrated regional and international societies only slowly. For centuries, Europeans did not concede equal status to most non-Christian political units. This gradually changed, and in the first decade of the twentieth century Japan was treated as a first-class power. However, in the United States, Japanese Americans were regarded as second-class citizens and Japan was asked to limit emigration.[111] It was not until the second half of the twentieth century that liberal democracies became the norm, so much so that authoritarian regimes were increasingly described as outliers, if not downright deviants. This status has not prevented such regimes or done much to hinder their flourishing.

International society has nevertheless been affected by changes in many of its more developed and powerful units, but lags behind them. Until very recently, as noted, standing was achieved primarily on the basis of military might, and secondarily, on the basis of cultural, scientific, and other achievements. In the postwar era wealth became increasingly important in its own right, and Scandinavia, Canada, the Netherlands, and South Korea, among others, claim standing on the basis of the wealth and the percentage of it they share with less affluent members of the international community. The two principles of justice have not merged the way they have in many Western societies. International society still has a dominant hierarchy, with the great powers or superpowers at the

---

[108] Hedley Bull, *The Anarchical Society: A Study of Order in World Politics* (New York: Columbia University Press, 1977); Hedley Bull and Adam Watson, eds., *The Expansion of International Society* (Oxford: Oxford University Press, 1984); R. J. Vincent, *Human Rights and International Relations* (Cambridge: Cambridge University Press, 1986); Andrew Linklater and Hidemi Suganami, *The English School of International Relations: A Contemporary Assessment* (Cambridge: Cambridge University Press, 2006).

[109] Lebow, *National Identifications and International Relations*, for elaboration.

[110] Mervyn Frost, "Tragedy, Ethics, and International Relations," and James Mayall, "Tragedy, Progress, and International Order," in Toni Erskine and Richard Ned Lebow, eds., *Tragedy and International Relations* (London: Palgrave-Macmillan, 2012), pp. 21–43 and 44–52 for a debate on the extent of these differences.

[111] David Reynolds, *Long Shadow The Legacies of the Great War in the Twentieth Century* (New York: Norton, 2015), p. 120; Naoko Shimazu, *Japan, Race, and Equality* (London: Routledge, 2009), pp. 80–96.

apex. Regional systems, some of them based on different principles, have nevertheless developed. This hierarchy, and its fairness-based principle of order, constitute something of an atavism in today's world, and is increasingly challenged. Practices based on equality (e.g., one state, one vote in many international fora) are widespread and often in sharp conflict with the hierarchy that places great powers at its apex. In effect, two principles of order are in conflict, and many different outcomes are possible.[112]

International society is deeply divided, in large part because its members subscribe to different principles and framings of justice and want them instantiated in often opposing ways. It is an open question as to whether this conflict is destructive or productive. We hope our analysis will shed some light on this question and highlight ways in which the latter outcome might be made more likely.

[112] Lebow, *National Identifications and International Relations*, ch. 7.

3

Justice in Confucianism

All political and social orders rest on principles of justice. This is as true for political systems of China as well as for those of the West. In the preceding chapter we examined principles of justice in Western history, focusing especially on fairness and equality. In this chapter and the next we do the same for China. At first blush it might be questionable whether we can find equivalent discussions of justice in Chinese history, let alone the principles of fairness and equality. One student of Chinese philosophy asserts that "there is not even a term for 'justice' in the classical lexicon of Confucius."[1] This claim is wide of the mark. Confucianism embodies a very rich theory of justice, and its concept of justice, *yi* 義, is central to its vocabulary. The Confucian theory of justice remains understudied, as do the theories of justice of other schools of Chinese thought.

We fill this gap by examining Confucian, Mohist, Legalist, and Daoist thoughts about justice, based on a close reading of their original texts. These four schools of thought are widely acknowledged as the most important in China's intellectual history. Each has made unique contributions to the development of Chinese civilization. Together with Buddhism, which was imported from India and adapted to Chinese conditions in the first millennium, they have formed the intellectual and cultural core of Chinese politics, society, and ways of life.

Every major intellectual movement is pioneered by a few great thinkers. In Western theories of justice, as we have seen, these include Plato and Aristotle in ancient Greece; Hume, Smith, Hobbes, and Kant during the Enlightenment; and Nietzsche, Martin Buber, and others in the contemporary era. Chinese theories of justice reveal a similar pattern: a small number of great thinkers of ancient China whose foundational ideas set the tone for their subsequent development. For Confucianism the indisputable masters are Kongzi (conventionally known as Confucius, 551–479 BCE), Mengzi (conventionally

---

[1] R. P. Peerenboom, "Confucian Justice: Achieving a Humane Society," *International Philosophical Quarterly* 30, no. 117 (1990), pp. 17–32, at p. 17.

Justice and International Order: East and West. Richard Ned Lebow and Feng Zhang, Oxford University Press.
© Oxford University Press 2022. DOI: 10.1093/oso/9780197598399.003.0003

known as Mencius, 372–289 BCE), and Xunzi (298–238 BCE). It is true that Confucianism underwent an intellectual transformation during the Song-Ming period (960–1644 CE), culminating in a more inward-looking and metaphysically conscious doctrine known as Neo-Confucianism. But insofar as justice theory is concerned, Neo-Confucianism made no serious modifications.

We begin our discussion with the concept of justice *yi* 義 and its two meanings in classical Confucianism—as a personal virtue and as social standards. Two additional concepts, *ren* (仁 humaneness) and *li* (禮 ritual propriety), provide the foundation for the Confucian theory of justice, serving respectively as the internal grounding and external manifestation of justice. Confucian justice espouses a strong principle of fairness and a subdued principle of equality. A tension has always existed between these two principles in the history of Confucian thought. In the imperial age when Confucianism was the dominant intellectual force, fairness always trumped equality. In the twentieth century, Chinese intellectuals, armed with imported Western ideas of equality, freedom, and democracy, launched a ferocious attack on Confucian ritual hierarchy and its principle of fairness. The Confucian tradition itself appeared in danger of extinction during the May Fourth movement of 1919 and the Cultural Revolution of 1966–1976. It withstood these onslaughts and staged a remarkable comeback, first in Hong Kong and Taiwan after the 1950s, and then on the Chinese mainland since the 1990s. In the new Confucianism of mainland China, fairness again appears to be having the upper hand.

Yi 義 as Justice

The Chinese concept that bears the closest resemblance to justice in Western intellectual history is *yi* 義. *Yi* has a wide conceptual scope and is variously translated as "appropriateness," "rightness," "duty," "righteousness," or "morality." In its earliest historical origins, it referred to the appropriateness of conduct in religious ceremonies.[2] All later Chinese thinkers draw on this sense of *yi* as uncodified rules and standards. Roger T. Ames provides perhaps the best philosophical definition of *yi* as "an achieved sense of appropriateness that enables one to act in a proper and fitting manner, given the specifics of a situation." This sense of appropriateness should be understood in terms of not only its aesthetic and moral connotations, but also its social and religious implications.[3]

---

[2] Li Zehou [李澤厚], *Lishi Bentilun* [歷史本體論 Historical Ontology] (Beijing: SDX, 2008), p. 381.

[3] Roger T. Ames, *Confucian Role Ethics: A Vocabulary* (Honolulu: University of Hawai'i Press, 2011), p. 205; Roger T. Ames and Henry Rosemont Jr., *The Analects of Confucius: A Philosophical Translation* (New York: Ballantine Books, 1998), p. 55.

Kongzi, the earliest and greatest Confucian thinker of all time, regards *yi* as "a kind of cultivated sense of what is right and morally proper."[4] He says: "Exemplary persons [*junzi* 君子] in making their way in the world have no predispositions for or against anything; rather, they go with what is appropriate [*yi* 義]."[5] *Yi* 義 is the ultimate criterion by which personal conduct is to be regulated.

Kongzi further remarks: "Having a sense of appropriate conduct [*yi* 義] as one's basic disposition [*zhi* 質], developing it in observing ritual propriety [*li* 禮], expressing it with modesty, and consummating it in making good on one's word [*xin* 信]: this then is an exemplary person."[6] Here he seems to be introducing two different meanings of *yi*. He understands *yi* as a personal disposition or virtue. However, in welding *yi* to *li* 禮 (ritual propriety), which denotes social norms and conventions, and suggesting *li* as the embodiment of *yi*, he introduces a sense of *yi* as social values or standards by which personal conduct is evaluated.

This second meaning of *yi* as social standards can be illustrated by Kongzi's views on personal gain or benefit (*li* 利). In a famous passage he says "exemplary persons understand what is appropriate [*yi* 義]; petty persons understand what is of personal gain [*li* 利]." This seems to pit *yi* against self-interest, as a kind of altruism. But this interpretation would be misleading. Kongzi in fact acknowledges the legitimacy of personal interests. One of the four ways of being an exemplary person, he tells his disciples, is to be "generous in attending to the needs [*hui* 惠] of the common people."[7] Zhu Xi, one of the great Neo-Confucian thinkers of the twelfth century, glosses *hui* as meaning the love of gain (*ai li* 愛利).[8] Kongzi believes that unbridled pursuit of personal gain incurs resentment.[9] What he intends when pitting *yi* against personal gain is the admonition that the quest for the latter must be based on the former; put differently, self-seeking behavior must be constrained by the standards of justice. He summarizes this principle as "*jian*

---

[4] Edward Slingerland, trans., *Confucius Analects: With Selections from Traditional Commentaries* (Indianapolis: Hackett, 2003), p. 241.

[5] Huang Huaixin [黃懷信], *Lunyu huijiao jishi* [論語彙校集釋 Corrections and Exegeses of the Analects of Confucius] (Shanghai: Shanghai guji chubanshe, 2008), p. 326; Ames and Rosemont, *The Analects of Confucius*, p. 91; Slingerland, *Confucius Analects*, p. 32.

[6] Huang, *Lunyu*, p. 1407; Ames and Rosemont, *The Analects of Confucius*, p. 188; Slingerland, *Confucius Analects*, p. 181.

[7] Huang, *Lunyu*, p. 419; Ames and Rosemont, *The Analects of Confucius*, p. 99; Slingerland, *Confucius Analects*, p. 46.

[8] Huang, *Lunyu*, p. 420.

[9] Huang, *Lunyu*, p. 332; Ames and Rosemont, *The Analects of Confucius*, p. 91; Slingerland, *Confucius Analects*, p. 33.

li si yi [見利思義]"—when seeing a chance for gain one should think of appropriate conduct.[10]

In Kongzi the two senses of *yi* as personal virtue and social standards are often confounded. His two great successors, Mengzi and Xunzi, have respectively developed each of these at great lengths. Mengzi is commonly said to highlight *yi*'s personal dimension as an expression of a person's innate but incipient virtuous inclinations.[11] He defines *yi* as the "feeling of disdain [*xiu e zhi xin* 羞惡之心]," one of the four cardinal human virtues that he theorizes as being grounded in a person's innate emotional reactions.[12] In this sense *yi* may be translated as "righteousness," although we need to be aware that the biblical associations that attend the word "righteousness" as obedience to the will of God introduces a sense of an independent, objective, and divinely sanctioned standard of rightness or morality that has little relevance for *yi*.[13]

Elsewhere, Mengzi edges closer toward a sense of *yi* as social principles, including that of the division of labor. He says: "Some labor with their hearts; some labor with their strength. Those who labor with their hearts rule others; those who labor with their strength are governed by others. This is the appropriateness [*yi* 義] common to the world."[14] Mengzi thus portrays a society with a hierarchical division of labor between the ruler and the ruled. He is in part describing a prevalent historical practice and in part preaching the norm of social division between the "great people" (*da ren* 大人) and the "petty people" (*xiao ren* 小人). Zhu Xi comments that the exchange of goods between these two social strata is just the means by which they help each other, and not the means by which they harm each other.[15] For Mengzi, as for Zhu Xi and a great many other Confucians, such divisions are conducive to social harmony. We shall see later that such social divisions embody the principle of fairness in Confucian justice theory.

When Mengzi asserts that *yi* is "people's proper path," he can mean either personal righteousness or social appropriateness, although given the focus of his thought on inner virtues righteousness is assumed to be his dominant conception of *yi*.[16] With Xunzi, such ambiguity diminishes. To be sure, Xunzi at times

[10] Huang, *Lunyu*, p. 1260; Ames and Rosemont, *The Analects of Confucius*, p. 174; Slingerland, *Confucius Analects*, p. 158.

[11] Bryan W. Van Norden, *Introduction to Classical Chinese Philosophy* (Indianapolis: Hackett, 2011), p. 176.

[12] Jiao Xun [焦循], *Mengzi zhengyi* [孟子正義 Correct Exegeses of Mengzi] (Beijing: Zhonghua shuju, 1987), p. 757; Bryan W. Van Norden, trans., *Mengzi: With Selections from Traditional Commentaries* (Indianapolis: Hackett, 2008), p. 149.

[13] Ames, *Confucian Role Ethics*, p. 203.

[14] Jiao, *Mengzi*, p. 373; Van Norden, *Mengzi*, p. 70.

[15] Van Norden, *Mengzi*, p. 70.

[16] Jiao, *Mengzi*, p. 507; Van Norden, *Mengzi*, p. 95.

sees *yi* as a personal virtue, namely a tendency to adhere to moral requirements, and in this sense he is not too far apart from Mengzi. Nevertheless, he lays great emphasis on the social functions of *yi*, almost seeing it as an artificial construct to meet the human need for society.[17]

Xunzi is the first Chinese thinker to use the term *zheng yi* 正義, which now serves as the standard translation for "justice."[18] He uses *yi* to refer to a variety of qualities, including appropriateness, fairness, impartiality, uprightness, rightness, and rationality. Appropriateness is his dominant conception of *yi*. He says that through *yi* the exemplary person changes and adapts to circumstances, because he knows when it is appropriate to bend and straighten.[19]

Another important example where Xunzi intends *yi* to denote appropriate principles of social action is his intervention in the Confucian debate of *li-yi* initiated by Kongzi. He asserts that "actions performed for the sake of profit [*zheng li* 正利] are called 'work' while those performed for the sake of *yi* [正義] are called 'moral conduct.' "[20] And further, "Those who put *yi* first and profit second will attain honor; those who put profit first and *yi* second will attain disgrace."[21] The argument is exactly the same as Kongzi's mentioned earlier. *Yi* as justice is seen as a moral constraint on people's pursuit of goals and benefits and is best translated as "standards of appropriateness." It is a non-consequentialist, nonutilitarian idea.[22]

The Inner Sources of *Yi* 義

Where does *yi*, understood as either a personal virtue or social appropriateness, come from? This is a question about the grounding of the Confucian conception of justice. Kongzi's answer is the most influential of all Chinese thought and has set the tone for Chinese humanism. He proposes *ren* 仁 as the inner source

---

[17] Van Norden, *Introduction to Classical Chinese Philosophy*, p. 176.

[18] Huang Yushun [黄玉順], *Zhongguo zhengyilun de xingcheng: Zhou Kong Meng Xun de zhidu lunlixue chuantong* [The Development of China's Theory of Justice: The Tradition of Institutional Ethics of the Duke of Zhou, Kongzi, Mengzi, and Xunzi] (Beijing: Dongfang chubanshe, 2015), p. 311.

[19] Wang Tianhai [王天海], *Xunzi jiaoshi* [荀子校釋 Corrections and Exegeses of the *Xunzi*] (Shanghai: Shanghai guji chubanshe, 2005), p. 91; Eric L. Hutton, trans., *Xunzi: the Complete Text* (Princeton, NJ: Princeton University Press, 2014), p. 18.

[20] Wang, *Xunzi*, p. 882; Hutton, *Xunzi*, p. 236.

[21] Wang, *Xunzi*, p.127; Hutton, *Xunzi*, p. 25.

[22] Joseph Chan, *Confucian Perfectionism: A Political Philosophy for Modern Times* (Princeton, NJ: Princeton University Press, 2014), p. 164.

not only of *yi* but of the whole gamut of personal conduct and social practice. Confucianism is sometimes referred to as the doctrine of *ren* owing to the pivotal role it imparts to that concept. *Ren* does not just embody a sense of justice, as some scholars suggest.[23] It is the psychological and ethical foundation of Confucian justice.

Kongzi does not offer a single, precise definition of *ren*, but instead discusses its varying meanings in different contexts in order to encompass all its connotations. The breadth and depth of the concept are reflected in Roger T. Ames and Henry Rosemont Jr.'s enunciation of it as "one's cultivated cognitive, aesthetic, moral, and religious sensibilities as they are expressed in one's ritualized roles and relationships."[24] *Ren*, in other words, reflects one's entire person. It is variously translated as humaneness, humanity, benevolence, love, compassion, sympathy, goodness, and consummate person or conduct. There are, however, two basic senses in which Kongzi uses *ren*: as universalizable affection, and as a personal virtue. Of the two, the first sense of *ren* as affection is the more fundamental in his thought.

Ren as affection stands for a basic and universalizable aspect of human feelings manifested as "love" or care for others. Kongzi says "*ren* is to *ai* [愛 love or care for] others."[25] He is appealing to a prominent human emotion embedded in every person's psychical reservoir that is capable of being aroused. Once aroused, it can lead to a process of "growing" (*sheng* 生) human relationships into robust participation in the human community. The kind of love that Kongzi wishes to call forth is an emotional response, not a principle of action. Love as a principle, as Bertrand Russell suspected, does not seem to be genuine.[26] Kongzi does not ignore intellectual reason or rationality, however. He believes that reason builds on emotion; a holistic and healthy rationality is therefore both cognitive and affective, but emotion—or affective rationality—is in the final analysis more fundamental than cognitive reason.[27] This privileging of emotion over reason stands out as a most distinguishing feature of Chinese thought in comparison with the reason-infused Western philosophy from Plato to Descartes to Leibniz to Kant.

---

[23] Erin M. Cline, "Two Senses of Justice: Confucianism, Rawls, and Comparative Political Philosophy," *Dao*, no. 6 (2007), pp. 361–81.

[24] Ames and Rosemont, *The Analects of Confucius*, p. 49.

[25] Huang, *Lunyu*, p. 1132; Ames and Rosemont, *The Analects of Confucius*, p. 159; Slingerland, *Confucius Analects*, p. 136.

[26] Bertrand Russell, *The Basic Writings of Bertrand Russell*, edited by Robert E. Egner and Lester E. Denonn (London: Routledge, 2009), p. 349.

[27] Li Zehou [李澤厚], *Lunyu jindu* [論語今讀 Reading the Analects of Confucius Today] (Beijing: Sanlian, 2008), p. 32.

Mengzi emphasizes the emotional underpinnings of *ren* even more strongly than Kongzi. In a famous passage about the "four human sprouts" he remarks:

> The reason why I say that all humans have hearts that are not unfeeling toward others is this. Suppose someone suddenly saw a child about to fall into a well: anyone in such a situation would have a feeling of alarm and compassion—not because one sought to get in good with the child's parents, not because one wanted fame among one's neighbors and friends, and not because one would dislike the sound of the child's cries. From this we can see that if one is without the feeling of compassion, one is not human. . . . The feeling of compassion is the sprout of humaneness [*ren* 仁]. The feeling of disdain is the sprout of righteousness [*yi* 義]. The feeling of deference is the sprout of propriety [*li* 禮]. The feeling of approval and disapproval is the sprout of wisdom [*zhi* 智].[28]

Just as Mengzi defines *yi* 義 as the feeling of disdain, so he defines *ren* 仁 as the feeling of compassion, and also an inherent emotional quality. Zhu Xi, who builds his Neo-Confucianism on the basis of Mengzi's emotional theory of human nature, suggests that compassion, disdain, deference, and approval and disapproval are emotions (*qing* 情), while humaneness, righteousness, propriety, and wisdom are human nature (*xing* 性). Linking and controlling emotions and human nature is *xin* (心 heart-and-mind).[29] He further argues that humaneness, righteousness, propriety, and wisdom are the more fundamental aspects of human nature in that they give rise to emotions such as compassion, disdain, deference, and approval and disapproval. Zhu Xi is right in making the distinction between emotions and human nature in Mengzi's thought, but he inverts their logic relationship. For Mengzi, emotions are the "sprouts" from which human nature springs, not the other way around.[30]

Xunzi likewise grounds *yi* 義 in *ren* 仁. The exemplary person, he says, "dwells in *ren* by means of *yi*, and only then is it *ren*."[31] *Ren* is care, and so it makes for affection; *yi* is reason (*li* 理), and so it makes for proper conduct.[32] It is clear that Xunzi regards *ren* as an emotion and *yi* as a principle of action. *Ren* and *yi* have a mutually constitutive relationship in that *ren* is the inner source of *yi*, while *yi* is the behavioral requirement of *ren*.

---

[28] Jiao, *Mengzi*, pp. 232–34; Van Norden, *Mengzi*, pp. 46–47.
[29] Van Norden, *Mengzi*, p. 47.
[30] Huang, *Zhongguo zhengyilun de xingcheng*, p. 208.
[31] Wang, *Xunzi*, pp. 1044–45; Hutton, *Xunzi*, pp. 292–93.
[32] Wang, *Xunzi*, pp. 1044–45; Hutton, *Xunzi*, pp. 292–3.

How, then, is *ren* as love or care manifested or practiced? Kongzi again provides the fundamental answer, which may be summarized into the principle of universal but differential care. Differential care means that a person practicing *ren* should start with one's family and then extend to other people. Kongzi observes that filial and fraternal responsibility is the root of *ren*.[33] One should love both his father and a stranger, but not equally; the love of his father must come first and should be stronger than the love of a stranger. Mengzi says much the same thing in a conversation with a king eager to hear advice about how to expand his power: "Treat your elders as elders, and extend it to the elders of others; treat your young ones as young ones, and extend it to the young ones of others, and you can turn the world in the palm of your hand."[34]

At the same time that love is differentiated, it must be extended. Humane persons, Mengzi says, "extend from what they love to what they do not yet love."[35] This suggests *ren* as universal affection through the mechanism of "extension" (*tui* 推). Although it is Mengzi who gives the concept of "extension" prominence, the idea is already manifest in Kongzi, who has developed what might be called the Confucian Golden Rule. It incorporates a negative and positive principle. The former says: "Do not impose upon others what you yourself do not want."[36] The latter says: "Humane persons establish others in seeking to establish themselves and promote others in seeking to get there themselves."[37] And further, "Being able to take what is near at hand as an analogy could perhaps be called the method of humaneness."[38]

Both the negative and positive principles are known as *shu* 恕 (putting oneself in the other's place).[39] Together they teach that humane persons identify themselves with the whole myriad things of the world and harmonize their desires with the desires of the world. They extend their affection from near to far through a continuous gradation, eventually making it permeate the whole world. By caring for others while trying to realize themselves, and by trying to achieve public interests in this way, humane persons overcome their personal desires without eliminating them.[40] *Shu* is not altruism since it starts with oneself, but

---

[33] Huang, *Lunyu*, p. 30; Ames and Rosemont, *The Analects of Confucius*, p. 71; Slingerland, *Confucius Analects*, p. 1.

[34] Jiao, *Mengzi*, p. 86; Van Norden, *Mengzi*, p. 11.

[35] Jiao, *Mengzi*, p. 953; Van Norden, *Mengzi*, p. 185.

[36] Huang, *Lunyu*, p. 1068; Ames and Rosemont, *The Analects of Confucius*, p. 153; Slingerland, *Confucius Analects*, p. 126.

[37] Huang, *Lunyu*, p. 551; Ames and Rosemont, *The Analects of Confucius*, p. 110; Slingerland, *Confucius Analects*, p. 63.

[38] Huang, *Lunyu*, p. 551; Ames and Rosemont, *The Analects of Confucius*, p. 110; Slingerland, *Confucius Analects*, p. 63.

[39] Ames, *Confucian Role Ethics*, p. 195.

[40] Huang, *Lunyu*, pp. 552–53.

it acquires an other-regarding generosity as it requires taking into consideration the interests of others.[41] It dissolves the self-other dichotomy and integrates personal interests with public interests in the building of a common humanity.

The External Manifestations of *Yi*

Internally *yi* 義, the Confucian notion of justice, is grounded in the emotional foundation of *ren* 仁 practiced through the principle of universal but differential care. What are the behavioral implications of this internal source of *yi*? Kongzi's answer is already evident. Earlier we quoted him saying that the exemplary person develops *yi* 義 in observing ritual propriety (*li* 禮). Mengzi illustrates the relationship between *yi* and *li* by likening *yi* to the path and *li* to the door, remarking that only an exemplary person can follow this path and go in and out through this door.[42] Xunzi is more forthright: the exemplary person "carries out *yi* by means of *li*, and only then is it *yi*."[43]

Li 禮, then, is the Confucian answer to the externalization of *yi* 義 or the behavioral manifestation of justice. Originally referring to ritual practices, *li* has come to encompass rules, norms, and institutions of personal etiquette and social conduct that become the hallmarks of the traditional Chinese society. Kongzi remarks with regard to personal etiquette: "Deference unmediated by observing ritual propriety [*li* 禮] is lethargy; caution unmediated by observing ritual propriety is timidity; boldness unmediated by observing ritual propriety is rowdiness; candor unmediated by observing ritual propriety is rudeness."[44] He posits a direct relationship between *ren* and *li*: "Restraining yourself and returning to ritual propriety [*li* 禮] constitutes humaneness [*ren* 仁]."[45]

There is a strong consensus among leading scholars that Kongzi's conception of the relationship between *ren* and *li* is among the most profound of his thoughts. The historian Ying-shih Yü observes that Kongzi reinterpreted *ren* as the spiritual kernel of *li*.[46] The philosopher Li Zehou similarly argues that Kongzi is trying to explain *li* by means of *ren*, emphasizing *li* not just as rites but as propriety with an emotional foundation. Such an emphasis makes eminent sense

---

[41] Ames, *Confucian Role Ethics*, p. 195.

[42] Jiao, *Mengzi*, p. 723; Van Norden, *Mengzi*, p. 141.

[43] Wang, *Xunzi*, pp. 1044–45; Hutton, *Xunzi*, pp. 292–93.

[44] Huang, *Lunyu*, p. 673; Ames and Rosemont, *The Analects of Confucius*, p. 120; Slingerland, *Confucius Analects*, p. 78.

[45] Huang, *Lunyu*, p. 1060; Ames and Rosemont, *The Analects of Confucius*, p. 152; Slingerland, *Confucius Analects*, p. 125.

[46] Ying-Shih Yü, *Chinese History and Culture, Volume 1: Sixth Century BCE to Seventeenth Century* (New York: Columbia University Press, 2016), Kindle ed., location 746–48.

because religious rites in antiquity were impregnated with the psychological qualities of awe, deference, loyalty, and sincerity. It is these qualities that Kongzi hopes to rationalize into the overarching concept of *ren*, embedding therein a psychology and ethic of universal affection that he wishes to put into practice. In this way he gives a psychological and ethical explanation of *li* through *ren*.[47]

Xunzi is ancient China's preeminent theorist of *li*, and gives greater prominence to the social function of *li*. He considers *li* the "ultimate in the human way" and the consummate solution to the ideal sociopolitical order.[48] Proper conduct of *li* by all social groups is the foundation of social order and harmony; its breakdown, a prelude to disorder and conflict. Xunzi remarks that "If their lives are without *li*, then people cannot survive. If affairs are without *li*, in them success does not thrive. If state and clan are without *li*, for them peace does not arrive."[49] Indeed, he sometimes uses the concept of *fa* 法 (law or regulation) interchangeably with *li*, taking both to mean social norms and institutions.[50] Nevertheless, being a true Confucian he does not fail to highlight *li*'s foundation in *ren* and *yi*. As he says, *li* "achieves proper form for love and respect, and brings to perfection the beauty of carrying out *yi*."[51]

The Requirements of *Yi*

Yi requires its internal grounding in *ren* and external realization in *li*. According to Kongzi, however, *li* is liable to alterations (*you sunyi* 有损益) in different historical circumstances, even though its foundation in *ren* and *yi* makes it possible to understand its continuities and changes.[52] This observation points to situational flexibility as a requirement of practicing *yi* or justice. Wang Xianqian (1842–1917), a leading commentator of Xunzi's thought, when pondering on Xunzi's remark that the exemplary person changes and adapts to circumstances through *yi*, comments that "*yi* has no fixed yardstick but changes with circumstances."[53]

Situational flexibility is another distinguishing feature of the Chinese conception of justice in comparison with that in the Western tradition. *Yi* is a matter of one's response to a situation, and relates to one's understanding of the situation

[47] Li Zehou [李澤厚], *You wu dao li, shi li gui ren* [由巫到禮,釋禮歸仁 From Shamanism to Propriety, from Propriety to Humaneness] (Beijing: SDX, 2015).

[48] Wang, *Xunzi*, p. 768; Hutton, *Xunzi*, p. 205.

[49] Wang, *Xunzi*, p. 49; Hutton, *Xunzi*, p. 10.

[50] Huang, *Zhongguo zhengyilun de xingcheng*, p. 345.

[51] Wang, *Xunzi*, p. 779; Hutton, *Xunzi*, p. 209.

[52] Huang, *Lunyu*, p. 181; Ames and Rosemont, *The Analects of Confucius*, p. 81; Slingerland, *Confucius Analects*, p. 15.

[53] Wang, *Xunzi*, p. 93.

and one's values, motives, and goals in practice.[54] Each response is considered unique; situational specificities, not moral absolutes, are the basis for the application of yi.[55] Based on an elastic ethic of universal but differential care, Confucian justice has none of the connotation of an absolute moral standard found in some Western conceptions of justice.

Confucian thinkers suggest two dimensions along which the situational flexibility of yi might be considered: the spatial and the temporal. Ames describes them in terms of synchronical and diachronical action:

> Synchronically yi action attempts to extend the context as broadly as possible, attending to the full range of possibilities involved, and taking under consideration the sometimes competing yet still legitimate interests of all concerned. Diachronically yi action in the present moment locates the immediate circumstances within the continuities it has with both past and future activity, making a comprehensive consideration of the continuing present the best way to make full use of those resources inherited out of past experience and the most productive way of anticipating what is yet to come.[56]

In addition to flexibility, Ames suggests resolve as the second practical requirement of justice.[57] This reading finds support in Kongzi's remarks that "to fail to cultivate moral excellence, to fail to practice what I have learned, to be unable to follow through on what has been deemed to be the most appropriate course of action [yi 義], and to be unable to reform conduct that is not efficacious—these are the things I worry about."[58] Kongzi seems to be advocating a two-step theory of justice linking thought and action: one must first determine what justice requires or entails in a given situation and then act upon that determination with firmness. The theory is already implicit in his elucidation of the qualities of the exemplary person mentioned earlier: such a person must have yi as a basic disposition and realize it with li (ritual propriety), sun (modesty), and xin (trustworthiness).[59]

---

[54] Chung-Ying Cheng, "Critical Reflections on Rawlsian Justice versus Confucian Justice," *Journal of Chinese Philosophy* 24, no. 4 (1997), pp. 417–26, at p. 420.

[55] Christophe Duvert, "How Is Justice Understood in Classic Confucianism?" *Asian Philosophy* 28, no. 4 (2018), pp. 295–315, at p. 297.

[56] Ames, *Confucian Role Ethics*, p. 202.

[57] Ames, *Confucian Role Ethics*, p. 204.

[58] Huang, *Lunyu*, p. 565; Ames and Rosemont, *The Analects of Confucius*, p. 111; Slingerland, *Confucius Analects*, p. 64.

[59] Huang, *Lunyu*, p. 1407; Ames and Rosemont, *The Analects of Confucius*, p. 188; Slingerland, *Confucius Analects*, p. 181.

Harmony as the Consummation of Justice

Justice and ritual combine, so the Confucians hope, to produce a sublime order of harmony (*he* 和). *He* refers to an ideal state of order as well as a process of reaching that ideal, and in the latter sense it is more appropriately rendered as "harmonization." In its earliest origin *he* describes how various sounds of animals, people, and instruments respond to one another in an appropriate way. Harmonization is the process whereby "various sounds respond to one another in a mutually promoting, mutually complementing, and mutually stabilizing way."[60] But it does not imply perfect agreement. Harmony presupposes the diversity rather than sameness of things, because diversity produces a lively world while sameness stymies growth.[61] Kongzi famously remarks that "exemplary persons seek harmony not sameness; petty persons seek sameness not harmony."[62] Because of diversity, a degree of disagreement and tension is inherent in the process of harmonization. They are nevertheless manageable disagreements and creative tensions that can be channeled to bring about harmony in the end. Harmonization is the process of overcoming strife; strife is necessary to achieve greater harmony in a continual process. For Confucians, overcoming strife does not mean eliminating conflict in toto. Rather, it means ameliorating and keeping conflict under control by turning antagonistic opposition or rivalry into cooperative opposition or accommodation. Harmony is achieved by striking a balance—the middle way or due proportion (*zhongyong* 中庸)—between diverse and opposing forces and eventually reconciling them into a peaceful and pleasant coexistence.[63]

Harmony embodies Confucian affective rationality rooted in the psychology and ethic of universal care, as noted earlier. For Confucians, the world exists not just for one kind of thing, but for the "myriad things." Nothing in the world can claim absolute superiority over everything else. Parties to a harmonious relationship are both the condition for and the constraint on each other's growth. A harmonious relationship implies mutual complementarity and mutual support between the parties. Harmony produces mutual benefit for the parties, but it cannot be reduced to the satisfaction of individual motives. Its ultimate

[60] Chenyang Li, "The Confucian Ideal of Harmony," *Philosophy East & West* 56, no. 4 (2006), p. 583–603, at p. 584.

[61] Li, "The Confucian Ideal of Harmony," pp. 584–85; Xinzhong Yao, "The Way of Harmony in the *Four Books*," *Journal of Chinese Philosophy* 40, no. 2 (2013), pp. 252–68, at pp. 255–56.

[62] Huang, *Lunyu*, p. 1210; Ames and Rosemont, *The Analects of Confucius*, p. 169; Slingerland, *Confucius Analects*, p. 149.

[63] Li, "The Confucian Ideal of Harmony," p. 591; Yao, "The Way of Harmony in the *Four Books*," p. 253.

purpose is to provide "a context for each party to have optimal space to flourish" and to create a fluid, dynamic, and productive order embodying human affection and obligation.[64]

Harmony across multiple levels of the family, the community, the nation, and the world is the highest ideal of order for the Confucian tradition.[65] *Zhongyong* (中庸 The Middle Way), a foundational text on Confucian metaphysics, declares that "harmony is the great way under Heaven."[66] *Yijing* (易經 Classic of Changes), another metaphysical text, speaks of "grand harmony" (太和 *taihe*), the idea that the world is full of different things and yet all these things harmonize even as they constantly change. Perhaps the best illustration of this Confucian ideal is Kongzi's description of a Golden Age society of *datong* 大同 (Great Harmony or Grand Union) as related through a dialogue between the master and one of his students in *The Book of Rites* (*liji* 禮記):

> Zhongni [Kongzi] was once present as one of the guests at the *Ji* Sacrifice; when it was over, he went out and paced back and forth on the terrace over the Gate of Proclamations, looking sad and sighing. What made him sigh was the state of Lu. Yan was by his side and asked him, "Master, why are you sighing?" Kongzi replied, "I have never seen the practice of the Grand Dao and the eminent men of the Three Dynasties, but I aspire to follow them. When the Grand Dao was pursued, a public and common spirit ruled all under the heaven [*tianxia weigong* 天下為公]; they chose men of talent, virtue, and ability for public service; they valued mutual trust and cultivated harmony. They did not treat only their own parents as parents, nor treat only their own sons as sons. Provision was secured for the aged till their death, employment for the able-bodied, and the means of growing up for the young. People showed kindness and compassion to widows, orphans, childless men, and those who were disabled by disease, so that they were all sufficiently provided for. Men had work and women had homes. Possessions were not wastefully discarded, nor were they greedily hoarded. People enjoyed laboring for others. In this way selfish scheming was discouraged and did not arise. Robbers, thieves, and rebellious traitors were unknown, and doors remained open and unlocked. Such was the Grand Union [*datong* 大同].[67]

---

[64] Li, "The Confucian Ideal of Harmony," p. 589.

[65] Li, "The Confucian Ideal of Harmony"; Yao, "The Way of Harmony in the *Four Books*."

[66] Li, "The Confucian Ideal of Harmony," p. 588.

[67] This translation is adopted from Chan, *Confucian Perfectionism*, p. 6.

The Principle of Fairness

What are the principles of justice that might lead to harmony? We explained earlier that situational flexibility is a practical requirement of *yi* as justice, so *yi* is not associated with any rigid or absolute moral injunctions as is Kant's categorial imperative.[68] Nevertheless, we can find in Confucian thought a strong principle of fairness and a subdued principle of equality. Neither is formulated in the manner of a universal law; both are nonetheless clear principles of justice.

There are two main conceptions of fairness in Confucian thought: fairness based on merit, virtue, or status, and fairness based on the reciprocity of obligations. The outstanding theorist of the first conception is Xunzi, who embeds his theory of fairness within a larger theory of *li* (禮 ritual propriety). Xunzi's theory of *li* is a magnificent, if ultimately flawed, attempt at explaining social order. As noted earlier, like Kongzi and Mengzi, Xunzi grounds *li* in *ren* and *yi*. He goes beyond them to propound an elaborate theory to explain *li*'s origins and functions. It is in this explanation that he claims fairness as a central principle of *yi* or justice.

Xunzi begins his theory with human desires and needs. He argues that humans are born with desires and must seek some means to satisfy them. If there are no limits and degrees to their seeking, they will invariably fall to wrangling with one another. From wrangling comes disorder and from disorder comes exhaustion. Humans live in social groups, but without proper distinctions to separate their statuses and roles, struggles for resources between groups are bound to occur. Xunzi claims that China's ancient kings hated such disorder and established ritual norms (*li* 禮) based on standards of appropriateness (*yi* 義) to create social divisions (*fen* 分) among their subjects and achieve distributive justice in fair hierarchies. The aim was to train their desires and provide for their satisfaction, so that desires did not go beyond the means available for their satiation and material goods did not fall short of what was desired.[69]

Xunzi roots the cause of disorder in the lack of *fen* 分—the proper divisions in social statuses, roles, classes, or occupations, and the appropriate distribution of resources in accordance with them. *Fen* implies hierarchy based in part on a rank ordering of status. This understanding of hierarchy, it might be noted, is in perfect harmony with the ancient Greek conception that one of us has documented elsewhere.[70] Xunzi recognizes that a society coheres not by gathering identical

---

[68] Immanuel Kant, translated and edited by Mary Gregor and Jens Timmermann, rev. ed., *Groundwork of the Metaphysics of Morals* (Cambridge: Cambridge University Press, 2012).

[69] Wang, *Xunzi*, pp. 346, 430, 751; Hutton, *Xunzi*, p. 201.

[70] Richard Ned Lebow, *A Cultural Theory of International Relations* (Cambridge: Cambridge University Press, 2008), p. 64.

units, but by harmonizing different units into hierarchical but fair divisions. The existence of identical units, each with its own selfish and uncompromising desires, would only lead to competition and conflict. Hierarchy, provided it is based on *yi* 義 and is thus seen as just, can forestall conflict by creating reasonable social divisions and correspondingly fair distributions of resources.[71]

A hierarchical order may be unequal, but it need not be unfair. In a fair hierarchy, one's honor or disgrace reflects one's degree of virtue (*de* 德);[72] and virtue is matched by position, ability by office, rewards by meritorious accomplishments, and penalties by offenses.[73] It is important, Xunzi urges, that a sage ruler should develop the cognitive ability of *bian* 辨 to recognize and improve the justice of social hierarchy.[74]

For Xunzi, *fen* (分 divisions) achieves harmony by means of *yi* or justice. Humans need *fen* to form communities, but such *fen* must be based on *yi* (義 justice). *Yi*-based *fen* is fairness, and it is this kind of *fen* that is conducive to harmony. As he remarks:

> When a humane person is in power, the farmers devote all their strength to their fields, the merchants devote all their cleverness to their earnings, and the hundred craftsmen devote all their skillfulness to their products. From the officers and high ministers up to the dukes and marquises, no one fails to devote all his humaneness, generosity, intelligence, and capabilities to fulfilling his official position. This is called the utmost fairness [*ping* 平].[75]

The last word in this passage, *ping* 平, can be rendered as either "fairness" as in *gongping* 公平 or "equality" as in *pingdeng* 平等. Here it decidedly means fairness. Yang Jing, a ninth-century commentator of Xunzi, explains that utmost fairness is a situation in which the noble and the base each act according to their station in spite of the inequality of their social positions. Zhang Jue, a modern commentator of Xunzi, takes *ping* to mean good governance based on fairness and order.[76] Elsewhere in Xunzi *ping* 平 may be translated as impartiality or evenhandedness, as in the remark that "public-spiritedness [*gong* 公] and impartiality [*ping* 平] are one's scales in holding a position, and the means of due

[71] Wang, *Xunzi*, p. 419; Hutton, *Xunzi*, p. 83.

[72] Wang, *Xunzi*, p. 15; Hutton, *Xunzi*, p. 3.

[73] Wang, *Xunzi*, p. 714; Hutton, *Xunzi*, p. 188.

[74] Masayuki Sato, *The Confucian Quest for Order: The Origin and Formation of the Political Thought of Xun Zi* (Leiden: Brill, 2003), pp. 356–61.

[75] Wang, *Xunzi*, p. 155; Hutton, *Xunzi*, p. 30.

[76] Wang, *Xunzi*, p. 157.

proportion [*zhongyong* 中庸] is one's plumb line in judging affairs."[77] But here fairness can serve as the translation just as well.

There are two interesting parallels between Xunzi's conception of justice as fairness and Western conceptions of justice. Xunzi holds that people should conduct themselves according to the differences in their moral excellence, ability, or social position, and that they should receive their rewards and punishments accordingly. The first view is essentially one of fairness based on one's merit or desert, which, as we have seen in chapter 2, is also a prominent tradition in the Western conception of justice.[78] The second view on the fair distribution of resources likewise echoes the ancient Greek and Roman law tradition of distributive justice as rendering to every man his due.[79] Nevertheless, one should not equate Xunzi's idea of fairness with that of the Greek philosophers, for Xunzi grounds his theory of fairness on the psychology and ethic of *ren* (仁 humaneness), which is distinctively Confucian.

Moving on to Xunzi's larger theory of *li* (禮 ritual propriety) in which his theory of fairness is embedded, *li* functions like an essential glue that holds a hierarchical order together and puts *yi* into practice. A *li*-based order begins by differentiating social statuses. Each status corresponds to a distinct role with a set of explicit obligations and implicit rights. The robustness of order depends on the extent to which the reciprocal obligations between social roles are performed. Roles and obligations are based on *yi* as justice, so order ultimately rests on the appeal of principles of justice. If the normative pull of *li* is strong enough, an order should be able to sustain itself almost effortlessly. *Yi* embodies the prevailing principles of justice that legitimate social divisions and hierarchical stratifications. *Li*, on the other hand, is the supreme method for creating and maintaining such a hierarchical order.

Mengzi expounds a slightly different theory of fairness on the basis of division of labor. Since no one individual can provide for his or her own sustenance entirely on his or her own, everyone relies on others through social division of labor for his or her flourishing. The diversity and differences among humans and other things make it possible to attain a harmonizing division of labor that fosters human community. As he says:

> There are activities of the great people and the affairs of the petty people. Furthermore, the products of the various artisans are available to each person. If one can make use of them only after one has made them oneself, this will lead the whole world to run around to the point

---

[77] Wang, *Xunzi*, p. 346; Hutton, *Xunzi*, p. 69.

[78] See also D. D. Raphael, *Concepts of Justice* (New York: Oxford University Press, 2001), p. 5.

[79] Raphael, *Concepts of Justice*, p. 33.

of exhaustion. Hence it is said, "Some labor with their hearts; some labor with their strength. Those who labor with their hearts rule others; those who labor with their strength are governed by others." Those who are governed by others feed others; those who govern others are fed by others. This is the appropriateness [*yi* 義] common to the world.[80]

By "the great people" Mengzi means rulers and their officials whose obligation it is to rule, teach, and inspire the common people, whom he refers to as "the petty people." The petty people are divided into farmers, artisans, and merchants according to their occupations.[81] Rulers serve the common people by providing good governance, while the common people serve rulers by producing material goods. Those who rule do not plow; those who plow do not rule. Mengzi thus paints a hierarchical society with clearly demarcated social divisions. Although he does not use the word *fen* (分 divisions) as Xunzi does, it is evident that it is this *fen* as fairness that he holds to be "the appropriateness [*yi* 義] common to the world."

The hierarchy that Mengzi depicts is not one of rigid class ossifications based on birth alone, but also one of statuses and roles in accordance with people's merit and virtue and is thus in principle fluid. The principle of hereditary aristocracy as an immutable fabric of political and social structure had already been torn down by Kongzi, who was of noble descent but identified himself as an elevated intellectual—the first of its kind in Chinese history. Kongzi transformed the basis of the distinction between the "exemplary person" and "petty person" from one of birth to one of virtue or moral excellence. The status of "exemplary person" was no longer inherited but became a goal for which everyone could strive. He held that officials should be selected on the basis of merit and virtue rather than nobility or class background. By this doctrine he hastened the decline of aristocracy and paved the way for a more popular form of politics, although in practice family or class background continued to exercise its hold in subsequent Chinese history.[82]

So far, we have been discussing a conception of fairness based on merit, virtue, or status. There is another notion of fairness that may be characterized as the reciprocity of obligation or duty. The language of obligation or duty, not that of right, suffuses the Confucian discourse. And obligation or duty, as pointed out earlier, may serve as a translation for *yi* 義 as justice. Here justice is understood as fairness because the relational duties it manifests are mutual and reciprocal.

---

[80] Jiao, *Mengzi*, p. 373; Van Norden, *Mengzi*, p. 70.

[81] Jiao, *Mengzi*, p. 372.

[82] Xu Fuguan [徐復觀], *Zhongguo renxinglunshi* [中國人性論史 A History of the Chinese Theory of Human Nature] (Beijing: Jiuzhou chubanshe, 2014), p. 59.

It is important to observe, moreover, that the language of obligations can easily be translated into one of rights, since obligations and rights entail each other.[83] The Confucian ritual order is one in which social statuses correspond to distinct roles with sets of explicit obligations and implicit rights. Xunzi is arguably the most articulate exponent of this conception, a conception to which all Confucians subscribe. Mengzi, who is usually regarded as the polar opposite of Xunzi within classical Confucianism, has this advice to give to a king:

> An enlightened ruler must regulate the people's livelihood to ensure that it is sufficient, on the one hand, to serve their fathers and mothers, and on the other hand, to nurture their wives and children. In good years, they are always full. In years of famine, they escape death. Only then do they rush toward the good, and thus the people follow the ruler easily. . . .
>
> If Your Majesty wishes to put this into effect, then why not return to the root? Plant every household of five acres with mulberry trees to cultivate silkworms, and fifty-year-olds can wear silk. Let the nurturing of chickens, pigs, and dogs not be neglected, and seventy-year-olds can eat meat. If you do not disturb the seasonal work in each field of one hundred acres, a clan with eight mouths need not go hungry. If you are careful that the schools engage in instruction, explaining the duties of filiality and brotherliness, then those with gray hair will not carry loads on the roads. It has never happened that a person fails to become the King when his old people wear silk and eat meat, and the black-haired people are neither hungry nor cold.[84]

As Ying-shih Yü notes, here Mengzi is giving a detailed account of what kinds of duty a true king is under to his people.[85] But if we translate his language of duties into the language of rights, it will immediately become clear that people have various rights including those to the use of land, to be left alone during agricultural seasons, and to education. Fairness underpins such a hierarchical relationship between the ruler and the people with their explicit obligations and implicit rights.

Another case in point are the so-called three bonds and five principles (*sangang wuchang* 三綱五常), a dominant social structure that ran through imperial China (221 BCE–1911 CE). The three bonds refer to the three hierarchical

[83] Ying-Shih Yü, *Chinese History and Culture, Volume 2: Seventeenth Century through Twentieth Century* (New York: Columbia University Press, 2016), Kindle ed., location 9264.

[84] Jiao, *Mengzi*, pp. 94–95; Van Norden, *Mengzi*, pp. 14–15.

[85] Yü, *Chinese History and Culture, Volume 2*, Kindle ed., location 9259.

relationships between ruler and subject, father and son, and husband and wife. The subject is expected to be loyal to the ruler, the son filial to the father, and the wife faithful to the husband. To the modern mind these relationships reek of unilateral and unfair submission of the weak or oppressed to the strong or privileged.

This sense of submission, however, reflects a distinct modern cast of mind, which is itself in part a result of changing conceptions of justice in the modern world, and does injustice to historical contexts. Historically the three bonds were regarded as constituting a mutual and reciprocal relationship marked by explicit obligations and implicit rights. Thus, while the subject is expected to display loyalty to the ruler, the ruler is expected to show grace to the subject; while the son is expected to be filial, the father is expected to be loving; while the wife is expected to be faithful, the husband is expected to be just. These paired obligations—loyalty and grace, filial piety and parental love, faithfulness and justice—are mutually constituted norms of behavior, not unilateral or one-sided oppression. The relationships based on these norms are undoubtedly unequal, but they may claim a sense of fairness in the mutuality or reciprocity of obligation. The parties to these relationships, although they occupy unequal social positions and roles, are nonetheless expected to take the concerns of each other into account, thereby avoiding abuse arising from social inequality.

The Principle of Equality

Fairness is the dominant Confucian principle of justice in a hierarchical political and social order, but it is not the only one. Confucians also acknowledge equality as a principle of justice. They conceive of equality in four different ways. The first might be called the equality of dignity and respect. Earlier we described Kongzi's Golden Rule or the principle of *shu* 恕, namely that one should put oneself in the other's place. This principle implies a certain reciprocity between oneself and others in their social relationships. It embodies the Confucian affective rationality of universal care, requiring one to take into consideration the interests of others. In both respects *shu* carries the implication of equality derived from basic human dignity and respect.[86] This notion of equality may be traced to pre-Confucian times, especially the prominent Western Zhou dynasty (c. 1100–771

---

[86] Gao Ruiquan [高瑞泉], *Pingdeng guannianshi luelun* [平等觀念史略論 A Brief Treatise on the History of the Concept of Equality] (Shanghai: Shanghai renmin chubanshe, 2011), p. 55; Xu Fuguan [徐復觀], *Rujia sixiagn yu xiandai shehui* [儒家思想與現代社會 Confucian Thought and Modern Society] (Beijing: Jiuzhou chubanshe, 2014), p. 144.

BCE) idea of people as the representative of Heaven and thus by implication an equality between people and the ruler.[87] By Kongzi's time, the Mandate of Heaven (*tianming* 天命), which had been used to legitimate dynastic politics, was also thought to have been conferred on the individual, resulting in a direct line of communication between Heaven and individual humans.[88]

Second, Confucianism promotes an equality or even identity of human nature inherent in all human beings.[89] "Everyone," says Mengzi, "can become a Yao or a Shun," Yao and Shun being China's sage rulers in antiquity.[90] The reason is that "the Way of Yao and Shun is nothing other than filiality and brotherliness," and this everyone can attain, regardless of their social positions.[91] Most important, the Way of Yao and Shun is ultimately the way of *ren* (仁 humaneness) and *yi* (義 appropriateness), and these qualities everyone is able to possess or aspire to.[92] Equality in these discussions amounts to equality in every human being's nature and moral potential. Believing human nature to be the same and good in every person, Mengzi holds that all may attain sageliness as long as they emulate the moral life of past sages such as Yao and Shun. Mengzi's theory of human nature thus provides the premise for human equality in the moral realm.[93]

In contrast to Mengzi, Xunzi holds a jaundiced view of human nature. "Peoples' nature is bad," he says; "their goodness is a matter of deliberate effort."[94] Yet this contrary theory of human nature ends up in the same position that human beings have the same moral potential and are thus equal in this sphere. Xunzi argues that anyone can become a Yu, another ancient sage ruler like Yao and Shun. They do this because they are *ren*, *yi*, lawful, and correct. *Ren*, *yi*, lawfulness, and correctness have patterns that can be known and practiced. Ordinary people possess the resources for knowing *ren*, *yi*, lawfulness, and correctness, and for practicing these qualities. It is in this way that they become a Yu.[95] In highlighting people's ability to practice moral virtues, Xunzi's argument is the same as Mengzi's. The difference lies in Xunzi's emphasis on the importance of practice or "deliberate effort" in achieving moral excellence, since he starts from the premise that human nature is bad.[96]

---

[87] Xu, *Rujia sixiagn yu xiandai shehui*, pp. 143–44.

[88] Yü, *Chinese History and Culture, Volume 1*, Kindle ed., location 793.

[89] Gao, *Pingdeng*, p. 54.

[90] Jiao, *Mengzi*, p. 810; Van Norden, *Mengzi*, p. 159.

[91] Jiao, *Mengzi*, p. 816; Van Norden, *Mengzi*, p. 159.

[92] Jiao, *Mengzi*, p. 810.

[93] Gao, *Pingdeng*, p. 56.

[94] Wang, *Xunzi*, p. 934; Hutton, *Xunzi*, p. 248.

[95] Wang, *Xunzi*, p. 950; Hutton, *Xunzi*, p. 254.

[96] Wang, *Xunzi*, p. 951; Hutton, *Xunzi*, p. 254.

Thus, both Mengzi and Xunzi believe in the equality of people's moral potential and the necessity of moral cultivation.[97] That it is an equality of potential and is therefore more theoretical than practical is important to observe. In the same passage where Xunzi touts the potential of common people to become a sage like Yu, he emphasizes that it is not necessarily the case that anyone will be able to become a Yu. One is not always able to do what one can do; potential does not mean achievement or entitlement.[98] Kongzi, great thinker though he was, never claimed to be a sage, although he was lauded as such by posterity. Mengzi was lionized by his followers as a "secondary sage" (ya sheng 亚圣) only.

In the Confucian conception of political and social order, equality of moral potential is largely an ideal. In practice, fairness—and its associated inequality—is held by all Confucians to be the dominant principle of justice in a hierarchical society guided by the norms of li (禮 ritual propriety). Not only is Confucian equality in theory different from the modern notion of equality of political and individual rights, but in practice it tends to strengthen the hold of hierarchical and thus unequal social norms. There is thus a very prominent tension between equality and fairness in Confucian theory, with fairness nearly always trumping equality.

Yet a sense of political equality—the third sense in which Confucians think of equality—is not wholly absent. Mengzi, for example, is famous for his astonishing declaration that "The people are the most important, the altars to the land and grain are next, and the ruler is the least important."[99] This is the boldest assertion of the political agency and primacy of the people in traditional China.[100] It might have been influenced by Kongzi's view that "in education there is no such thing as social classes."[101] The removal of class barriers in education prepared the ground for imperial China's famed civil examination system, which for 1,300 years provided an institutional channel for building a wide-ranging meritocracy under absolute monarchy. This equal access to education in turn lessened class divisions and contributed to the near extinction of hereditary aristocracy after the Song dynasty (960–1279).

Yet the result was not a true political equality. Mengzi's idea was never realized. Instead, as noted, Confucians turned inward by focusing on personal moral cultivation rather than actuating outward political equality. Even in the sphere of

---

[97] Chenyang Li, "Equality and Inequality in Confucianism," Dao 11, no. 3 (2012), pp. 295–313, at p. 297.

[98] Wang, Xunzi, p. 954; Hutton, Xunzi, p. 255.

[99] Jiao, Mengzi, p. 973; Van Norden, Mengzi, p. 187.

[100] Xu, Rujia sixiagn yu xiandai shehui, p. 145.

[101] Huang, Lunyu, p. 1440; Ames and Rosemont, The Analects of Confucius, p. 192; Slingerland, Confucius Analects, p. 189.

education, equal opportunity was largely meant for the educated elite of the lite-rati class (*shi* 士), not peasants, artisans, or merchants, the other three categories of people in traditional China. Traditional China was still an elite-based hierar-chical society, with a steady supply and screening of elites from the literati class through a competitive examination system. The system, while creating political mobility for the literati, shut out most of the other social classes.[102] Even down to Ming-Qing times, family background was still an important justification for office; no one would be admitted to the civil service examination until he could show a clear and clean family record.[103]

Finally, Confucian ethics on friendship manifest a sense of interpersonal equality. Kongzi has numerous remarks on friendship, the most famous of which is perhaps the second opening question in his *Analects* that "is it not a source of enjoyment to have friends come from afar?"[104] He holds trustworthiness (*xin* 信) to be the most important virtue of friendship, and trustworthiness, by embodying a reciprocity of promise-keeping, implies equality.[105]

A more illuminating discussion of friendship comes from Mengzi. When asked about the principle of making friends, Mengzi replies that "One does not become someone's friend by presuming upon one's age or social status or family relationship. One befriends the virtue of another person. There may not be an-ything else one presumes upon."[106] Moral excellence, not social status, is held to be the true marker of friendship. "If you are one of the finest nobles in a village," Mengzi continues, "then befriend the other fine nobles of that village. If you are one of the finest nobles in a state, then befriend the other fine nobles of that state. If you are one of the finest nobles in the world, then befriend the other fine nobles of the world."[107] As has been pointed out, Mengzi's notion of equality with regard to friendship is akin to Aristotle's in that both stress virtue as an im-portant foundation of friendship.[108]

Modern Standing

Kongzi, Mengzi, and Xunzi—the three pioneering thinkers of classical Con-fucianism in ancient China before the Qin unification in 221 BCE—inaugurated

---

[102] Gao, *Pingdeng*, p. 65.

[103] Yü, *Chinese History and Culture, Volume 2*, Kindle ed., location 1385.

[104] Huang, *Lunyu*, p. 22; Ames and Rosemont, *The Analects of Confucius*, p. 71; Slingerland, *Confucius Analects*, p. 1.

[105] Gao, *Pingdeng*, p. 73.

[106] Jiao, *Mengzi*, p. 690; Van Norden, *Mengzi*, p. 134.

[107] Jiao, *Mengzi*, p. 725; Van Norden, *Mengzi*, p. 141.

[108] Gao, *Pingdeng*, p. 75.

the tradition of intellectual and spiritual Confucianism in Chinese history. This tradition was developed and, in some ways, transformed by the Neo-Confucianism of the Song-Ming period (960–1644) in the hands of such brilliant scholars as Zhu Xi (1130–1200) and Wang Yangming (1472–1529). Pre-Qin classical Confucianism and Song-Ming Neo-Confucianism represent two epochs of Confucianism as an intellectual movement in Chinese history.[109] Intellectualism aside, Confucianism also offered itself as a legitimating ideology and governing tool for the imperial Chinese state; in this marriage with politics it is best distinguished as political or institutional Confucianism. By the time of the Han dynasty (206 BCE–220 CE), Confucianism had become the foundation of state ideology and the only valuable scholarship sanctioned by the imperial court. By the end of the Song dynasty (920–1279), Zhu Xi had canonized the *Analects*, *Mengzi*, and two other Confucian classics as the Four Books, which became the major source for imperial examination.

With the collapse of the last imperial dynasty of the Qing in 1911, Confucianism entered its third and bleak historical epoch. Political Confucianism came to an end and intellectual Confucianism encountered a fierce backlash under the double onslaught of domestic turmoil and foreign aggression. But it did not die out. Confucianism in the modern era—from the founding of the Republic of China in 1912 onwards—is marked by four turning points: the 1920s when a new movement called Contemporary New Confucianism was initiated, the 1940s when the philosophies of this new Confucianism were formulated, the 1960s when a narrow version of Contemporary New Confucianism flourished in Hong Kong and Taiwan, and the 1980s when the movement acquired an international dimension and significantly influenced the rise of new Confucianism on the Chinese mainland.[110]

From the perspective of justice theory, however, a different, four-wave periodization makes better sense. The first wave came in the late nineteenth century when some Confucian scholars—most notably Kang Youwei—sought to find the equivalents of modern Western ideas of equality and democracy in the Confucian classics. Still holding faith in the intellectual and political power of Confucianism, they wished to save China with a reformed and modernized version of that tradition.

With the second wave, symbolized by the May Fourth movement in 1919, the intellectual temperament had changed utterly. Protagonists of this new cultural

---

[109] Liu Shu-hsien [劉述先], *Lun rujia zhexue de sange dashidai* [論儒家哲學的三個大時代 The Three Epochs of Confucian Philosophy] (Hong Kong: The Chinese University of Hong Kong Press, 2015).

[110] Shu-hsien Liu, "Contemporary Confucianism," in William Edelglass and Jay L. Garfield, eds., *The Oxford Handbook of World Philosophy* (Oxford: Oxford University Press, 2011), pp. 95–106.

movement, blaming Confucianism for China's backwardness, unleashed a merciless attack on it with slogans such as "Down with the Confucian shop." Abhorred by the perceived evil of the Confucian principle of fairness embodied by ritual hierarchy, they sought nostrums in the modern Western ideas of equality and democracy.

The third wave began in the 1950s when new Confucian scholars based in Hong Kong and Taiwan, troubled by this radicalism, began to undertake a more balanced examination of Confucianism and tried to reconcile its doctrines with modern Western ideas. In the Chinese mainland after the founding of the People's Republic in 1949, Confucianism suffered a worse blow in the "anti-Kongzi" frenzy during the Cultural Revolution of 1966–1976 than it did during the May Fourth movement. Thanks to the New Confucianism from Hong Kong and Taiwan, it recovered in the 1980s and rose to prominence after the 1990s. A remarkable feature of this fourth wave of Confucian renaissance in mainland China is the return to the principle of fairness in major scholarly and political writings.

Kang Youwei (1858–1927) was a scholar, official, and reformer whose pioneering ideas exerted a powerful influence on modern Chinese thought. His *Book on Great Harmony*, written in 1901–1902 while in exile in India, is a clarion call for equality not just in China but throughout the world.[111] It urges economic equality, especially that between different social classes. It exhorts social equality, including gender equality. It demands equality between nations and even the abolition of national borders, so as to eliminate the inequality brought about by international competition. Foreign aggression at the end of the nineteenth century made equality between China and the imperial powers a matter of national survival, but Kang made his appeal not on the basis of parochial nationalism but a sort of transnational universalism that he argued would ensure universal equality in a just world order.

In his thorough advocacy of equality, Kang was clearly influenced by Western ideas, which had by his time crept into the learned quarters of Qing China. Without this Western influence, he probably would not have made the leap from the subdued notion of equality in traditional Confucianism to his bold new conception. As we have seen, Confucianism offered theoretical support for the equality of human nature and moral potential, but had achieved little in the way of actual equality in Chinese politics and society. Recognizing this, Kang elevated equality from the abstract level of moral potential to a major practicable social principle. But he was not dismissive of traditional Confucian teachings,

---

[111] Kang Youwei [康有為], *Kang Youwei quanji, Vol. 7* [康有為全集 The Completed Works of Kang Youwei] (Beijing: Zhongguo renmin daxue chubanshe, 2020).

even though his classical scholarship was highly eccentric. In fact, he praised Kongzi for uprooting the aristocracy and the imperial examination system for upholding merit as the sole criterion of selecting officials. And his universalism was obviously inspired by Kongzi's vision of a Golden Age of Great Harmony mentioned earlier. In this first wave of Confucian reformation in the modern era, Confucianism was still held in high esteem—albeit considered in need of some Western enrichment.

It soon ceased to be so. Tan Sitong (1865–1898), a radical thinker and reform-minded official who became a martyr to the failed "Hundred Days' Reforms" of 1898, launched a fierce attack on Confucian hierarchy, setting his target especially on the Confucian ritual stricture of "three bonds and five principles," as mentioned earlier. In the place of this stricture he urged the adoption of friendship as the criterion of all social relationships because friendship, according to him, more than anything else manifests the principles of equality, freedom, and autonomy. Tan held Kongzi in respect, but dismissed all later Confucians as accomplices in social inequality. He wanted to dismantle the old principle of fairness and erect a new, largely Western-inspired principle of equality.[112] For his rejection of traditional Chinese ethics, and for his contemplation of violent revolution as a means to achieve social change—a cause to which he gave his life—Tan heralded Chinese radicalism in the twentieth century. This radicalism also inaugurated the second wave of modern Confucianism—a Confucianism under siege.

The siege reached its climax in the May Fourth movement of 1919, especially by the writers of the highly influential intellectual journal *New Youth*. Chen Duxiu (1879–1942), a founder of the journal, a leader of the May Fourth movement, and the first secretary-general of the Chinese Communist Party, pounced upon Confucian ethics, especially ritual hierarchy. He faulted Confucian ritual for depriving the independence and autonomy of individuals, which he regarded as being central to "modernity." Borrowing from Nietzsche, he held that Confucian virtues such as dutifulness and filial piety are not "subjective morality" but "slave morality." He urged Chinese youth to develop a modern individuality of independence, equality, autonomy, and freedom.[113] To build a modern Chinese state, he said, "the basic task is to import the foundation of Western society, that is, the new belief in equality and human rights. We must be thoroughly aware of the incompatibility between Confucianism and the new belief, the new society,

---

[112] Tan Sitong [譚嗣同], *Tan Sitong ji* [譚嗣同集 The Collected Works of Tan Sitong], Vol. 2 (Hangzhou: Zhejiang guji chubanshe, 2018).

[113] Ren Jianshu [任建樹], ed., *Chen Duxiu zhuozuo xuanbian* [陳獨秀著作選編 The Selected Works of Chen Duxiu], Vol. 1, 1897–1918 (Shanghai: Shanghai renmin chubanshe, 2014), pp. 159, 199.

and the new state."[114] He famously espoused two concepts that he termed "Mr. Democracy" and "Mr. Science" as the key opponents to Confucian tradition-alism. Like Tan, his fascination with the modern Western ideas of equality, de-mocracy, and science led him to abhor the traditional Confucian principle of fairness.

This anti-Confucian radicalism prompted a backlash in the form of New Confucianism. This New Confucianism was developed by scholars who had fled the mainland to Hong Kong and Taiwan after the Communist vic-tory in 1949. Thus began the third wave of modern Confucianism. In 1958, four distinguished new Confucian scholars published a "Manifesto for a Reappraisal of Sinology and Reconstruction of Chinese Culture," in which they reaffirmed the value of the traditional Confucian conception of the equality of human potential and suggested that it was a source—or at least a seed—of democracy.[115]

Xu Fuguan, one of these four scholars, tried to reconcile the traditional Confucian principle of hierarchical fairness with the modern conception of equality. He defends Xunzi's theory of ritual-based hierarchy, as described earlier, on the grounds that order requires hierarchical divisions. But he criticizes Xunzi for neglecting the internal grounding of humaneness as emphasized by Kongzi. Without humaneness as its spiritual foundation, a hierarchical order of ritual norms is at risk of lapsing into coercion and oppression. Unlike the anti-Confucian radicals, however, Xu does not put the blame on ritual per se but points to the lack of humaneness as the more fundamental flaw of the Confucian ritual order. Turning his attention to the modern Western order of freedom and equality, he suggests that the Western order is unlikely to achieve a balance be-tween rights and obligations if it is destitute of humaneness. The implication is that order requires a judicious combination of equality and fairness underpinned by the Confucian ethic of humaneness.[116]

With the rise of Confucianism in the Chinese mainland after the 1990s—the fourth wave of modern Confucianism—the balance in the emphasis be-tween the principles of equality and fairness tipped again, this time to fairness. Two scholars, Jiang Qing, an eccentric thinker modelling himself on traditional

---

[114] Quoted in Jonathan D. Spence, *The Search for Modern China*, 2nd ed. (New York: Norton, 1999), pp. 303–4.

[115] Mou Zongsan [牟宗三], Xu Fuguan [徐復觀], Zhang Junmai [張君勱], and Tang Junyi [唐君毅], "Wei zhongguo wenhua jinggao shijie renshi xuanyan—women dui zhongguo xueshu yanjiu ji zhongguo wenhua yu shijie wenhua qiantu zhi gongtong renshi" [為中國文化敬告世界人士宣言—我們對中國學術研究及中國文化與世界文化前途之共同認識 A Manifesto for a Reappraisal of Sinology and Reconstruction of Chinese Culture], in Xu Fuguan [徐復觀], *Lun wenhua* [論文化 On Culture] (Beijing: Jiuzhou chubanshe, 2014), Vol. 1, pp. 254–313.

[116] Xu, *Zhongguo renxinglunshi*, pp. 235–36.

Confucians, and Daniel A. Bell, a Canadian political theorist based in China, illustrate this development.

Jiang advocates a new sort of political Confucianism that would have been unthinkable in the People's Republic of China before the 1990s. He wants to promote Confucianism to the status of state or civic religion so that it can be firmly implanted into the minds of the Chinese people, and he champions a Confucian constitutionalism based on the "kingly way" as a rival system to Western liberal democracy.[117] Jiang maintains that China must transform itself into a "republic under a symbolic monarchy" in which the direct descendants of Kongzi should be the monarch. He proposes a tricameral legislature composed of a House of the Great Confucians that represents the will of Heaven, a House of Nation that represents the history and culture of the country, and a House of the People that represents popular legitimacy. These ideas are so radical that even the ruling Communist Party finds them too much to stomach. It is all too clear that Jiang, wanting none of the modern values of equality, freedom, and democracy, yearns to take China back to a mythical Confucian Golden Age where hierarchical fairness rules.

Bell, like Jiang, is critical of liberal democracy and contends that China should build a new system of meritocracy based on the experience of imperial examination and recommendation. The aim is to select the most capable, skilled, and virtuous national leaders. Unlike Jiang, he nevertheless maintains that a certain degree of electoral democracy is essential for China in the modern world. The challenge for China is how to consummate the marriage of meritocracy and democracy. Bell's emphasis on leaders' ability and virtue accords closely with the traditional Confucian conception of fairness based on merit, virtue, or status examined earlier. He removes status from his criteria of meritocracy for the obvious reason that aristocracy has lost its appeal in the modern world; at any rate it became extinct in China after the Song dynasty (960–1279).

The contemporary renaissance of Confucianism on the Chinese mainland is not only a scholarly phenomenon; it has also received notable official sanction. President Hu Jintao, who was the top leader of China from 2003 to 2012, tried to harness Confucianism by proposing "harmonious society" and "harmonious world" as his governing values. He set up hundreds of Confucius Institutes around the world to promote the study of Chinese language and culture. President Xi Jinping has offered equally strong endorsements. In November 2013, he visited the birthplace of Kongzi in Shandong and praised Kongzi's teachings. In September 2014, he delivered a keynote speech at the international

---

[117] Jiang Qing, *A Confucian Constitutional Order: How China's Ancient Past Can Shape Its Political Future* (Princeton, NJ: Princeton University Press, 2013).

conference in memory of Kongzi's 2,565th birthday, in which he remarked that Chinese Communists "have consciously absorbed nutrition from the teachings of Kongzi to those of Sun Yat-sen."[118]

Yet many scholars suspect that this may be the latest iteration of the historical pattern of state cooption of Confucianism for cultural leadership and regime consolidation. The novelty today is that Confucianism is pressed into serve as an ideology subordinate to the official orthodoxy of Marxism-Leninism in the construction of "socialism with Chinese characteristics." Intellectual Confucianism will be at risk, again, of losing its autonomy and moral power if it forfeits its critical stance and degenerates into political Confucianism.[119]

Conclusion

Yi 義, the Chinese concept of justice, denotes an achieved sense of appropriateness that enables one to act in a proper manner. Confucians understand *yi* either as a personal virtue, in which case it may be translated as righteousness, or as social standards by which personal conduct is evaluated, in which case it is best rendered as appropriateness. In both cases, Confucians take *yi* to be a moral constraint on the pursuit of material interests. It is a nonutilitarian idea.

Confucians build an elaborate theory of justice with two additional concepts: *ren* (仁 humaneness) and *li* (禮 ritual propriety). They ground justice internally in the emotional foundation of *ren* practiced through the principle of universal but differential care, and identify its external realization in the rules, norms, and institutions of *li*. Justice, in this account, is founded on humaneness and manifested in ritual practices. Because Confucian justice is based on an elastic ethic of universal but differential care, it has none of the connotation of an absolute moral standard found in some Western conceptions of justice. Because Confucianism takes harmony to be the ultimate goal of social and political order, harmony can be seen as the goal of Confucian justice.

Confucian justice espouses a strong principle of fairness and a subdued principle of equality. It conceives of fairness in two ways: fairness based on merit, virtue, or status, and fairness based on the reciprocity of obligations. It suggests four senses of equality: equality of human dignity and respect, equality of human nature and especially moral potential, political equality, and equality

---

[118] Yi-Huah Jiang, "Confucian Political Theory in Contemporary China," *Annual Review of Political Science*, no. 21 (2018), pp. 155–73, at pp. 169–70.

[119] Jiang, "Confucian Political Theory in Contemporary China," p. 171; Shufang Wu, "The Revival of Confucianism and the CCP's Struggle for Cultural Leadership: A Content Analysis of the *People's Daily*, 2000–2009," *Journal Contemporary China* 23, no. 89 (2014), pp. 971–991, at pp. 990–91.

in friendships. Political equality and the equality of moral potential are largely ideals. In practice, fairness—and the inequality associated with it—is held to be the dominant principle of justice in a hierarchical society dominated by absolute rulers and the educated elite. There is an inescapable tension between fairness and equality in Confucian thought, with fairness nearly always trumping equality.

Confucianism has exercised a profound influence on Chinese politics, ethics, life, art, and ways of thinking. It is useful to distinguish between intellectual or spiritual Confucianism and political Confucianism. Intellectual Confucianism has contributed to the formation of a Chinese cultural-psychological system that Li Zehou refers to as practical or pragmatic rationality.[120] It can lay claim to a long and distinguished line of thinkers from Kongzi, Mengzi, and Xunzi in ancient China, to Zhu Xi and Wang Yangming in Song-Ming Neo-Confucianism (960–1644), to Liang Shuming and Qian Mu in modern Confucianism. Political Confucianism was pressed into service by Chinese rulers since the Han dynasty (206 BCE–220 CE) as an ideology for legitimating their rule. Part of the modern attack on Confucianism targets its role as this sort of imperial ideology.

Confucianism in the modern era has undergone astonishing vicissitudes. It teetered on the brink of destruction during the May Fourth movement of 1919 and even more so during the Cultural Revolution of 1966–1976, yet it blossomed into a new Confucianism in Hong Kong and Taiwan after the 1950s and received a state-sanctioned renaissance on the Chinese mainland after the 1990s. The vicissitudes apply equally to its theory of justice; the principle of fairness, after being battered by numerous critics in the twentieth century, is receiving a fair and even elevated treatment in mainland Confucianism in the twenty-first century. The tenacity and resilience of Confucianism are extraordinary. There is no reason to believe that it will lose its appeal in the future, even though it may not be able to reclaim its dominant status as in the imperial age.

---

[120] Li Zehou [李澤厚], *Zhongguo gudai sixiangshilu* [中國古代思想史論 On Traditional Chinese Thought] (Beijing: Sanlian, 2008), p. 25.

4

Justice in Mohism, Legalism, and Daoism

In this chapter we examine conceptions of justice in Mohism, Legalism, and Daoism, three major intellectual rivals to Confucianism. The master of Mohism is Mozi (479–438 BCE), an artisan, perhaps a carpenter, of humble origin. The great synthesizer of Legalist thought is Han Fei, who was a pupil of Xunzi and was active in practical politics until his death in 233 BCE. The founder of Daoist thought is Laozi, who lived sometime from the sixth to the fourth century BCE and whose precise lifespan is unknown. He was followed by Zhuangzi (c. 369–286 BCE), the second great Daoist thinker. As with the three Confucian thinkers in the previous chapter, we now examine these Mohist, Legalist, and Daoist masters' thought on justice based on the best scholarly editions of their writings.

Like Confucianism, Mohism, Legalism, and Daoism each has its unique conceptions of justice. Mohism offers a consequentialist theory of justice—the first of its kind in Chinese history—that takes justice to be a means for achieving material benefits. Legalism contains a notion of retributive justice, but one that is overshadowed by its glorification of the ruler and the efficacy of the use of force. Daoism sets forth an admirable naturalist theory of justice and a thoroughgoing defense of the natural equality of all things that has no equivalents in Chinese intellectual history. Viewed in terms of the principles of fairness and equality, Confucianism is the most elaborate protagonist of fairness, and Daoism is the most thorough advocate of equality. In between stands Mohism, which espouses a combination of equality and fairness. Legalism reflects a restrictive notion of equality and not at all fairness.

Justice and International Order: East and West. Richard Ned Lebow and Feng Zhang, Oxford University Press.
© Oxford University Press 2022. DOI: 10.1093/oso/9780197598399.003.0004

The Mohist Theory of Consequentialist Justice

Confucianism aside, Mohism provides the most elaborate theory of justice in ancient China. Mohism shares some aspects of its doctrine with Confucianism, notably the use of common concepts such as *ren* 仁 and *yi* 義, and Mozi himself received Confucian teaching in his early life. The similarities, however, are largely superficial. In his later life Mozi led a thoroughgoing rebellion against Confucianism. His theory of justice, a central part of this rebellion, is all but an inversion of the Confucian theory. Confucianism is a non-consequentialist or non-utilitarian doctrine, emphasizing right action guided by ethical principles while downplaying the consequences of action. Mohism, by contrast, offers the first major theory of consequentialism in Chinese history, judging justice solely according to the consequences of action rather than the adherence of moral principles.

The concept of justice, *yi* 義, occupies a pivotal place in Mohist thought. "Of the ten thousand things," Mozi declares, "there is none more valuable than justice [*yi* 義]."[1] It is so important that "when the world has justice, it 'lives'; when it lacks justice, it 'dies.' When it has justice, it is rich; when it lacks justice, it is poor. When it has justice, it is well ordered; when it lacks justice, it is disordered."[2] A key purpose of the Mohist doctrine is the realization of such justice in the world.

The Mohist justice, while owing its terminological origin to Confucianism, is in other respects radically different from it. Mohists hold that "justice is but the attainment of benefit [*li* 利]."[3] Wise rulers in ancient times, Mozi says, realized justice by "benefiting Heaven, ghosts, and ordinary people."[4] Because justice can benefit people, it is "the world's excellent treasure."[5] To Mohists, justice is a means to an end, the end being benefits, with economic wealth and political order being the most important of them.[6] Justice, in this conception, is a function of the benefit that might be accrued from action. It is a consequentialist ethic par excellence. It is important to note, however, that this consequentialism is of a communitarian rather than individualistic

---

[1] Wang Huanbiao [王煥鑣], *Mozi jigu* [墨子集詁 Collected Interpretations of Mozi] (Shanghai: Shanghai guji chubanshe, 2005), p. 1041; Ian Johnston, *The Mozi: A Complete Translation* (Hong Kong: The Chinese University Press, 2010), p. 660.

[2] Wang, *Mozi*, p. 638; Johnston, *The Mozi*, p. 235.

[3] Johnston, *The Mozi*, p. 381.

[4] Wang, *Mozi*, pp. 438–40; Johnston, *The Mozi*, p. 183.

[5] Wang, *Mozi*, p. 1013; Johnston, *The Mozi*, p. 649.

[6] Huang Weihe [黃偉合], "Mozi de yiliguan" [墨子的義利觀 Mozi's View on Justice and Benefit], *Zhongguo Shehui Kexue* [Chinese Social Sciences], no. 3 (1985), pp. 115–24, at p. 117.

nature.[7] Mozi always privileges the benefits of the community over those of the individual. The economic wealth and political order that he emphasizes are collective, even public in nature. As he puts it, "The business of the humane person must be to seek assiduously to promote *the world's* benefits and to eliminate *the world's* harms."[8] Confucians, as we saw earlier, reject such consequentialism out of hand. For them, *yi* or justice acts as a moral constraint on the pursuit of benefit, not as a means of gaining them. In this respect the Mohist and Confucian ethics of justice are diametrically opposed.[9]

Mohist and Confucian theories of justice diverge in other ways too. We explained earlier that Kongzi grounds *yi* in the emotional foundation of *ren* (仁 humaneness) practiced through the principle of universal but differential care. Mozi agrees on universal care but repudiates the role of human emotions and with it the doctrine of differential care. Indeed, taking a pointed swipe at that doctrine, he proposes "universal and impartial care" (*jian ai* 兼愛) as the foundation of ethics. In his vision of "impartial mutual love and mutual benefit" (*jian xiang ai, jiao xiang li* 兼相愛交相利), "people would view others' states as they view their own states, people would view others' houses as they view their own houses, and people would view other people as they view themselves."[10]

Embedded in the Mohist doctrine of impartial care are four conceptions of equality that bear interesting similarities and contrasts to Confucian ones. Most notably, impartial care itself conveys a sense of moral equality, that is, each person should treat every other person as he or she would treat himself or herself. Mozi contends that "mutual discrimination" among people is the source of the world's harms, and so it must be changed through impartial care (*jian yi yi bie* 兼以易別). The thoroughness of this doctrine of equality is especially clear in comparison with the Confucian scheme of differential care. Differential care is essentially familial in nature, requiring one to love one's close kin before other people. This is exactly what Mozi condemns as "discrimination" (*bie* 別). The logic of differential care, if interpreted only in terms of consequence, would lead to self-interest maximization since it begins with loving oneself. Thus, Mohists put into the mouth of a follower of the doctrine of differential care the frightening thought that "I would kill another to benefit myself rather than be killed myself to benefit another."[11]

---

[7] Chris Fraser, "Major Rival Schools: Mohism and Legalism," in William Edelglass and Jay L. Garfield, eds., *The Oxford Handbook of World Philosophy* (Oxford: Oxford University Press, 2011), pp. 58–67, at p. 62.

[8] Wang, *Mozi*, p. 346; Johnston, *The Mozi*, p. 147 (emphasis added).

[9] Huang, "Mozi de yiliguan," p. 118.

[10] Wang, *Mozi*, p. 311; Johnston, *The Mozi*, p. 139.

[11] Wang, *Mozi*, p. 1028; Johnston, *The Mozi*, p. 655.

Confucians would object that Mohists have ridden roughshod over the role of emotion-based affective rationality and the principle of *shu* (putting oneself in the other's place) in differential care. As we showed in chapter 3, *shu*, properly understood, already carries the implication of equality derived from basic human dignity and respect, since it requires taking others' interests into account. Practicality is also an important issue: is it really possible for one to treat another person's father as one would treat one's own? Mengzi certainly does not think so, and to him Mozi's doctrine of universal and impartial love is tantamount to "not having a father."[12] This is about as savage an attack as is possible from a Confucian. Recognizing this problem, Mozi is compelled to offer a long defense for the feasibility of his doctrine.[13] The fundamental difference between the Confucian and Mohist doctrines of care seems to lie in their understanding of the nature of rationality. Confucians emphasize affective reason and would love to have it play a great part in human motivation, but they do not dismiss instrumental reason. Mohists abhor affective reason and have only consequentialism in their motivational vocabulary. The Confucian understanding of human motivation is more comprehensive and less flawed than that of Mohism.

The second Mohist conception of equality might be called the equality of reciprocity, a reciprocity that is different from the Confucian reciprocity of mutual but unequal obligations. Mozi remarks:

> If a person loves others then others must, as a result, love that person. If a person benefits others then others must, as a result, benefit that person. If a person hates others then others must, as a result, hate that person. If a person harms others then others must, as a result, harm that person.[14]

Here Mozi advocates a complete and uncompromising reciprocity of action, regardless of the nature or form of action. In the previous chapter we described a Confucian conception of fairness based on the reciprocity of obligations. These two kinds of reciprocity are different. The Confucian reciprocity applies to mutual but hierarchically differentiated obligations in unequal relationships (e.g., ruler and subject, father and son, husband and wife); this is why it manifests fairness rather than equality. The Mohist reciprocity is supposed to apply to all forms of relationship and tends to flatten their hierarchy; it is thus better seen as a reflection of equality.

---

[12] Jiao, *Mengzi*, p. 456; Van Norden, *Mengzi*, p. 85.

[13] Wang, *Mozi*, pp. 346–93; Johnston, *The Mozi*, pp. 146–65.

[14] Wang, *Mozi*, p. 323; Johnston, *The Mozi*, p. 141.

Third, Mohists exhibit a notion of equality akin to the redress or correction (*zheng* 正) of the imbalance in power, wealth, status, and ability, so as to restore and maintain political and social order. Justice is equated with correction and correction with order; this is, in effect, an argument that order rests on justice.[15] Mozi explains:

> Heaven's intention is not to want great states to attack small states, or great houses to bring disorder to small houses, or the strong to oppress the weak, or the many to tyrannize the few, or the cunning to deceive the gullible, or the noble to be arrogant towards the lowly. These are the things that Heaven's intention does not want. But it does not stop at this. It wants those with strength to help others, those who know the Way to teach others, and those with wealth to distribute it.[16]

This teaching later evolved into a spirit of chivalry (*xia* 俠) to help the underdog. Chivalry and appropriateness coalesced to form a composite concept of *xia-yi* 俠義, and the conception of justice embodied by this spirit was especially prominent in the lower rungs of the Chinese society. It has permeated, for example, the moral codes of secret societies up to this day. It was also the spiritual glue of numerous peasant rebellions in Chinese history.[17]

The fourth area in which the Mohist conception of equality has left its mark is political equality, and here again the Mohist doctrine is more comprehensive than Confucianism. Confucians, although they acknowledged the political agency of the people and their equal access to education—the precondition for political advancement—favored the literati class, to which most of them belonged. They frowned upon peasants, artisans, merchants, and soldiers, doubting their potential to become "exemplary persons" and worthy rulers. Mohists do not discriminate this way. Mozi remarks:

> The sage kings of ancient times, in the conduct of government, gave precedence to virtue and exalted worthiness so, although someone might be a farmer, or a craftsman, or a merchant, if he had ability then they promoted him, conferring on him high rank, giving him a generous salary, entrusting him with important matters, and providing him with executive power. . . . Thus officials were not necessarily assured of permanent nobility and ordinary people were not necessarily lowly

---

[15] Wang, *Mozi*, p. 691; Johnston, *The Mozi*, p. 263.

[16] Wang, *Mozi*, p. 658; Johnston, *The Mozi*, p. 247.

[17] Li, *Zhongguo gudai sixiangshilu*, p. 68.

for their whole lives. Those with ability were advanced. Those without ability were demoted.[18]

Ability or merit is one of the criteria by which Confucians judge people's worth, but they are nowhere as open to flattening the class divisions as Mohists are; social positions or statuses are as important as ability in determining the Confucian political order. That is why Confucians preach justice as fairness at the expense of equality. Mohists, by basing their doctrine of equality thoroughly on individual worthiness, attack aristocracy and the privileged class of nobles and literati in a way that no Confucian would venture. No wonder Xunzi rebukes Mozi for "disdaining ranks and classes" and for failing to "accept distinctions and differences or discriminate between lord and minister."[19]

But is the gulf between Mohists and Confucians so wide as Xunzi makes it out to be? Mohism contains brilliant thoughts on equality, but it is also entangled with the notion of fairness. In the latter respect it converges to an important degree with Confucianism. The Mohist conception of fairness manifests itself in three respects. First, Mohists wholeheartedly agree on the need for a hierarchical social and political order. Indeed, the doctrine of impartial care is meant to realize such an order. As Mozi puts it:

> Impartiality is the Way of the sage kings. It was the means whereby kings, dukes and great officers brought peace, and the means whereby the ten thousand people had enough clothing and food. So, for the exemplary person, there is nothing equal to carefully examining impartiality and assiduously practicing it. It makes rulers necessarily kind, it makes ministers necessarily loyal, it makes fathers necessarily compassionate, it makes sons necessarily filial, it makes old brothers necessarily well disposed, and it makes younger brothers necessarily respectful. And, for an exemplary person, there is nothing equal to wishing to be a kind ruler, or a loyal minister, or a compassionate father, or a filial son, or a well-disposed older brother, or a respectful younger brother, so it is right that impartiality cannot but be put into practice.[20]

The hierarchal relationships between ruler and minister, father and son, and older brother and younger brother and the ethical principles guiding them appear almost indistinguishable from Confucian teachings. Moreover, Mozi

[18] Wang, *Mozi*, pp. 129–30; Johnston, *The Mozi*, p. 59.

[19] Wang, *Xunzi*, p. 200; Hutton, *Xunzi*, p. 40.

[20] Wang, *Mozi*, pp. 388–89; Johnston, *The Mozi*, p. 165.

promotes, even if only in passing, a distributive justice based on the principle of virtue- and merit-based fairness that is very similar to that of Xunzi. He maintains that official ranks need to be based on virtue, responsibility for affairs on official position, rewards on meritorious accomplishment, and emoluments on achievement.[21] Mozi would also agree with Mengzi's hierarchical division of labor and the difference between the "great people" who rule and the "petty people" who are ruled, as mentioned earlier. The difference is that Mozi emphasizes the importance of the lower social classes and allows a much greater degree of fluidity between and mobility across class divisions. This is likely because the bulk of the early Mohists came from the disadvantaged classes of peasants and artisans, and they were speaking as much for their own interests as for the interests of political and social order as a whole.[22]

Second, Mohism exalts political unity centered on the ruler or the Son of Heaven. The Son of Heaven, selected for his virtue and ability, is given "the task of bringing unity to the principles of the world."[23] Thence, "what the Son of Heaven takes to be right, all must take to be right; what the Son of Heaven takes to be wrong, all must take to be wrong."[24] Therefore, "bringing order to the states of the world is like bringing order to a single family; making use of the people of the world is like making use of one person."[25] The ideal Mohist ruler appears more absolute and dictatorial than the Confucian sage king.

Finally, Mohism advocates a divinely sanctioned fairness that is lacking in Confucianism. Kongzi's attitude toward the spiritual world is one of agnosticism. While far from denying the existence of the other world, he does not dwell on it. When asked about death, he says: "Not yet understanding life, how could you understand death?"[26] When asked about how to serve the spirits and the gods, he replies: "Not yet being able to serve other people, how would you be able to serve the spirits."[27] As his disciples relate, Kongzi "has nothing to say about strange happenings, feats of strength, disorderly conduct, or the supernatural."[28] Confucianism as a whole retained such a this-worldly character throughout Chinese history. Even Neo-Confucianism after the Song period (906–1279),

---

[21] Wang, *Mozi*, p. 130; Johnston, *The Mozi*, p. 58.

[22] Li, *Zhongguo gudai sixiangshilu*, p. 50.

[23] Wang, *Mozi*, p. 237; Johnston, *The Mozi*, p. 99.

[24] Wang, *Mozi*, p. 229; Johnston, *The Mozi*, p. 95.

[25] Wang, *Mozi*, p. 288; Johnston, *The Mozi*, p. 127.

[26] Huang, *Lunyu*, p. 983; Ames and Rosemont, *The Analects of Confucius*, p. 115; Slingerland, *Confucius Analects*, p. 71.

[27] Huang, *Lunyu*, p. 983; Ames and Rosemont, *The Analects of Confucius*, p. 115; Slingerland, *Confucius Analects*, p. 71.

[28] Huang, *Lunyu*, p. 619; Ames and Rosemont, *The Analects of Confucius*, p. 115; Slingerland, *Confucius Analects*, p. 71.

while developing a metaphysic in response to the challenge from Buddhism, was ultimately concerned with affairs in this world.

Mohism, by contrast, bases its doctrines on the presumption of "Heaven's will" (*tian zhi* 天志). Heaven is presented as an anthropomorphic God, an omnipotent and omniscient being with intentions and desires. Heaven lays down rules, norms, and laws for terrestrial affairs, including the selection of the Son of Heaven whose reward or punishment as the ruler of this world it alone dispenses. Heaven sets the standard of justice, for rule by justice (*yi zheng* 義政) is nothing other than compliance with its will.[29] Heaven mandates the doctrine of impartial care, for Heaven loves everyone equally.[30] Heaven is the primordial source of every Mohist doctrine.

The Mohist fascination with Heaven and subordination of everything to Heaven's will is a major limitation of its thought. Because Heaven is worshipped as omnipotent and omniscient, the terrestrial order under its decree must be just. But in tracing justice to such a divine source, it elevates a spiritually derived fairness with Heaven at its apex over this-worldly equality that it otherwise so strenuously promotes. The divine hierarchy reduces the individual human being to no significance, thus drastically undercutting the appeal to equality that must be based on the worth of humans. This is perhaps one reason why Mohism fails to produce something approaching the modern notion of the equality of individual rights.[31] Confucianism fares better in never allowing ghosts and spirits to invade humans, even though its idea of equality was equally unproductive in the real world.

The Legalist Doctrine of Retributive Justice

The Legalist school stands out as the most violent opponent to both Confucianism and Mohism. It rejects the Confucian doctrine of moral cultivation and affective care, repeatedly accusing humaneness and appropriateness of being devoid of any practical utility. It repudiates the Mohist teaching of Heaven's will and impartial care, claiming that Mohism, like Confucianism, fastens upon the supposed Way of ancient sages whose truth cannot be ascertained.[32] It preaches instead the accumulation of state power, the subjugation of the individual to the

---

[29] Wang, *Mozi*, p. 647; Johnston, *The Mozi*, p. 240.

[30] Wang, *Mozi*, p. 658; Johnston, *The Mozi*, p. 265.

[31] Li, *Zhongguo gudai sixiangshilu*, p. 61.

[32] Chen Qiyou [陳奇猷], *Han Fei Zi xin jiaozhu* [韓非子新校注 New Exegeses of the *Han Fei Zi*] (Shanghai: Shanghai guji chubanshe, 2000), p. 1124; Burton Watson, trans., *Han Feizi: Basic Writings* (New York: Columbia University Press, 2003), p. 119.

ruler, the uniformity of thought, and the use of force.[33] Justice, whether inspired by morality or religion, is seldom its concern. Nevertheless, its ruthless champion of the law of punishment and reward implies a theory of retributive justice, albeit a very narrow and crude one.

To understand the Legalist rejection of Confucian justice, we must begin with its theory of human nature. Han Fei, the greatest Legalist thinker, holds that human nature is bad. People "like benefit [*li* 利] and fear harm," he says.[34] Benefit is the only motive force of social development, and material interests are the real basis upon which human relationships are forged, including even the relationship between parents and children.[35] We have seen in the previous chapter that Xunzi also believes human nature to be bad, but the social implications he draws from this premise are nowhere as bleak as those deduced by Han Fei. A pupil of Xunzi, Han Fei might have derived his understanding of human nature from him. He parted company with his master, however, by driving that assumption to its logical conclusion. While the Confucian Xunzi urges developing goodness in human nature through moral practice, especially ritual propriety, the Legalist Han Fei has no such faith in moral uplifting. He resorts instead to the crude instruments of punishment and reward, not to improve human nature but to orient it toward realizing the utilitarian ends of the wealth and power of the state. The Legalist obsession with material consequences of action might have been influenced by Mohism, but many consider it a cruel and contemptible doctrine in comparison because it has nothing of Mohism's concern with universal and impartial care. If we classify Mohist consequentialism as a sort of rule consequentialism that adheres to moral rules in the quest for benefit, then Legalist consequentialism is but a stripe of extreme consequentialism in total disregard of moral principles.[36]

Punishment (*xing* 刑) and reward (*shang* 賞) are essentially what Han Fei means by law (*fa* 法), from which Legalism derives its name. This notion of law is of a very different nature from law in Western history, which has given rise to the tradition of the rule of law. "By law," Han Fei asserts, "is meant statutes and orders formulated by the government, with punishments which will surely impress the hearts of the people. Rewards are therefore for those who obey the law and punishments are to be imposed on those who violate orders. These are things the ministers must follow."[37] In one sense this reflects a conception of

[33] Wing-Tsit Chan, *A Source Book in Chinese Philosophy* (Princeton, NJ: Princeton University Press, 1963), p. 251.

[34] Chen, *Han Fei Zi*, p. 893.

[35] Chen, *Han Fei Zi*, pp. 683–84.

[36] Huang, "Mozi de yiliguan," p. 120.

[37] Chan, *A Source Book in Chinese Philosophy*, p. 255.

retributive justice. But to speak of justice may be too high a compliment to Han Fei's philosophical system, for he makes clear that the purpose of such law is to prevent officials from becoming "rebellious."[38] It is not difficult to understand why this notion of law has led to the tradition of rule by law rather than rule of law in Chinese history.

Meanwhile Han Fei urges the ruler to adopt another tool for maintaining power—*shu* 術, which is variously translated as statecraft, techniques, or methods. This type of statecraft "involves appointing officials according to their abilities and demanding that actualities correspond to names."[39] Through its skillful and ruthless exercise the ruler judges the ability of his officials and determines their life and death. The ideal ruler, for Han Fei, must possess both law and state-craft: without statecraft, he will be ruined; without law, his ministers will become rebellious.[40]

It is in this doctrine of the supremacy of the law and statecraft for maintaining power that we may discern a notion of equality in the sense that everyone, with the all-important exception of the ruler, must be subject to law. As Han Fei puts it:

> The law no more makes exceptions for men of high station than the plumb line bends to accommodate a crooked place in the wood. What the law has decreed the wise man cannot dispute nor the brave man venture to contest. When faults are to be punished, the highest min-ister cannot escape; when good is to be rewarded, the lowest peasant must not be passed over. Hence, for correcting the faults of superiors, chastising the misdeeds of subordinates, restoring order, exposing error, checking excess, remedying evil, and unifying the standards of the people, nothing can compare to law.[41]

This belief in the universality of law is quite a contrast to the Confucian doc-trine of rule particularism as symbolized by the saying that "ritual is not conferred on the common people, nor is punishment meted out for the noblemen."[42] Fastidious about social divisions, Confucians demand particularism for different kinds of people. Indifferent to class backgrounds, Legalists insist on legal univer-salism. But this is universalism only up to a point. It is limited by its exemption

[38] Ibid.

[39] Ibid.

[40] Ibid.

[41] Chen, *Han Fei Zi*, p. 111; Watson, *Han Feizi*, p. 28.

[42] Yang Tianyu [楊天宇], *Liji yizhu* [禮記譯注 A Translation and Exegesis of the Book of Notes on Rituals] (Shanghai: Shanghai guji chubanshe, 2004), p. 27.

of the ruler from the jurisdiction of law. It is not equality before the law, but
equality before the law as laid down by the ruler—or authoritarian equality. The
ruler is the sole source of political power including law, since law is but an instru-
ment of power.[43] Moreover, equality itself has no intrinsic value for Legalists; it
is a mere means to an end, that end being the building of a strong and powerful
state. As Han Fei puts it, "in our present age he who can put an end to private
scheming and make men uphold the public law will see his people secure and his
state well ordered; he who can block selfish pursuits and enforce the public law
will see his armies growing stronger and his enemies weakening."[44]

Nor can Legalists' glorification of the ruler's absolute power and thus a top-
down, hierarchical political system be seen as reflecting fairness in any sense,
as one may contend with regard to Confucian and Mohist hierarchies. The
Confucian hierarchy is based on merit, virtue, or status, and the Mohist hierarchy rests in addition on divine sanction. The Legalist hierarchy, however, rises
solely through the accumulation of power and the use of force aided by the
instruments of law and statecraft. Exalting the efficacy of law and power, Han Fei
has only contempt for Confucian justice:

> If the ruler sheds tears when punishment is carried out according to
> law, that is a way to show humaneness [*ren* 仁] but not the way to con-
> duct a government. For it is humaneness that causes one to shed tears
> and wish for no punishment, but it is law that punishments cannot be
> avoided. Ancient kings relied on laws and paid no heed to tears. It is
> clear that humaneness is not adequate for a government. Moreover,
> people are submissive to power [*shi* 勢] and few of them can be
> influenced by the doctrines of appropriateness [*yi* 義]. Kongzi was
> a sage known throughout the world. . . . People within the Four Seas
> [i.e., China] loved his doctrine of humaneness and praised his doctrine
> of appropriateness. And yet only seventy people became his devoted
> pupils. The reason is that few people value humaneness and it is diffi-
> cult to practice appropriateness. That was why in the wide, wide world
> there were only seventy who became his devoted pupils and only one
> [i.e., Kongzi himself] who could practice humaneness and appropriate-
> ness. On the other hand, Duke Ai of Lu was an inferior ruler. When he
> sat on the throne as the sovereign of the state, none within the borders
> of the state dared refuse to submit. For people are originally submissive
> to power and it is truly easy to subdue people with power. Therefore

---

[43] Gao, *Pingdeng*, p. 87.
[44] Chen, *Han Fei Zi*, p. 91; Watson, *Han Feizi*, p. 22.

Kongzi turned out to be a subordinate and Duke Ai, contrary to one's expectation, became a ruler.[45]

In this doctrine there is no justice as fairness, only the material interests of the state. Han Fei elevates such material interests to *gongyi* 公義, which literally means "public justice" but is really a perversion of justice.[46] Confucians, as we have seen, do not shun material gains but pursue them under the moral constraint of justice. They are always in quest of sage rulers—usually in vain—who can realize their ethical visions. Legalists idolize autocrats who rule by force and subordinate the interests of the people to the alleged "public" interests of the state and its ruler, and their advice of "statecraft" often fell on receptive ears. The Legalist world is truly one in which might makes right. It resembles the claim of Thrasymachus, noted in chapter 2, in which justice is equated with the interests of the strong.

The Legalist doctrines of the law (*fa* 法), statecraft (*shu* 術), and power (*shi* 勢) have had a very substantial impact upon the course of Chinese history. It was instrumental in the unification of China by the First Emperor of the Qin dynasty in 221 BCE, who implemented Han Fei's callous teachings in a ruthless manner. It was soon blamed for bringing down the Qin only three years after the First Emperor's death, although the Qin regime's draconian and indiscriminate application of Legalist doctrines might have had more to do with its downfall than the doctrines themselves. To be fair to Han Fei, his doctrine of rule by force is based on a historicism completely missed by the Qin rulers. "Circumstances differ with the age," he says.[47] "Men of high antiquity strove for moral virtue; men of middle times sought out wise schemes; men of today vie to be known for strength and spirit."[48] It was for his own time of the so-called Warring States period (403–222 BCE), which Han Fei thought was characterized by "strength and spirit," that he preached the merciless doctrines of law and force. Had he lived beyond 221 BCE, when for longer periods China was unified and no longer subject to constant warfare, he might have reverted to counsel "wise schemes" or even "moral virtue."

Regardless, since Han Fei's time Legalism has been cherished by countless Chinese rulers as a treasure in authoritarian statecraft, even though its ostensible amoralism has driven it out of the public view. Han Fei marked both an end and a beginning: an end to the Legalist school and a beginning of China's long tradition of centralized bureaucratic statecraft. After him no Legalist thinker of eminence appeared.[49] But in Han Fei the idea of a strong

---

[45] Chen, *Han Fei Zi*, pp. 1096–97; Chan, *A Source Book in Chinese Philosophy*, p. 258.

[46] Chen, *Han Fei Zi*, p. 261; Watson, *Han Feizi*, p. 75.

[47] Chen, *Han Fei Zi*, p. 1092; Watson, *Han Feizi*, p. 100.

[48] Chen, *Han Fei Zi*, p. 1092; Watson, *Han Feizi*, p. 101.

[49] Chan, *A Source Book in Chinese Philosophy*, p. 251.

centralized state brought together by force and coercion culminated, an idea and tradition from which successive generations of Chinese rulers would draw inspiration. Indeed, the reality of Chinese politics throughout the ages is often summarized in the phrase "ornamentally Confucian and functionally Legalist" (*yin fa yang ru* 陰法陽儒).

The Daoist Thought of Natural Justice

Daoism is the most mystical and philosophical of all Chinese schools of thought. There is, however, no mystery in its rejection of Confucian justice in favor of a naturalist conception of justice chiefly in terms of equality. Zhuangzi, the second great Daoist thinker after Laozi, wants to "cast away humaneness [*ren* 仁] and appropriateness [*yi* 義]" so as to unify the virtue of the people of the world.[50] Laozi is more circumspect. He says that "When the great Dao [道 the One] declined, the doctrines of humaneness and appropriateness arose."[51] This is not disdain for humaneness and appropriateness per se, but mainly a point about their relative unimportance when Dao permeates the world.[52] It is nevertheless a censure of Confucianism because Laozi clearly ranks the Confucian notions of humaneness, appropriateness, and ritual propriety, which together form the edifice of the Confucian theory of justice, far below Dao or the One.[53]

Dao is at once the beginning of all things and the way in which all things pursue their course. When it is possessed by individual things, it becomes its character or virtue (*de* 德). The ideal life for the individual, the ideal order for society, and the ideal type of government are all based on it and guided by it. This ideal manifests simplicity, spontaneity, tranquility, and most important of all, action without artifice (*wu wei* 無為). Action without artifice is not inactivity but rather taking no action that is contrary to Nature. In other words, it requires "letting Nature take its own course."[54] As Laozi puts it:

Dao produces the ten thousand things. Virtue fosters them. Matter gives them physical form. The circumstances and tendencies complete

[50] Chen Guying [陳鼓應], *Zhuangzi zhushi ji pingjie* [莊子今註今譯 A Contemporary Exegesis and Translation of the Zhuangzi] (Beijing: Zhonghua shuju, 2009), p. 284; Brook Ziporyn, trans., *Zhuangzi: The Essential Writings* (Indianapolis: Hackett, 2009), Kindle ed., location 2025.

[51] Chen Guying [陳鼓應], *Laozi zhushi ji pingjie* [老子註釋及評介 An Exegesis and Commentary on the Laozi] (Beijing: Zhonghua shuju, 2009), p. 132; Chan, *A Source Book in Chinese Philosophy*, p. 148.

[52] Chen, *Laozi*, p. 132.

[53] Chen, *Laozi*, p. 206; Chan, *A Source Book in Chinese Philosophy*, p. 158.

[54] Chan, *A Source Book in Chinese Philosophy*, p. 136.

them. Therefore the ten thousand things esteem Dao and honor virtue. Dao is esteemed and virtue is honored without anyone's order. They always come spontaneously. Therefore Dao produces them and virtue fosters them. They rear them and develop them. They give them security and give them peace. They nurture them and protect them. Dao produces them but does not take possession of them. It acts but does not rely on its own ability.[55]

There is a very profound naturalism in this philosophy. The essence of Dao is Nature, the beginning of all things, human and non-human alike. It follows that in the original state—or the state of nature, to borrow a term prominent in Western thought—all things are equal, including human beings. This is a radical doctrine of the natural equality and even identity of all things. Altogether we may identify five Daoist conceptions of equality, two individualist and three social.

The first individualist conception is equality between Heaven and humans. Laozi says that "Dao is great. Heaven is great. Earth is Great. And Human is also great. There are four great things in the universe, and Human is one of them."[56] He is the first thinker in ancient China to challenge the metaphysical and religious dominance of Heaven over humans. Heaven and humans are equal; they are both preceded by Dao. Similarly, Zhuangzi proclaims that "Heaven and Earth are born together with me, and the ten thousand things and I are one."[57] We noted earlier that both Confucianism and Mohism espouse the moral equality of human beings, but they have never ventured to assert human equality with Heaven. Kongzi holds the mandate of Heaven in awe; Mozi worships the will of Heaven. Daoists deprive Heaven of its mystical authority, regarding it as a natural being just like humans and other things. Heaven does not dominate humans, nor is it controlled by humans. Heaven and humans are both part of Nature, whose rights to existence and propensities to a harmonious coexistence must be respected and encouraged.[58]

Daoism's second individualist conception of equality is the equality of human beings, including possibly gender equality. "Leveling all things into one,"

---

[55] Chen, *Laozi*, p. 254; Chan, *A Source Book in Chinese Philosophy*, p. 163.

[56] Chen, *Laozi*, p. 159; Chan, *A Source Book in Chinese Philosophy*, p. 152.

[57] Chen, *Zhuangzi*, p. 80; Ziporyn, *Zhuangzi*, location 648-52.

[58] Li Xia [李霞], "Daojia pingdeng sixiang jiqi xianshi yiyi" [道家平等思想及其現實意義 Daoist Thought on Equality and Its Practical Significance], *Anhui daxue xuebao* [安徽大學學報 Journal of Anhui University] 25, no. 4 (2001), pp. 81–86, at p. 84.

Zhuangzi asks, "what is long or short?"[59] "From the point of view of Dao," he argues, "no one thing is more valuable than any other."[60] Zhuangzi would have none of the social divisions and class privileges prevalent in the Confucian order. "From the point of view of Dao," he remarks, "the reciprocal overflowing of things are such that nothing can be definitively called worthy [*gui* 貴] or unworthy [*jian* 賤]."[61] The distinction between worthy and unworthy, or what Mengzi refers to as the gulf between "the great people" and "the petty people," is an absolute foundation of Confucian hierarchy. It is a manifestation, as we have explained earlier, of the Confucian theory of justice as fairness. But it is exactly this kind of fairness that Zhuangzi seeks to root out. Inverting the distinction between the "exemplary person" and the "petty person," he says that "he who to Heaven is a petty person is to the people an exemplary person, while he who to Heaven is an exemplary person is to the people a petty person."[62]

Laozi and Zhuangzi value the pristine times of great virtue when Dao is possessed by all things. In that kind of natural equality, no need to distinguish the exemplary person and the petty person arises. Zhuangzi accuses the Confucian sages of spoiling Nature by promoting the artifices of humaneness, appropriateness, and propriety. As he puts it with great eloquence:

> In the age of perfect virtue, the people lived together with the birds and beasts, bunched together with all things. What did they know about "exemplary person" and "petty person"? All the same in knowing nothing, their undivided virtue never left them. They were all the same in wanting nothing: that is what it means to be undyed and unhewn. It was by being left undyed and unhewn that the inborn nature of the people reached its full realization. Then along came the sages. Limping and staggering after humaneness, straining on tiptoe after appropriateness, they filled everyone in the world with self-doubt. Lasciviously slobbering over music, fastidiously obsessing over ritual, they got everyone in the world to take sides. For unless the undyed and unhewn are mutilated, what can be made into libation goblets? Unless the white jade is broken, what can be made into the ritual scepters and batons? And unless you drop Dao and virtue, how can you take up humaneness and appropriateness? Unless our inborn nature and our uncontrived condition are dismembered, what use will there be for ritual and

---

[59] Chen, *Zhuangzi*, p. 456; Ziporyn, *Zhuangzi*, Kindle ed., location 2217.
[60] Chen, *Zhuangzi*, p. 452; Ziporyn, *Zhuangzi*, Kindle ed., location 2186.
[61] Chen, *Zhuangzi*, p. 456; Ziporyn, *Zhuangzi*, Kindle ed., location 2217.
[62] Chen, *Zhuangzi*, p. 213; Ziporyn, *Zhuangzi*, Kindle ed., location 1539–40.

music? Unless the Five Colors are in chaos, what can be formed into designs and decorations? Unless the Five Tones are in chaos, what can be forced into step with the Six Modes? The mutilation of the unhewn raw material to make valued vessels is the crime of the skilled carpenter. The destruction of Dao and virtue to make humaneness and appropriateness is the fault of the sages.[63]

Daoism brooks no hierarchy whatsoever. Confucianism, as we have seen, sets forth a doctrine about a hierarchical but harmonious order of political and social divisions on account of the moralizing influence of the principles of humaneness, appropriateness, and propriety. Mohism and Legalism, on the other hand, advocate social mobility on the basis of utilitarian achievements in an authoritarian system dominated by an absolute ruler. Daoism rejects humaneness, appropriateness, propriety, benefit, care, law, statecraft, and power as artificial virtues—or worse, artificial vices. They all carry intentionality or purpose in more or less arbitrary ways. They thus violate the spontaneity and freedom of Dao and consequently damage the natural order of things. It is interesting to observe that this Daoist critique of artificial virtues bears an intriguing resemblance to David Hume's theory of "artificial justice," as noted in chapter 2.

Daoism may also be seen to support, at least implicitly, gender equality by virtue of its belief in the mutability of the weak and the strong and the dialectical relationship between them. Confucians, Mohists, and Legalists, in spite of their numerous doctrinal differences, all assume the primacy or dominance of men. Daoism never exalts the greatness of men. On the contrary, it holds in high esteem seemingly female qualities such as quietism, weakness, deference, simplicity, and sincerity. Laozi is famous for believing that "the weak and the tender can overcome the hard and the strong."[64] He does not mention gender directly, but in a contest between the strong and the weak he would side with the weak. This position stems from his observation that what is seemingly weak is in fact resilient and durable while those ostensibly strong often too easily expose themselves and therefore cannot endure.[65]

Individual existence, freedom, and security is a central ontological premise of Daoism, from which issues the individualist conceptions of equality between humans and Heaven and equality among humans. Daoism also expounds three social conceptions of equality, in politics, economics, and the realm of ideas respectively. Its conception of political equality is manifest in its denunciation of despotism. Laozi accuses rulers of "robbery and extravagance" when they

---

[63] Chen, *Zhuangzi*, p. 270; Ziporyn, *Zhuangzi*, Kindle ed., location 1944–56.
[64] Chen, *Laozi*, p. 198; Chan, *A Source Book in Chinese Philosophy*, p. 157.
[65] Chen, *Laozi*, p. 202.

"accumulate wealth and treasures in excess" while "the fields are exceedingly weedy" and "the granaries are exceedingly empty."[66] He urges rulers not to oppress the lives of the people, telling them that "it is because you do not oppress them that they are not oppressed."[67] He pours scorn on their habit of coercion in a famous question: "The people are not afraid of death. Why, then, threaten them with death?"[68] And of course, Laozi's and Zhuangzi's rebuke of hierarchy is itself an appeal to political equality.

Daoists believe that much of political ill stems from too much action by the ruler, that is, coercion against the people and intervention in their lives through the use of state power.[69] Their ideal politics is action without artifice (*wu wei* 無為), or letting Nature take its own course. On the part of the ruler, this principle urges them to refrain from interfering with people's lives. As Laozi remarks:

> The sage manages affairs without action. And spreads doctrines without words. All things arise, and he does not turn away from them. He produces them, but does not take possession of them. He acts, but does not rely on his own ability. He accomplishes his task, but does not claim credit for it. It is precisely because he does not claim credit that his accomplishment remains with him.[70]

On the part of the people, action without artifice encourages them to take their own initiatives and govern themselves by following their own nature rather than bowing to authority. This almost laissez-faire attitude is an affirmation of the individual person's worth and freedom. Human worth in a less complete form that Confucians and Mohists also value, but not freedom. Freedom flows from the politics of action without artifice, and action without artifice is the supreme Daoist method for realizing political and social justice. The politics of action without artifice has some interesting affinities with modern constitutional government. The modern constitutional government is constrained in its power by law; the politics of action without artifice is circumscribed by Dao. It does not appear fanciful to compare Dao with the conception of natural and then constitutional law in Western history. After all, Dao reflects the essence of Nature.[71]

---

[66] Chen, *Laozi*, p. 262; Chan, *A Source Book in Chinese Philosophy*, p. 164.

[67] Chen, *Laozi*, p. 319; Chan, *A Source Book in Chinese Philosophy*, p. 173.

[68] Chen, *Laozi*, p. 325; Chan, *A Source Book in Chinese Philosophy*, p. 173.

[69] Chen, *Laozi*, p. 327; Chan, *A Source Book in Chinese Philosophy*, p. 174.

[70] Chen, *Laozi*, p. 60; Chan, *A Source Book in Chinese Philosophy*, p. 140.

[71] Lǚ Xichen [呂錫琛], "Lun daojia dui shehui zhengyi de suqiu" [論道家對社會正義的訴求 On the Daoist Aspirations to Social Justice], *Hubei daxue xuebao* [湖北大學學報 Journal of Hubei University] 32, no. 6 (2005), pp. 632–37.

Daoism defends economic equality. Laozi says that "the Dao of Heaven" reduces whatever is excessive and supplements whatever is insufficient, while "the way of the people" reduces the insufficient to offer to the excessive.[72] He thus excoriates "the way of the people," the economic policies of injustice committed by rulers during his day, for worsening inequality by benefiting the rich and powerful at the expense of the poor and weak. The Dao of Heaven is to be preferred because it favors the poor by bringing them livelihood, tranquility, and peace. This Dao is economic equality and social moderation.

Finally, Daoism exudes a tolerant and inclusive attitude toward all ideas, and thus may be seen as traditional China's rare advocate of the freedom of thought and expression.[73] This inclusiveness is a natural outcome of the Daoist doctrine that everything is in some way a manifestation of Dao and thus possesses its own value. Laozi remarks that "He who knows the eternal is all-embracing. Being all-embracing, he is impartial."[74] This all-embracing quality certainly includes tolerance and acceptance of the diversity of ideas. Zhuangzi at times edges to philosophical relativism; he doubts whether there is any universal or objective standard by which to evaluate truth claims.[75] He may even be seen as an anti-intellectual.[76] In reality he is a pluralist, and in chapter 7 we will apply his pluralist ethics of difference to the amelioration of Sino-American ideological rivalry.

Modern Standing

Mohism was a vigorous competitor to Confucianism and Daoism in ancient China. After the Qin unification and especially after the Western Han dynasty (206 BCE–8 CE), however, it disappeared as an intellectual movement. Its doctrine of universal and impartial care was a major cause of this decline. In a society where hierarchical divisions modeled on the family were entrenched, the Mohist appeal to complete equality and impartial care was noble but impractical. Although a product of Chinese culture, Mohism failed to appreciate, as Confucianism did, the Chinese familial-cultural core based on the affective reason of ren (仁 humaneness). It was dealt a final blow by the decision of Emperor Wu of the Western Han (r. 141–87 BCE) to establish Confucianism as the orthodoxy of imperial thought.

---

[72] Chen, *Laozi*, p. 334; Chan, *A Source Book in Chinese Philosophy*, p. 174.

[73] Li, "Daojia pingdeng sixiang jiqi xianshi yiyi," p. 83.

[74] Chen, *Laozi*, p. 121; Chan, *A Source Book in Chinese Philosophy*, p. 147.

[75] Gao, *Pingdeng*, p. 99.

[76] Ying-Shih Yü, *Chinese History and Culture, Volume 2: Seventeenth Century through Twentieth Century* (New York: Columbia University Press, 2016), Kindle ed., location 1303.

Even though Mohism was no longer a living tradition, it continued to exercise a subtle influence through the lure of its teachings, even if not always its signature doctrine of universal and impartial care. Some of these teachings affected Confucianism, Legalism, and Daoism. It has been pointed out, for example, that the Confucian vision of Great Harmony, mentioned in the previous chapter, was so close to Mohist teachings that it might have been Mohist in origin. The Mohist appeals to equality, merit, thrift, and practical utility were upheld as important values by various scholar-officials throughout the imperial age.[77]

Mohism underwent a remarkable revival at the dawn of the modern era, a revival bound up with Chinese efforts to save the country from foreign predations. Chinese reformers at the turn of the twentieth century were staggered by the material power of the West and its underlying intellectual ideas, especially freedom, equality, and scientific thinking. And yet, when they scoured Mohist writings they were amazed to find strong appeals to equality, a utilitarian ethic, and echoes of modern scientific and logical thinking. If these ideas could be resuscitated and married to the latest Western advances in science and politics, China might be able to stave off predatory imperialism. Liang Qichao (1873–1929), a distinguished pupil of the Confucian reformer Kang Youwei whom we discussed in the previous chapter, and one of modern China's most influential thinkers, was an ardent admirer of Mohism for precisely this reason. He went so far as to say that "only Mohism can save China today."[78] But his infatuation with Mohism derived less from a thorough study of how Mohism might help China to navigate competitive modernity than from a desire to overturn Confucianism and establish a new, indigenously grounded culture.

Mohist thinking also nourished republican revolution in the early twentieth century. Sun Yat-sen (1866–1925), China's most famous revolutionary before Mao Zedong, and the provisional first president of the Republic of China in January 1912, drew inspiration from Mohism for his theory of the Three Principles of the People. He pointed out that among ancient Chinese thinkers Mozi was most inclined to discuss the concept of love. Mozi's universal and impartial love, according to him, was the same as Christian love. Applauding the Mohist love as a good virtue of the Chinese tradition, he urged the new Chinese nation to uphold it as an essential moral principle.[79] Universal love, along with

[77] Xue Baicheng [薛柏成], "Qinhan yihou de mojia sixiang jiqi yingxiang" [秦漢以後的墨家思想及其影響 Mohism and Its Influence after the Qin-Han Period], *Qilu xuekan* [齊魯學刊 Qilu Journal] 174, no. 3 (2003), pp. 60–63.

[78] Liang Qichao [梁啟超], *Liang Qichao quanji, Vol. 4* [梁啟超全集 The Complete Works of Liang Qichao] (Beijing: Zhongguo renmin daxue chubanshe, 2018), p. 354.

[79] Sun Yat-sen [孫中山], *Sun Zhongshan quanji, Vol. 9* [孫中山全集 The Complete Works of Sun Yan-sen] (Beijing: Zhonghua shuju, 2011), p. 245.

freedom and equality, formed the foundation of Sun's revolutionary thought. And his revolutionary activities were likewise spurred by the Mohist spirit of chivalry, which, in extremis, called for personal sacrifice for the cause of justice—a sacrifice revolutionaries must be prepared to make.[80]

Finally, Mohism facilitated the transformation of modern Chinese ethics. This transformation can by no means be attributed to Mohism alone. Confucian ethics evolved and became hospitable to a new merchant culture that had emerged by the sixteenth century.[81] The new treaty ports that Western powers forced upon China in the nineteenth century added a practical impetus to the new commercialism. But the transition from the traditional Confucian ethics that looked askance at merchants to a new utilitarian ethic embracing commerce was no doubt eased by the Mohist doctrine of "impartial mutual love and mutual benefit." As we have seen, a central proposition of the Mohist theory of justice is that justice is the attainment of welfare for all, especially that of economic wealth and political order. Such a theory of justice would appear particularly pertinent in the modern era when wealth and order were sorely needed in China's struggle to fend off foreign imperialism. Indeed, modern China's persistent search for wealth and power, although triggered by foreign predation and influenced by Social Darwinism, has an indigenous source in the Mohist doctrine that "diligence ensures wealth and lack of diligence must result in poverty."[82]

Like Mohism, Legalism receded into the background during the imperial age, since nobody wanted to be publicly associated with its amoral outlook. But it never lost its utility as a practical albeit surreptitious philosophy guiding imperial statecraft. After the Western Han dynasty, Legalist statecraft was absorbed into Confucian institutions, a blend that imparted an ornamentally Confucian and functionally Legalist character to imperial politics. Some scholars call this the "Confucian-Legalist state," in which the ruler accepted Confucianism as the state ideology while Confucian scholar-officials administered the country with an amalgam of Confucian ethics and Legalist regulations and techniques.[83]

In the modern era, especially during Maoist China (1949–1976), Confucianism lost its utility even as an ornament, giving way to Marxism-Leninism and Mao Thought as the official ideology of the People's Republic of

---

[80] Xue Baicheng [薛柏成], "Mojia sixiang dui zhongguo 'xiayi' jingshen de yingx" [墨家思想對中國"俠義"精神的影響 Mohism and Its Influence on China's Spirit of "Chivalry"], Dongbei shida xuebao [東北師大學報 Journal of Northeast Normal University] 217, no. 5 (2005), pp. 115–20.

[81] Ying-Shih Yü, Chinese History and Culture, Volume 1: Sixth Century BCE to Seventeenth Century (New York: Columbia University Press, 2016), Kindle ed., location 8045.

[82] Wang, Mozi, p. 914; Johnston, The Mozi, p. 345.

[83] Dingxin Zhao, The Confucian-Legalist State: A New Theory of Chinese History (New York: Oxford University Press, 2015), p. 14.

China. The functional utility of Legalism, however, was not only retained but strengthened. Mao, an avowed admirer of the First Emperor of the Qin, China's most famous and ruinous Legalist ruler, applied Legalist statecraft to shore up his new regime. For two years during the Cultural Revolution (1974–1975), Legalism was officially promoted at the expense of Confucianism.[84] Legalist influence in practical politics continues to the present day. President Xi Jinping, the foremost intellectual heir of Mao, elevated rule by law as one of his governing philosophies.[85] A notable example is the national security law for Hong Kong promulgated in June 2020.[86] The law brought the mainland's rule-by-law approach to a Hong Kong accustomed to the British tradition of rule of law, setting the stage for a clash between two governance systems.

Legalism wields an enduring appeal for another reason: whenever the external environment appears so dangerous as to put China's survival in jeopardy, Legalism's emphasis on the wealth and power of the state presents itself as a viable path for national salvation. Such was the case during the Warring States period (403–222 BCE) when Han Fei synthesized Legalist thought. Such was also the case from the mid-nineteenth century to 1949—the so-called century of national humiliation—when China fell prey to European and Japanese predations. Some intellectuals at the time called the period "a new Warring States era."[87] They set out to rediscover and apply the supposed virtues of Legalism to the cause of national salvation. Liao Qichao, who had contended that only Mohism could save China, as mentioned earlier, asserted that "Legalism was the only doctrine capable of saving China today," apparently untroubled by these contradictory claims.[88] Even the New Confucian scholar Xiong Shili (1885–1968) felt impelled to promote Han Fei's Legalist doctrines during the exigencies of the Japanese invasion of China (1937–1945).[89] A sense of desperation was palpable in the thinking of these intellectuals: any doctrine would do as long as it could

---

[84] Yu Zhong [喻中], "Xianyin zhijian: bainian zhongguo de 'xin fajia' sichao" [顯隱之間：百年中國的"新法家"思潮 between Prominence and Obscurity: China "New Legalist" Thought in a Century], *Huadong zhengfa daxue xuebao* [華東政法大學學報 Journal of the East China University of Political Science and Law], no. 1 (2011), pp. 73–82, at p. 80.

[85] Feng Zhang, "The Xi Jinping Doctrine of China's International Relations," *Asia Policy* 14, no. 3 (2019), pp. 7–23, at p. 22.

[86] Chris Buckley, Keith Bradsher, and Tiffany May, "New Security Law Gives China Sweeping Powers over Hong Kong," *New York Times*, June 29, 2020, https://www.nytimes.com/2020/06/29/world/asia/china-hong-kong-security-law-rules.html (accessed 15 July, 2020).

[87] Yu, "Xianyin zhijian," p. 78.

[88] Liang Qichao [梁啟超], *Liang Qichao quanji, Vol. 5* [梁啟超全集 The Complete Works of Liang Qichao] (Beijing: Zhongguo renmin daxue chubanshe, 2018), p. 430.

[89] Xiong Shili [熊十力], *Hanfeizi pinglun; yu youren lun Zhang Jiangling* [韓非子評論; 與友人論張江陵 A Commentary on Hanfeizi and Correspondence with a Friend on Zhang Jiangling] (Shanghai: Shanghai guji chubanshe, 2018), p. 9.

make China strong. We should not be surprised if Legalism makes a third comeback in an era of competition between China and the United States.

Legalism also holds an intriguing significance for Chinese law. We observed earlier that Legalism promotes equality of all before the law except the ruler. In this doctrine there is a glaring conflict between its legal universalism, which is commendable, and political absolutism, which is an unfortunate consequence of ruthless power politics during the Warring States period. This conflict is the underlying reason why rule by law at the hands of the ruler, rather than rule of law institutionalized by an independent judiciary, has prevailed in the Chinese legal tradition.

Some contemporary Chinese scholars, however, suggest that Legalism may be compatible with an independent judiciary and is thus not an insuperable obstacle to the rule of law. They reason that Legalism upholds the sanctity of legal justice and restricts the abuse of power by setting limits to the reach of political offices. Although initially developed to serve monarchical absolutism, it may be reinterpreted and adjusted for building a new, modern legal system. So it may be, but it seems that the experience of the People's Republic of China at most gives one the hope of a truncated rule-of-law system whereby a judiciary carries out its remit, without fear of interference from other branches of the party and government, across all fields except the top leadership. The top leadership is exempt because its sanctity is needed to allow this semi-independent judiciary to function. This is not bona fide rule of law. Nevertheless, it will still be an improvement on the existing judicial system if it comes to pass.[90]

Daoism's influence over the development of Chinese civilization is pervasive. "No one," writes Wing-Tsit Chan, "can hope to understand Chinese philosophy, religion, government, art, medicine—or even cooking—without a real appreciation" of its merits.[91] In philosophy its pioneering concepts, methods, and doctrines have influenced and outshined all other schools, including Confucianism, and formed the kernel of Chinese thought.[92] In politics and culture, especially the art of government and the cultivation of individual life, it is fully the equal of Confucianism. Unlike Mohism and Legalism, it continues to be openly espoused in the modern era. It is never the target of such vituperative attacks or periodic persecutions as has befallen Confucianism; nor has it been upheld as an orthodox ideology like Confucianism. Its influence has been deeply penetrating and yet subtle.

---

[90] Wang Renbo [王人博], "Yige zuidi xiandu de fazhi gainian" [一個最低限度的法治概念 A Minimum Rule of Law Concept], *Faxue luntan* [法學論壇 Legal Forum] 18, no. 1 (2003), pp. 13–26.

[91] Chan, *A Source Book in Chinese Philosophy*, p. 136.

[92] Chen, *Zhuangzi*, p. 5.

For Chinese theories of justice, Daoism's significance lies in its radical insistence on natural equality and freedom as a reflection of the supreme Dao and thus the dominant principle of justice.[93] This doctrine of justice as equality, like the Mohist conception of equality through impartial care, is one to which successive generations of Chinese have appealed in their search for equality, individualism, and freedom. Chen Guying, a modern scholar of Daoism, relates that while living under the "white terror" of the National Party in Taiwan before its democratization, it was the reading of Zhuangzi and Nietzsche that spurred him to carry on his intellectual pursuit.[94] In China's long history there have been numerous individuals who, like Chen, found solace in Daoism and made peace with the harshness of life. In this respect Daoism plays a role for the Chinese similar to that of Stoicism for the Greeks and Romans.

Conclusion

After Confucianism, Mohism offers ancient China's second most elaborate theory of justice. It represents an inversion of the Confucian theory. While Confucianism is non-utilitarian, Mohism is the first major theory of consequentialism in Chinese history. It takes justice to be only a means for achieving the utilitarian ends of benefit, especially that of economic wealth and political order. Mohism's most distinctive doctrine is impartial care, within which four conceptions of equality are embedded. These are the moral equality of human beings, equality of reciprocity, corrective equality, and political equality. But in practice Mohists are as much in favor of a hierarchical order as are Confucians. Moreover, they exalt a divinely sanctioned fairness based on the will of Heaven, a religious conception alien to Confucianism. As in Confucianism, equality and fairness exist in an uneasy tension in Mohism.

No such tension is apparent in Legalism, for this is a doctrine unconcerned with fairness. Equality it supports with the doctrine that everyone, with the notable exception of the ruler, must be subject to the law of punishments and rewards. If this notion of equality reflects retributive justice, it is a very narrow one because it exempts the ruler from the jurisdiction of law. The ruler is in fact extolled as the sole source of law, and being the lawgiver he sits above law. Indeed, Legalism is infamous for its glorification of the accumulation of state power, the subjugation of the individual to the ruler, the uniformity of thought, and the use of force.

---

[93] Mo Daoming [莫道明], *Zhongdu daodejing* [重讀道德經 A Heavy Reading of Daodejing] (Beijing: Dongfang chubanshe, 2018), p. 2.
[94] Chen, *Zhuangzi zhushi ji pingjie*, p. 3.

Daoism, like Legalism, contains no tension between equality and fairness, but for a different reason: its defense of equality is so thorough that fairness can find no place. Daoism's radical doctrine of the natural equality of all things derives from its assumption that Dao, a metaphysical entity whose essence is Nature itself, is at once the beginning of all things and the way in which all things pursue their course. Daoism manifests five conceptions of equality, two individualist and three social. The individualist conceptions are equality between Heaven and humans and equality of human beings. The social conceptions are political equality, economic equality, and the equality of thought and expression. Of all the intellectual traditions in Chinese history, Daoism is the most thoroughgoing advocate of equality, and its doctrine of justice is but a doctrine of equality.

The Confucian, Mohist, Legalist, and Daoist theories of justice are products of rapid social and political changes in ancient China from the sixth to the third century BCE, a period rightly hailed as the golden age of Chinese thought. They offer various recipes for progress, reform, or revolution. Confucianism is conservative in its defense of a mythical hierarchical order of sagely humaneness, but is progressive in urging people to strive for justice and morality even at the expense of personal lives. Mohism is admirable for its doctrine of impartial care but lamentable for its worship of an omnipotent Heaven. Legalism is contemptible for its amoral statecraft and glorification of absolutism, and is for this reason delightful to autocrats and their minions. Daoism is lovable for its thorough pursuit of equality and freedom and its defense of the weak and underprivileged; its revolt against orthodoxy and authority is a mark of its courage.

The unification of the Qin in 221 BCE ushered in China's long imperial tradition of centralized bureaucratic statecraft, and this may seem to indicate the dominant practical influence of Legalism. But this is too partial a view to be taken seriously. Legalism itself was influenced by Daoism, Confucianism, and Mohism. And after the Qin unification it lost the intellectual ground to Confucianism and Daoism. In practice, these four schools of thought, each in its own way, continued to influence the development of Chinese civilization during the imperial era. Their hold on Chinese thought was broken first by Buddhism in the first millennium and then, in a more painful manner, by the modern West in the last two centuries of the second millennium. Despite these epochal challenges, they have continued to exert varying degrees of influence on Chinese thought and practice in the modern world.

5

Comparing East and West

We argued in the Introduction that there is as much diversity concerning conceptions of justice within Western and Chinese thought as there is between them. The last three chapters drove home this point. They described intellectual traditions in both cultures that frame justice differently, justify it in different ways, and have different expectations about its implications for state behavior. There are nevertheless many striking parallels, and they are the focus of this chapter.

The similarities, we contend, reflect the common humanity of Chinese and Westerners. People everywhere share similar needs, emotions, and aspirations, and it is not at all surprising that their societies have sought to address them in roughly similar ways. All societies foster justice discourses, practices supportive of them, and procedures to deal with violators. In China and the West—and presumably elsewhere as well—equality and fairness are foundational to these discourses. They are also evident in other mammalian societies that live in groups.[1] It may be, as we argued earlier, that fairness and equality are the glue that holds together any society. If so, it is hardly surprising that there is considerable homology between the West and China.

All but the smallest societies have hierarchies in which a minority of people at the apex receive disproportionate rewards. These hierarchies are often at odds with the principles of justice used to justify them. The tension between theory and practice exists everywhere and most often results in elite attempts to explain it away and suppress dissent. It also gives rise to efforts to hold the feet of elite to the fire. One means toward this end is the propagation of counter-discourses about justice and the better, or even ideal, worlds to which its principles could lead. The development of justice discourses in China and the West follows this pattern. The consequences of this ideological tug of war is an empirical question

---

[1] See chapter 1 for discussion and references.

Justice and International Order: East and West. Richard Ned Lebow and Feng Zhang, Oxford University Press. © Oxford University Press 2022. DOI: 10.1093/oso/9780197598399.003.0005

beyond the scope of this study. However, the discourses themselves are of great interest because they not only foreground principles of justice but specify domains to which they should be applied, and often how they should be put into practice.

There are many ways we could structure our comparison of justice discourses. As our ultimate interest is a peaceful and collaborative international order, we focus on categories that seem the most germane to this end. This is a purely intellectual exercise, although our goal is ultimately a political one. We must accordingly include a follow-on step in our analysis: the factoring in of the political acceptability and appeal of the intellectual traditions with which particular understandings of justice are associated. If we are to build on local understandings of justice, they must be ones that find wide resonance and political acceptance. At first sight this seems a particular problem for Sino-Western relations given the cultural, intellectual, and political divergences of the two cultures. We contend that the gulf is not as wide as it appears; China and the West both feature equality and fairness as central principles of justice, albeit in different expressions and forms.

Our comparisons within and across cultures indicate several possible foundations for regional and international orders. We describe them in this chapter but elaborate their possible applications in subsequent ones. The diversity and competition among different conceptions of justice present an obvious problem for order building and maintenance. It is nevertheless a welcome development, as pluralism has numerous advantages, which we enumerate in due course. China and the West have long learned to live with multiple philosophies and value systems, although to be sure there has been considerable competition between them, which at times has become violent. Deep divides remain in both cultures over values and understandings of justice. These divisions exist in regional and international societies and will, without doubt, continue for the foreseeable future. By comparing conceptions of justice within and across cultures we can gain a better understanding of these conflicts at every level of society. We might also learn from domestic experiences about how the negative consequences of the differences might be muted and their positive benefits exploited.

Conceptions of Justice

China and the West developed conceptions of justice early in their history. In the West they were initially imported from Mesopotamia and Israel. The Jewish people influenced what became Western culture indirectly through Christianity. The ancient Greeks made a separate and equally significant contribution.

Western conceptions of justice are a mix of religious and secular traditions. Jewish and Christian ethics have religious roots, and the latter has always been justified with reference to a deity.

The Greek contribution to ethics does not fit neatly into the religious-secular binary. It is secular in the sense that neither the playwrights nor the philosophers turn to gods for justifications. But there was no clear distinction between the religious and secular in ancient Greece. The word *hieron* refers to a sacred place and applied to temples, but also to many of the venues where plays were performed. It was not until the Enlightenment that purely secular conceptions of justice began to compete with religious ones. They are quite varied, develop new meanings of fairness and equality, and reflect the shift from fairness to equality as the favored principle of justice. There are sharp differences between modern secular and traditional religious conceptions of ethics, the latter being anchored in a deity and many of the former in reason. From Nietzsche on, many philosophers and social scientists have recognized that there are no firm foundations for ethical principles.

In China, the origins of ethical conceptions also have a mixed provenance, although religious influence steadily gives way to secular thought. In prehistoric times, before the Zhou dynasty (c. 1100–256 BCE), the worship of Heaven as an anthropomorphic god who watched over people and dispensed rewards and punishments was pervasive. After the Zhou, Heaven ceased to be anthropomorphic and evolved to become a supreme principle or law of nature. It was conceived of as the ultimate source of natural phenomena from which norms of human behavior could be derived.[2] The conception of Heaven did not produce a theology, but it did give rise to a system of ethics grounded in Heaven's mystical and naturalistic authority over human behavior. Morality was now conceived to be the nature of Heaven, which produced order in human affairs; disorder was thus a manifestation of immorality. To this day the notion of *tian ren he yi* (天人合一 the unity of heaven and humanity) has remained a central trope of Chinese culture.[3]

Another important source of Chinese ethics is the dominance of the family. Once China emerged from the tribal age, family became the primary organizational unit of society and politics. The Zhou dynasty developed a famous kinship-based clan system known as "lineage law" (*zongfa* 宗法) in which the Zhou king was at once the political overlord of regional rulers and the head of the "primary line" of the royal lineage—a dual role that greatly facilitated his authority. This system later broke down, but the dominance of the family endured.

---

[2] Ying-Shih Yü, *Chinese History and Culture*, vol. 1: *Sixth Century BCE to Seventeenth Century* (New York: Columbia University Press, 2016), Kindle ed., location 727.

[3] Ibid., location 929.

The essence of family ethics is a hierarchical and paternalistic order in which the patriarch rules—at its best—with love and affection. Extending this principle to society and politics results in a normative hierarchy where each person—father and son, husband and wife, brother and sister, ruler and subject—needs to find their proper place.[4] Such a structure leaves no private sphere for individuals, which is in marked contrast to the separation of the public and private spheres in the West.[5]

There are interesting parallels in the early framing of justice in China and the West. In both cultures it was initially indirect. The Hebrew Bible, the *Tanakh*, has many references to justice without elaboration of any principles on which they might rest. Exodus 21:23–25 stipulates that a wrongdoer should suffer the same harm as he has caused. In this book the Egyptians suffer such a fate. Every other subsequent book addresses justice in some form. In Leviticus 19:9–10, for example, god reminds the children of Israel not to harvest all the crops in their fields but to leave some for the poor, strangers, widows, and orphans; in Deuteronomy 24:19–22, god repeats his harvest command; Amos 5:21–24 ends with this phrase "let justice roll down like waters, and righteousness like an ever-flowing stream." Proverbs 31:8–9 is explicitly political. It declares that everyone has the god-given rights to life and liberty and freedom from all forms of oppression and injustices. The *Tanakh* describes three kinds of justice: distributive, in the form of fair dealing; public, with regard to punishment and rewards; and rectitude or personal integrity. Justice in the *Tanakh* is always individual, but it is applied equally to leaders as well as ordinary people.

The *Tanakh* has no single word for justice but terms that describe qualities or procedures that make it possible. A *tzadik* (צַדִּיק) is a righteous person. This honorific applies to people who have sublimated their natural animal-like instincts, have accordingly overcome material and other temptations, and are capable of experiencing fully the love and awe of God. *Mishpat ivri* (עברי משפט) refers to Jewish law and jurisprudence, but is also frequently translated as justice in the sense of giving people their appropriate rewards or punishments. The law and righteousness are meant to be reinforcing because the proper administration of justice depends on the character of judges.

The Confucian tradition places great emphasis on *yi* 義, which in certain contexts can be translated as righteousness. It does not represent justice but that which instantiates it or follows from it. This includes duty, responsibility,

---

[4] Cai Yuanpei, *Zhongguo lunlixueshi*, p. 11.

[5] Liang Zhiping [梁治平], *Xunqiu ziran zhixu zhongde hexie: zhongguo chuantong falü wenhua yanjiu* [尋求自然秩序中的和諧：中國傳統法律文化研究 Searching for Harmony in the Natural Order: A Study of China's Legal Tradition from a Cultural Perspective] (Beijing: The Commercial Press, 2013), p. 18.

and appropriateness. *Yi* is personal but also social because propriety requires adherence to social norms. In Confucianism, as in Judaism, the foundation of justice is individual character that leads to righteous behavior. Mengzi, who foregrounds the personal dimension of *yi*, pinpoints it as a natural characteristic incipient in the hearts-and-minds (*xin* 心) of all people.[6] Confucianism, however, also emphasizes the relational and situational contexts in which justice is obtained. Although Confucians frequently speak of virtues such as humaneness, justice, courage, and wisdom, they conceive of these virtues differently from Western virtue ethics derived from Aristotle. *Ren* (humaneness 仁), the foundation of justice in Confucianism, is not just a personal virtue but an all-encompassing quality that reflects one's entire person in his or her lived roles and relations. *Yi*, from which justice follows, "involves persons disposing themselves in this or that manner within particular contexts."[7] If *yi* is a virtue, it is not static but dispositional and context-dependent. Justice in the West is for the most part an abstract virtue. Justice in China is more a malleable contextual property determined by the demands of personal character, social norms, and situational flexibility. Confucian justice tends to be unique and particular rather than general and abstract, leaving no place for absolute or universal rules. This traditional conception of justice is still exerting its grip on modern China, explaining in no small part the difficulty for rule of law—a Western import—to take root.

Righteousness in Judaism is dictated by god in the *Tanakh* and infuses the Ten Commandments. God is an overwhelming presence, but humans are the source of ethical behavior and principles. This is not that dissimilar from Confucianism. *Ren* (humaneness) and *li* (禮 ritual propriety) are linked with awe, deference, loyalty, and sincerity. In their earliest manifestations they were associated with religious rituals. Over time, they became rooted in a more secular philosophy. Ancient Greek ethical practices also have religious roots.[8] By the fifth century BCE they were anchored in the polis and avowedly civic practices, some of which, like the Dionysia festival where plays were performed, nevertheless had religious origins.[9] Christianity is the outlier. For Roman Catholics, early Protestants, and present-day evangelicals, god speaks directly on all kinds of issues, so the entire moral code is regarded as His will and immutable.

[6] David L. Hall and Roger T. Ames, *Thinking through Confucius* (Albany: State University of New York Press, 1987), p. 91.

[7] Ibid., p. 105.

[8] Robert Parker, *Athenian Religion: A History* (Oxford: Oxford University Press, 1996).

[9] Simon Goldhill, "The Great Dionysia and Civic Ideology," in John J. Winkler and Froma I. Zeitlin, eds., *Nothing to Do with Dionysos? Athenian Drama in Its Social Context* (Princeton, NJ: Princeton University Press, 1990), pp. 97–129.

Jewish and Confucian understandings of justice also overlap in substance. Both place great emphasis on helping others. *Tzedakah* (צדקה) has a wide lexical field. It signifies justice, righteousness, and fairness, but is most commonly used to mean charity. It indicates the extent to which justice find expression in righteous behavior, making it close in meaning to its Confucian counterpart. The association of charity with *tzedakah* is a late development, arising in the post-exilic, rabbinic era. In the Middle Ages, Maimonides (Moses ben Maimon) conceived of an eight-level hierarchy of *tzedakah*, where the highest form is to give a gift, loan, or partnership that will result in the recipient's becoming self-sufficient in lieu of living off others. Traditional Jews commonly practice *ma'sar kesafim*, the giving of 10 percent of their income to support the needy. From the earliest times Jewish conceptions of charity differ from Greek and Christian ones in that *tzedakah* is intended to be anonymous. Because it is conceived of as an act of righteousness it should have no practical advantages; it is enough that it is known to god.[10]

From whence does righteousness arise? For Confucianism, it is associated more with emotions (*qing* 情) than with reason (*zhi* 知). Confucianism is an empirical mode of thought in that it derives its ethical and political doctrines from historical and everyday experiences rather than from the pure intellect. From this experiential foundation it advances the concept of the heart-and-mind (*xin* 心), a composite notion implicitly treating the emotional and the intellectual as inseparable in a way that has no parallel in the West.[11] The emotional heart, which is the bigger part of the *xin*, Kongzi characterizes as *ren* (仁 humaneness). Confucianism is in an important sense the study of the heart-and-mind (*xin xue* 心學), a tradition of which Mengzi is an outstanding pioneer. Mengzi says: "What distinguishes exemplary persons from others is that they preserve their hearts [*xin* 心]. Exemplary persons preserve their hearts with humaneness (*ren* 仁) and propriety (*li* 禮). The humane love others, and those who have propriety revere others. Those who love others are generally loved by others. Those who revere others are generally revered by them."[12]

Daoism repudiates as artificial the Confucian conception of justice centered on *ren*, *yi*, and *li*, and thus also rejects Confucian emotivism. In contrast to the Confucian project of cultivating human emotions in the direction of

[10] Anonymity has nevertheless lapsed among many contemporary Western Jews, who, like their Christian counterparts, often seek public recognition (e.g., names of plaques, buildings, programs) for their giving.

[11] Michael Slote, *A Sentimentalist Theory of the Mind* (Oxford: Oxford University Press, 2014), p. xviii.

[12] Bryan W. Van Norden, trans., *Mengzi: With Selections from Traditional Commentaries* (Indianapolis: Hackett, 2008), p. 111.

humaneness, Daoism advocates an emotionally cool and indifferent way of life. Laozi identifies human desires as a main cause of war and social disorder; desires and emotions are at the core of the "human problem," that is, the problem of achieving the same degree of natural functionality among humans as in the natural order of "heaven and earth." Laozi, like Kongzi, urges personal cultivation, but one that is focused on minimizing desires and their corresponding emotions.[13] He asserts that desires spoil our tastes, our contentment, and, ultimately, our social harmony. He is even hostile to the desire for knowledge, advising that the ruler should persistently "make the people have no knowledge and no desires."[14] Desires, knowledge, and the inventions and techniques that result from applied knowledge are prone to cause emotional trouble. Unsurprisingly, Daoism is often faulted for its anti-intellectualism and emotional aridity.

Zhuangzi, the second great Daoist thinker after Laozi, takes a similar, albeit much richer, approach to emotion. Like Laozi, Zhuangzi equates ordinary human emotions with psychological disturbance that is apt to cause personal tensions and social disorder. In what has been referred to as his "virtuoso view of emotion," Zhuangzi advocates accepting the inevitable in life without experiencing intense emotions. "Virtuosos," or persons of *de* (德), "nurture a state of inner calm and ease, without consciously dwelling on their own welfare."[15] He allows for certain mild emotions such as a general sense of ease, calm, and harmony; what he opposes are emotions of the intense and turbulent sort, including humaneness as emphasized by Confucians. Humaneness may be positive and pleasant, but there are always negative emotions of its opposites lurking in the background to take its place when the condition for its obtainment lapses. Thus, even emotions of love and happiness are deficient in a good life.

Zhuangzi's position of emotional equanimity is consistent with his philosophical commitments. Daoism holds that all things are created and nurtured by Dao in a natural flow of the cosmos. Interrupting or resisting this Dao with emotional investments is futile; better to "be content with this time and dwell in this order."[16] Emotional equanimity also chimes with Zhuangzi's epistemology: ordinary emotions blind people from seeing things clearly and get in the way of their exercise of agency in changing contexts; equanimity, by contrast, enables them to achieve clear understanding and become aware of the plurality

---

[13] Hans-Georg Moeller, *The Philosophy of the Daodejing* (New York: Columbia University Press, 2006), p. 87.

[14] Ibid., p. 95.

[15] Chris Fraser, "Emotion and Agency in Zhuangzi," *Asian Philosophy* 21, no. 1 (2011), pp. 97–121, at p. 100.

[16] Songyao ren, "The Zhuangist Views on Emotions," *Asian Philosophy* 28, no. 1 (2018), pp. 55–67, at p. 58.

of perspectives.[17] This epistemology has affinity with the modern Western philosophy of mind initiated by Descartes insofar as the goal of clear and distinct thinking is emphasized in both traditions; in all other respects Daoism diverges from Cartesian reason.

If the Daoist conception of emotion is characterized by equanimity, the Legalist view is insensitive to emotions. Legalists take into account only observable behavior and its consequences, not mental or psychological states such as personal intentions, desires, and emotions. An anecdote that Han Fei relates is an excellent illustration of this attitude. When a lord gets drunk and falls asleep, the royal hat keeper protects him from the wind by covering him with a royal robe. Rather than rewarding the attendant for his good intentions, the lord punishes him for overstepping the boundaries of his role.[18] Legalists ignore intentions and emotions—even good ones—because they are held to be remote from consequences; worse, they may represent manipulation and deception, thwarting the realization of material interests. Unsurprisingly, Legalists reject Confucianism's emotionally grounded conception of emotion.

Mohism also offers a sharp contrast to Confucianism, Daoism, and Legalism. Like Confucianism, it exalts the value of justice, but not from an emotional point of view such as Confucian humaneness. In its celebration of justice it differs from Daoism and Legalism, but it shares to some extent with Daoism and Legalism their indifference to or repudiation of emotion. Mohists downplay emotion and substitute consequentialist reason in their defense of justice. Their signature doctrine—inclusive care—is justified on the grounds of the reciprocity of mutual benefit, not with reference to affection or altruism. Although "care" (ai 愛) may be accompanied by emotions, it need not involve a feeling of affection or any other emotional state; it may simply indicate a preference.[19] Inclusive care is conceived of as a reciprocal ideal that contributes to the benefit of all, one that appeals to people with some capacity for learning and reasoning. If people can understand that inclusive care will benefit everyone, they will adopt it as a principle of action because it serves their interests; emotion is not required for this reasoning process. The Mohist doctrine of inclusive care can be contrasted with the Kantian principle of regarding humanity as an end in itself. Like Kant, who admonishes treating others merely as a means to one's own ends, Mohists promote caring about others for their own sake. But the Kantian principle is individualistic in that it is grounded in the respect for the dignity of each individual

---

[17] Ibid., p. 64.

[18] Hans-Georg Moeller and Paul J. D'Ambrosio, *Genuine Pretending: On the Philosophy of the Zhuangzi* (New York: Columbia University Press, 2017), p. 221.

[19] Chris Fraser, *The Philosophy of Mozi: The First Consequentialists* (New York: Columbia University Press, 2016), p. 159.

as an autonomous, rational agent. The Mohist view is communitarian, based on a commitment to the welfare of humanity as a whole, of which each individual is a part.[20]

Western philosophy reveals the same division between emotion and reason. Much of it is within traditions. Judaism and Christianity understand emotion and reason as equally valid pathways to god. Tensions nevertheless arise when both religions became increasingly intellectualized, giving rise to periodic attempts to restore the role, even primacy, of emotions. In Judaism, this was most evident in the Hasidic movement, which began in Eastern Europe in the eighteenth century. It stressed the joy and happiness of worship and religious life and the value of ordinary people over scholars.[21] Christianity began as a religion rooted in emotion. Paul's epiphany and conversion, which took place on the road to Damascus, circa 34–37 CE, is the paradigmatic example. Saul/Paul was overcome by emotion and fell to ground in response to his revelation.[22] Christianity was subsequently intellectualized by Jerome, Augustine, and, in the Middle Ages, by Thomas Aquinas. Medieval and early modern philosophers of ethics argued that god endowed humans with reason so they might discover him and the way to a righteous life.

In the late eighteenth century, David Hume did his best to puncture this pretention. He excoriated philosophers for building systems on logic or moral assumptions rather than on observation of human life. He pointed out the irony that Christian systems of ethics were both descriptive and prescriptive. They assert that god provided natural dispositions to human beings but then urge people, without notable success, to act in accord with them.[23] Hume sought to downplay reason and substitute impressions and emotions as the basis for inference and behavior.[24] Hume and his fellow Scot Adam Smith followed Rousseau in rooting human kindness and other ethical behavior in natural sympathy. Immanuel Kant, by contrast, sought to uphold the power of reason and make it the foundation of all ethical principles. Enlightenment philosophers continued but secularized the long-standing conflict between emotion and reason.

Another important and related cleavage concerns the relative importance of practice versus belief. Here, too, the divide is more within cultures than between

---

[20] Ibid., p. 263.

[21] Rachel Elior, *The Mystical Origins of Hasidism* (Liverpool: Littman Library of Jewish Civilization, 2006); Martin Buber, *Tales of the Hasidim*, trans. Olga Marx, 2 vols. (New York: Schocken Books, 1991 [1947]).

[22] 1 Corinthians, 15:3–8; Galatians 1:11–16; Acts 9:3–9.

[23] David Hume, *A Treatise of Human Nature*, ed. David Fate Norton and Mary J. Norton (Oxford: Oxford University Press, 2000), Introduction, 7–8.

[24] Richard Ned Lebow, *Reason and Cause: Social Science in a Social World* (Cambridge: Cambridge University Press, 2020), ch. 4.

them. Confucians emphasize practices, and historically have been fairly rigid about their character and performance. They promote personal cultivation through lifelong education and learning, for the purpose of making contribution to public affairs. Kongzi's greatest achievement lies in establishing a body of thought and learning, by means of which the scholar as "exemplary person" can advance in office, and which he can apply in practical fashion.[25] The ideal of a consummate Confucian person as set down by Kongzi is "sageliness within and kingliness without" (neisheng waiwang 內聖外王), which is a combination of deep learning and effective practice. This ideal is encapsulated by ren (仁 humaneness), the foundational concept of Confucianism. Ren begins with emotion and ends in action. In the realm of personal cultivation, it reflects private morality; applied to practice, it expresses social ethics and political principles.[26]

There is a strong parallel here to Judaism, which also stresses practice. What makes one a good Jew among the orthodox is performance of mitzvot (god's commandments). Love of god is assumed, but there is little or no dogma or debate about what constitutes it. Most arguments are about interpreting practices and the domains in which they apply. Many modern Jews are agnostic or even atheist but strongly identify as Jews and perform differing degrees of practices.

Daoism too is practice-based. It teaches disciplines for attaining perfection by becoming one with the unplanned rhythms of the universe. Daoist ethics differ across schools, but all stress wu wei (無為 action without artifice) that is manifested in simplicity, spontaneity, and the three treasures of compassion, frugality, and humility.[27] Compared with Confucianism and Mohism, Daoism is passive in that it offers methods of withdrawal and quiescence whereby the individual could preserve his own safety and be at ease with himself. But there is also an uplifting positive side. Skeptical about the efficacy of government, Laozi and Zhuangzi set out to affirm the value of the individual. The preservation of life and the free expression of human nature become the ultimate goals of their political philosophy.[28] Negative or positive, both sides of Daoism teach an individualistic way of life based on freedom and equality.

Once again, Christianity is the outlier. For almost all denominations, belief is all-important and practices secondary. This is manifested in catechisms that teach doctrine, self-definition in terms of belief, and often fierce conflicts over dogma within and between denominations. Occasionally, practices can

---

[25] Kung-chuan Hsiao, trans. F. W. Mote, A History of Chinese Political Thought, vol. 1: From the Beginnings to the Sixth Century AD (Princeton, NJ: Princeton University Press, 1979), p. 86.

[26] Ibid., pp. 102–3.

[27] Wing-Tsit Chan, A Source Book in Chinese Philosophy (Princeton, NJ: Princeton University Press, 1963), p. 171.

[28] Hsiao, History of Chinese Political Thought, pp. 277, 282.

also generate conflict, a case in point being the persecution by the Russian government of Old Believers who maintain the liturgical and ritual practices of the Eastern Orthodox Church as they were before the reforms of Patriarch Nikon of Moscow between 1652 and 1666.[29] More recently, in the 1960s, the Roman Catholic Church began celebrating mass in local languages. Traditional Catholics objected strongly and demanded a return to Latin.[30]

Harmony vs. Conflict

More than most people, philosophers like to have their cake and eat it too. Many invoke principles of justice to imagine societies in which there is little to no conflict. This utopian vision is equally evident in both cultures. In Chinese culture the most remarkable utopia originated with Confucianism. In chapter 3, we quoted Kongzi's description of a Golden Age society of *datong* (大同 Great Harmony or Grand Union). Confucians hope that justice and ritual might combine to produce a sublime order of harmony (*he* 和). They recognize that there will also be disagreements but hope they might prove a vehicle for harmonization. They do not expect conflict to disappear, but think they can be managed without much difficulty if people limit their personal ambitions and feel a strong degree of solidarity with others. Harmonization is the Confucian problem-solving strategy par excellence. It shows striking parallels with the ancient Greek concept of *medan agan* (the middle way), inscribed at the temple at Delphi, and made central to Aristotle's understanding of ethics. It is also central to Islam.[31]

Mohists, although they attack Confucians' teaching of differential care and their ritual extravagances, borrow from key Confucian insights and expound an even more radical utopia. Mozi identifies human selfishness as the cause of social disorder and therefore preaches "impartial mutual love" (*jian xiang ai* 兼相愛) as a substitute, using the lure of mutual benefit (*jiao xiang li* 交相利) to

---

[29] Robert O. Crummey, *The Old Believers and the World of Antichrist: The Vyg Community and the Russian State* (Madison: University of Wisconsin Press, 1970), and "Eastern Orthodoxy in Russia and Ukraine in the Age of the Counter-Reformation," in Michael Angold, ed., *The Cambridge History of Christianity*, vol. 5: *Eastern Christianity* (Cambridge: Cambridge University Press, 2006), pp. 302–24.

[30] Zita Ballinger Fletcher, "The Latin Mass Becomes a Cult of Toxic Tradition," *National Catholic Reporter*, 5 November2019, https://www.ncronline.org/news/opinion/latin-mass-becomes-cult-toxic-tradition; Christopher Lamb, "Pope Rails against Attempts to Restore Old-Style Catholic Worship," *Religious News Service*, 25 August 2017, https://religionnews.com/2017/08/25/pope-rails-against-attempts-to-restore-old-style-catholic-worship/ (both accessed 3 December 2020).

[31] Mohammad Hashim Kamali, *The Middle Path of Moderation in Islam: The Qur'ānic Principle of Wasaṭiyyah* (New York: Oxford University Press, 2015).

increase his appeal of impartial care. The Mohist "care" appears to be a variation of the Confucian notion of humaneness, only more radical in that it is supposed to be impartial and capable of being understood and accepted through consequentialist reasoning. Confucians promote universal care on a differential basis, recognizing the impossibility of bypassing the natural human inclination to love one's family more than others. Mohists deny this impossibility and wish to transcend differential care and achieve Great Harmony directly from the principle of impartial care.[32]

Daoism, through the ideal of *wu wei* (無為 action without artifice), propounds a different sort of utopia. With *wu wei*, according to Laozi, there is nothing that is not governed. The first principle of *wu wei* is to decrease the things done by government and to reduce the scope of governmental activity to the very lowest levels and smallest degrees possible. The people should be permitted to do as they wish, and then superior and inferior can live together in peace, each achieving what is most appropriate to him or her. Forceful intervention by the government will only lead to confusion and disturbance. Daoists prefer simplicity and quiescence. Not only must desires be limited, but the search for knowledge must also be abandoned. When desires are few and knowledge ignored, Laozi asserts, then humankind can be as full of power and efficacy as a newborn infant. His ideal of *wu wei* presents a utopian lifestyle that involves satisfying only the lowest level of human needs; civilization as we know it, and the comforts it produces, are to be swept away.[33]

In the West, Plato and Aristotle make arguments somewhat analogous to those of Confucianism and Mohism. Plato's *Republic*, founded on the principle of fairness, envisages a society with the most basic level of comforts, high degree of solidarity, and minimum of conflict.[34] Plato nevertheless acknowledges that such a world would still decay over time as a result of internal dissension. Aristotle distinguishes a *homonoia* (a perfectly harmonious society) from a *koinonia* (the best that can be achieved in the real world). A koinonia rests on common agreement about fundamental principles, but differences still arise. There is nevertheless a fundamental consensus about underlying values that minimizes the nature of conflict and the cost of being on the losing end. To maintain this level of solidarity, actors must accept compromise instead of outright victory in their disputes.[35]

[32] Hsiao, *History of Chinese Political Thought*, p. 233.

[33] Ibid., p. 298.

[34] Plato, *Republic*, in Plato, *The Collected Dialogues*, eds. Edith Hamilton and Huntington Cairns (Princeton, NJ: Princeton University Press, 1961).

[35] Aristotle, *Politics* II.1.1261a18, III.1.1275b20, in *The Complete Works of Aristotle: The Revised Oxford Translation*, 2 vols., ed. Jonathan Barnes (Princeton, NJ: Princeton University Press, 1984).

In the modern era, Rousseau makes a claim similar to Aristotle's. Invoking the concept of the general will, he argues that if everyone asks what is best for the community as a whole they will come up with the same answers and policies.[36] Rousseau was nevertheless dubious about the possibility of such a community as civilization had corrupted man by substituting *amour propre* (a form of self-love where one's opinion of oneself is dependent on what other members of society think) for *amour de soi* (narrow self-love that is natural and benign in its implications).[37] Like Plato and Aristotle, Rousseau envisages his ideal society as a utopia. Karl Marx would insist that such a world was realizable. Post-revolutionary socialism would create a classless world; more accurately, do away with all but the working class. As all conflict was class-based, socialist society would be harmonious and the state—whose only purpose was the repression of one class by another—would wither away.[38] Mao Zedong on the other hand had no such illusion. He thought that conflict was eternal, that a harmonious world order was unlikely, and that even communist bureaucracies needed periodic purging and renewal.[39]

A different Western tradition recognizes, even emphasizes, conflict but disagrees about its consequences. Tragedy portrays conflict as inevitable and destructive. Modern liberalism also sees conflict as inevitable but regards it as benign if effectively constrained by laws and norms. Conflict is described as competition, and theorized as the mechanism responsible for economic and intellectual development. The newly emergent field of evolutionary psychology also sees conflict as inevitable and benign as it creates an environment in which only the fittest survive.

Developed by Athenian poets in the fifth century BCE, tragedy is one of the West's oldest conceptual and ethical frameworks.[40] Writing in the aftermath of the Peloponnesian War, Thucydides applied it to international relations.[41]

---

[36] Jean-Jacques Rousseau, *Du contrat social* (Paris: Editions Garnier Frères, 1962).

[37] Jean-Jacques Rousseau, *Discourse on Science and the Arts* (First Discourse), in Roger D. Masters and Judith R. Masters, trans., *First and Second Discourses* (New York: St. Martin's Press, 1969), pp. 1–76.

[38] Friedrich Engels, *Anti-Dühring. Herr Eugen Dühring's Revolution in Science* (Moscow: Progress Publishers, 1947), part 3, ch. 2; Kenneth Surin, "Marxism(s) and 'The Withering Away of the State'," *Social Text* 27 (1990), pp. 35–54.

[39] Li Zehou [李澤厚], *Zhongguo xiandai sixiangshilun* [中國現代思想史論 On Contemporary Chinese Thought] (Beijing: Sanlian, 2008), pp. 196–200.

[40] M. S. Silk, *Tragedy and the Tragic: Greek Theatre and Beyond* (Oxford: Oxford University Press, 1998); Edith Hall, *Greek Tragedy: Suffering under the Sun* (Oxford: Oxford University Press, 2010); Simon Critchley, *Tragedy, the Greeks, and Us* (New York: Vintage, 2020).

[41] Thucydides, *The Landmark Thucydides: A Comprehensive Guide to the Peloponnesian War*, ed. Robert B. Strassler (New York: Free Press, 1996); Richard Ned Lebow, *Tragic Vision of Politics*, chs. 3–4, and *Reason and Cause: Social Science in a Social World* (Cambridge: Cambridge University Press, 2020), chs. 2–3, on reading Thucydides as tragedy.

The tragic poets describe four kinds of tragedy: those of unmerited suffering, the result of character, hard choices, and moral dilemma. Each poses a different kind of ethical and political challenge.[42]

Tragedies of character are most often associated with hubris, a form of excessive self-confidence. Successful people become overconfident in their ability to control others and their environment, and their initiatives can bring about outcomes the very opposite of those they sought. Tragedies of character are endemic to international relations. World War I was tragic because of the miscalculations of Austrian and German leaders. They unreasonably counted on fighting a limited war in the Balkans, but Russian support for Serbia began a chain reaction that transformed a local war into first a European war and then a world war. In an attempt to strengthen their empires, Vienna and Berlin set in motion a chain of events that destroyed them and created the conditions for an even more destructive war a generation later.

Tragedies of hard choice arise from scarce financial or human resources. Governments and non-governmental organizations (NGOs) must constantly make all kinds of difficult choices. In the medical realm these concern such things as what research to fund, which drugs and treatments to pay for, what populations to prioritize, how much money should go to health care as opposed to other research and services, and who should get vaccinated first. Deserving people are bound to suffer, if not entire categories of them. Some of these difficult choices might to some degree be finessed or mitigated in part by more astute political skill and moral courage, but there will still be tragic outcomes.

Tragedies of moral dilemma derive from conflicting ethical imperatives. In Sophocles' *Antigone*, first performed in 441, Thebes has just survived an internal uprising. One of the leaders was Polyneices, the sister of Antigone. She is engaged to Haemon, son of the ruler Creon. Intent on demonstrating his authority, Creon decrees that none of the rebels are to be buried but their corpses left to rot outside the city or be eaten by dogs. Antigone, committed to her family and Greek customs, ignores his dictate and buries her brother. An enraged Creon walls her up and leaves her to starve. Antigone hangs herself and Haemon—Creon's son and her betrothed—discovers her body and stabs himself in grief. Creon's extreme and unflinching commitment to civil order, and Antigone's to family and religion, lead to an intense, escalating conflict destructive of family and city alike.

Moral dilemmas of this sort are recognized by early Chinese thinkers, although not framed in tragic terms. The Mohists, in particular, build their

---

[42] Catherine Lu, "Tragedies and International Relations, in Toni Erskine and Richard Ned Lebow, eds., *Tragedy and International Relations* (London: Palgrave-Macmillan, 2012), pp. 158–71.

thought on the intractability of competing norms and end up with the nostrum of authoritarianism. Like Thomas Hobbes, they hold that disagreement over the conceptions of justice (*yi* 義) and the values and norms that emanate from them is the root cause of disorder. Such disagreement intensifies competition and violence. Mohists propose uniformity in norms as the solution—norms resting on a uniform conception of justice from which all benefit. It is to be achieved through the unchallenged exercise of political authority.[43] This is a reflection of their doctrine of identifying upward or agreeing with the superior (*shang tong* 尚同). Moral education geared toward this end encourages everyone to "identify upward" with the good examples set by social and political leaders. Government should take the form of a centralized bureaucratic state led by a virtuous monarch and managed by a hierarchy of appointed officials. Competent and virtuous officials should serve as role models for the population. This system would instantiate the Mohists' doctrine of identifying upward with an additional principle of promoting the worthy (*shang xian* 尚賢).[44]

The aim of Mohist politics is to remove disagreement about moral norms by imposing uniform principles of justice. One may rightly question whether the supposed problem of moral disagreement warrants the proposed answer of moral uniformity. Uniformity in norms is all but impossible in the absence of authoritarianism. This was to a large degree realized in imperial China. If applied to international relations, it is apt to generate even greater conflicts among states than if the diverse norms are allowed to coexist. Perhaps Mohists can rethink their program by encouraging respect or toleration toward others' norms and values while jointly pursuing those commonly shared. Such an alternative approach is more consistent with their ideal of impartial care and reciprocal benefit than their own authoritarian system is.[45] Confucianism and Daoism are on firmer grounds in their response to conflicts arising from normative differences: the former advocates diversity rather than sameness as embodied in the concept of harmony, while the latter promotes exploring different possibilities of fulfilling the plurality of value frameworks.

Conflicts of moral dilemma as foregrounded by the tragic poets and Mohists are commonplace in contemporary international relations. They arise in the first instance from the diversity of values and beliefs and the different goals and commitments to which they lead. Western commitments to democracy and equality, and tolerance of differences and dissent—admittedly, often honored more in the breach than in practice—are strikingly at odds with beliefs and

---

[43] Hsiao, *History of Chinese Political Thought*, p. 235.
[44] Fraser, *The Philosophy of Mozi*, p. 17.
[45] Ibid., p. 102.

practices in most other parts of the world. Conflict is inevitable if any culture attempts to impose its beliefs and practice on another.

A final source of tragedy is unwillingness to compromise. Disputes about money or property, or other substantive issues, lend themselves to compromise solutions. They are not either-or in nature. Compromise of one form or another results in one side or the other getting a little more or less of whatever is at dispute. This is more difficult, and often unacceptable, if fundamental values are believed to be at stake. When people frame conflicts in terms of justice they are correspondingly reluctant to compromise. Being not entirely honest, honoring a commitment only in part, or tolerating only some kinds of speech or religion is difficult, perhaps contradictory, and certainly more difficult to defend logically and politically to oneself and important constituencies.

Transforming differences over interests into conflicts over principles is all too frequent a phenomenon in politics. It encourages maximalist demands, refusal to compromise, and greater willingness to resort to force to achieve one's goals. Consider the conflict between Israelis and Palestinians, one of the most intractable of disputes associated with partitioned countries that were once parts of empires.[46] Israelis frame their relations with the Palestinians largely in terms of security. Palestinians understand it more as one of self-esteem. They define themselves as an oppressed group in search of recognition and physical control of a homeland. Almost everything the Israelis do to enhance their security threatens Palestinian self-esteem, and much of what Palestinians do to buttress their self-esteem threatens Israel's security. Until these two goals can be disaggregated and to some degree satisfied, there is no chance of compromise and an agreed-upon political solution. These two peoples are Antigone and Creon writ large.

Tragedy teaches us that people and political units only function effectively as members of communities. Communities constitute individuals and political units by conferring recognition, assigning or confirming roles, and enabling affiliations. Neither people nor states can formulate interests intelligently outside of them. Their first commitment is to uphold their community and its values because they make possible security, wealth, and status. Tragedy also alerts us to the parochial nature of our beliefs, especially of our conceptions of justice. It also makes us aware of the often unpredictable consequences of our actions. These reinforcing insights have the potential to make people more tolerant, cautious, respectful of uncertainty, and humble. A tragic view of life and politics arguably also has the potential to reduce the frequency of tragedy.[47]

[46] On the origins of this kind of conflict, Gregory Henderson, Richard Ned Lebow, and John G. Stoessinger, eds., *Divided Nations in a Divided World* (New York: David McKay, 1974).

[47] Erskine and Lebow, *Tragedy and International Relations*, for a series of essays that debates this question.

Modern liberalism is in most ways the antithesis of tragedy. It is a quintessential Enlightenment project in its foundational belief that humans can use reason to reorder their societies to limit, if not do away with, superstition, oppression, poverty, and war.[48] It found an early expression in the writings of John Locke, who argued that individuals were possessors of their bodies, minds, and life choices. They accordingly have a "natural" right to life, liberty, and property, and governments must respect and uphold these rights.[49] In the nineteenth century, liberalism took on an economic component, and by the mid-twentieth century was closely associated with the position that government should not regulate the economy but allow the market, and the unrestricted competition, to do so. Liberals claimed that the market would do a better—more efficient—job than the government and that government interference was a violation of individual freedom.[50]

Liberal thought developed in diverse ways but most liberals are individualist, egalitarian, and universalist. Their common starting point is the individual, understood as autonomous and egoistic. In the middle decades of the twentieth century, liberals maintained that their tradition was the constitutive ideology of the West. This move was made possible by the Cold War and America's need for a counter-ideology to communism.[51]

Liberalism makes no claim to produce a harmonious society, only a happier one by virtue of greater freedom and affluence. It puts a positive gloss on conflict, provided it takes place within a set of rules and norms. These rules should above all guarantee the equality of actors, freedom of expression, protection of property rights, and enforcement of contracts. Liberals envisage political conflict as beneficial because it provides information to the electorate. Economic conflict promotes efficiency; the best and cheapest products drive out the competition. Intellectual conflict is also regarded as a kind of marketplace where good ideas drive out the bad. John Stuart Mill, closely associated with this claim, made a subtler one in defense of free speech. Ideas, once established as orthodoxy, lose their power and become "dead truths." People only recognize

---

[48] Duncan Bell, "What Is Liberalism?" *Political Theory* 42, no. 6 (2014), pp. 682–715; Edmund Fawcett, *Liberalism: The Life of an Idea* (Princeton, NJ: Princeton University Press, 2014); John Gray, *Liberalism* (Minneapolis: University of Minnesota Press, 1995); Pierre Manent and Jerrold Seigel, *An Intellectual History of Liberalism* (Princeton, NJ: Princeton University Press, 1994).

[49] John Locke, "Second Treatise," in John Locke, *Two Treatises of Government* (New York: Cambridge University Press, 1988).

[50] Joseph Schumpeter, *Capitalism, Socialism, and Democracy* (New York: Harper and Brothers, 1942); Friedrich Hayek, *The Road to Serfdom* (Chicago: University of Chicago Press, 2007 [1944]); Milton Friedman, *Capitalism and Freedom* (Chicago: University of Chicago Press, 1962).

[51] Gray, *Liberalism*; Bell, "What Is Liberalism?"

the importance of the beliefs and live by them when they must be constantly defended.[52]

Evolutionary psychology has nothing positive to say about harmony but rather embraces conflict.[53] It reveals a distinct bias in its emphasis on the selfish and aggressive side of human nature. It ignores or explains away more benign features of human behavior, such as altruism.[54]

Analogizing from apes and their hierarchies, some writers assume a universal human drive for dominance.[55] Others describe aggressiveness as highly functional, at least at certain stages of human development. Richard Wrangham and Dale Peterson assert: "Male coalition warfare is primal." We are part of a group within the apes where males hold sway by combining into powerful, unpredictable, status-driven and manipulative coalitions. This explains "why humans are cursed with males given to vicious, lethal aggression."[56] A related argument, known as the "male warrior" hypothesis, maintains that tribalism developed in response to external threats or an early version of what John Herz would call the security dilemma. In-group members are treated well and out-groups malevolently. Cognitive mechanisms develop to encourage coalitions of in-group "male warriors" as they confer an advantage in the competition for security and

[52] John Stuart Mill, "On Liberty," in John Stuart Mill, *On Liberty, Utilitarianism and Other Essays* (Oxford: Oxford University Press, 2015 [1859]).

[53] Azar Gat, "So Why Do People Fight? Evolutionary Theory and the Causes of War," *European Journal of International Relations* 15, no. 4 (2009), pp. 571–600; Mark Van Vugt, "The Male Warrior Hypothesis: The Evolutionary Psychology of Intergroup Conflict, Tribal Aggression, and Warfare," in Shackelford and Weekes-Schakelford, *Oxford Handbook of Evolutionary Perspectives on Violence, Homicide and War* (Oxford: Oxford University Press, 2012), pp. 291–300; Robert Wright, *The Moral Animal. Why We Are, the Way We Are: The New Science of Evolutionary Psychology* (New York: Vintage, 1995); Richard Wrangham and Dale Peterson, *Demonic Males: Apes and the Origins of Human Violence* (New York: Vintage, 1995); Stephen P. Rosen, *War and Human Nature* (Princeton, NJ: Princeton University Press, 2007), pp. 89–90, 95; Bradley Thayer, *Darwinism and International Relations: On the Evolutionary Origins of War and Ethnic Conflict* (Lexington: University of Kentucky Press, 2004).

[54] W. D. Hamilton, "The Genetical Evolution of Social Behavior," *Journal of Theoretical Biology* 7 (1964), pp. 1–52; R. L. Trivers, "The Evolution of Reciprocal Altruism," *Quarterly Review of Biology* 46 (1971), pp. 35–57, and "Parent-Offspring Conflict," *American Zoologist* 14 (1974), pp. 249–64; Christopher Boehm, *Hierarchy in the Forest: The Evolution of Egalitarian Behavior* (Cambridge, MA: Harvard University Press, 1999), and *Moral Origins: The Evolution of Virtue, Altruism, and Shame* (New York: Basic Books, 2012).

[55] E. O. Wilson, *Sociobiology: The New Synthesis* (Cambridge, MA: Harvard University Press, 1975); Richard Dawkins, *The Selfish Gene* (Oxford: Oxford University Press, 1976); Irenaus Eibl-Eisbesfeldt, *The Biology of Peace and War: Men, Animals, and Aggression* (New York: Viking, 1979), and *Human Ethology* (New York: de Gruyter, 1989).

[56] Richard Wrangham and Dale Peterson, *Demonic Males: Apes and the Origins of Human Violence* (New York: Vintage, 1995).

scarce resources.[57] War is simply an extension of this behavior on a larger scale. According to Goreik, Shackelford, and Weekes-Shackelford, "institutional, regional, and global violence are rooted in our adaptations to seek, acquire, maintain, and utilize limited resources needed for survival and reproduction."[58]

What is most striking about evolutionary psychology is its arbitrary identification of some features of today's world—male dominance, aggression, hierarchy, and inequality—and equally arbitrary assumption that these attributes must have been selected for their benefits they conferred at some earlier stage of development.[59] Evolutionary psychologists reason backwards to find explanations and then use these speculative narratives as justifications for the present state of affairs, including such features as war and the subordination of women. Competition among genes, individuals, or groups is the mechanism that drives evolution and thus is to be welcomed. Evolutionary psychology is very similar to its nineteenth-century predecessor, Social Darwinism. Both offered "scientific" justifications for practices at odds with conventional principles of justice and increasingly opposed by reformers.

While there are differences within China and the West regarding harmony and conflict, there are even greater differences between them. Broadly speaking, with the exception of Legalism which embraces conflict, Chinese philosophies value harmony, although Confucians, Mohists, and Daoists differ in their understanding of it. Confucians value mediated diversity, Mohists lean toward authoritarian uniformity, and Daoists prefer natural plurality. They envisage harmony as an ideal and not likely to be attained in the real world. In China, the Confucian and communist traditions are reinforcing in this regard, although they have very

[57] Mark Van Vugt, "The Male Warrior Hypothesis: The Evolutionary Psychology of Intergroup Conflict, Tribal Aggression, and Warfare," in T. K. Shackelford and V. A. Weekes-Schakelford, eds., *The Oxford Handbook of Evolutionary Perspectives on Violence, Homicide and War* (Oxford: Oxford University Press, 2012), pp. 291–300; M. M. MacDonald, C. D. Navarrete, and M. Van Vugt, "Evolution and the Psychology of Intergroup Conflict: The Male Warrior Hypothesis," *Philosophical Transactions of the Royal Society–Biological Sciences* 367, no. 1589 (2012), pp. 670–679.

[58] Gregory Gorelik, Todd K. Shackelford, and Viviana A. Weekes-Shackelford, "Resource, Acquisition, Violence, and Evolutionary Consciousness," in Shackelford and Weekes-Schakelford, *Oxford Handbook of Evolutionary Perspectives on Violence, Homicide and War* (Oxford: Oxford University Press, 2012), pp. 506–23.

[59] For critiques, Stephen J. Gould, "Darwinian Fundamentalism," and "Evolution: The Pleasures of Pluralism," *New York Review of Books*, 26 June and 14 August 1997, pp. 34–37 and 47–52; Rudolf Valentine Dusek, "Sociobiology Sanitized: The Evolutionary Psychology and Gene Selectionism Debates," *Science and Culture* 8, no. 2 (1999), pp. 129–70; Duncan Bell, "Beware of False Prophets: Biology, Human Nature and the Future of International Relations Theory," *International Affairs* 82, no. 3 (2006), pp. 493–510; Richard Ned Lebow, "You Can't Keep a Bad Idea Down: Evolutionary Biology and International Relations," *International Politics Reviews* 1, no. 1 (2013), pp. 1–9; F. B. M. de Waal and P. L. Tyack, *Animal Social Complexity: Intelligence, Culture, and Individualized Societies* (Cambridge, MA: Harvard University Press, 2003).

different understandings of what constitutes harmony and how it is achieved. Conflict retains its bad name in China, even though its presence at every level of society is widely, although not officially, recognized.

The West went down a different intellectual pathway in the modern era. The framing of individuals as autonomous and egoistic and the rise of liberalism brought about a significant reversal in the perceived value of harmony and conflict. This shift was further facilitated by the rise of secularism and the concomitant decline in belief in any kind of cosmic order. Conflict was not only accepted as the norm but reconceived as beneficial because of its potential to reward clever and industrious actors and produce efficiency, framed as a benefit to society at large. For conflict to have these positive effects it had to be constrained by law that kept it in bounds and treated competing agents as equals. Liberalism is the expression of a fundamental reframing of the relationship between people and their society that privileges the former over the latter. It is unique to the West, although selective aspects of it now find some resonance in other parts of the world.

Marxism is, of course, a Western innovation, and a radical reformulation of an older utopian tradition.[60] Beginning with Hesiod's *Works and Days* and the Book of Genesis, utopias posit golden ages and subsequent declines from them. These theodicies were initially a form of nostalgia, but also intended to justify suffering in the present. In the modern era they were projected into the future and framed as realizable. Utopias, including Marxism, have had considerable resonance in the West, in large part because they offer an alternative to the competition, hierarchy, and alienation of the modern industrial world. Evangelical religion has made a comeback for much the same reasons.[61] Marxism envisages a harmonious world but one that can only be achieved by means of violent conflict. Marxism-Leninism's emphasis on revolution and its export legitimizes violence in a way that most other philosophical traditions do not.

Marxism became the official ideology of the People's Republic of China, where it supplanted earlier philosophical traditions. But this is Marxism of a Sinicized sort. Chinese Marxists, especially Mao Zedong, were most drawn to the epistemology of historical materialism and its attendant doctrine of class conflict. Class conflict became Chinese Marxism par excellence during the Maoist era because it provided a rationale for, as well as the means of, revolution. Mao also drew on Marxist dialectics, which he found congenial to the dialectical spirit of the traditional Chinese school of war as represented by Sunzi's *Art of War*. Traditional Chinese military thought propounded the importance of grasping

---

[60] Richard Ned Lebow, *The Politics and Ethics of Identity: In Search of Ourselves* (Cambridge: Cambridge University Press, 2012), ch. 2.

[61] Ibid., ch. 6, for a comparison of Marxism and radical evangelism.

the main contradiction of a situation—a form of dialectics—and conceived of the object of inquiry as a target in constant change resulting from close interaction with the subject conducting the inquiry.[62] This is strikingly similar to Marxist dialectics that perceive both the subject and object, both the knower and the thing known, as in a continual process of mutual adaptation.[63] Chinese and Marxist dialectics also agree that the main purpose of inquiry should be to change the world rather than simply to understand it. Chinese Marxism is thus a blend of the materialism and dialectics of the original Marxism with China's pressing need for peasant revolution and the dialectics of its military tradition, united by a common practice orientation.

The influence of Marxism on modern Chinese history has been profound and paradoxical. On the one hand, it armed the Communists with a potent ideology, which, through Mao's brilliant military leadership, helped deliver one of the most consequential peasant revolutions in Chinese history. A new China with a decisive break with the past was created. On the other hand, it wreaked havoc on a society constantly gripped by Mao's obsession with class struggle and continuous revolution, culminating in the disaster of the Cultural Revolution. It is worth noting that this catastrophe was attributable in no small part to a common utopia shared by Marxism and Mao's romanticism. Just as Marxism envisaged a utopia of harmony to be achieved only by means of violent conflict, so Mao imagined a world of Great Harmony (*datong* 大同) realizable only through class struggle. In June 1949, on the eve of the Communist victory against the Nationalists, Mao proclaimed that the only way to achieve a Great Harmony for the world was eliminating classes, state power, and political parties by establishing people's republics led by the working class—or a political system he called "people's democratic dictatorship."[64]

Mao's "struggle philosophy" was predicated on the assumption of inevitable conflict between the proletariat and the bourgeois and between socialism and capitalism. Nothing resembling this type of cosmic conflict can be found in traditional Chinese thought; although Legalism embraces conflict, it is conflict of a different sort. It is through Mao's belief in the unique value of perpetual struggle and the political upheavals this belief unleashed that Marxism exerted its greatest influence on modern China.[65]

These differences between East and West carry over into international relations. China has a long-standing tradition of seeking harmonious relationships

---

[62] Li, *Zhongguo xiandai sixiangshilun*, pp. 180–81.

[63] Bertrand Russell, *History of Western Philosophy* (London: Routledge, 2004), p. 707.

[64] Mao Zedong [毛澤東], *Mao Zedong xuanji* [毛澤東選集 The Selected Works of Mao Zedong] (Beijing: Renmin chubanshe, 1991), pp. 1469–75.

[65] Li, *Zhongguo xiandai sixiangshilun*, pp. 196, 199.

with neighbors, and the West does not. Nevertheless, the ideas of conflict and struggle, whether locally grounded or externally stimulated, have loomed large from time to time to influence the course of Chinese history. *Realpolitik* harks back to Hobbes and has been invoked to justify the use of force and subordination of weaker political units. Conflict is equally evident in liberalism, which might be considered a parallel to Marxism in that its triumph is expected to lead to a peaceful world. In contrast to Marxists, most liberals envisage the transition of democratic, capitalist states as largely nonviolent. The democratic peace research program is built on this foundation. Subsequent chapters will explore further the implications of these differences.

Fairness and Equality

There are two main conceptions of fairness in Confucian thought: one based on merit, the other on the reciprocity of obligations. In the Confucian ritual order each status is associated with distinct roles and with them, explicit obligations and implicit rights. Xunzi is arguably the most articulate exponent of this conception of society. He maintains fairness as a central principle of *yi* or justice. Xunzi offers an historical narrative of the origins of justice that bears a striking resemblance to those of Plato and David Hume: population grows, conflict arises because of competition, and norms must be devised to discipline people and preserve society.

Like Plato, Xunzi envisages hierarchy as a means of reducing conflict by teaching everyone their proper place. Xunzi proposes a version of the classic fairness argument: those with more rewards are required to perform more services. Nevertheless, one should not equate Xunzi's idea of fairness with that of the Greek philosophers. Xunzi grounds his theory of fairness on the psychology and ethic of *ren* (仁 humaneness), which is distinctively Confucian. Greek conceptions derive from a core defense of aristocracy: that people have different talents and needs and that hierarchy is natural but needs constraining. That constraint is external and in the form of rule packages, the violation of which invites shaming. For Xunzi, the constraints are internal and a function of good character.

Modern Western philosophy introduced the concepts of rights. They are central to the French and American constitution and most modern accounts of social relations. The language of obligation or duty, not of rights, suffuses the Confucian discourse. An obligation or duty, as noted earlier, can serve as a translation for *yi* 義 as justice. Mengzi, however, comes close at places to referring to rights, such as those to education and of farmers to work their land. He nevertheless bases his theory of fairness on the division of labor. Roles and resulting hierarchies to which they give rise exploit human diversity in productive ways and build community in the process. Mengzi's formulation of social order is not that distant from Adam Smith's. But his concept of the division of labor is more like Plato's *Republic*, with its philosophers at the apex and ordinary people at the bottom. Like Plato, his hierarchy is based on individual abilities and virtue, not birth.

Mengzi offers some fascinating remarks on hierarchy in international relations, especially principles of conduct in the relationship between a big and a small country. He uses the concept *shi* 事, meaning "to serve," to describe the mutuality of such a relationship, but argues that it requires different principles from the big and small countries respectively:

> Only the humane [*ren* 仁] are able to serve the small with the big.... Only the wise [*zhi* 智] are able to serve the big with the small.... Those who serve the small with the big delight in Heaven; those who serve the big with the small are in awe of Heaven. Those who delight in Heaven care for the world; those who are in awe of Heaven care for their state.[66]

Here Mengzi is making an ethical argument for the big country with the emotion of humaneness (*ren*) and a prudential argument for the small country with the virtue of wisdom (*zhi*). The ethical argument, according to Neo-Confucian scholar Zhu Xi, is that the heart of the humane ruler of the big country is too generous to maximize his country's self-interest on account of its superior power; even if the ruler of the small country is not deferential enough, the humane ruler of the big country cannot help caring for it.[67] This is an ethical argument based on the emotion of *ren*. The prudential argument for the wise ruler of the small country is that he should recognize the principles of justice and the trends of time—that is, the power disparity—in order to protect his country; even if the big country somehow infringes upon his country, he should not disregard the propriety of serving it. This is a pragmatist argument appealing to what we now call the "national interest" of the small country.

It is noteworthy that Mengzi uses the language of emotion to describe this hierarchy of relations. The humane ruler of the big country cares for the world; he derives Heaven's delight in serving the small country because his affection for the small country is a manifestation of Heaven's virtue. Although the argument for the wise ruler of the small country is mainly prudential, Mengzi uses "awe" (*wei* 畏) to describe the wise ruler's feeling of respect for and fear of Heaven. As long as the ruler respects Heaven's principles and maintains a proper degree of

---

[66] Van Norden, *Mengzi*, p. 18.

[67] Zhu Xi [朱熹], *Sishu zhangju jizhu* [四書章句集注 The Collected Exegeses of the Four Books] (Beijing: Zhonghua shuju, 2016), p. 215.

fear for the consequence of violating these principles, he should be able to protect his country.

If Mengzi had developed his tantalizing thoughts on hierarchical international relations into a full-blown theory, he might have gone down the direction of Greek philosophers. He already implies the mutuality of obligations between the humane ruler of the big country and the wise ruler of the small country, namely one between humaneness and deference. It is not clear if he thinks that in addition to conforming with Confucian ethical principles, such a hierarchy of obligations also serves the best interests of both countries. Nor is it clear if he thinks that this pattern of relations is conditional in the sense that changes in the approach of one party would prompt changes in the policies of the other. That is, if the big country is no longer humane, the small country will no longer need to be deferential; if the small country is no longer deferential, the big country will have reason to withhold its humanness. Mengzi appears to be too much of a moralist in his advice for the big country to continue with humaneness even in the face of the small country's intransigence and that for the small country to keep up deference regardless of the big country's coercion.

Mengzi by no means ignores the importance of material interests. He is particularly concerned with the duties of a benevolent government to teach and nourish the people, including enriching their livelihood, decreasing taxes and imposts, and bringing wars to an end. Nor does he preach blind subservience to the powerful; in fact, he is the boldest among Confucians to argue that it is just to kill a tyrannical ruler.[68] It is plausible to deduce from these positions that in his conception of hierarchical relations he values both ethics and interests and allows for conditionality in the mutual obligation between humaneness and deference.

Mengzi's thinking on hierarchy bears striking resemblance to the Greek conception in which those at the top gain honor in return for providing practical benefits to those at the bottom.[69] His notion of *wangdao* (王道), literally meaning "the kingly way" but perhaps better translated as "humane authority," is akin to the Greek concept of *hēgemonia*. As he elucidates:

> One who uses power to feign humaneness is a Hegemon [*ba* 霸]. A Hegemon must have a large state. One who uses moral excellence [*de* 德] to put humaneness into effect is a King [*wang* 王]. A King does not depend on size. . . . If one makes others submit with power, their hearts do not submit. Power is inadequate to make their hearts

---

[68] Hsiao, *History of Chinese Political Thought*, pp. 150, 157.

[69] Richard Ned Lebow, *A Cultural Theory of International Relations* (Cambridge: Cambridge University Press, 2008), pp. 64, 84.

submit. If one makes others submit with moral excellence, they are pleased in their hearts and genuinely submit, like the seventy disciples who served Kongzi.[70]

Wangdao is the approach whereby the king uses his virtue to put humaneness into effect and make others submit; humaneness and morality will bring practical benefits to those who accept the king's superiority and leadership. In a similar vein, *hēgemonia* in the Greek context describes an honorific status conferred on a leading power by others because of the service it has provided to the community. It represents a clientelist approach to politics: the powerful attain honor by providing benefits to the weak; the latter willingly accept their inferior status in return for economic and security benefits and the constraints such an arrangement imposes on the powerful.[71]

The similarities in Chinese and Western constructions of fairness are striking. Philosophers East and West invoke fairness to justify hierarchy and defend it as beneficial to everyone for roughly the same reasons. The main difference is that Confucian fairness appeals to the ethics of humaneness upon which the conception of a just order is based, whereas Greek fairness emphasizes honor and how it enables the innate human drive of spirit to realize its goal of self-esteem.[72] Another difference is the relative legitimacy and importance of fairness versus equality, which we will now address.

Almost all Chinese philosophical traditions advocate equality in one form or another. Confucians explicitly acknowledge it as a foundational principle of justice. Mengzi maintains that people deserve equal dignity and respect because all human beings share the same nature.[73] Xunzi argues for it on the grounds that all people have the same moral potential. Confucian expressions of political equality are more muted. Mengzi famously declared that "The people are the most important, the altars to the land and grain are next, and the ruler is the least important."[74] Confucians nevertheless turned inward to focus on personal moral cultivation and were more often than not co-opted by rulers. Their notion of equality was also restricted to the elite, to the literati class (*shi* 士). Only they were allowed to sit exams to enter the bureaucracy.

---

[70] Van Norden, *Mengzi*, p. 43.

[71] Feng Zhang and Richard Ned Lebow, *Taming Sino-American Rivalry* (Oxford: Oxford University Press, 2020), pp. 155–56.

[72] Lebow, *A Cultural Theory of International Relations*, p. 64.

[73] Gao Ruiquan [高瑞泉], *Pingdeng guannianshi luelun* [平等觀念史略論 A Brief Treatise on the History of the Concept of Equality] (Shanghai: Shanghai renmin chubanshe, 2011), p. 54.

[74] Jiao Xun [焦循], *Mengzi zhengyi* [孟子正義 Correct Exegeses of Mengzi] (Beijing: Zhonghua shuju, 1987), p. 973; Van Norden, *Mengzi*, p. 187.

Equality is central to Mohism, which propagates its version of the golden rule. Moral equality dictates that everyone treat others as they would treat themselves. Mozi identifies inequality—what he calls "mutual discrimination" among people—as the source of the world's evils. It needs to be overcome through impartial care (*jian yi bie* 兼以易別). The Confucian reciprocity is based on fairness and finds expression in hierarchically differentiated obligations in unequal relationships (e.g., ruler and subject, father and son, husband and wife). Mohist reciprocity, by contrast, is more egalitarian and intended to apply to all forms of relationships. Mohists nevertheless embraced a hierarchical social and political order. Over time, the doctrine of impartial care was interpreted as a means of realizing and sustaining such an order. The Mohist conception of political equality is still more comprehensive than Confucianism. Mohists exhibit a notion of equality akin to the redress or correction (*zheng* 正) of the imbalance in power, wealth, status, and ability, so as to restore and maintain political and social order.

Mohism develops a consequentialist theory of justice. It understands justice as a means of achieving collective material benefits. Mozi led a thoroughgoing rebellion against Confucianism. In a near complete inversion of Confucianism, Mozi described "justice as the attainment of benefit [*li* 利]."[75] He nevertheless always privileges the benefits of the community over those of the individual. According to Mozi: "The business of the humane person must be to seek assiduously to promote *the world's* benefits and to eliminate *the world's* harms."[76] Consequentialism treats people as equals but its benefits are still realized in a hierarchy.

Daoism is the most egalitarian of traditional Chinese philosophies. It is rooted in a theory of justice that asserts the natural equality of all people. Daoism expounds political, economic, and intellectual equality. It can even be read to support gender equality.[77] Its conception of political equality is manifest in its denunciation of despotism. Laozi accuses rulers of "robbery and extravagance" when they "accumulate wealth and treasures in excess" while "the fields are exceedingly weedy" and "the granaries are exceedingly empty."[78] Daoism

---

[75] Ian Johnston, *The Mozi: A Complete Translation* (Hong Kong: The Chinese University Press, 2010), p. 381.

[76] Wang Huanbiao [王煥鑣], *Mozi jigu* [墨子集詁 Collected Interpretations of Mozi] (Shanghai: Shanghai guji chubanshe, 2005), p. 346; Johnston, *The Mozi*, p. 147 (emphasis added).

[77] Chen Guying [陳鼓應], *Zhuangzi zhushi ji pingjie* [莊子今註今譯 A Contemporary Exegesis and Translation of the Zhuangzi] (Beijing: Zhonghua shuju, 2009), p. 456; Brook Ziporyn, trans., *Zhuangzi: The Essential Writings* (Indianapolis: Hackett, 2009), Kindle ed., location 2217.

[78] Chen Guying [陳鼓應], *Laozi zhushi ji pingjie* [老子註釋及評介 An Exegesis and Commentary on the Laozi] (Beijing: Zhonghua shuju, 2009), p. 262; Wing-Tsit Chan, *A Source Book in Chinese Philosophy* (Princeton, NJ: Princeton University Press, 1963), p. 164.

is based on the concept of Dao, understood as the origin of all things and the way in which they develop or proceed. Possession of Dao builds character and promotes virtue (*de* 德). They are the foundation for ideal order among individuals and governments. It is with reference to such a primal yet omnipotent Dao that Daoism justifies its appeal to equality.

Confucianism and Mohism contain unresolved tensions between fairness and equality. To the degree that they are partially resolved, it is in the direction of fairness. Hierarchy is central to both philosophies and equality is subordinate to it. Daoism and Legalism are free of these tensions and for different reasons. Daoism is so committed to equality that it has no place for fairness. Legalism rejects Confucianism and Mohism and glorifies state power. It subjugates the individual to the ruler and his use of force.[79] It has little to no concern for justice, so need not make choices between fairness and equality.

China and the West reveal interesting differences in the evolution of fairness and equality. In Chinese, *ping* 平 can be rendered as either "fairness" as in *gongping* 公平 or "equality" as in *pingdeng* 平等. This overlap reveals early recognition of the linkages between the two concepts. In West, the lexicography is more complicated. Ancient Greek reveals little overlap between fairness and equality. There is no distinct word for fairness, but *epieikeia* is commonly rendered as reasonable, fairness, goodness, and even clemency.[80] *Isos* connotes equality in number and distribution, but also equal relations and rights.[81] *Isonomos* means equal rights. *Dikaios*, often translated as just, also indicates well-ordered, righteous, and later assumed the connotations of balanced, fair, and impartial, lawful, real, and genuine.[82] Justice was associated with fairness, reciprocity, and carrying out one's obligations. It was not until the modern era that it also came to encompass equality.

There is a second notable difference that follows from the first and pertains to the tensions between our two principles of justice. In Confucianism and

---

[79] Chan, *A Source Book in Chinese Philosophy*, p. 251.

[80] Hippocrates, *De fracturis*, 31, Perseus Digital Library, http://www.perseus.tufts.edu/hopper/text?doc=Perseus%3Atext%3A1999.01.0248%3Atext%3DFract; Aristotle, *Topics*, 141a16, and *Nichomachean Ethics*, 1175b24; Isocrates, *Speeches*, 18.34, Perseus Digital Library; Thucydides, 3.40, 48, 5.86 (both accessed 20 October 2020).

[81] Sappho, ἴσος (equal), 91 (dub.); Herodotus, *The Histories*, trans. George Rawlinson (New York: Knopf, 1997), 7.135; Aristotle, *Politics*, 1295b25; Homer, *Odyssey*, trans. Richmond Lattimore (New York: Harper, 2007), 9.42; Thucydides, 8.89.

[82] Homer, Odyssey, 3.52, 9.175, 8.5, and *Iliad*, trans. Robert Fagles (New York: Viking Penguin, 1990), 13.6, 11.832; Herodotus, *Histories*, 2.177, 7.108; Thucydides, 3.44, 3.54, 5.98, Antiphon, *Speeches*, Perseus Digital Library, 1.8, http://perseus.uchicago.edu/perseus-cgi/citequery3.pl?dbname=GreekTexts&query=Antiph.%201.8&getid=1 (accessed 20 October 2020); Aristotle, *Nicomachean Ethics*, 1129a34, 1131b25, 27, 1134b18.

Mohism they are internal, as these philosophies invoke both principles. In the West, fairness and equality are largely embedded in different philosophies. In ancient Greece they were associated with different political structures—oligarchy and democracy—each with different procedures for selecting rulers and making policies. These differences were not academic but very real, leading to acute strife and even civil war within cities. In China, these distinctions overlap. Tensions between principles of justice remained the concern of philosophers, owing to the early founding of a unified empire in 221 BCE. Fairness as the dominant principle, in thought as well as practice, was not challenged and overcome until the onslaught of Western ideas in the late nineteenth century.

In the West, beginning in Greece, principles of justice became motives and justifications for political action. Fairness was the principle of the aristocracy and used to justify its privileges. Equality was the principle of the demos, who sought to impose democracy. Knowledge of these conflicts and of democracy as an alternative to kingship and aristocracy served as a spur to philosophizing and acting on them in the modern era. The American Declaration of Independence and the French Revolution drew on this tradition.

In the West there was also greater awareness of these two principles and the tensions between them. This encouraged philosophers to find ways of reducing these tensions by striking some balance between the principles or somehow trying to harmonize them. Plato's *Republic* is one of the first efforts of this kind. As we noted, it makes fairness its guiding principle but creates its hierarchy on the basis of talent, not birth, thus anchoring it in one kind of equality. Thomas More's *Utopia*, an early modern example, strikes a different balance, one favoring equality.[83] These and other utopias reveal a progression from fairness to equality as the dominant principle. From the nineteenth century on, with rare exceptions, equality is paramount. William Morris and Karl Marx are cases in point.[84] In Morris's *News from Nowhere*, London is transformed into a quasi-rural, pre-modern economy run along socialist lines where everyone has access to food, education, culture, and the material possessions essential for a fulfilling life. There is no money or credit, but a collective joy in producing goods of high artistic quality and providing them to people who need and appreciate them.[85] In the twentieth century, fairness comes back into the picture, although it remains a secondary principle. The most prominent liberal formulation of utopia is by

---

[83] Plato, *Republic* and *Laws*, in Hamilton and Cairns, *Collected Dialogues*; Thomas More, *Utopia*, ed. George M. Logan and Robert M. Adams, rev. ed. (Cambridge: Cambridge University Press, 2002).

[84] Karl Marx, *Critique of the Gotha Program* (Rockville, MD: Wildside Press, 2008).

[85] William Morris, *New from Nowhere*, ed. Krishan Kumar (Cambridge: Cambridge University Press, 1995 [1890]).

John Rawls.[86] Everyone earns the same amount, but exceptions can be made for people who significantly increase the wealth of the community.[87] Public opinion polls in developed countries, but especially in the United States, reveal considerable support across income groups for such a distribution of wealth.[88]

There is also a tradition in the West that tries to incorporate both principles in actual constitutions, but in full recognition that they are in competition. It begins with Aristotle, who speaks favorably of a *politeia*, a constitution that mixes oligarchy and democracy.[89] As previously noted, the US Constitution incorporates both principles and its evolution indicates a move away from fairness towards equality. The Fourteenth Amendment, ratified in 1868, made African Americans, and anybody else born in the United States, citizens. The Fifteenth Amendment, which came into effect in 1870, extended the franchise to African Americans. Senators were originally chosen by state legislatures as the Senate was envisaged as a body of wealthy, educated, and sophisticated people that would serve as a check on the demos. The Seventeenth Amendment, ratified in 1913, stipulated their direct election by the people. The Nineteenth Amendment, ratified in 1920, extended the vote to women. These several amendments, and more recently, anti-discrimination legislation and gay marriage, were justified in the name of equality. Both principles have also been incorporated in the Charter of the United Nations, although not in the European Union.

Hierarchies and Tensions

Primitive societies and small communities like communes and kibbutzim function largely, if not exclusively, on the basis of equality. All larger social units are hierarchical in one form or another. Hierarchies generate tensions because wealth, status, and access to sexual partners, leisure, and health and longevity are unevenly distributed. Generally, those who work the most and in the hardest jobs receive the least. We noted at the outset and in chapter 2 that societies develop fairness as a principle of justice to legitimate these uneven distributions

---

[86] John Rawls, *A Theory of Justice*, rev. ed. (Cambridge, MA: Harvard University Press, 1999).

[87] Ibid.

[88] Sidney Verba and Gary R. Orren, *Equality in America: The View from the Top* (Cambridge, MA: Harvard University Press, 1985), pp. 127–28, 133; Jerald Greenberg and Ronald L. Cohen, *Equality and Justice in Social Behavior* (New York: Academic Press, 1982); Morton Deutsch, *Distributive Justice* (New Haven, CT: Yale University Press, 1985); Melvin J. Lerner and Susan Clayton, *Justice and Self-Interest: Two Fundamental Motives* (New York: Cambridge University Press, 2011), pp. 40–58.

[89] Aristotle, *Politics*, books 7 and 8, who also uses the term more generally to describe a constitution.

and propagate discourses to explain away the discrepancies that always exist between the theory of fairness and its implementation. Fairness is the more difficult principle to sustain in theory and practice when the principle of equality finds roots in the population. This shift is, of course, a defining feature of the modern world.

In traditional societies, the tensions associated with hierarchy were muted. Outside of Greece, the principle of equality had not been theorized as an alternative to fairness or applied in a fully explicit way to politics. In these societies the mass of ordinary people were illiterate, uneducated, unorganized, and had low expectations of justice. Most philosophies could and did emphasize fairness and describe hierarchy as a natural and benign foundation of social order. Daoism is an important exception, as it brooks no hierarchy whatsoever.

Confucian philosophy theorizes *li* 禮 as the vehicle of righteousness. Originally associated with religious sacrifice, *li* took on the meanings of ceremony, ritual, decorum, rules of propriety, good form, and appropriate custom. Confucians believe that performing rituals and etiquette correctly links the terrestrial and celestial realms, bringing about harmony and making their relationship palpable. Confucian philosophy justified the hierarchical social structure through the three bonds and five principles (*sangang wuchang* 三綱五常). The bonds refer to hierarchical relationships between ruler and subject, father and son, and husband and wife. The subject is expected to be loyal to the ruler, the son filial to the father, and the wife faithful to the husband. Obligations, however, extend in both directions. Parents and husbands are expected to be caring and loving and rulers responsible and just. This conception of social structure dominated imperial China from 221 BCE up to the proclamation of a republic in 1912. Mengzi also portrays the ideal society as a hierarchy. He accepts the existing social division between the "great people" (大人 *da ren*) and the "petty people" (小人 *xiao ren*) as just. Zhu Xi maintains that the exchange of goods and services between these two strata is beneficial to both. For Mengzi, Zhu Xi, and other Confucians, social divisions are conducive to social harmony.

There are parallels here with Jews and ancient Greeks. The *Tanakh* assumes a strong family hierarchy with the father at the apex. He had near absolute control over his family and slaves. No one questioned Jacob's rite to sacrifice Isaac, and he was stopped only by god. There is also a long history of familial piety in Greece. In Homer and the later Greek tragedies there is little distinction between the *oikos* (family) and the *polis* (city). *Patér* derivatives are widespread and important in ancient Greek. There are also lots of references to the "fatherland," which was also used in reference to patrimony and property. The husband and father was *kyrios* (lord and master) at home as political leaders were in the *polis*. Citizens were *kyrios* in democracies and to avoid shame had to show that they were also masters of their household. Household and polis were reinforcing institutions. According to Barry Strauss: "The Athenian family was politicized and . . . Athenian politics was familialized."[90]

This relationship was kept alive during the Middle Ages and early modern era. As the modern state undermined the kinship power network of the medieval aristocracy it fostered household patriarchy as a model of the new royal patriarchy. Influenced by John Locke, it would move further away from the household model as liberalism emerged.[91] But metaphors linking family and state continued to have meaning. To this day in the United States, George Washington is routinely referred to as "the father of his country."

In China, justice is connected with early religious practices and took on social meanings, which often kept their religious connotations. This is equally true in ancient Greece. *Xenia* (guest friendship) was a core Greek value. It required people to offer food and shelter to visitors, and visitors not to abuse the hospitality they received. These obligations were deemed sufficiently important that hospitality was made one of the epithets of the father of the gods: Zeus Xenios.[92] Even in the polis, this connection was evident. The most honored religious shrines were ancestral. To carry out a religious rite was called *patriazein* (to take after one's fathers). In contrast to China, Athenians had little interest in ancestors beyond their great-grandfathers.

For Mengzi, personal righteousness and social appropriateness come together, as they do for Greeks, Christians, and Jews, although not always in the same ways. Mengzi's concept of hierarchy finds resonance in the West in Plato's *Republic* and Christian notions of cosmic hierarchy. For medieval Christians, God is at the apex, and beneath him come the angels, stars, and planets, and finally the earth at the center. On earth, Jerusalem is at the center, and earthly hierarchies resembled heavenly ones with the pope and kings at the apex and ordinary folk beneath them, and animals at the base.[93] Even those Christians who sought to escape from government and society and lead a monastic life did so in highly organized and hierarchical orders.[94] Christians were nevertheless more ambivalent about hierarchies than Confucians. Early Christians rejected them, and Augustine, who embraced them—and the Roman Empire—nevertheless

[90] Barry S. Strauss, *Fathers and Sons in Athens: Ideology and Society in the Era of the Peloponnesian War* (Princeton, NJ: Princeton University Press, 1993), p. 12.

[91] Lawrence Stone, *The Family, Sex and Marriage in England, 1500–1800* (New York: Harper & Row, 1977).

[92] Moses I. Finley, *The World of Odysseus* (New York: Viking, 1978), pp. 99–101.

[93] Edward H. Dahl and Jean-François Gauvin, *Sphaerae Mundi* (Montreal: McGill-Queen's Press, 2003); Jonathan T. Pennington, *Heaven and Earth in the Gospel of Matthew* (Amsterdam: Brill, 2007).

[94] C. H. Lawrence, *Medieval Monasticism*, 3rd ed. (Harlow: Pearson, 2001); Eleanor Shipley Duckett, *The Gateway to the Middle Ages: Monasticism* (Ann Arbor: University of Michigan Press, 1988).

regarded the latter as a necessary evil.[95] These tensions in Christianity were readily visible in the era of the Reformation. Many Protestant sects spurned hierarchies and some rejected governments.[96] Contemporary Christianity runs the gamut on this score.

In China, the Confucian hierarchy is based on merit, virtue, or status, and the Mohist one rests in addition on divine sanction. The Legalist hierarchy rises solely through the accumulation of power and the use of force aided by the instruments of law and statecraft. In the West, hierarchy was most often based on birth, and the aristocracy remained the dominant political force until the twentieth century. This was not true, of course, for tribal groups like the Germans at the time of the Roman Empire or the Vikings in the Middle Ages. It was not until the modern era that alternate forms of hierarchies were theorized, initially by liberals. They sought to replace hierarchies of birth with those of merit, and by doing so, assert and justify their claim to power and status. Achieved status ultimately triumphed over ascribed status in the West. In recent decades, celebrity has emerged as an alternate basis for claiming wealth and status, and even power as indicated by the election of Hollywood and television stars to office in the United States.

Hierarchies come with rule packages. These rules are central to Homer, were practiced to varying degrees in *oikos* and *polis*, and reached their apotheosis in intra-Greek relations in the form of *hēgemonia*.[97] At all levels of social aggregation, hierarchy was characterized by mutual obligations. Lesser family members, dependent people, and weaker powers were expected to honor fathers, leading figures, and powerful states. In return, they were required to look after the practical needs of those who honor them. For the Greeks, this procedure extended to the gods, to whom sacrifices were made in the hope of divine intervention in one's favor. Similar practices developed in China, where they also extended to relations with other countries thought to be civilized. The Confucian principles of propriety established ethical relationships from which all parties benefited. Ming emperors practiced "expressive hegemony." When it prevailed, China was honored by its neighbors and provided practical benefits (i.e., trade and security) to them in return for recognition of Chinese cultural dominance, adoption of the Chinese calendar, and the payment of symbolic tribute.[98]

[95] Augustine of Hippo, *The City of God*, trans. R. W. Dyson (Cambridge: Cambridge University Press, 1988).

[96] Thomas A. Howard, *Remembering the Reformation: An Inquiry into the Meanings of Protestantism* (Oxford: Oxford University Press, 2016); Alister E. McGrath, *Christianity's Dangerous Idea* (New York: HarperOne, 2007).

[97] Richard Ned Lebow, *The Tragic Vision of Politics: Ethics, Interest, and Orders* (Cambridge: Cambridge University Press, 2003), chs. 2 and 3.

[98] Ibid., pp. 7, 21–22.

Liberalism gave rise to a different form of hierarchy. Status is acquired on the basis of wealth. Affluence must be displayed and recognized by others. This is not a novel phenomenon, as ancient rulers everywhere built temples, monuments, palaces, and gardens as means of displaying their power and wealth. In seventeenth- and early eighteenth-century France, Louis XIV built Versailles and gardens, sponsored theater and opera, and supported the arts and science. He was widely emulated by other European rulers.[99] Conspicuous consumption, as Thorstein Veblen called it, became a prominent feature of bourgeois life as many newly wealthy people sought to emulate the lifestyle of the aristocracy or of one another.[100] Bourgeois hierarchies differed from aristocratic ones in that they were constrained by few, if any, rules. Rich people employed servants but were not necessarily shamed by their peers if they did not look after them well. The requirement of public service, which took the form of *noblesse oblige* in the earlier aristocratic age, also waned. Alexis de Tocqueville, an astute observer of equality and its effects, worried that wealth and power, cut free from constraints and responsibilities, could result in a new and horrible form of tyranny.[101]

As noted, liberal hierarchies confront a basic contradiction. Liberalism is rooted in the principle of equality. However, the societies in which liberal laws and norms predominate have often led to increased inequality. Liberals have found several ways to square this circle, at least in theory. Some argue that everyone's relative wealth is much higher due to liberalism, so inequality should not matter so much.[102] Other liberals defend hierarchies if they arrived at fairly. With level playing fields and equal opportunity to compete, whatever hierarchies emerge are the result of some combination of talent, hard work, and luck and are thus largely justified.[103] These arguments have appeal to a particular segment of intellectuals and businesspeople at the apex of the hierarchy. Lower down, they have found less traction. Public opinion polls indicate that in countries where disease and religious and ethnic violence are not immediate concerns, people feel most threatened by inequality.[104]

---

[99] Richard Ned Lebow, *A Cultural Theory of International Relations* (Cambridge: Cambridge University Press, 2008), ch. 7 on the competition for standing in eighteenth-century Europe.

[100] Thorstein Veblen, *The Theory of the Leisure Class: An Economic Study in the Evolution of Institutions* (New York: Modern Library, 1934).

[101] Alexis de Tocqueville, *Democracy in America*, trans. and ed. Harvey C. Mansfield and Debra Winthrop (Chicago: University of Chicago Press, 2000), II.4.6, p. 663.

[102] Diedre N. McCloskey, *Bourgeois Equality: How Ideas, Not Capital or Institutions, Enriched the World* (Chicago: University of Chicago Press, 2016), ch. 1.

[103] Rawls, *Theory of Justice*, for the most elegant, if unconvincing, theoretical defense.

[104] Jacob Poushter, "What Is the Greatest Threat in the World? Depends on Where You Live," *Pew Research Center*, Spring 2014 world survey, http://www.pewresearch.org/fact-tank/2014/10/16/what-is-the-greatest-threat-to-the-world-depends-on-where-you-live/ (accessed 16 May 2020).

There is a third kind of hierarchy, one that rests on no principle of justice but rather on force. Legalism in China comes the closest to offering support for such a social order. It promotes the equality of all before the law—except for the ruler. In effect, it sanctions political absolutism. Legalism is the unfortunate legacy of ruthless power struggles of the Warring States period (c. 475–221 BCE). The closest Western equivalent is probably Social Darwinism in the nineteenth and early twentieth centuries. It invoked the biological mechanism of natural selection to justify war and the domination of the weak by the powerful.[105] The realist paradigm in international relations offers some support for the rule of the powerful, but in far more muted form. Most realists do not defend international relations as ethical, although classical realists make the case for foreign policy in accord with accepted ethical principles.[106] Only *Realpolitik* dispenses with any ethical considerations and justifies the unconstrained pursuit of power.[107]

Scope and Appeal

All three hierarchies, and principles of justice more generally, were initially applied to family or tribal groupings, later to larger political units, and finally, to regional and international societies. This progression is a natural one because it mirrors the social organization of our species. We started in families, small groups, and tribes, and over time became organized in increasingly larger units. Most people still privilege loyalty to family even though identification with the nation has everywhere grown in intensity. So too in the postwar era has identification with even larger entities. A 2018 Eurobarometer survey revealed that 89 percent of Europeans felt attached to their city, town, or village and 93 percent to their country. Fully 56 percent also feel attached to the European Union, and 65 percent to Europe.[108]

As social aggregations have grown in size and complexity, principles of justice, initially developed in the context of small groups characterized by face-to-face

---

[105] D. Paul Crook, *Darwinism, War and History: The Debate over the Biology of War from the "Origin of Species" to the First World War* (Cambridge: Cambridge University Press, 1994); Mike Hawkins, *Social Darwinism in European and American Thought 1860–1945: Nature and Model and Nature as Threat* (Cambridge: Cambridge University Press, 1997); Robert C. Bannister, *Social Darwinism: Science and Myth in Anglo-American Social Thought* (Philadelphia: Temple University Press, 1979).

[106] Lebow, *Tragic Vision of Politics*; ch. 4, and *Ethics and International Relations: A Tragic Perspective* (Cambridge: Cambridge University Press, 2020), ch. 2.

[107] John Bew, *Realpolitik: A History* (Oxford: Oxford University Press, 2018).

[108] European Commission, "Standard Eurobarometer 89 Spring 2018: Report," March 2018, file:///Users/nedlebow/Downloads/eb_89_citizenship_en.pdf (accessed 17 October 2020), p. 5.

relations, have been extended and reformulated to encompass interactions among people unlikely to know or even to have encountered one another. This process gives rise to a set of interesting questions that we can raise though certainly not hope to answer in this chapter. Of most interest perhaps are the mechanisms that enable these extensions of principles of justice. Next is the extent to which all levels of aggregation are treated equally or one privileged over the others. Finally comes the degree to which the principles of justice involved are open to evolution in theory and practice.

Expanding circles is one important pathway of extending principles to higher levels of aggregation. Confucians start with love of family and extend this sentiment out to community and nation. There is no reason why it cannot be applied beyond the nation, and in various periods of Chinese history Confucian scholar-officials did so with some success. Jews also focus on the family and later extended ethics to embrace other members of the Jewish community and, in the rabbinic era, people more generally.

The principal mechanism for these extensions is friendship. Kongzi and Mengzi emphasize how they promote equality and vice versa. Kongzi holds trustworthiness (*xin* 信) to be the most important quality of friendship. Mengzi takes virtue, not status, to be the true marker of friendship. At a deeper level, the Confucian conception of friendship derives from its role in ethics. Confucianism conceives of human beings as role-bearing persons, as did ancient Greeks and Romans—not as abstract autonomous individuals so familiar in modern Western thought. The conception of role-bearing persons emphasizes the sociality and relationality of human beings; in all their roles they are defined in large measure by the others with whom they interact. Friendship is the basic role for entrance to the world outside the family, and it is one of the most important relations for role-bearing persons. The role of friend requires the same emotional responses as familial ones, although not in the same degree: love, trust, nurturance, loyalty, and the joy of contributing to the friend's flourishing.[109]

Trustworthiness, which Kongzi takes to be the most important virtue of friendship, embodies reciprocity. But it is a different sort of reciprocity than that envisaged by the Western social contract. The social contract rests on the presumption of the autonomous individual and transactions among such individuals in a market society. This notion is alien to traditional China and East Asia. East Asian reciprocity is embodied in the specific roles of people rather than in their transactions. When I dine at my friend's house, he is the benefactor and I am the beneficiary. The beneficiary role evokes a set of responses

---

[109] Henry Rosemont Jr., "How to Think about Morality without Moral Agents," in Michael J. Sandel and Paul J. D'Ambrosio, eds., *Encountering China: Michael Sandel and Chinese Philosophy* (Cambridge, MA: Harvard University Press, 2018), pp. 197–227, at p. 216.

appropriate to that position. They include gratitude, obedience, attentiveness, and so on, whereas the benefactor must demonstrate such attitudes as care, sensitivity, and courage.[110] This is relational reciprocity predicated on role performance, not individualistic reciprocity based on contract obligations. Confucians rely on relational reciprocity as the mechanism to extend ethics to ever wider circles of friendship.

Friendship was also considered the cement of society in ancient Greece. It encouraged loyalty, self-restraint, and generosity based on the principle of reciprocity. It was similar in many ways to the Confucian understanding. It was anchored in roles, which required people to behave in certain ways, as noted earlier in the example of *xenia*. As with Confucians, it was expected to scale up from individuals to families, to cities, and to relations among them. According to Aristotle, *philia* (friendship) created solidarity among people and sustained the community. *Philoi* (friends) created expanding circles of affective networks that formed the foundation of the civic project.[111] Plato valued friendship because it created an atmosphere of trust in which meaningful dialogue and acceptable disagreements became possible.[112] In his funeral oration, Thucydides has Pericles exhort Athenians to think of themselves as lovers (*erastai*) of their polis.[113] Pericles extends friendship from people to city-states. Without intended irony, Athenian playwrights describe as "demos-lovers" people who had the same degree of affection for their polis as for their family and friends.

Here the parallel ends. Greek beliefs in regionalism were limited to the Greek political units that constituted Hellas. Hellenes and Christians developed a more universal understanding of community and ethics that differs notably from Confucianism. Confucian ethics is at once local and universal. Its local nature is manifested in its doctrine of rule particularism, which asserts that "ritual is not conferred on the common people, nor is punishment meted out for the noblemen."[114] Fastidious about social divisions, Confucians demand particularism for different kinds of people. This doctrine might well be applied to

[110] Ibid., p. 217.

[111] Aristotle, *Politics*, 1253a2–3, 1280b39, and *Nicomachean Ethics*, 1155a14, 1159b25, 1161a23, 1161b12.

[112] Plato, *Republic*, 509d–511d, 531d–534c.

[113] Thucydides, 2.36–46.

[114] Eric Brown, "Hellenistic Cosmopolitanism," in Mary Louise Gill and Pierre Pellegrin, eds., *A Companion to Ancient Philosophy* (Oxford: Blackwell, 2006), pp. 549–558; David Konstan, "Cosmopolitan Traditions," in Ryan K. Balot, ed., *A Companion to Greek and Roman Political Thought* (Chichester: Wiley-Blackwell, 2009), pp. 473–84; for quote, Yang Tianyu [楊天宇], *Liji yizhu* [禮記譯注 A Translation and Exegesis of the Book of Notes on Rituals] (Shanghai: Shanghai guji chubanshe, 2004), p. 27.

premodern Europe, where different rights, penalties, and procedures applied to aristocrats and commoners.

But Confucian ethics also urges the "petty person" to acquire the emotion of humaneness, develop the sense of justice, and learn ritual propriety just like the "exemplary person." Confucians wish to extend their whole ethical edifice from the family to the community to the nation and eventually to the whole world. The concept of *tianxia* (天下), literally meaning "all under Heaven," denotes the last category of the whole world, and it is a concept to which virtually all Chinese schools of thought subscribe. *Tianxia* represents a Chinese universalism that is especially manifest in Confucianism but is accepted by all Chinese elites. It places China at the center of the known world and holds its values to be universally imitable. But it is a universalism distinct from the later activist and even aggressive Christian and liberal universalisms. Chinese universalism is more restrained and passive in that it encourages other peoples to learn from the Chinese civilization and imitate its culture and practices rather than actively seeking to export them. It is not a priori universalism of the Hellenistic, Christian, or liberal sort describing a logical necessity or prescribing a destination. Rather, it is a kind of civilizational and humanist universalism grounding itself on aspects of human nature (*xing* 性) thought common to all people.[115]

Confucianism and Judaism work up the social aggregation ladder in their ethical commitments. Mohism and Christianity work their way down. Mohists exalt political and ethical unity centered on the ruler or the Son of Heaven. The Son of Heaven, selected for his virtue and ability, is given "the task of bringing unity to the principles of the world."[116] It follows that "what the Son of Heaven takes to be right, all must take to be right; what the Son of Heaven takes to be wrong, all must take to be wrong."[117] "Bringing order to the world's political units" is therefore "like bringing order to a single family, and making use of the people of the world is like making use of one person."[118] The ideal Mohist ruler appears more absolute and dictatorial than the Confucian sage king.

Christians envisaged themselves as members of a world community long before they imagined themselves as nations. By medieval times, they had a full-blown cosmology. It distinguished terrestrial from celestial regions, with the latter including everything from the moon to the limits of the universe. The land portion was known to the Greeks as *oikoumene*, and referred to the three connected continents of Europe, Asia, and Africa. The *oikoumene* was envisaged

---

[115] Francois Jullien, *On the Universal, the Uniform, the Common and Dialogue between Cultures* (Cambridge: Polity, 2014), p. 74.

[116] Wang, *Mozi*, p. 237; Johnston, *Mozi*, p. 99.

[117] Wang, *Mozi*, p. 229; Johnston, *Mozi*, p. 95.

[118] Wang, *Mozi*, p. 288; Johnston, *Mozi*, p. 127.

as a universal, regulative ideal.[119] The idea of a human community gradually gave way to one of human diversity, explained with reference to the prior dispersion of peoples. This belief became more concrete in the fifteenth century, facilitated by cartographical advances motivated by search for cheap and safe routes to the East Indies. The earth was now depicted as a single sphere with a common center of gravity. From this perspective it was easy to imagine humans spread out over the globe. The oceans were no longer limits but routes of communication connecting these land masses. This construction of space made it possible, even easy, to divide the world by well-known geometrical methods and use those divisions to demarcate empires and states. This procedure provided the justification for sovereignty, stories of nationhood, and outward expansion by European states.

Some philosophies of justice based on expanding circles claim to apply to all levels of social aggregation. They develop at one level—usually the family—but do not privilege this level over others. This even-handedness is even more evident among philosophies that developed on a top-down basis. They generate a cosmic order that applied to all kind of human relations. A second dimension is degree of universality: do the principles apply across countries and cultures, or are they intended to be local due to cultural or class distinctiveness? The big divide here is within bottom-up philosophies, which vary on both dimensions.

In China, Mohism is a top-down philosophy that applies to all levels of social aggregation and is universal in its claims. Daoism is a bottom-up philosophy that uses the notion of Dao—the primordial root of all things—to explain the natural world and all levels of social aggregation. These Mohist and Daoist principles are supposed to be universal. Confucianism is the most intriguing in its suggestion of both local limits and universal implications.

Emotions, virtues, and principles embodying the three most important Confucian notions of *ren* (humaneness), *yi* (justice), and *li* (ritual propriety) start with the family but are believed to be extendable to expanding circles. Confucianism assumes a universal human nature but contends that it is manifested differently depending on a society's level of cultural or civilizational attainment. Kongzi rejected race as a criterion by which to distinguish between the *yi* (夷), which is conventionally translated as "barbarians" but should be properly rendered as "culturally inferior foreign peoples," and the *xia* (夏 people of Chinese culture). Once Kongzi expressed an intention to go and live among

---

[119] Jens Bartelson, *Visions of World Community* (Cambridge: Cambridge University Press, 2009).

the Eastern *yi* and was asked what he would do about their crudeness. He replied, "Were an exemplary person to live among them, what crudeness could there be?"[120]

Kongzi accordingly believed in the potential of Chinese culture to influence, assimilate, and even transform foreign peoples of a low cultural breeding. He used culture to distinguish between the *yi* and *xia*. The distinction was not fixed but fluctuated according to rising or falling cultural levels, thus losing all its racial significance and becoming a purely cultural term. A *yi* could become a *xia* and a *xia* could become a *yi*, depending on their cultural excellence. Kongzi clearly intended the *xia* to mean "civilized country" or people from such a country, but not "the Chinese race."[121] No trace of nationalism was discernable in his thinking, only a simultaneous localism and universalism linked by the mechanism of extending humaneness. Such a mechanism was necessary because just as some of the *yi* were nearer and others were farther away from the Chinese cultural center, so some had been practicing humaneness longer than others.[122] Extending humaneness from the near to the far is the Confucian method of ethics. Confucian ethics is in this respect one of distance and sequence.

In the West, we also find both traditions. Ancient Greeks long assumed that their customs and norms were given by the gods but by the fifth century came to appreciate the diversity of human practices and beliefs. Herodotus tells the amusing tale of an encounter of Greeks and Indians in which each is shocked by how the other disposes of dead bodies.[123] Greeks made an even sharper distinction than did Confucians when dealing with other peoples. They were all considered different, if not barbarians, and the rules regulating relations among Greeks did not extend to them.

Christians in theory were committed to universalism, but in practice made sharp decisions between themselves and others. The dissonance created by such contradictions had to be reduced by perceptual sleights of hand. Spanish conquerors initially denied human status to the native Americans they conquered and enslaved. In the Valladolid debate of 1550–1551, priests and scholars argued opposite sides of the question.[124] Colonists everywhere devised stereotypes of

---

[120] Roger T. Ames and Henry Rosemont Jr., *The Analects of Confucius: A Philosophical Translation* (New York: Ballantine Books, 1998), p. 129.

[121] Hsiao, *History of Chinese Political Thought*, p. 140.

[122] Ibid., p. 142.

[123] Herodotus, *Histories*, book 3.16, 38, 4.73–75.

[124] Juan Keen and Benjamin Friede, eds., *Bartolomé de las Casas in History: Toward an Understanding of the Man and his Work* (DeKalb: Northern Illinois University Press, 1971).

the colonized to reconcile their Christian beliefs with the barbaric treatment of those they colonized. In Ireland, the British stereotypes initially characterized the Irish as uncivilized and later, childlike, and in need of a firm hand. In the nineteenth century, when race entered the lexicon, the Irish were described as inferior and, as the satirical magazine *Punch* put it, the missing link between apes and Africans.[125]

These differences among philosophies find resonance in today's debate between cosmopolitans and communitarians.[126] Cosmopolitans insist that all human beings are, or could or should be, members of a single community. They hold varying views of what constitutes this community and may stress moral standards, economic practices, political structures, or cultural forms. In international relations, cosmopolitans argue strongly for the application of single standard of ethics and international law.[127] Communitarian critics advocate localism and reject top-down approaches in favor of bottom-up ones. They emphasize the connection between the individual and the community and argue that ethics are embedded in local cultures and practices and cannot be imposed from the outside.[128] Communitarianism is a legitimate philosophy. It also provided a rhetorical cover and justification in the 1990s for authoritarian practices and violations of human rights by Asian leaders. The concept of "Asian values" in contrast to Western ones was advocated by Mahathir Mohamad of Malaysia and Lee Kuan Yew of Singapore, strong leaders who bolstered their credentials with the economic success of their countries.[129]

---

[125] Richard Ned Lebow, *White Britain and Black Ireland: Stereotypes and Colonial Policy* (Philadelphia: Institute for the Study of Human Issues, 1971).

[126] Duncan Bell, ed., *Ethics and World Politics* (Oxford: Oxford University Press, 2010).

[127] Daniele Archibugi and David Held, eds., *Cosmopolitan Democracy. An Agenda for a New World Order* (Cambridge: Polity Press, 1995); Kwame Anthony Appiah, *World of Strangers* (London: Penguin Books, 2007); Gillian Brock and Harry Brighouse, *The Political Philosophy of Cosmopolitanism* (Cambridge: Cambridge University Press, 2005); Seyla Benhabib, *The Rights of Others: Aliens, Residents and Citizens* (Cambridge: Cambridge University Press, 2004); Onora O'Neill, *Bounds of Justice* (Cambridge: Cambridge University Press, 2000); Gerard Delanty, ed., *Routledge International Handbook of Cosmopolitanism Studies*, 2nd ed. (London: Routledge, 2018).

[128] Daniel Bell, *East Meets West: Human Rights and Democracy in East Asia* (Princeton, NJ: Princeton University Press, 2000); Martha Nussbaum, *The Cosmopolitan Tradition: A Noble but Flawed Ideal* (Cambridge, MA: Harvard University Press, 2019); Amitai Etzioni, *The New Golden Rule* (New York: Basic Books, 1996); Michael J. Sandel, *Liberalism and the Limits of Justice* (Cambridge: Cambridge University Press, 1998).

[129] Michael D. Barr, *Cultural Politics and Asian Values: The Tepid War* (London: Routledge, 2004); Josiane Cauquelin, Paul Lim, and Birgit Mayer-König, eds., *Asian Values: Encounter with Diversity* (London: Routledge, 2014); Amartya Kumar Sen, *Human Rights and Asian Values* (Washington, DC: Carnegie Council on Ethics and International Affairs, 2003).

Conclusion

Philosophical traditions reveal varying degrees of malleability. Chinese philosophies are on the whole less adaptable than Western ones. Confucianism has survived for more than two millennia with a core vocabulary handed down by Kongzi. Since the rise of classical Confucianism, it underwent only two periods of further significant evolution: during the Song-Ming dynasties (960–1644) that gave rise to Neo-Confucianism, and a further reformulation that began in the twentieth century.[130] Daoism gained sophistication over the centuries and spawned a popular religious movement, but no major doctrinal shift occurred. Mohism disappeared from the scene in the last century before the Common Era. Nobody ventured to take Legalism further because its doctrines are too amoral for anyone to uphold publicly, even though in practice many ambitious men followed them with glee.

In the West, there is considerable variation. Deity-anchored philosophies are the least malleable, as is most evident with conservative, evangelical sects. Another critical factor is the degree of institutionalization. For this reason, Roman Catholicism has proven less flexible with regard to ethics than many of its Protestant counterparts, although Pope Francis came out in favor of same-sex unions.[131] Liberal Protestant sects have changed their views in the last half-century on such issues as capital punishment, female ministers or priests, birth control, abortion, premarital sex, remarriage, and gay marriage. The Anglican Church, which is also hierarchical, has found change on these issues more difficult.[132]

Secular philosophical traditions have evolved more rapidly, as have liberalism, political conservatism, and Marxism. Lenin and the Bolsheviks, and later rulers of the Soviet Union, sought to control Marxist doctrine as tightly as the Catholic Church does Christian doctrine. This effort proved self-defeating and

---

[130] Liu Shu-hsien [劉述先], *Lun rujia zhexue de sange dashidai* [論儒家哲學的三個大時代 The Three Epochs of Confucian Philosophy] (Hong Kong: The Chinese University of Hong Kong Press, 2015).

[131] Harriet Sherwood, "Pope Francis Backs Same-Sex Civil Unions," *Guardian*, 20 October 2020, https://www.theguardian.com/world/2020/oct/21/pope-francis-backs-same-sex-civil-unions (accessed 20 October 2020).

[132] Hervé Picton, *A Short History of the Church of England: From the Reformation to the Present Day* (Newcastle upon Tyne: Cambridge Scholars Publishing, 2015); Miranda Hassett, *Anglican Communion in Crisis: How Episcopal Dissidents and Their African Allies Are Reshaping Anglicanism* (Princeton, NJ: Princeton University Press, 2007); Rowan Williams, *Anglican Identities* (London: Darton, Longman & Todd, 2003).

may well have accelerated the diversity and rate of change of Marxist thinking.[133] Liberalism, based on equality, and conservatism, rooted in fairness, have evolved considerably in the last 150 years.[134] There are now many competing understandings of these philosophical traditions.

We end with a word about ethical violations. Confucians recognize that their highest ideals are too lofty for most people to live up to. Kongzi developed those ideals out of a deep concern about the political and moral decay of the Spring and Autumn period (770–475 BCE). As much as he had wanted to arrest it, he failed in his endeavors and was thus fully attuned to the difficulties. In the end, he turned inward and focused on cultivating personal virtues, especially humaneness (*ren*). The Confucian moral vision nevertheless provided a critical inspiration for generations of Chinese literati, contributing to the making of a more humane and just society in spite of ethical violations.[135]

The Daoist conception of ethical violations is very different. In contrast to Kongzi, Zhuangzi does not advocate a particular way of life as an ethical model to emulate. His ethics of difference holds that a truly moral person "is one who can naturally, spontaneously, and effortlessly recognize and respect the equal value of diverse ways of life."[136] Imposing one's own values and ways of life on others is immoral. Ethical violations take place when people do not regard other ways of life as having equal worth; correspondingly, these people can no longer deserve the respect from others. Zhuangzi is not a relativist for whom ethical violations do not occur; he is a virtue ethicist who urges us to respect the difference of others.[137]

Jews and Christians acknowledge human imperfections and do not expect people to live fully up to their moral codes. Roman Catholics require confession and allow penance for most sins. Jews have a yearly reckoning with god on Yom Kippur where individuals, acting in conjunction with other members of the Jewish community, ask forgiveness for not having honored their vows. As everybody publicly acknowledges all misdeeds, only those who have committed them know of their transgressions. In Germany, *Vergangenheitsbewältigung* (coming to terms with the past) involves public acceptance of responsibility for Nazi crimes,

---

[133] Eric Hobsbawm, *The History of Marxism*, vol. 1: *Marxism in Marx's Day* (Bloomington: Indiana University Press, 1982); Leszek Kołakowski, *Main Currents of Marxism* (New York: W. W. Norton, 2005).

[134] Fawcett, *Liberalism*; Gray, *Liberalism*; Manent and Seigel, *An Intellectual History of Liberalism*.

[135] Feng Zhang, *Chinese Hegemony: Grand Strategy and International Institutions in East Asian History* (Stanford, CA: Stanford University Press, 2015), p. 179.

[136] Yong Huang, "Respecting Different Ways of Life: A Daoist Ethics of Virtue in the *Zhuangzi*," *Journal of Asian Studies* 69, no. 4 (2020), pp. 1049–69, at p. 1059.

[137] Ibid.

educational programs, and diverse forms of commemoration.[138] Forgiveness and reconciliation tribunals are an increasing common practice in international relations.[139]

In chapter 2 we quoted Kant to the effect that most people performed behavior mandated by society because they recognized that it was in their interest to be respected by others. When they routinely acted this way they made good behavior habitual. By this means, the "crooked timber" of humanity was able to sustain societies that incorporated principles of justice.[140] There is just as much reason to think that people look for ways of circumventing justice and avoiding its obligations when they are seen as costly or in some other way disadvantageous. Daryl Bem, father of self-perception theory, argues that how we behave shapes our self-understandings.[141] If the arrow of influence points in both directions, as Bem suggests, behavior at odds with values, if repetitive in nature, can alter conceptions of self. By extension, as Thucydides was the first to recognize in writing, it can also reshape our language and ethical codes.[142]

The tension between values and practice is more acute for most organizations, including governments. They invoke principles of justice, but instantiate them even less than individuals. This may be because they have more power to act this way and often a greater ability to keep what they do from the public eye.

---

[138] Norbert Frei, *Vergangenheitspolitik. Die Anfänge der Bundesrepublik und die NS-Vergangenheit* (Munich: Beck, 1996); Jeffrey Herf, *Divided Memory: The Nazi Past in the Two Germanys* (Cambridge, MA: Harvard University Press, 1997); Wulf Kansteiner, *In Pursuit of German Memory: History, Television, and Politics after Auschwitz* (Athens: University of Ohio Press, 2006); Andreas Maislinger, *Coming to Terms with the Past: An International Comparison. In Nationalism, Ethnicity, and Identity: Cross National and Comparative Perspectives* New Brunswick, NJ: Transaction Publishers, 2004).

[139] Priscilla Hayner, *Unspeakable Truths: Transitional Justice and the Challenge of Truth Commissions*, 2nd ed. (London: Routledge, 2010); Rachel Kerr and Eirin Mobekk, *Peace and Justice: Seeking Accountability after War* (London: Polity, 2007); Naomi Roht-Arriaza and Javier Mariezcurrena, *Transitional Justice in the Twenty-first Century: Beyond Truth versus Justice* (Cambridge: Cambridge University Press, 2007); Richard A. Wilson, *The Politics of Truth and Reconciliation in South Africa: Legitimizing the Post-Apartheid State* (Cambridge: Cambridge University Press, 2001); Rebekka Friedman, *Competing Memories: Truth and Reconciliation in Sierra Leone and Peru* (Cambridge: Cambridge University Press, 2017).

[140] Immanuel Kant, "Idea for a Universal History with a Cosmopolitan Purpose," in Hans Reiss, ed., H. B. Nisbet, trans., in *Kant's Political Writings*, 2nd ed. (Cambridge: Cambridge University Press, 1991), pp. 41–53, and *Anthropology from a Pragmatic Point of View*, Robert Louden, ed. (Cambridge: Cambridge University Press, 2006); Seán Molloy, *Kant's International Relations: The Political Theology of Perpetual Peace* (Ann Arbor: University of Michigan Press, 2017), pp. 94–96, 100–11.

[141] Daryl J. Bem, "Self-Perception Theory," in L. Berkowitz, ed., *Advances in Experimental Social Psychology* (New York: Academic Press, 1972), vol. 6, pp. 1–62, and "Self-Perception: An Alternative Interpretation of Cognitive Dissonance Phenomena," *Psychological Review* 74 (1967), pp. 183–200.

[142] Thucydides, 3.82.

There is accordingly a complex, uncertain, and highly context-dependent relationship between justice and order. They are only fully supporting and reconcilable in utopias. In real worlds, they are more often in conflict, even though all successful orders rest on principles of justice. Sometimes this conflict is destructive of order, but on other occasions the tension between them is productive. In the next part of our book we look at ways in which we might design orders, based on the principles we have examined, that maximize the chances of adherence by China, the United States, and other states.

PART II

6

International "Order"

Western studies of international relations and foreign policy routinely refer to something called the postwar order. Most take it for granted that such a thing exists, although they rarely discuss in any detail its nature and scope. They are less likely still to elaborate a theoretical understanding of what an order is and what it requires in practice. To the extent that they discuss order, it is in terms of its structure and effects. By structure, most Western commentators mean polarity or international liberal economic institutions and practices. By effects, they usually have in mind the preservation of political units and economic intercourse and limits on the use of force.[1]

In China, political order has traditionally been defined in terms of low taxes and the provision of public goods.[2] In foreign relations, China used to think of itself as the center of the known world, preeminent especially in political and

---

[1] Hedley Bull, *The Anarchical Society: A Study of Order in World Politics* (New York: Columbia University Press, 1977), p. 53, defines order in terms of preservation of its units. Also, Andrew Linklater, *Violence and Civilization in the Western States-System* (London: Cambridge, 2016), pp. 468–71; Alexander Wendt, *Social Theory of International Politics* (Cambridge: Cambridge University Press, 1999), who describes three kinds of order, distinguished by the robustness of international society and its ability to restrain or eliminate the use of force. Ian Clark, *The Hierarchy of States: Reform and Resistance in the International Order* (Cambridge: Cambridge University Press, 1989), who identifies a minimal order that acknowledges the use of force but imposes limits on it, and a more robust order that at least in part delegitimizes force. Alexander Cooley and Daniel Nexon, *Exit from Hegemony: The Unraveling of the American Global Order* (New York: Oxford University Press, 2020), p. 31, describe order as "relatively stable patterns and relationships." Christian Reus-Smit, *On Cultural Diversity: International Theory in a World of Difference* (Cambridge: Cambridge University Press, 2018), pp. 79–80, suggests that international relations scholars use the term as a synonym for stability or a description for a particular arrangement of international relations.

[2] Jean-Laurent Rosenthal and R. Bin Wong, *Before and beyond Divergence: The Politics of Economic Change in China and Europe* (Cambridge, MA: Harvard University Press, 2011), pp. 189–90.

Justice and International Order: East and West. Richard Ned Lebow and Feng Zhang, Oxford University Press.
© Oxford University Press 2022. DOI: 10.1093/oso/9780197598399.003.0006

cultural affairs.[3] This order was destroyed by the Western colonial powers and Japan in the second half of the nineteenth century, causing a Chinese ambivalence—and at times hostility—toward the Western order that has lingered to the present day. Nevertheless, since the late 1970s China has embraced the agenda of "modernizing" international order, that is, reforming aspects of the existing order from within rather than overthrowing it from without.[4]

Those who speak favorably of the so-called postwar order give bipolarity or American hegemony credit for maintaining the great power peace and stimulating remarkable economic growth on a worldwide basis.[5] Critics often focus on its hierarchy and efforts to uphold it by those at its apex.[6] Many consider Cold War bipolarity, the postwar American quest for hegemony, or the great power "club" responsible for costly regional wars and the relative subordination and exploitation of much of the Global South. Those who consider the current order benign believe it to be threatened and in desperate need of shoring up.[7] Those who oppose it see it as robust and difficult to challenge with any chance of success.

These near-mirror images of international relations share a common starting point: the belief that there is some kind of international order. The most vocal dissenters are those realists who deny its existence or recognize only a weak, fragile, impermanent, and emergent order. Instead of talking about international

---

[3] John K. Fairbank, ed., *The Chinese World Order: Traditional China's Foreign Relations* (Cambridge, MA: Harvard University Press, 1968); Feng Zhang, *Chinese Hegemony: Grand Strategy and International Institutions in East Asian History* (Stanford, CA: Stanford University Press, 2005).

[4] Wang Honggang, "Xiandai guoji zhixu de yanjin yu zhongguo de shidai zeren" [The Evolution of Modern International Order and China's Responsibility of the Times], *Xiandai guoji guanxi* [Contemporary International Relations], no. 12 (2016), pp. 1–14.

[5] For a critique of this claim, Simon Reich and Richard Ned Lebow, *Good-Bye Hegemony! Power and Influence in the Global System* (Princeton, NJ: Princeton University Press, 2014), ch. 2; Christopher Fettweis, "Unipolarity, Hegemony, and the New World Peace," *Security Studies* 26, no. 3 (2017), pp. 423–51.

[6] Alexander Cooley, *Logics of Hierarchy: The Organization of Empires, States, and Military Occupations* (Ithaca, NY: Cornell University Press, 2005); Alexander Cooley and Hendrik Spruyt, *Contracting States Sovereign Transfers in International Relations* (Princeton, NJ: Princeton University Press, 2009); Vincent Pouliot, *Pecking Orders* (Princeton, NJ: Princeton University Press, 2016); Ayşe Zarakol, ed., *Hierarchies in World Politics* (Cambridge: Cambridge University Press, 2017); Maya Spanu, "The Hierarchical Society: The Politics of Self-Determination and the Constitution of New States after 1919," *European Journal of International Relations* 26, no. 2 (2020), pp. 372–96.

[7] Special Issue, "Is the Liberal Order in Peril?" *Foreign Affairs*, May–June 2017, https://www.for eignaffairs.com/ask-the-experts/liberal-order-peril (accessed 1 January 2021); James Kirchick, *The End of Europe: Dictators, Demagogues, and the Coming Dark Age* (New Haven, CT: Yale University Press, 2017). Stephen G. Brooks and William C. Wohlforth, "The Rise and Fall of the Great Powers in the Twenty-first Century: China's Rise and the Fate of America's Position," *International Security* 40, no. 3 (2015/2016), pp. 7–53.

"society," as most liberals and constructivists do, they speak of the international "system." They characterize it as anarchical with a de facto hierarchy arising from the number of actors and their relative power.[8] International order is not, of course, the same thing as international or global society. The latter relies on informal rules, norms, and procedures and requires some degree of solidarity to function. There is a controversy among scholars about the extent to which there is such a thing as an international society, how it should be described, and, if so, who its members are, and what authority this society has vis-à-vis states.[9]

We accordingly open this chapter with a general discussion of international order. It provides the conceptual foundation for our subsequent analysis of the composition, evolution, relative robustness of international orders. We argue that both society and order exist at the international level. International society is thin because there is no consensus about fundamental values or goals. International order is fragile and best understood as a patchwork of multiple and often overlapping orders, some of them regional in nature, others functionally specific, and each with varying degrees of robustness. The international order is partly the product of design and partly an emergent property. Regional orders are weighted more in the direction of the former. Design does not mean that orders function as intended, as they assume a life of their own that often bears only a partial relationship to what their founders anticipated.

We turn next to the evaluation of these orders, with a focus on the dominant, so-called, liberal order. Orders are only worth evaluating if there is some prospect of changing them. We briefly look at how international relations scholars differ on this question; some think orders cannot be altered by design, others think efforts to do so likely to make matters worse. However, there are many scholars, representing different approaches to international relations, who believe reform to be a reasonable and desirable, if difficult goal.

We then address the current dominant order: the liberal one fostered by the United States after World War II and embedded in numerous regional and international institutions. It is widely supported by developed capitalist states, although less so by many of their citizens, and is also deeply resented in many parts of the world. A review of the relevant literature indicates that orders are defended or criticized on the basis of their goals, how well they achieve them, at what cost, and how their benefits and costs are seen to be distributed. These judgments draw on beliefs about what is politically possible and desirable, and

---

[8] Kenneth N. Waltz, *Theory of International Politics* (Reading, MA: Addison-Wesley, 1979).

[9] On the first point see the debate between Mervyn Frost, "Tragedy, Ethics and International Relations," and James Mayall, "Tragedy, Progress and the International Order," in Toni Erskine and Richard Ned Lebow, eds., *Tragedy and International Relations* (London: Palgrave-Macmillan, 2012), pp. 21–43 and 44–52.

this latter judgment ultimately rests on conceptions of what theorists and other analysts think is just. Those supportive of the liberal order describe it as fair, and those opposed condemn it for its inequality. In this respect, international relations mirrors domestic politics in many countries where the principles of fairness and equality are often at odds. The more powerful an actor, the more likely it is to seek special privileges or advantages and defend them on the basis of fairness. Those who are less powerful mobilize the principle of equality in an effort to restrain the powerful and protect and advance their interests.

International relations scholars have proposed all kinds of changes, and we examine diverse suggestions for reforming the liberal order or restructuring international relations more generally. We conclude with our own assessment of what would have to be done to reorder international relations in ways to promote peace and development more effectively and reduce current sources of tension and conflict, or at least mitigate their effects. Our analysis forms the basis for the succeeding chapters that explore different pathways toward these orders.

International Order

Understandings of order, its origins, robustness, its actors, and its consequences vary within and across paradigms. Among those realists who acknowledge the possibility of order, most think about it as an emergent property arising from the behavior of states that results in certain kinds of predictable behavior like balancing and bandwagoning.[10] Some realists associate order with war avoidance, or its limitation, and attribute to balancing or bi- or unipolarity.[11] For other realists, meaningful order requires a hegemon that has the power to impose and enforce rules.[12] Liberals stress the hegemon's ability to take the lead in creating international institutions, norms, and regimes capable of constraining violence and managing international economic relations.[13] Liberal theorists of the democratic

---

[10] John Mearsheimer, *The Tragedy of Great Power Politics* (New York: W. W. Norton, 2001); Clark, *Hierarchy of States*, p. 1.

[11] Waltz, *Theory of International Politics*; Charles Krauthammer, "The Unipolar Moment," *Foreign Affairs* 70 (1990/1991), pp. 23–33; William Wohlforth, "Stability of a Unipolar World," *International Security* 24, no. 2 (1999), pp. 5–41; Samuel P. Huntington, "Lonely Superpower," *Foreign Affairs* 78 (1999), pp. 35–49.

[12] Ian Clark, *Hegemony in International Society* (Oxford: Oxford University Press, 2011), pp. 23–28; Stephen G. Brooks and William C. Wohlforth, *World out of Balance: International Relations and the Challenge of American Primacy* (Princeton, NJ: Princeton University Press, 2008); Fareed Zakaria, *The Post-American World* (New York: W. W. Norton, 2008).

[13] Stanley Hoffman, *Janus and Minerva: Essays in the Theory and Practice of International Politics* (Boulder, CO: Westview, 1987), pp. 85–87; Stephen D. Krasner, ed., *International Regimes* (Ithaca, NY: Cornell University Press, 1983); Robert Keohane, *After Hegemony: Cooperation and Discord*

peace go further in their claim that war would not exist in a world of democratic states. However, they attribute this result to domestic structure, not to any kind of order at the international level.[14] Liberals also emphasize the role of states, and particularly the institutions they create. But they recognize the importance of non-state actors and what some describe as the increasingly important role of global civil society. Constructivists emphasize society as the source of order and the ways in which it has the potential to bind actors to one another and the rules and norms they establish to govern their relations. These rules do not necessarily prohibit violence or war but do seek to regulate and constrain it.[15] Like liberals, constructivists recognize actors beyond states.

Theorists also vary in their preferences for top-down versus bottom-up orders. Realists believe that any robust order must be top-down and a hegemon its source. Liberals also value hegemons but describe international institutions as

in the World Political Economy (Princeton, NJ: Princeton University Press, 1984); David A. Lake, "Leadership, Hegemony, and the International Economy: Naked Emperor or Tattered Monarch with Potential?" *International Studies Quarterly* 37 no. 4 (1993), pp. 459–89; G. John Ikenberry, *After Victory: Institutions, Strategic Restraint, and the Rebuilding of Order after Major War* (Princeton, NJ: Princeton University Press, 2001), and *The Liberal Leviathan* (Princeton, NJ: Princeton University Press, 2011).

[14] Nils P. Gleditsch, "Democracy and Peace," *Journal of Peace Research* 29, no. 4 (1992), pp. 369–76; James Lee Ray, *Democracy and International Conflict* (Columbia: University of South Carolina Press, 1995); Rudolph J. Rummel, *Power Kills: Democracy as a Method of Nonviolence* (Piscataway, NJ: Transaction Publishers, 1997); John R. Oneal and Bruce Russett, "The Kantian Peace: The Pacific Benefits of Democracy, Interdependence, and International Organizations," *World Politics* 52, no. 1 (1999), pp. 1–37; Bruce Russett and John R. Oneal, *Triangulating Peace: Democracy, Interdependence, and International Organizations* (New York: W. W. Norton, 2001); Gilat Levy and Ronny Razin, "It Takes Two: An Explanation for the Democratic Peace," *Journal of the European Economic Association* 2, no. 1 (2004), pp. 1–29; Hyung Min Kim and David L. Rousseau, "The Classical Liberals Were Half Right (or Half Wrong): New Tests of the 'Liberal Peace,' 1960–88," *Journal of Peace Research* 42, no. 5 (2005), pp. 523–43. For critical evaluation, Steve Chan, "In Search of Democratic Peace: Problems and Promise," *Mershon International Studies Review* 41, no. 1 (1997), pp. 59–91; David Kinsella, "No Rest for the Democratic Peace," *American Political Science Review* 99, no. 3 (2005), pp. 453–57; Gunther Hellmann and Benjamin Herborth, "Fishing in the Mild West: Democratic Peace and Militarised Interstate Disputes in the Transatlantic Community," *Review of International Studies* 34, no. 3 (2008), pp. 481–506; Errol Henderson, *Democracy and War, the End of an Illusion?* (Boulder, CO: Lynne Rienner, 2002); Fred Chernoff, "The Study of Democratic Peace and Progress in International Relations," *International Studies Review* 6, no. 1 (2004), pp. 1079–760; Michael Haas, *Deconstructing the "Democratic Peace": How a Research Agenda Boomeranged* (Los Angeles: Publishing House for Scholars, 2014); Dan Reiter, "Is Democracy a Cause of Peace?," *Oxford Research Encyclopedia of Politics*, 25 January 2017, https://oxfordre.com/politics/view/10.1093/acrefore/9780190228637.001.0001/acrefore-9780190228637-e-287 (accessed 13 March 2021).

[15] Richard Ned Lebow, *A Cultural Theory of International Relations* (Cambridge: Cambridge University Press, 2008); Hendrik Spruyt, *The World Imagined: Collective Beliefs and Political Order in the Sinocentric, Islamic and Southeast Asian International Societies* (Cambridge: Cambridge University Press, 2020).

another source of order. Constructivists emphasize the importance of bottom-up orders and the role of a wider range of non-state actors. The twentieth century witnessed a phenomenal growth in non-governmental organizations that operate regionally or internationally. By 2000 there were thousands of firms engaged in international business; some 5,000 yearly international congresses; and more than 50,000 international non-governmental organizations (INGOs), nearly 90 percent of which came into existence after 1970.[16] These INGOS include charities, religious organizations, lobbying groups, think tanks, and environmental and scientific, health, educational, and legal organizations. They are largely or entirely independent of governments but network with one another, governments, and the media.[17] According to John Keane, they form "a highly complex ensemble of differently sized, overlapping form of structured social action" with a striking "momentum or power" of their own."[18] Deborah Avant, Martha Finnemore, and Susan Sell contend that these actors "solve problems, change outcomes, and transform international life."[19]

Governments have long been accused of extending their control into all walks of life. Rajhi Kothari asserts with some reason that in the modern era "Governance has been usurped by governments."[20] But domestically and internationally, bottom-up, non-governmental organizations have spread their tentacles and become increasingly important. It is no longer possible to ignore the role in international governance.[21] Keane claims that governments and intergovernmental organizations "are now feeling the pinching effects of this global civil society."[22] These top-down and bottom-up organizations have made inroads on one another, and one of the interesting questions is the degree to which these

[16] John Keane, *Global Civil Society* (Cambridge: Cambridge University Press, 2003), pp. 4–5, 9; Helmut Anheier, Marlies Glasius, and Mary Kaldor, eds., *Global Civil Society 2001* (Oxford: Oxford University Press, 2001).

[17] Deborah D. Avant, Martha Finnemore, and Susan K. Sell, *Who Governs the Globe?* (Cambridge: Cambridge University Press, 2010), for essays elaborating this theme.

[18] Keane, *Global Civil Society*, p. 11.

[19] Avant, Finnemore, and Sell, *Who Governs the Globe?*, p. 1.

[20] Rajhi Kothari, "On Human Governance," *Alternatives* 12, no. 8 (1987), pp. 277–290.

[21] Joseph S. Nye Jr. and John D. Donohue, eds., *Governance in a Globalizing World* (Washington, DC: Brookings, 2000); James N. Rosenau and Ernst-Otto Czempiel, eds., *Governance without Government: Order and Change in World Politics* (Cambridge: Cambridge University Press, 1992); Keane, *Global Civil Society*; Avant, Finnemore, and Sell, *Who Governs the Globe?*; Joel M. Podolny and Karen L. Page, "Network Forms of Organization," *Annual Review of Sociology* 24 (1998), pp. 15–27; Daphné Josselin and William Wallace, eds., *Non-State Actors in World Politics* (New York: Palgrave-Macmillan, 2002); Anne Clunan and Harold Trinkunas, eds., *Ungoverned Spaces: Alternatives to State Authority in an Era of Softened Sovereignty* (Stanford, CA: Stanford University Press, 2010).

[22] Keane, *Global Civil Society*, p. 15.

patterns and interactions differ in domestic, regional, and international affairs, and if so, their respective implications for governance.

Influence often requires naming. The conceptualization of the "self," "class," "race," and "the unconscious" had profound effects on elite and popular consciousness and people's thinking and behavior.[23] The same is arguably true of "global civil society." Keane notes that it is a recent neologism that reflects

> new awareness, stimulated by peace and ecological movements, of ourselves as members of a fragile and potentially self-destructive world system; the widespread perception that the implosion of Soviet-type communist systems implied a new global political order; the world-wide growth spurt of neo-liberal economics and market capitalist economies; the disillusion with the broken and unfulfilled promises of post-colonial states; and the rising concern about the dangerous and misery producing vacuums open up by the collapse of empires and states and the outbreak of civil wars.[24]

Keane and others contend that what we call bottom-up governance and the dense network of relations among NGOs, their participants, and the people they affect have the potential to increase global awareness of mutual dependency and the correspondingly great need for tolerance and cooperation. Some allege that they might encourage people to develop transnational identities.[25] Back in 1917—surely a low point in international solidarity—classicist and Versailles Conference participant Alfred Zimmern imagined the future emergence of what he dubbed "planetary patriotism."[26] Margaret Keck and Kathryn Sikkink made the strongest—and some would say most naïve—case for transnational networks of bottom-up organizations governed by principles instead of interests successfully advancing a progressive human rights agenda.[27] Today we recognize that NGOs and the transnational networks to which they give rise have just

[23] On the emergence of the concept of self, see Jerrold Seigel, *The Idea of the Self: Thought and Experience in Western Europe since the Seventeenth Century* (Cambridge: Cambridge University Press, 2005); Richard Ned Lebow, *The Politics and Ethics of Identity* (Cambridge: Cambridge University Press, 2012), ch. 1.

[24] Keane, *Global Civil Society*, pp. 1–2.

[25] Ibid., p. 11; Paul Wapner, "The Normative Promise of Non-State Actors: A Theoretical Account of Global Civil Society," in Paul Wapner and Lester Edwin J. Ruiz, eds., *Principled World Politics: The Challenge of Normative International Relations* (Lanham, MD: Rowan & Littlefield, 2000), pp. 261–74; Avant, Finnemore, and Sell, *Who Governs the Globe?*, pp. 7–8.

[26] Keane, *Global Civil Society*, p. 52, citing an unpublished 2001 paper by Frank Trentmann.

[27] Margaret Keck and Katheryn Sikkink, *Activists beyond Borders: Activist Networks in International Politics* (Ithaca, NY: Cornell University Press, 1998).

as much potential to intensify nationalism, religious intolerance, violence, and inward-looking policies.[28] There has also been a state-level backlash against organizations that promote democracy and the rule of law.[29] George Soros and the several institutions he funds have become the whipping boy of nationalist movement in central Europe and the centerpiece of right-wing conspiracy theories.[30] There have been up to 500,000 negative tweets about him daily.[31] Authoritarian governments everywhere have restricted or banned transnational organizations with liberal and internationalist agendas.[32]

Ian Clarke describes international relations as a hierarchy of states, whose degree of order depends on whether leading states balance against one another or form some kind of concert of powers.[33] He is among many who recognize that hierarchy can be a form of domination because it formally recognizes stratification based on inequalities. These inequalities can be economic, military, or cultural, or all three, as critics contend they have been throughout much of the modern era. Christian Reus-Smit agrees that "orders are best conceived as systematic configurations of political authority." But to gain legitimacy and stability, he insists, the inequalities of power must be transformed into political authority. "Might has to become right."[34]

---

[28] Larry Diamond, Mark F. Plattner, and Christopher Walker, eds., *Authoritarianism Goes Global* (Baltimore: Johns Hopkins University Press, 2016); Anna Lührmann and Staffan I. Lindberg, "A Third Wave of Autocratization Is Here: What Is New About It?" *Democratization* 26, no. 7 (2019), pp. 1095–113.

[29] Lisbeth Zimmermann, *Global Norms with a Local Face* (Cambridge: Cambridge University Press, 2017), ch. 1.

[30] Emily Tamkin, "Five Myths about George Soros," *Washington Post*, 6 August 2020, https://www.washingtonpost.com/outlook/five-myths/five-myths-about-george-soros/2020/08/06/ad195582-d1e9-11ea-8d32-1ebf4e9d8e0d_story.html; David Klepper and Lori Hinnant, "George Soros Conspiracy Theories Surge as Protests Sweep US," Associated Press reported in *San Diego Union-Tribune*, 21 June 2020, https://www.sandiegouniontribune.com/business/nation/story/2020-06-21/george-soros-conspiracy-theories-surge-as-protests-sweep-us (both accessed 30 December 2020).

[31] Ben Salesjta, "What You Need to Know about George Soros, Center of Conspiracy Theories," *Jerusalem Post*, 9 September 2020, https://www.jpost.com/diaspora/antisemitism/what-you-need-to-know-about-george-soros-center-of-conspiracy-theories-641553 (accessed 30 December 2020).

[32] Darrin Christensen and Jeremy M. Weinstein, "Defunding Dissent: Restrictions on Aid to NGOs," *Journal of Democracy* 24, no. 2 (2013), pp. 77–91; Kendra Dupuy, James Ron, and Aseem Prakash, "Hands Off My Regime! Governments' Restrictions on Foreign Aid to Non-Governmental Organizations in Poor and Middle-Income Countries," *World Development* 84 (2016), pp. 299–311.

[33] Clark, *Hierarchy of States*, p. 1. Also, David Lake, *Hierarchy in International Relations* (Ithaca, NY: Cornell University Press, 2009).

[34] Christian Reus-Smit, *On Cultural Diversity: International Theory in a World of Difference* (Cambridge: Cambridge University Press, 2018), p. 13. See also Zarakol, *Hierarchies in World Politics*.

Top-down orders attempt to impose consistency and predictability in behavior and meet resistance when they run roughshod over local values and practices. As noted, hierarchy is a central feature of order. It is as central to regional and international relations as it is to domestic societies. One of the enduring features of modern international relations is the attempt by powerful actors, or coalitions of them, to impose their values and practices on others. This is a long-standing effort, and one that was officially recognized at the Congress of Vienna in 1815. Great power status has endured, but the rule package associated with it has evolved; it has become both more embracing and constraining. Post-1945 efforts to create equality through national self-determination and the UN General Assembly led to a proliferation of state actors but created new inequalities in the form of post-imperial hierarchies.[35]

Today's great powers have responsibilities for economic management as well as security but can no longer act solely on the basis of agreements among themselves. They have additional responsibility for post-conflict reconstruction, prevention of genocide, and looking after refugees dislocated by domestic and international conflicts.[36] During the Cold War, the United States and Soviet Union attempted to gain more authority vis-à-vis other states by propagating the concept of a bipolar world and, with it, their status as superpowers. Since the end of the Cold War and collapse of the Soviet Union, the United States has sought special privileges on the basis of its claim to hegemony.[37]

Most, although not all, realists and liberals value these attempts to impose order, but it also arouses opposition. Back in 1940, realist E. H. Carr observed that liberal institutions, laws, and processes designed to transform international politics only abetted the politics of narrow self-interest. They were used by the great powers as a screen behind which they could operate as they always had.[38] In 1971, Ada Bozeman described the rule of law as a Western cultural artefact whose advocates envisaged it as "the main carrier of shared values, the most effective agent of social control, and the only reliable principle capable of moderating and reducing the reign of passion, arbitrariness, and caprice in human life."[39] This expectation was carried over to international law, where it no longer rested on common cultural foundations. The spread of international law in these circumstances "intensified power politics beneath the thin veneer

---

[35] Spanu, "Hierarchical Society."

[36] Gareth Evans, *The Responsibility to Protect: Ending Mass Atrocity Crimes Once and For All* (Washington, DC: Brookings, 2008); Hannes Hansen-Magnusson and Antje Vetterlein, eds., *The Rise of Responsibility in World Politics* (Cambridge: Cambridge University Press, 2020).

[37] Reich and Lebow, *Good-Bye Hegemony!*

[38] Carr, *Twenty Years' Crisis.*

[39] Ada Bozeman, *Future of Law in a Multicultural World* (Princeton, NJ: Princeton University Press, 1971), p. 38.

of an increasingly ineffectual legalistic order."[40] This kind of conflict has since been theorized in the dispute between universalism and communitarianism, especially with regard to human rights.[41]

In nineteenth-century Europe, great powers acting in concert represented a single source of top-down authority. Such unity—short-lived to be sure—is a thing of the past. In today's world, the great powers rarely, if ever, act in concert. The United States, China, and Russia are each trying to foster their own regional or international orders. All have used force toward this end. We accordingly confront two levels of conflict: among great powers, over the scope and influence of their respective top-down orders, and, within these orders, conflict between top-down and bottom-up actors.

If many realists deny the possibility of exiting from anarchy and a violent world characterized by great power conflict and domination, some liberals and constructivists may have erred in the other direction by predicting the emergence of a benign international environment. In the immediate aftermath of the Cold War, James Rosenau suggested that global governance might be separated to a certain degree from government. He defined governance as the prevention or adjudication of conflicts among members, procuring necessary resources, and framing and implementing the policies necessary to achieve these goals. Governance is a "broad framework arrangements governing activities of . . . members of society over a wide range of specific issues."[42] It involves the "dispersion of power among key actors, hierarchical differences among them, rules that govern their interactions and understandings about the kinds of interactions that are acceptable." Somewhat like Keane, Rosenau envisaged governance as issue-based in the tradition of functionalism.[43] Not every liberal follows Rosenau and Keane in rooting for the emergence of a powerful global society; others, especially liberal institutionalists, remain wary of such a development and place more trust in government-sponsored international institutions.[44]

---

[40] Ibid., p. 186.

[41] For an overview of the origins of this debate, David Rasmussen, *Universalism vs. Communitarianism Contemporary Debates in Ethics* (Cambridge, MA: MIT Press, 1990).

[42] Rosenau, "Governance, Change, and Order in World Politics," in Rosenau and Czempiel, *Governance without Government*, pp. 1–29. Also, Bull, *Anarchical Society*; Evelyn Goh, *The Struggle for Order: Hegemony, Hierarchy, and Transition in Post–Cold War East Asia* (Oxford: Oxford University Press, 2013), who stress the importance of common goals for order. Goh, *Struggle for Order*, p. 7, describes order in South Asia "as an arrangement that sustains the primary goals of the society states."

[43] On functionalism, Jens Steffek, "The Cosmopolitanism of David Mitrany: Equality, Devolution and Functional Democracy beyond the State," *International Relations* 29, no. 1 (2014), pp. 23–44.

[44] Robert Keohane and Joseph Nye Jr., *Power and Interdependence*, 4th ed. (New York: Routledge, 2011); Ikenberry, *After Victory*, and *Origins, Crisis, and Transformation of the American World Order*; Beth A. Simmons and Lisa L. Martin, "International Organizations and Institutions," in Walter Carlsnaes, Thomas Risse, and Beth A. Simmons, eds. *Handbook of International Relations*, (Thousand Oaks, CA: Sage, 2002), pp. 192–211.

For societies—domestic or international—to achieve a reasonable degree of solidarity, top-down and bottom-up orders must be at least as much reinforcing as they are competitive. This requires limits on top-down orders and at least partial autonomy for their bottom-up counterparts. Top-down orders must be more consensual than imposed and accommodate as far as possible local traditions and practices. Bottom-up orders must in turn accept, within reason, the authority of their top-down counterparts. Ideally, both kinds of order should become more co-constitutive and collaborative than antagonistic. In present-day international relations we observe symbiosis and conflict. Some NGOs in some circumstances work closely with governments, providing useful information and contacts, and mobilizing support for or implementing policies in ways governments would find difficult, expensive, or politically costly. Non-governmental organizations also lobby for policies governments oppose, and publicize governmental violations of international law, neglect of responsibilities, and commission of illegalities and atrocities.

As many international relations scholars have noted, a key distinguishing feature of any international order is the extent to which it legitimates and encourages the use of force or delegitimates and constrains it. We further need to differentiate orders that are largely peaceful because they depend on force or the threat of force for compliance from those that exhibit a high degree of voluntary compliance because actors accept them and their rules as legitimate.[45] This distinction is not a binary but a continuum, with all orders at every level of social aggregation found somewhere between these extremes. Realists on the whole describe international order as something that rests more on coercion than consent. Many liberals, by contrast, emphasize voluntary compliance, at least by developed, democratic countries.[46] This book goes to press as Russia has invaded Ukraine. This violent act appears to offer evidence to the realist claim. However, it has provoked revulsion almost everywhere, and if it and Putin fail in the long-term, it might strengthen the norm of the non-use of force in the absence of authorization from the United Nations Security Council.

Compliance and legitimacy are closely related and both are connected to justice. Aristotle, Machiavelli, and Max Weber all argue that for political orders to survive they must appeal to, and to some degree instantiate, principles of justice that resonate with their populations. Justice is a fundamental human concern

---

[45] Bruce Gilley, *The Right to Rule: How States Win and Lose Legitimacy* (New York: Columbia University Press, 2009); Arthur Isak Applbaum, *Legitimacy: The Right to Rule in a Wanton World* (Cambridge, MA: Harvard University Press, 2019); Jack Knight and Melissa Schwartzberg, eds., *Political Legitimacy*, Nomos 61 (New York: NYU Press, 2019).

[46] For the classic statement of this position, H. John Ikenberry, *After Victory: Institutions, Strategic Restraint, and the Rebuilding of Order after Major Wars* (Princeton, NJ: Princeton University Press, 2000), and *The Origins, Crisis, and Transformation of the American World Order* (Princeton, NJ: Princeton University Press, 2011).

and a metric people use for judging their orders. This is because it is a means—even a prerequisite—to many important ends, among them security, intimacy, status, and material well-being. In an ideal world, order and justice would be mutually reinforcing, but this is rarely, if ever, the case. They are almost always to some degree at odds, and often very much so. This is certainly true in contemporary international relations as it is in many domestic societies.

At every level of governance, authorities invoke principles of justice to justify their behavior. As we ascend the level of social aggregation from bottom-up to top-down orders, and from national governments to regional and international organizations, the discrepancy between proclaimed principles and observable behavior generally becomes more pronounced. For this reason, all political orders, and especially international ones, must rely on other incentives to get others to conform to their laws, rules, and norms. We theorize four mechanisms of compliance: fear, interest, *thumos*, and habit. The first three appeal to human needs: survival, material well-being, and self-esteem. Habit is the product of long-term conformity to laws, rules, and norms to, or near, the point where it becomes almost a reflex reaction. For most of us, stopping at a red light is a good example. Robust orders rely on habitual compliance and are in trouble when it ceases. To stay with the driving example, an increase in running red lights, failing to signal for turns, and parking in spaces reserved for others, including the disabled, are early signs of disorder. Once enough people violate traditional norms and practices it becomes increasingly difficult to enforce them.[47]

As noted, orders require some degree of solidarity among their members. They also need psychological as well as political boundaries, and solidarity helps to define and mark off who belongs and who does not. Belonging is a precondition of solidarity, but not a sufficient one. Solidarity became a pressing concern for nineteenth-century sociologists because they recognized its importance in holding together increasingly large and impersonal societies. They disagreed among themselves about whether modernity would create a new basis for solidarity or undermine the sense of community on which existing social and political orders rested, leaving alienation and anomie in its place.[48] Most nineteenth-century thinkers, while not blind to nationalism, did not grasp the extent to which it would provide the most important social glue for states, but also become the principal source of domestic and international conflict and violence. More recent students of nationalism are acutely aware of its Janus-faced nature. They describe solidarity as both the basis of nationality and its

---

[47] Richard Ned Lebow, *Self-Interest from Tocqueville to Trump* (London: Palgrave-Macmillan, 2018), ch. 1, for running red lights and its broader political and social implications.

[48] Lebow, *Rise and Fall of Political Orders*, ch. 2, for a comparative analysis of nineteenth-century sociologists and the problem of order.

consequence.[49] There is, of course, nothing similar at the international level to provide solidarity and act as a catalyst for Zimmern's hope of planetary patriotism.

Our analysis of order rests on four substantive assumptions. First, disorder is the default of all top-down orders; they are more fragile and shorter-lived than bottom-up orders. Second, to achieve any degree of stability, top-down and bottom-up orders alike must justify themselves to relevant actors with reference to accepted principles of justice. Third, the stability of orders is threatened when their principles of justice are challenged and the discrepancy between them and practice becomes unacceptable. Fourth, all top-down orders—and many bottom-up orders—are hierarchical and require some degree of solidarity to soften the unequal distribution of honor and wealth.[50]

Can Orders Be Reformed?

To argue for or against an order assumes the possibility of changing it for the better. It further assumes that change can be brought about by conscious design as opposed to uncontrolled evolution. Critiques of existing orders implicitly assume that directed change is not only possible but can confer important benefits. Arguments against change rest on several premises. The first and most common line of argument is that the current order is worth defending because it is better than other plausible alternatives. A second, related contention is that attempts to change the existing order could undermine it, promote chaos, and make everybody worse off. A third position, one that we will elaborate in this section of the chapter, is that orderly change by design is simply not possible because any attempt will meet strong resistance and ultimately fail. A fourth argument that we also consider is that reform is not worth the effort as orders are essentially alike and little more than systems for maintaining inequality and

[49] Hans Kohn, *The Idea of Nationalism: A Study in Its Origins and Background* (New York: Macmillan, 1944); Karl W. Deutsch, *Nationalism and Social Communication* (Cambridge, MA: MIT Press, 1953); Benedict R. Anderson, *Imagined Communities: Reflections on the Origin and Spread of Nationalism* (London: Verso, 1983).

[50] On hierarchy, Max Weber, "The Profession and Vocation of Politics," in Peter Lassman and Ronald Speirs, trans. and eds., *Political Writings* (Cambridge: Cambridge University Press, 2000), pp. 309–69; Susan T. Fiske, "Interpersonal Stratification: Status, Power, and Subordination," in Susan T. Fiske, Daniel T. Gilbert, and Gardner Lindzey, eds., *Handbook of Modern Psychology*, vol. 2 (New York: Wiley, 2010), pp. 941–82. On solidarity, Jean-Jacques Rousseau, *Discourse on Political Economy*, in Roger D. Masters and Judith R. Masters, trans., *First and Second Discourses* (New York: St. Martin's Press, 1969), pp. 77–229, and *The Government of Poland*, trans. Wilmore Kendall (Indianapolis: Hackett, 1985); Emile Durkheim, *The Division of Labor in Society*, trans. W. D. Halls (New York: Macmillan, 1984), pp. 229–30.

exploitation. At best, they are what English School founder Hedley Bull calls "imperialism with good manners."[51]

Diplomatic historian F. H. Hinsley and international relations scholar Ian Clark represent the third position. Hinsley observes that at the end of every major war since the eighteenth century, the great powers "made a concerted effort, each one more radical than the last, to reconstruct the system on lines that would enable them . . . to avoid a future war." These efforts "all came to nothing."[52] Clark makes a comparison with domestic orders, many of which have been successfully restructured over the last 200 years. He follows Hinsley in believing that repeated attempts to reform international order by developing group norms, especially those intended to limit great power abuse of power and subordination of others, have consistently failed.[53]

Oran Young offers a strong version of the fourth argument, contending that what change there has been is negative in its effects. The international polity expanded geographically and in its number of units but, Young insists, political, economic, and military power has become more concentrated in the hands of the few. Having spent much of his career trying to bring about international cooperation in the Arctic, he is increasingly pessimistic: "Many inequalities in the international polity have exhibited a marked tendency to become more extreme rather than less extreme in modern times. With respect to material wealth this has become quite dramatic over the last hundred years."[54] This argument, as we will see, is echoed by critics of the American liberal order who describe it as a vehicle for domination and exploitation.[55]

Realists are divided in their take on the prospect of progress. Many tend to dismiss plans for reforms, let alone transformations, of the international order as unrealistic and more likely to lead to dystopias than utopias.[56] The most

---

[51] Bull, *Anarchical Society*, p. 209. Also, E. H. Carr, *The Twenty Years' Crisis, 1919–1939* (London: Palgrave-Macmillan, 2016).

[52] F. H. Hinsley, "The Rise and Fall of the Modern State System," *Review of International Studies* 8, no. 1 (1982), pp. 1–8.

[53] Clark, *The Hierarchy of States*, pp. 210, 94.

[54] Oran Young, "On the Performance of the International Polity," *British Journal of International Studies* 4, no. 3 (1978), pp. 191–208.

[55] Branco Milanovic, *Global Inequality: A New Approach for the Age of Globalization* (Cambridge, MA: Harvard University Press, 2018), ch. 1. Dan Rodrik, *The Globalization Paradox: Democracy and the Future of the World Economy* (New York: W. W. Norton, 2012), argues that growth in advanced economies is more likely to redistribute than to add to wealth.

[56] Peter Wilson, "Carr and His Early Critics: Responses to the Twenty Years' Crisis, 1939–46," in Michael Cox, *E. H. Carr: A Critical Appraisal* (Basingstoke: Palgrave-Macmillan, 2000); Brian Schmidt, ed., *International Relations and the First Great Debate* (London: Routledge, 2012); William E. Scheuerman, *Morgenthau: Realism and Beyond* (Cambridge: Polity, 2009); Alexander Reichwein, *Hans J. Morgenthau und die Twenty Years' Crisis: Eine kontextualisierte Interpretation des realistischen Denkens in den IB* (Heidelberg: Springer, 2020).

prominent contemporary spokesman for pessimism is John J. Mearsheimer. In his most recent book he argues that American attempts to spread liberal democracy, foster an open international economy, and build international institutions have inevitably failed. They transformed the United States into a highly militarized state willing to initiate wars whose effects are to undermine peace, harm human rights, and threaten domestic liberal values.[57] Realists like Mearsheimer nevertheless acknowledge that some degree of order is possible under conditions of anarchy. A minimal, emergent order can arise through the balance of power, or a more robust one if imposed by a hegemon or concert of powers.[58]

Mearsheimer is not alone in believing that new orders do not emerge by consensus but through fiat imposed by powerful states, and usually at the end of wars. This is a core assumption of power transition theory.[59] Adam Tooze has recently argued in support of the conservative realist and power transition position. Since 2008, he observes, American order is in serious crisis. It is not surprising that there are multiple calls for new institutional design. We should be careful what we wish for, he warns. If history is anything to go by, that new order will not emerge from collective and enlightened acts of leadership. Rather, it will be the result of a "power grab by a new stakeholder determined to have its way." Better that "we should get comfortable with the new disorder."[60]

There is a more optimistic tradition within realism. John Herz considered the postwar order fragile, like all preceding orders, but thought improvement a realistic goal. Toward this end, he sought to create a synthesis of realism and liberalism anchored in international law.[61] In the early postwar years, Hans Morgenthau

---

[57] John J. Mearsheimer, *Tragedy of Great Power Politics*, and *The Great Delusion: Liberal Dreams and International Realities* (New Haven, CT: Yale University Press, 2019); Barry Posen, *Restraint: A New Foundation for U.S. Grand Strategy* (Ithaca, NY: Cornell University Press, 2015); Stephen M. Walt, *The Hell of Good Intentions: America's Foreign Policy Elite and the Decline of U.S. Primacy* (New York: Farrar, Straus & Giroux, 2018); Charles L. Glaser, "A Flawed Framework: Why the Liberal International Order Framework Is Misguided," *International Security* 43, no. 4 (2019), pp. 51–87. Also, Stephen D. Krasner, *Sovereignty: Organized Hypocrisy* (Princeton, NJ: Princeton University Press, 1999).

[58] See above for realist cites. For a critique of the balance of power, Stuart J. Kaufman, Richard Little, and William C. Wohlforth, *The Balance of Power in World History* (New York: Palgrave-Macmillan, 2007).

[59] For compelling critiques of power transition, Steve Chan, *China, the U.S., and the Power-Transition Theory: A Critique* (London: Routledge, 2008); Richard Ned Lebow and Benjamin A. Valentino, "Lost in Transition: A Critique of Power Transition Theories," *International Relations* 23, no. 3 (2009), pp. 389–410; Richard Ned Lebow and Daniel Tompkins, "The Thucydides Claptrap," *Washington Monthly*, June 28, 2016.

[60] Adam Tooze, "Everything You Know about Global Order Is Wrong," *Foreign Policy*, January 2019, https://foreignpolicy.com/2019/01/30/everything-you-know-about-global-order-is-wrong/ (accessed 6 January 2021). Also, Adam Tooze, *Crashed: How a Decade of Financial Crises Changed the World* (London: Penguin, 2019).

[61] John H. Herz, *Political Realism and Political Idealism* (Chicago: University of Chicago Press, 1951); Peter Stirk, "John H. Herz: Realism and the Fragility of the International Order,"

rejected international reform as unrealistic and dangerous, making him an articulate representative of our second strategy. He later insisted on the need to supersede national sovereignty to deal with the nuclear and environmental threats, and in his last decade thought these goals more feasible.[62] Herz, Morgenthau, and more recent proponents of reform like Amitav Acharya have more limited goals than Zimmern. They agree with realists, in the words of Acharya, that "absolute peace is illusory" but contend that we can reasonably aim for "relative stability." By this he means the prevention of genocide, war among the major powers, and the management of regional conflicts to minimize their human costs.[63]

For the Current Order

References to a "global order" are most often a shorthand for the Western-led, liberal capitalist, political and economic order. It is far from universal in its reach or consistent in its adherence to its proclaimed principles. Much of the theoretical literature on this order originates in the Anglosphere and tends to exaggerate its benefits and those of American power. The English School valued the postwar order but insisted that it was dependent on a common culture. Martin Wight and Hedley Bull feared for its survival with the emergence of so many non-Western states.[64] Henry Kissinger makes a similar argument. He applauds Western power, its principles, and the order it has imposed. The rise in power of non-Western states, he insists, is almost certain to fuel disorder.[65] Bertrand Badie suggests—and not without reason—that people like Bull and Kissinger live(d) in a world of "imagined order," based on the now

---

Review of International Studies 31, no. 2 (2005), pp. 285–306; Casper Sylvest, "John H. Herz and the Resurrection of Classical Realism," *International Relations* 22, no. 4 (2008), pp. 441–55, and "Realism and International Law: The Challenge of John H. Herz," *International Theory* 2, no 3 (2010), pp. 410–45.

[62] Richard Ned Lebow, *The Tragic Vision of Politics: Ethics, Interests, and Orders* (Cambridge: Cambridge University Press, 2003), ch. 5; Seán Molloy, "Truth, Power, Theory: Hans Morgenthau's Formulation of Realism," *Diplomacy and Statecraft* 15, no. 1 (2010), pp. 1–34; William E. Scheuerman, *The Realist Case for Global Reform* (New York: Polity, 2011); Reichwein, *Hans J. Morgenthau und die Twenty Years' Crisis*.

[63] Amitav Acharya, *The End of American World Order*, 2nd ed. (London: Verso, 2018), p. 15.

[64] Martin Wight, *System of States* (Leicester: Leicester University Press, 1977); Bull, *Anarchical Society*. Robert Jackson, *Quasi-States: Sovereignty, International Relations, and the Third World* (Cambridge: Cambridge University Press, 1990), and *The Global Covenant: Human Conduct in a World of States* (Oxford: Oxford University Press, 2000), is more open to cultural diversity.

[65] Henry Kissinger, *World Order: Reflections on the Character of Nations and the Course of History* (London: Allen Lane, 2014), pp. 8–10.

increasingly out-of-date Westphalian system. Incapable of envisaging an alternative, they foresee only chaos.[66]

For most realists, the problem is not culture but power. In the aftermath of the Cold War and collapse of the Soviet Union, some naïvely proclaimed that "unipolarity" would encourage or compel others to imitate American political and economic structures and values. In the last decade, the pendulum has swung away from such unjustified euphoria to deepening pessimism.[67] Realists emphasize different threats depending on their political and theoretical frameworks, but there is a consensus that the liberal, democratic order is on the defensive. They see the major threat to order as a rising China, and secondarily, a revanchist Russia.[68]

For liberal supporters of the current order, the principal threat is internal, from challenges to democracy by authoritarian politicians and political parties.[69] Some liberals also worry about the defection from the liberal order by weaker states who hope to escape from pressures to conform to liberal economic and social practices. Equally worrisome, others insist, is the damaging behavior of the self-proclaimed hegemon, beginning with its invasions of Afghanistan and Iraq, irresponsible economic behavior, and, of course, the disastrous presidency of Donald Trump.[70]

[66] Bertrand Badie to Ned Lebow, email, 6 February 2021.

[67] Thomas Wright, *All Measures Short of War: The Contest for the Twenty-first Century and the Future of American Power* (New Haven, CT: Yale University Press, 2017).

[68] Aaron L. Friedberg, *A Contest for Supremacy: China, America, and the Struggle for Mastery in Asia* (New York: W. W. Norton, 2012), "Competing with China," *Survival* 60, no. 3 (2018), pp. 7–64, and "Getting the China Challenge Right," *The American Interest*, 10 January 2019, https://www. the-american-interest.com/2019/01/10/getting-the-china-challenge-right/ (accessed 6 February 2019); Mearsheimer, *Tragedy of Great Power*, p. 400, "China's Unpeaceful Rise," *Current History* 105 (2006), pp. 160–62, and "The Gathering Storm: China's Challenge to US Power in Asia," *Chinese Journal of International Politics* 3, no. 4 (2010), pp. 381–96; Christopher Layne, "The Waning of U.S. Hegemony: Myth or Reality?" *International Security* 34, no. 1 (2009), pp. 147–72, and "The US-China Power Shift and the End of the Pax Americana," *International Affairs* 94, no. 1 (2018), pp. 89–111; Steven W. Mosher, *Hegemon: China's Plan to Dominate Asia and the World* (San Francisco: Encounter Books, 2000); Stefan Halper, *The Beijing Consensus: How China's Authoritarian Model Will Dominate the Twenty-first Century* (New York: Basic Books, 2010); Graham Allison, *Destined for War: Can America and China Escape Thucydides's Trap?* (Boston: Houghton Mifflin Harcourt, 2017).

[69] Larry Diamond, *Ill Winds: Saving Democracy from Russian Rage, Chinese Ambition, and American Complacency* (New York: Penguin, 2019); G. John Ikenberry, *A World Safe for Democracy: Liberal Internationalism and the Crises of Global Order* (New Haven, CT: Yale University Press, 2020); Michael Tomasky, *If We Can Keep It: How the Republic Collapsed and How It Might Be Saved* (New York: Liveright, 2019).

[70] Cédric Jourde, "The International Relations of Small Neoauthoritarian States: Islamism, Warlordism, and the Framing of Stability," *International Studies Quarterly* 51, no. 2 (2007), pp. 481–503; Parag Khanna, *The Second World: How Emerging Powers Are Redefining Competition in the Twenty-first Century* (New York: Random House, 2008); Stacie E. Goddard, "Embedded Revisionism: Networks, Institutions, and Challenges to World Order," *International Organization* 72,

Dire predictions abound on all sides.[71] Some of them have been realized, as with Russia's invasion of Ukraine. We should acknowledge the problems faced by the American-led order but also its enduring strength. The United States retains considerable influence over its allies and others by virtue of the security, economic benefits, and political support it provides. But we should not make the mistake of so many American realists and liberals and confuse this set of arrangements with world order. Joseph Nye, long a defender of the liberal, democratic project, rightly observes that support for it is "largely limited to a group of like-minded states centered on the Atlantic littoral."[72] Alexander Cooley and Daniel Nexon argue, also with some justification, that to the extent there is any global order, "it takes the form of an assemblage of many different orders at different scales."[73] World order is not monolithic but multiple, with different states and societies participating more or less in the political, economic, military, and social values and activities of different orders. Some of these orders (e.g., the US liberal order and the European Union) share much in common and might be said to constitute components of a larger community. Others (e.g., the US liberal order, Russia's efforts to organize a Moscow-centric order in its near abroad, efforts at creating Islamic-based orders by Saudi Arabia and Iran) are sharply at odds and in competition with one another. And still others (the US liberal order and China's efforts at establishing a Beijing-centered regional, if not world, order) reveal a mix of cooperation and conflict.

In the opinion of many, China is seeking to construct an alternative to the American liberal order. It is seen to be challenging not only America's material power, but also its liberal values. Some analysts hold that the challenge to American values is the more important because it will potentially erode fundamental human rights, freedom of thought and expression, and self-government around the world. According to Nadège Rolland, the Chinese vision of

---

no. 4 (2018), pp. 763–97; Christopher Walker, "The Authoritarian Threat: The Hijacking of Soft Power," *Journal of Democracy* 27, no. 3 (2016), pp. 49–63, and "What Is Sharp Power?" *Journal of Democracy* 29, no. 3 (2018), pp. 9–23; Cooley and Nexon, *Exit from Hegemony*, on these threats and how they are reinforcing.

[71] For example, Charles A. Kupchan and Peter L. Trubowitz, "Dead Center: The Demise of Liberal Internationalism in the United States," *International Security* 32, no. 2 (2007), pp. 7–44; Georg Sörensen, *A Liberal World Order in Crisis: Choosing between Imposition and Restraint* (Ithaca, NY: Cornell University Press, 2011); Acharya, *End of American Order*; Gideon Rose, "The Fourth Founding: The United States and the Liberal Order," *Foreign Affairs* 98, no. 1 (2019), pp. 10–21; Ian Buruma, "The End of the Anglo-American Order," *New York Times Magazine*, 29 November 2016; Michael J. Boyle, "The Coming Illiberal Era," *Survival* 58, no. 2 (2016), pp. 35–66; Kirchick, *The End of Europe*; Cooley and Nexon, *Exit from Hegemony*; Patrick Porter, *The False Promise of the Liberal Order* (London: Polity, 2020).

[72] Joseph S. Nye Jr., "Will the Liberal Order Survive? The History of an Idea," *Foreign Affairs* 96, no. 1 (2017), pp. 10–16.

[73] Cooley and Nexon, *Exit from Hegemony*, p. 32.

order draws inspiration from traditional Chinese thought and past historical experiences. It is an order in which China enjoys partial hegemony over large portions of the Global South—a space that would be free from Western influence and purged of liberal ideals.[74]

The Chinese project represents a different conception of order, one that is capitalist but authoritarian. Yet China is not exporting authoritarianism, as the United States has tried to do with liberalism; it is instead fighting a defensive ideological battle against liberal norms of democracy and human rights.[75] China might be said to straddle two worlds, as it is also a participant in the American-designed and -led order, in which it plays an increasingly prominent and powerful economic role. It has been pragmatically revising the American order and working around its constraints, rather than rejecting it wholesale. In a wide-ranging empirical analysis, Alastair Iain Johnston argues that China is not challenging the liberal international order as much as the dominant narrative in the United States suggests.[76] Many Chinese scholars concur. Shiping Tang, for example, understands China's ideal international order as a durable post-1945 Westphalian order with economic liberalization.[77]

Given the novelty of Chinese efforts, we will concentrate on the long-established reality of the American efforts to structure a world order. Some supporters of this order insist that it approximates the best of all worlds because it has prevented great power conventional or nuclear war for over seventy years.[78] They are at a loss to imagine an alternative other than chaos, and accordingly urge Washington to maintain its military advantage and continued international engagement and leadership. Liberals assert that the American-led order has fostered a vast improvement in wealth and well-being on a global scale. Other liberals give it responsibility as well for the decline of interstate war by creating institutions capable of managing conflict and encouraging the emergence of democracy. The most extreme version of this claim is the democratic peace research program.[79] Some liberals famously assert that democratization and globalization

[74] Nadège Rolland, "China's Vision for a New World Order," NBR Special Report 83, January 2020.

[75] Jessica Chen Weiss, "A World Safe for Autocracy? China's Rise and the Future of Global Politics," *Foreign Affairs* 98, no. 4 (2019), pp. 92–102.

[76] Alastair Iain Johnston, "China in a World of Orders: Rethinking Compliance and Challenge in Beijing's International Relations," *International Security* 44, no. 2 (2019), pp. 9–60.

[77] Shiping Tang, "China and the Future of International Order(s)," *Ethics & International Affairs* 32, no. 1 (2018), pp. 31–43.

[78] Waltz, *Theory of International Politics*, for the strongest claim.

[79] For example, Bruce Russett, *Grasping the Democratic Peace: Principles for a Post–Cold War World* (Princeton, NJ: Princeton University Press, 1993); Michael E. Brown, Sean M. Lynn-Jones, and Steven E. Miller, *Debating the Democratic Peace* (Cambridge, MA: MIT Press, 1996). Andrew Lawrence, "Imperial Peace or Imperial Method? Skeptical Inquiries into Ambiguous Evidence for

would usher in a new peaceful and productive era, even bringing history to an end—a claim that in retrospect seems increasingly hollow.[80] Enthusiasm for globalization among liberals, which reached its high point in the aftermath of the Cold War, has increasingly given way to a more cautious or even jaundiced view of its consequences.[81]

In a recent, sophisticated, and elegant defense of the liberal project, John Ikenberry acknowledges that liberal values and institutions have suffered serious setbacks, but insists this is not the first time they have faced such challenges.[82] His thoughtful book focuses on political liberalism, defined as the organization of the international order in a manner conducive to the protection and flourishing of democracy. He acknowledges the ways in which the post–Cold War extension of the liberal project has made the liberal order "wider but narrower" and has "hollowed out" its social purposes. He also recognizes that the political-economic bargain at the heart of the liberal order—American security protection and open markets in return for absorbing the dollars associated with the US balance-of-payments deficit—has lost its utility and appeal.[83] Ikenberry nevertheless believes that liberal democracy will prevail in the long run because it is the most appropriate response to modernity.

the 'Democratic Peace,'" in Richard Ned Lebow and Mark I. Lichbach, eds., *Theory and Evidence in Comparative Politics and International Relations* (New York: Palgrave-Macmillan, 2007), pp. 188–228.

[80] Daniel Bell, *The End of Ideology: On the Exhaustion of Political Ideas in the 1950s* (Glencoe, IL: Free Press, 1960); Francis Fukuyama, *The End of History and the Last Man* (New York: Free Press, 1992); Thomas Friedman, *The Lexus and the Olive Tree* (New York: Farrar, Straus & Giroux, 1999); Alexander L. Wendt, "Why a World State Is Inevitable," *European Journal of International Relations* 9, no. 4 (2003), pp. 491–542. Andrew Hurrell, *On Global Order: Power, Values, and the Constitution of International Society* (Oxford: Oxford University Press, 2007), ch. 3, for a thoughtful treatment of globalization and liberal claims of convergence.

[81] John Gray, *False Dawn: The Delusions of Global Capitalism* (New York: Free Press, 2000); Joseph Stiglitz, *Globalization and Its Discontents* (New York: W. W. Norton, 2002), and *Globalization and Its Discontents Revisited: Anti-Globalization in the Era of Trump* (New York: W. W. Norton, 2020); Dani Rodrik, *The Globalization Paradox: Democracy and the Future of the World Economy* (New York: W. W. Norton, 2012); Hurrell, *On Global Order*, ch. 8; Klaus Schwab. "We Need a New Narrative for Globalization," *World Economic Forum*, 17 March 2017, https://www.weforum.org/agenda/2017/03/klaus-schwab-new-narrative-for-globalization/ (accessed 1 January 2021); Porter, *False Promise of the Liberal Order*, pp. 148–49; Randall D. Germain, ed., *Globalization and Its Critics: Perspectives from Political Economy* (Houndmills: Macmillan, 2000).

[82] Ikenberry, *A World Safe for Democracy*.

[83] Ibid., pp. 258–59, 269–72. On the political-economic arrangement and its decline, see Michael Mastanduno, "System Maker and Privilege Taker: US Power and the International Political Economy," in G. John Ikenberry, Michael Mastanduno, and William C. Wohlforth, eds., *International Relations Theory and the Consequences of Unipolarity* (Princeton, NJ: Princeton University Press, 1999), pp. 142–47.

Many realists and liberals vaunt the alleged advantages of American hegemony. With the active support of developed capitalist countries, the United States is alleged to have created a rule-based liberal order from which everyone benefits. It provides public goods, including defense, monetary stability, free trade, and freedom of the seas. American engagement should continue in their view, along with its support for a range of international institutions in which it has traditionally played a major role.[84] This perspective on world order is widely propagated by such institutions as the Council on Foreign Relations, the World Economic Forum at Davos, and the Brookings Institution.

Most realists and liberals maintain that any shift in the global distribution of power away from unipolarity, or at least away from US dominance, would be destabilizing. Some fear this is already happening, but a minority deny this or describe it as a very long-term process.[85] The most significant cleavage among those who vaunt American hegemony is the degree to which they believe it is threatened, and by what or whom, and how any decline can be halted or reversed. On the whole, most realists and liberals who write about hegemony favor tighter alliances and enough defense spending for the United States to remain the dominant military power, although they are deeply divided over the use of this power.[86] Many attribute the perceived decline in the US position to

[84] Examples of optimists include Mortimer Zuckerman, "A Second American Century," *Foreign Affairs* 7, no. 3 (1998), pp. 18–31; Walter Russell Mead, *Power, Terror, Peace and War: America's Grand Strategy in a World at Risk* (New York: Knopf, 2004); Stephen G. Brooks and William C. Wohlforth, *World out of Balance: International Relations and the Challenge of U.S. Primacy* (Princeton, NJ: Princeton University Press, 2008); William C. Wohlforth, "The Stability of a Unipolar World," *International Security* 24, no. 1 (1999), pp. 5–41, and "U.S. Strategy in a Unipolar World," in G. John Ikenberry, ed., *America Unrivaled: The Future of the Balance of Power* (Ithaca, NY: Cornell University Press, 2002), pp. 98–120; Ikenberry, *Liberal Leviathan*, p. 4, and Ikenberry, ed., *Power, Order, Change in World Politics* (Cambridge: Cambridge University Press, 2014); Joseph S. Nye Jr., Condoleezza Rice, Nicholas Burns, Leah Bitounis, and Jonathan Price, *The World Turned Upside Down: Strategies to Expand US Engagement in a Competitive World Order* (Washington, DC: Center for a New American Security, 2016); Stephen G. Brooks and William C. Wohlforth, *Why the Sole Superpower Should Not Pull Back from the World* (New York: Oxford University Press, 2016).

[85] Brooks and Wohlforth, "Rise and Fall of the Great Powers in the Twenty-First Century," and Brooks and Wohlforth, *Why the Sole Superpower Should Not Pull Back from the World*; Joseph S. Nye Jr., "American Hegemony or American Primacy? Project Syndicate, 9 March 2015, https://www.proj ect-syndicate.org/commentary/american-hegemony-military-superiority-by-joseph-s--nye-2015-03?barrier=accesspaylog (accessed 3 January 2021); Michael Beckley, *Unrivaled: Why American Will Remain the World's Sole Superpower* (Ithaca, NY: Cornell University Press, 2018); Rebecca Lissner and Mira Rapp-Hooper, *An Open World: How American Can Win the Contest for Twenty-first Century Order* (New Haven, CT: Yale University Press, 2020). For an overview and critique of unipolarity, Acharya, *End of American World Order*, pp. 20–46.

[86] Richard Haass, "The Age of Nonpolarity: What Will Follow US Dominance," *Foreign Affairs* 87, no. 3 (May/June 2008), pp. 44–56. Christopher Layne, "The Waning of U.S. Hegemony—Myth or Reality? A Review Essay," *International Security* 34, no. 1 (2009), pp. 147–72; Robert Kagan, *The*

a shift in power caused by the rise of other states, notably China.[87] Realists and liberals alike tend to depict China as selfish, mercantilist, strident, and opposed to human rights at home and abroad.[88] The pessimists among them fear that the United States is in the final stages of its role as global leader and must take dramatic action if it is to sustain its hegemonic role.[89]

Some conservative critics of American foreign policy attribute America's decline to Washington's restraint. In their view, this takes the form of trying to cloak what is in effect an empire with the language and practices of liberalism.[90] Liberals strongly resist this framing and describe illiberal and authoritarian practices as aberrations that are prejudicial and damaging to American influence.[91] Many conservatives, on the other hand, are willing to acknowledge America's empire but with the caveat that it is more benign than any its predecessors.[92] Patrick

Jungle Grows Back: America and Our Imperiled World (New York: Knopf, 2018). For non-American perspectives, Dilip Hiro, *After Empire: The Birth of a Multipolar World* (New York: Nation Books, 2009); Giovanni Grevi, *The Interpolar World: A New Scenario* (Paris: European Union Institute for Security Studies, 2009); Luis Peral, ed., *Global Security in a Multipolar World* (Paris: European Union Institute for Security Studies, 2009); Thomas Renard, *A BRIC in the World: Emerging Powers, Europe and the Coming Order* (Brussels: Academic Press for the Royal Institute of International Relations, 2009); Álvaro de Vasconcelos, "Multilateralising Multi-Polarity: Between Self-Interest and a Responsible Approach," in Luis Peral, ed., *Global Security in a Multi-polar World* (Paris: European Institute for Security Studies, 2009); Kishore Mahbubani, *The New Asian Hemisphere: The Irresistible Shift of Global Power to the East* (New York: Public Affairs Press, 2008).

[87] Zakaria, *The Post-American World*.

[88] Shirong Chen, "China Defends Africa Economic and Trade Role," BBC Website, http://www.bbc.co.uk/news/mobile/world-asia-pacific-12069624?SThisEM, 23 December 2010; Martin Wolf, *Fixing Global Finance: How to Curb Financial Crisis in the 21st Century* (New Haven, CT: Yale University Press, 2008). On human rights, "China Rejects US Criticism of Human Rights Record," 11 May 2011, http://www.bbc.co.uk/news/world-asia-pacific-13358081 (both accessed 28 December 2020).

[89] James Traub, "Wallowing in Decline," *Foreign Policy*, 24 September 2010, http://www.foreignpolicy.com/articles/2010/09/24/wallowing_in_decline (accessed 27 December 2010); Stephen M. Walt, "The Virtues of Competence," *Foreign Policy*, 22 September 2010, http://walt.foreignpolicy.com/posts/2010/09/22/the_virtues_of_competence (accessed 27 December 2010); Kurt M. Campbell and Ely Ratner, "The China Reckoning," *Foreign Affairs*, 13 February 2018, https://www.foreignaffairs.com/articles/china/2018-02-13/china-reckoning (accessed 2 January 2021); Wright, *All Measures Short of War*.

[90] Porter, *False Promise of the Liberal Order*, leads the charge here.

[91] Cooley and Nexon, *Exit from Hegemony*, p. 23, *Porter, False Promise of the Liberal Order*, pp. 5–8.

[92] Robert Kagan, "The Benevolent Empire," *Foreign Policy*, no. 111 (1998), pp. 24–35; Andrew Bacevich, *American Empire: The Realities and Consequences of U.S. Diplomacy* (Cambridge, MA: Harvard University Press, 2002); Niall Ferguson, "Hegemony or Empire?" *Foreign Affairs* 82, no. 5 (2003), pp. 154–61; Deepak Lal, *In Praise of Empires: Globalization and Order* (New York: Palgrave-Macmillan, 2004); Max Boot, "The Case for American Empire," *Weekly Standard*, 15 October 2001, https://www.washingtonexaminer.com/weekly-standard/the-case-for-american-empire (accessed 1 January 2021); Daniel Nexon and Thomas Wright, "What's at Stake in the American Empire Debate," *American Political Science Review* 101, no. 2 (2007), pp. 253–71.

Porter offers the most extensive version of this argument. He contends that pretensions to a liberal order mask a love-hate relationship with empire. The world "is too conflict-ridden and dangerous to be governed liberally" and efforts to spread democracy abroad are only undermining it at home. The "dark" side of American foreign policy is not an aberration, as policymakers and pundits often claim, but actually constitutive of the international order. Anarchy and competition result in violent struggles for dominance. This thoroughly illiberal process gives rise to a hierarchy and those at the top, if rational, use all means at their disposal to maintain their position and the advantages it confers. Ordering is "an inherently imperial undertaking." International relations is tragedy, he insists, with any commitment to liberal values periodically giving way to the brutal exercise of power. All international orders are built and maintained on the basis of coercion regardless of their rhetorical claims. America should recognize this truth and get on with their empire.[93]

These claims have not gone unchallenged. A school of critics accepts the description of American order as an empire, but rejects its characterization as benign in any way or one cheered on by other states. They describe most cooperation with the United States as merely instrumental and not indicative of any kind of positive commitment by other countries and their leaders.[94] Early post–Cold War expectations that Russia and China, or democracies like South Africa, India, or Brazil, would become part of a larger liberal order have been dashed.[95] Harsher critics characterize American order as more a form of dominance than cooperation. In the words of Robert Cox, "the structure of power maintains itself through these institutions."[96] More recently, Samuel Moyn has depicted liberal internationalism as nothing more than a bid for global hegemony.[97]

Other scholars deny that hegemony has any empirical basis. They argue that the United States exercised a regional hegemony in the Western Hemisphere and short-lived dominance elsewhere because of its extraordinary and short-lived economic and military advantages at the end of World War II.[98] In 1944,

[93] Porter, *False Promise of the Liberal Order*, p. 21, for an overview of the argument.

[94] Mlada Bukovansky, "The Responsibility to Accommodate Ideas and Change," in T. V. Paul, ed., *Accommodating Rising Powers: Past, Present, and Future* (Cambridge: Cambridge University Press, 2016), pp. 87–108.

[95] Andrew Hurrell, "Narratives of Emergence: Rising Powers and the End of the Third World?" *Brazilian Journal of Political Economy* 30, no. 2 (2013), pp. 203–31.

[96] Robert Cox, *The New Realism: Perspective on Multilateralism and World Order* (New York: St. Martin's 1997).

[97] Samuel Moyn, "Beyond Liberal Institutionalism," *Dissent*, Winter 2017, pp. 108–14, and *Not Enough: Human Rights in an Unequal World* (Cambridge, MA: Harvard University Press, 2018). Also, Bacevich, *American Empire*; Perry Anderson, *The H-Word: The Peripeteia of Hegemony* (London: Verso, 2017).

[98] Reich and Lebow, *Good-Bye Hegemony*, ch. 2.

US GDP peaked at 35 percent of the world total, a figure that had dropped to 25 percent by 1960 and 20 percent by 1980.[99] Western Europe and Japan not only rebuilt their economies but also regained much of their self-confidence; both developments reduced the need and appeal of American leadership. The Korean War stalemate in the early 1950s demonstrated the limits of this supposed hegemony, as did the failure of intervention in Indochina in the 1960s and 1970s and the delinking of the dollar from the gold standard in 1971. Of equal importance, these critics contend, the United States has abused what power and influence it has, making it a source of political and economic instability.

Against the Current Order

Critiques of the so-called American liberal order are economic, political, and psychological in nature. They also differ in the extent to which they think this order can be reformed or must be replaced with something significantly different.

The economic critique focuses on the destructive consequences of capitalism. The principal distinction here is between those, mostly Marxists, who portray it as the inevitable consequences of this mode of production, and those who are more favorably inclined to capitalism and believe that its practices might be reformed.[100] Pro-capitalist critics identify neo-liberalism as the principal evil. Georges Soros, an early critic of global, neo-liberal capitalism, emphasizes how it legitimizes greed. It differs from earlier understandings of business and finance because its "intensification of the profit motive and its penetration into areas that were previously governed by other considerations." As a result, Soros argues, "money rules people's lives to a great extent than ever before."[101]

Ned Lebow argues that unrestrained greed is part of a broader shift away from self-interest defined at least partly in communal terms, with more people today willing to consider and advance their interest independently of and often at the expense of their community.[102] He documents this shift in a qualitative and quantitative content analyses of six decades of presidential inaugural and

---

[99] Angus Maddison, *Monitoring the World Economy, 1820–1992* (Paris: Organization for Economic Cooperation and Development, 1995). Even Robert Gilpin, *War and Change in World Politics* (New York: Cambridge University Press, 1987), pp. 173–75, renowned proponent of hegemonic stability theory, acknowledges the fact that US global dominance was fleeting.

[100] For Marxist critiques, Jeanne Morefield, *Empires without Imperialism: Anglo-American Decline and the Politics of Deflection* (Oxford: Oxford University Press, 2014); Perry Anderson, *American Foreign Policy and Its Thinkers* (London: Verso, 2013); Inderjeet Parmar, "The US-Led Liberal Order: Imperialism by Another Name," *International Affairs* 94, no. 1 (2018), pp. 151–72.

[101] George Soros, *The Crisis of Global Capitalism* (New York: Public Affairs 1998), pp. 115–16.

[102] Lebow, *Rise and Fall of Political Orders*, ch. 5.

state of the union speeches, television sitcoms, and popular music. It is interesting to speculate whether these shifts in the understanding of self-interest— by no means restricted to the United States—made people more receptive to neo-liberalism possible, or whether Reaganism, Thatcherism, and neo-liberalism legitimated greed and encouraged people to focus more on themselves and frame their interests more narrowly. We suspect the process was reciprocal and that neo-liberalism and the policies it spawned may be an all but inevitable expression of late capitalism in cultures that have always stressed the autonomy and freedom of the individual.

In his intellectual history of neo-liberal globalism, Quinn Slobodian shows how Austrian economists Friedrich Hayek, Ludwig von Mises, and their followers, far from discarding the regulatory state, sought to inoculate capitalism from democratic interference.[103] As former German chancellor Gerhard Schröder put it, the world had to "be modernized by the unchecked forces of the market."[104] Neo-liberals used states and international institutions, including the League of Nations, the International Monetary Fund (IMF), the World Bank, European Court of Justice, the World Trade Organization, the European Central Bank, the North American Free Trade Agreement (NAFTA, and since July 2020 the United States-Mexico-Canada Agreement [USMCA]), and international investment law, to insulate the markets against states and democratic demands for greater equality and social justice. Neo-liberalism emerged less to shrink government and abolish regulations than to redeploy them at a global level, and by doing so, reduce the power of states. Neo-liberals have been extraordinarily successful in their project, but by giving free rein to banks, investors, and corporations at the international level they may have created a monster that threatens the economic and political order. Martin Wolf, the highly regarded economics editor of the *Financial Times*, notes the irony that the effort to depoliticize economic relations was a highly visible project that inevitably aroused considerable awareness of what was happening and opposition to it.[105]

---

[103] Friedrich A. Hayek, *The Constitution of Liberty* (Chicago: University of Chicago Press, 2011). Quinn Slobodian, *Globalists: The End of Empire and the Birth of Neoliberalism* (Cambridge, MA: Harvard University Press, 2018). See also Danny Nicol, *The Constitutional Protection of Capitalism* (London: Bloomsbury, 2010); Keller Easterling, *Extrastatecraft: The Power of Infrastructure Space* (New York: Verso, 2014); Ronen Palan, *The Offshore World: Sovereign Markets, Virtual Places, and Nomad Millionaires* (Ithaca, NY: Cornell University Press, 2003).

[104] Quoted in Wolfgang Streeck, *Buying Time: The Delayed Crisis of Democratic Capitalism* (London: Verso, 2014), p. 213; orders become fragile when their justifying discourses lose traction or the principle of justice on which an order is based loses its relative appeal or is largely supplanted by another.

[105] Martin Wolf, "Does the Trading System Have a Future?" *Jan Tumlir Political Essays*, European Centre for Political Economy, November 2009, https://ecipe.org/wp-content/uploads/2014/12/does-the-trading-system-have-a-future.pdf (accessed 27 January 2021).

Tooze explores some of these consequences of neo-liberalism for the international order. The early postwar era saw a continuation of wartime controls and it was not until 1958 that the Bretton Woods vision was implemented. International mobility of capital remained limited for anything other than long-term investment. The gradual abolition of exchange controls went hand in hand with the lifting of trade quotas, but the GATT did not accomplish much in this regard until the Kennedy Round of the 1960s. A comprehensive world trade organization was not in effect until 1995. It ushered in the age of the Washington Consensus. The neo-liberal order was the product of the emasculation of organized labor, government willingness to shift authority on key economic matters to international institutions, the collapse of the Soviet Union and communism, and China's decision to join the world economy. It is largely a post–Cold War phenomenon.[106]

The result, Tooze contends, was the strengthening of the technostructure's dollar-based hegemony in a manner that no macroeconomic approach limited to looking at the national accounts of states could possibly explain. Global finance fueled imbalanced dollar-denominated flows, and ultimately crashed in 2008. The global technostructure was preserved by America and China. In Europe, a similar bubble burst; banks made questionable loans and were only saved by intervention of the European Central Bank. Finance was rescued at the expense of the general public, and developed countries at the expense of less developed ones.[107] In practice, supposedly apolitical macroeconomic management wields enormous political power in support of powerful states and interests. Banks and governments shifted all the risks and losses arising from its irresponsibility onto the weak, callously telling them they must suffer the consequences of their alleged "profligacy." These developments fueled nationalism, racism, and geopolitical tensions.

Equally destructive was the dismantling of social protections in Europe and the United States, another key goal of neo-liberalism. John Ruggie argues that the economic foundation of the Cold War order was the reconciliation, as far as possible, of open markets with social protections.[108] Fostering open markets

---

[106] Tooze, "Everything You Know about Global Order.Is Wrong"; Philip Mirowski, "Neoliberalism: The Movement That Dare Not Speak Its Name," *American Affairs* 2, no. 1 (2018), pp. 1–20.

[107] Tooze, *Crashed*.

[108] John G. Ruggie, "International Regimes, Transactions, and Change: Embedded Liberalism in the Postwar Order," *International Organization* 76, no. 2 (1982), pp. 379–415. Also, Rawi Abdelal and John G. Ruggie, "The Principles of Embedded Liberalism: Social Legitimacy and Global Capitalism," in David Moss and John Cisternino, eds., *New Perspectives on Regulation* (Cambridge, MA: Tobin Project, 2009), pp. 151–62; Jeff D. Colgan and Robert O. Keohane, "The Liberal Order Is Rigged: Fix It Now or Watch It Wither," *Foreign Affairs* 96, no. 3 (2017), pp. 36–44; Mark Blyth, *Austerity: A History of a Dangerous Idea* (Oxford: Oxford University Press, 2013), and "Capitalism in Crisis: What

while removing much of the social net played into the hands of authoritarian and xenophobic politicians in the United States, Greece, Italy, Austria, Germany, Poland, Hungary, and elsewhere. In the absence of some progressive alternative, postmodern fascism is becoming increasingly attractive to large segments of European populations.

Another line of argument is more political, although it incorporates an important economic component. These critics maintain that the loss of US influence is not attributable to any relative decline in wealth or material capabilities, or challenges from external competitors or enemies. Rather, as Alexander Cooley and Daniel Nexon argue, it is the product of American mismanagement of its political and economic assets and responsibilities. They also attribute dissatisfaction with the global liberal order to the nature of that order itself, how it is imposed or enforced, and the lack of alternatives available for those who dissent.[109] They offer a different and more pessimistic vision of what it is likely to succeed a failed American-led liberal order: some kind of globalized oligarchy and kleptocracy.[110] A striking feature of the current order, they contend, is the ease with which oligarchs and other corrupt officials and entrepreneurs can exploit the means of this order to launder their money and reputations and sow doubts and conspiracy theories among democratic populations. Their ill-gained assets are safely stored in Western banks, investment, and property. Those in the West who facilitate these transfers invariably describe their clients as Westernizers in order to protect themselves. Oligarchs are a cause and expression of inequality, which is increasing almost everywhere. In the United States the richest 1 percent own 40 percent of the nation's wealth. Something similar prevails in Russia, and inequality is also on the rise in Britain, France, India, and China.[111] In all these countries the very wealthy park 30–40 percent of their assets offshore to avoid taxes.[112] This figure rises to over 60 percent among wealthy Russians.[113]

Went Wrong and What Comes Next?" *Foreign Affairs* 95, no. 4 (2016), pp. 172–79; Paul Collier, *The Future of Capitalism: Facing the New Anxieties* (London: Allen Lane, 2019); Ikenberry, *World Safe for Democracy*, pp. 275–78.

[109] Cooley and Nexon, *Exit from Hegemony*. See also John Gray, *The Two Faces of Liberalism* (Cambridge: Polity, 2000).

[110] Cooley and Nexon, *Exit from Hegemony*, pp. 196–200.

[111] Gabriel Zucman, "Global Wealth Inequality," *Annual Review of Economics* 33 (2019), pp. 119–38, https://doi.org/10.1146/annurev-economics-080218-025852 (accessed 2 January 2021).

[112] Guardian Investigation Team, "Pandora Papers: Biggest Ever Leak of Offshore Data Exposes Financial Secrets of Rich and Powerful," *The Guardian*, 3 October 2021, https://www.theguardian.com/news/2021/oct/03/pandora-papers-biggest-ever-leak-of-offshore-data-exposes-financial-secrets-of-rich-and-powerful (accessed 5 October 2021).

[113] Annette Alstadsaeter, Niels Johanneson, and Gabriel Zucman, "Who Owns the Wealth in Tax Havens? Macro Evidence and Implications for Global Inequality," *Journal of Public Economics* 162

Ned Lebow also makes the case that the United States lost influence because of the ways in which it has exploited its economic and military power at the expense of others.[114] He argues that for all its might, America is just another country, and one deeply resented by others when it abuses its political, economic, or military power. The United States should uphold and instantiate widely accepted norms governing foreign policy goals and methods. American leaders must further recognize that persuasion is more effective than coercion, multilateralism more efficacious than unilateralism, and that power, when exercised, needs to be masked, not publicized and paraded to buttress public self-esteem. Self-restraint is rarely perceived as weakness, contrary to the conventional wisdom in the national security establishment. Even more paradoxically, given how Americans think about the world, sitting back from time to time and letting others take the lead can build respect and influence in the longer term.

More radical critiques, as noted, regard the liberal order as a vehicle or cover for the expansion of US hegemony that at best pays lip service to its proclaimed liberal values.[115]

Radical critics contend that the United States behaves less like a hegemon and more like a free-rider or deviant. Beginning in the 1980s, the United States systematically reneged on its own liberal trading rules by introducing a variety of tariffs and quotas instead of bearing the costs of economic adjustments.[116] More recently, imperial overstretch was evident in the interventions in Afghanistan and Iraq. In each instance, the United States acted without the support of the United Nations or most of its closest allies and in the face of what they considered their best interests. America's capacity was found wanting and its strategic objectives were frustrated. The supposed "unipolar moment" of US power in the early 1990s was accompanied by an unprecedented number of intra-state wars, with the United States unable to impose solutions consistent with hegemony. These wars produced greater instability in the Middle East and

---

(2018), pp. 8–100; Alexander Cooley, John Heathershaw, and J. C. Sharman, "Laundering Cash, Whitewashing Reputations," *Journal of Democracy* 29, no. 1 (2008), pp. 39–53.

[114] Richard Ned Lebow, *A Democratic Foreign Policy: Regaining American Influence Abroad* (New York: Palgrave-Macmillan, 2019).

[115] Bacevich, *American Empire*; Samuel Moyn, "Beyond Liberal Institutionalism," *Dissent*, Winter 2017, pp. 108–14, and *Not Enough: Human Rights in an Unequal World* (Cambridge, MA: Harvard University Press, 2018); Perry Anderson, *The H-Word: The Peripeteia of Hegemony* (London: Verso, 2017).

[116] Charles P. Kindleberger, "Dominance and Leadership in the International Economy: Exploitation, Public Goods, and Free Rides," *International Studies Quarterly* 25, no. 2 (1981) pp. 242, 248; Simon Reich, *Restraining Trade to Invoke Investment: MITI and the Japanese Auto Producers: Case Studies in International Negotiation* (Washington, DC: Institute for the Study of Diplomacy, 2002); Reich and Lebow, *Good-Bye Hegemony!*

"blowback" at home. The American presence in Iraq and a puppet government in Baghdad strengthened fundamentalist forces in Saudi Arabia and throughout the Muslim world, as opponents of the war predicted.[117] They also compelled Middle East governments to distance themselves from Washington and seriously eroded American influence in the region.[118]

Around the world, the United States is widely believed to have abused its economic and military power in a way to make it a principal cause of economic and political instability. This perception became more pronounced during the presidency of Donald Trump. A 2017 Pew survey indicated that 39 percent of respondents across thirty-eight countries considered US influence and power a major threat to their countries, compared to 31 percent for both Russia and China.[119] After Donald Trump was in office for only a few months in office, another Pew survey of thirty-seven nations found just 22 percent of their respondents had confidence in him and the United States to do the right thing in international affairs.[120] A year later, a Gallup poll found that approval of US policy and leadership had dropped 40 percent in Canada and 28 percent in Mexico, and that around the world, trust in US leadership had dropped from 48 to 30 percent, putting it below Germany and China.[121] The Biden administration has proclaimed that "America is back," but as this book goes to press the only really positive response to date has been from domestic audiences.

Equally worthy of consideration is the argument that hegemony is unnecessary. According to K. J. Holsti, nineteenth-century European powers in an era of multipolarity successfully devised collaborative forms of stewardship to

---

[117] Chalmers Johnson, *Blowback: The Costs and Consequences of American Empire* (New York: Holt, 2000).

[118] "Islamic Nations Totally Reject Iraq War," *Al-Jazeera, News*, March 2003; Shibley Telhami, "Arab Public Opinion: A Survey in Six Countries," *San Jose Mercury*, 16 March 2003; Susan Page, "Poll: Muslim Countries, Europe Question U.S. Motives," *USA Today*, 21 June 2004; Amin Saikal, "Reactions in the Muslim World to the Iraqi Conflict," in Ramesh Thakur and Waheguru Pal Singh Sidhu, eds., *The Iraq Crisis and World Order: Structural, Institutional and Normative Challenges* (Tokyo: United Nations University Press, 2006), pp. 187–200.

[119] Jacob Poushter and Dorothy Manevich, "Globally, People Point to ISIS and Climate Change as Leading Security Threats," PEW Research Center, 1 August 2017, https://www.pewresearch. org/global/2017/08/01/globally-people-point-to-isis-and-climate-change-as-leading-security-thre ats/; Jamshed Baruah, "U.S. Is Greatest Threat to World Peace," *IDN-InDepth News*, 6 January 2020, https://www.indepthnews.net/index.php/opinion/3227-u-s-is-greatest-threat-to-world-peace (both accessed 27 December 2020).

[120] Richard Wike, Bruce Stokes, Jacob Poushter, and Janell Fetterolf, "U.S. Image Suffers as Publics around World Question Trump's Leadership," PEW Research Center, 26 June 2017, https:// www.pewresearch.org/global/2017/06/26/u-s-image-suffers-as-publics-around-world-question- trumps-leadership/ (accessed 27 December 2020).

[121] Gallup, "Rating World Leaders: 2018," file:///Users/nedlebow/Downloads/RatingWorld Leaders_Report_2018.pdf (accessed 27 December 2020).

create and maintain regional, and to some degree, international order.[122] Simon Reich and Ned Lebow maintain that polyarchy is equally applicable to present-day international relations.[123] Charles Kindleberger's hegemonic stability theory attributes three responsibilities to a hegemon.[124] The first is normative and entails the capacity to shape the policy agenda of global institutions or ad-hoc coalitions.[125] Second is economic management, which demands the management of risk through market signaling (information passed, intentionally or not, among market participants) and intergovernmental negotiations in a variety of venues. The intent, according to Kindleberger, is to stabilize and undergird the functions of the global economic system. Third is sponsorship that finds expression in the creation and maintenance of international institutions that develop and enforce global norms. Sponsorship requires material capabilities but relies primarily on diplomatic skill.

Reich and Lebow document how all three functions of hegemony require contingent forms of influence rather than the blunt exercise of power. Their application is becoming increasingly diffused among states, rather than concentrated in the hands of a single power. These functions are performed by multiple states, sometimes in collaboration with non-state actors. Global governance practices are sharply at odds with the formulations of realists and liberals alike. Western Europeans have made consistent efforts to extend their normative influence by promoting agendas well beyond those with which they are traditionally associated. These include environmental and human rights initiatives, but also security issues and corporate regulation. Asian states, most notably China, have increasingly assumed a custodial role, as is reflected in the China-centered Belt and Road Initiative and the Asian Infrastructure Investment Bank. In the United States, President Obama, and now President Biden, embraced a sponsorship role that ran parallel with efforts to rebuild bridges with traditional allies. The continuing quest for hegemony is not only unnecessary for global order, Reich and Lebow argue, but actually stands in its way.[126]

Another political critique looks at the global order from the standpoint of those who are non-Western, less developed, more vulnerable to political and

---

[122] K. J. Hosti, "Governance without Government: Polyarchy in Nineteenth-Century European International Politics," in Rosenau and Czempiel, eds., *Governance without Government*, pp. 30–57.

[123] Reich and Lebow, *Good-Bye Hegemony!*

[124] Charles P. Kindleberger, *The World in Depression, 1929–1939* (Berkeley: University of California Press, 1973), p. 305.

[125] Michael Barnett and Raymond Duvall, "Power in International Politics," *International Organization* 59, no. 1 (2005), pp. 39–75; Ian Manners, "Normative Power Europe: A Contradiction in Terms?" *Journal of Common Market Studies* 40, no. 2 (2002), pp. 235–58.

[126] Reich and Lebow, *Good-Bye Hegemony!*

economic disruption and exploitation, and all but excluded from any but a passive and disadvantaged role in this order.

Adam Pabst maintains that the liberal world order is illiberal, undemocratic, and intolerant of the cultural values of ordinary people in the West and the rest of the world. It has concentrated power in the hands of a relatively small number of Western leaders, officials, and bankers and Western institutions. These banks and international institutions and those who staff them are not accountable to Western publics, let alone people elsewhere.[127] According to Pabst, the liberal order is a source of economic injustice and social fragmentation. It is also responsible for a "culture war" between globalists and nativists. Far from defending the order and rules, liberal internationalists have consistently violated international law in seeking to impose market fundamentalism and their version of democracy promotion by military means.

In a series of books, Bertrand Badie has developed by far the most detailed and sophisticated critique of the current order from the vantage point of the "Global South."[128] His target is not only the liberal, capitalist order, but what might be considered the informal concert of great powers, which include Russia and China, that made order hierarchical and deprive those at the bottom of any real rewards. Badie writes about the often deliberate use of humiliation as a strategy by dominant Western powers. Humiliation, he argues, is the inevitable consequence of a Westphalian world where states are given legal license to do what their power allows. The conquest, marginalization, and resulting humiliation of political units and peoples was most acute in the era of colonialism but continues down to the present day. It takes the form of neo-colonialism, neo-liberal economic dominance, and a hierarchy of international organizations dominated by great powers that deny all but the wealthy and powerful any role in governance.[129] The ruling "clubs," among them, the UN Security Council, the

---

[127] Adam Pabst, *Liberal World Order and Its Critics* (London: Routledge, 2018).

[128] Bertrand Badie, *Les temps des humiliés: Pathologie des relations internationals* (Paris: Odile Jacob, 2014), now available in English translation: *Humiliation in International Relations, A Pathology of Contemporary International Systems* (Oxford: Hart, Bloomsbury, 2017). See also his *L'état importé. L'occidentalisation de l'ordre politique* (Paris: Fayard, 1992), *Qui gouverne le monde?* (Paris, La Découverte, 2017), *Quand le Sud réinvente le monde* (Paris, La Découverte, 2018), and *Intersocialités: La fin d'un monde géopolitique* (Paris: CNRS Éditions, 2020).

[129] On the reluctance to include non-Western States—Japan and China aside—in global economic and political institutions, see Robert Wade, "Protecting Power: Western States in Global Organization," in David Held and Charles Roger, eds., *Global Governance at Risk* (Cambridge: Polity, 2013), pp. 77–110. There has been expansion, however. See Fen Osler Hampson and Paul Heinbecker, "The 'New Multilateralism' of the Twenty-first Century," *Global Governance* 27, no. 3 (2011), pp. 299–310; Andrew Cooper and Vincent Pouliot, "How Much Is Global Governance Changing? The G20 as International Practice," *Cooperation and Conflict* 50, no. 3 (2015), pp. 334–50. On international organizations and their hierarchies more generally, Ayse Zarakol, "Theorising

G7, the World Bank, the International Monetary Fund, and NATO, confirm and reinforce the low status of the excluded. So too does the double standard that is applied with regard to human rights, economic exchange, and nuclear weapons. Non-proliferation treaties let the great powers and the allies develop weapons but not others, which if they try are labeled "rogue" states led by "immoral" leaders.[130]

Humiliation is a byproduct of inequality, but also a conscious political strategy of those who wield power to rob victims of their dignity and sense of self-worth.[131] Drawing on Nietzsche and Max Scheler, Badie describes how humiliation gives rise to "a powerful envy" that has profound psychological and social consequences for nations and peoples. Humiliation becomes an important part of their collective memory and a "founding" narrative of their identity.[132] This is most pronounced in the Arab World, sub-Saharan Africa, and countries like Iran and Pakistan, but is also evident in Turkey, Russia, and China, countries that have objectively overcome their former stigmatization and subordination. Humiliation has become the leading cause of international violence and conflict. Outraged and angry peoples and states strike out against an order and its perpetrators that they now define as the evil other. Increasing inequality and humiliation give rise to extreme nationalism, fundamentalism, and terrorism. Ironically, globalization and the Internet have made it easier for non-state actors like al-Qaeda and ISIS to mobilize support.

Badie identifies four distinct ways in which humiliation is manifested. The first is associated with colonialism and its aftermath, the memory of which endures throughout the Global South. As noted, the collective memory and identity colonialism constructed is the perceptual lens through which Western power and policies have continued to be viewed. It makes entire people extremely sensitive to discrimination, even when none is intended. The second type is associated with denial of equality and derives from a hierarchy with the great powers at the apex and everyone else well below. Humiliation arises

---

Hierarchies: An Introduction," *International Organization* 70, no. 3 (2017), pp. 623–54; Ian Hurd, *International Organizations: Politics, Law, Practice*, 4th ed. (Cambridge: Cambridge University Press, 2020).

[130] Badie, *Les temps des humiliés*, pp. 11–12.

[131] Ibid., pp. 2–3. On this point, see also Ervin Staub, *The Roots of Evil: The Origins of Genocide and Other Group Violence* (Cambridge: Cambridge University Press, 1989); Evelin G. Lindner, *Making Enemies: Humiliation and International Conflicts* (Boulder, CO: Praeger, 2006); Ayşe Zarakol, *After Defeat: How the East Learned to Live with the West* (Cambridge: Cambridge University Press, 2011), and "What Made the Modern World Hang Together. Socialisation or Stigmatisation?" *International Theory* 6, no. 2 (2014), pp. 311–32.

[132] Badie, *Les temps des humiliés*, pp. 3, 13–14.

when aspiring powers demand, but do not receive, what they consider appropriate respect from the dominant states, and especially the United States. Badie insists that the worldview and foreign policies of Russia and China cannot be understood without understanding their bitter feelings of resentment and the corresponding determination to gain respect. The third type, humiliation by abasement, arises from the formal and informal groupings of mostly Western states and organizations to address global problems, fora from which the weak are largely or completely excluded. The powerful and rich claim to know better than those they are allegedly trying to assist, which further ratchets up the humiliation their actions engender. Finally, there is humiliation through stigmatization. It shares the features of humiliation by denial of equality; the principal difference is that it comes about through the defamation of entire cultures. A prime example is Washington's stigmatization and punishment of Iraq and Iran during the 1980s that set the stage for the subsequent demonization of Islam.

Badie contends that the cumulative effect of these several forms of humiliation is to make people become angry readily and to rebel against the American order or feel sympathy for those who do. People in Beirut, Karachi, and Djakarta do not necessarily hate the United States or Americans, but they feel powerless and strike out against the country and culture because it is perceived to be at the top of an unjust hierarchy. This is among the most significant consequences of American primacy since the end of the Cold War and the collapse of the Soviet Union, but it is also a product of post–Cold War US military interventions in Afghanistan and Iraq, continuing support of authoritarian regimes that use violence on a large scale against their peoples or neighbors, and drone strikes that put people everywhere in turbulent countries at greater risk. The kind of blowback these policies have produced, Badie observes, was never envisaged by Cold War triumphalists.

Badie's arguments are seconded, at least in part, by Patrick Porter and Amitav Acharya. They concur that disorder is not only a product of American policy. China, in their view, has acted equally irresponsibly. It has also sought status and material rewards at the expense of others. The "rules" of the international system encourage this kind of behavior and accordingly need serious reexamination. The larger problem, both contend, is the degree of inequality in regional and international orders, and this in an age where equality has become the dominant principle of justice. Peoples and states at the bottom of the hierarchy are correspondingly more resentful of their relative deprivation of wealth, status, and physical well-being. A hierarchical order in which those at the bottom—rightly or wrongly—believe they have no stake in the system is a precarious order and one that must increasingly rely on coercion to keep the discontented in line.

Such a strategy must ultimately prove futile and invite a larger and more serious upheaval than would a negotiated restructuring.[133]

What Can Be Done?

We argue that declining orders are marked by a breakdown in solidary. This is most often attributable to elite violation of rule packages and the vividness it creates in the minds of ordinary people about the contradictions between practice and the principles of justice on which their orders rest. Consistent elite violations encourage others to follow suit and to violate norms, rules, and laws in pursuit of short-term self-interest. Communal solidarity is quickly undermined, exacerbating existing conflicts and creating new ones. In the longer term, orders and solidarity are threatened when foundational principles of justice, or formulations of them, lose their relative appeal or legitimacy. When both processes occur and are reinforcing, orders of all kinds become increasingly fragile.

Critiques of the US-sponsored postwar order do not analyze it in terms of our analytical categories. Many, if not most, of the critiques we have discussed accuse the self-proclaimed hegemon of having violated its own rule package. Instead of providing security for others, it is a major cause of their insecurity. Instead of stabilizing financial arrangements and markets, the United States has exploited its position in narrowly selfish ways that endanger the well-being of others. It has gone from being a lender of the last resort to the borrower of the first resort. It has fostered, and sometimes imposed via the so-called Washington Consensus, a liberal economic regime that benefits the rich at the expense of the poor.

Hegemony and hierarchies are rooted in the principle of fairness. As noted in earlier chapters, this principle assumes that those who contribute the most to society should be disproportionately rewarded. This unequal distribution is justified on the basis of the security, well-being, and other benefits the privileged elite allegedly provides for the less fortunate. There is a trade-off here based on the expectation that relative inequality is acceptable when it promotes greater absolute well-being and satisfaction for all. In ancient Greece and imperial China, fairness resulted in orders in which the hegemons received honor from others in return for providing security and material rewards. The powerful gained status but were constrained by elaborate rule packages that prohibited

---

[133] Porter, *False Promise of the Liberal Order*; Acharya, *End of American World Order*; Cooley and Nexon, *Exit from Hegemony*; Zarakol, "Theorising Hierarchies."

their exploitation of the greater relative power and required them to earn the respect of others by catering to their interest. Powerful and weak alike gained from such orders and recognized their benefits.

The current order, whether we describe it as the US-dominated liberal order, or more widely as a kind of minimal great power condominium, satisfies only one condition of a fairness-based order. It provides special privileges to the powerful, and does so at expense of weaker parties. The United States, its Western European allies, Russia, and China claim privileges on the basis of fairness but abuse their power in blatant ways. Most of the benefits increasingly flow in one direction. It is hardly surprising that they have generated so much opposition, and that so much of it is directed toward the United States. As Badie observes, the world's most powerful nation is the natural target for the disenfranchised, disgruntled, and humiliated.

Many American liberals claim that the United States lives up to the expectations of a fairness-based order. They further contend that by providing security and the conditions for successful development the Western order has enabled the kind of absolute improvement in security and material well-being that justifies American privileges and rewards. There are undoubtedly countries and regions where this argument resonates (e.g., some parts of Europe, Israel, South Korea, Taiwan) but many more where it does not. Public opinion polls cited earlier in this chapter indicate that publics in America's closest allies have significantly revised their opinion of its role in world affairs. It is no longer seen as an upholder of a system from which they benefit but a principal cause of insecurity and conflict. Liberal academics are not the relevant constituency for determining the justness of the liberal order. States and their peoples are, and the majority have found the United States and its order wanting.

One of the defining features of modernity is the extent to which the principle of fairness has given way to that of equality. Both are present and valued, but equality is increasingly seen as the more important of the two and the domains in which it is thought applicable have been extended. This process began in the West and was an underlying cause of political change. Almost everywhere, monarchies and aristocracies gave way to democracies. Not all of these democracies survived, but it is fair to say that everywhere in the West—and now in much of the rest of the world—democracy is perceived as the only legitimate form of government. As noted, the application of the principle of equality to regional and international relations was a more recent development. Fairness predominated, and still does to a large degree even though equality in principle has increasingly become the norm. We noted as evidence the perceived need for those demanding special status and privileges (e.g., India, Brazil, South Africa) to couch their demands in the language of equality. Hierarchies seen as exploitative are that much more unacceptable in a world where equality has become the dominant principle of justice. In such a world, *relative* wealth, status, longevity, and physical well-being assume a much greater importance.

What is to be done? In our view, a stable international order must be more equal in its governance, rely as much on bottom-up as top-down governance, give a wider range of actors strong incentives to support and participate, and significantly reduce the degree of alienation, humiliation, and anger felt by many non-Western peoples. As we will see, many of the suggested reforms fail to address, or do so only in part, these needs.

International political economists have advanced proposals for, among other things, corporate social responsibility and stakeholder capitalism, state capitalism, and using climate change as a lever for reform and redistribution, as well as a variety of technical and redistributive measures.[134] Even some successful capitalists now fashionably argue for reform and sustainability investment.[135] Most of these are not linked or embedded in the kinds of political changes and structures that would address the problem of order.

There are many voices urging a more fundamental rethinking about the nature of order and how it might be reformed or restructured. Amitav Acharya argues that the United States and its Western allies "must give up exclusive privileges" in return for "the trust and cooperation" of the rest of the world.[136] He envisages what he calls a "multiplex" world. It would consist of what remains of the American liberal order plus other emergent orders. In the world he envisages, standing and influence are not based on the number of powers or their relative power, but rather on the relationships among them. These may be bilateral or multilateral and embedded in institutions and their norms. Order will be hierarchical, but the relative standing of states will reflect more their influence than their power.

There would be no hegemon in Acharya's envisaged order but an increase in the number of actors who matter. Other features of the multiplex world include a global shift in economic power from "the West to the Rest," regional powers like China and India playing a more assertive role, new forms of globalization, and a less "US-centric" world in every respect. Regions and regionalism

[134] Elton Kessell, "Competition in the US Free Market Economy," *World Affairs* 15, no. 4 (2011), pp. 52–67; Thomas Piketty, *Capital in the Twenty-first Century*, trans. Arthur Goldhammer (Cambridge, MA: Harvard University Press, 2014), and *The Economics of Inequality* (Cambridge, MA: Harvard University Press, 2015); special issue on "The Future of Capitalism," *Foreign Affairs* (January/February 2020).

[135] Ray Dalio, *Principles of Navigating Big Debt Crises* (Westport, CT: Bridgewater, 2018); Caleb Silver, "The Next 20 Years, According to Ray Dalio," *Investopedia*, 16 October 2019, https://www.investopedia.com/ray-dalio-on-the-future-of-the-global-economy-markets-and-technology-4773303.

[136] Acharya, *End of American World Order*, p. xi.

will play a more important role in governance.[137] This will result in a "patch-work of institutions" and different and partly overlapping layers of order not under American control nor necessarily responsive to American initiative. The resulting political and economic arrangements and multilevel and multiregional governance would allow for greater pluralism in values, approaches to develop-ment, and even understandings of modernity.[138]

Acharya's proposals are implicitly rooted in a bottom-up understanding of order. Local actors, by no means all of the major regional powers, are expected to take on new functions, and play active roles in regional orders that emerge in part by negotiation and in part as emergent properties.[139] Acharya gives no indi-cation of how this state of affairs might be achieved and provides no reasons why it would prove to be a more stable and consensual order.

Badie offered perhaps the most negative assessment of global order. He nev-ertheless suggests that hostility and violence might be muted if Washington made serious efforts to redress the humiliation felt by middle-range powers and to include them in global decision-making. More generally, the West must rec-ognize and respect political, economic, and cultural diversity; it must do what it can to address the material and status needs of non-Western populations and states, and must make its governing institutions truly multilateral and more le-gitimate in the eyes of those who now feel humiliated. However, he sees little incentive—international or domestic—for American leaders to move in this di-rection.[140] Of equal importance, Badie believes that Western analysts and leaders are focused on the wrong source of disorder. In today's world, he argues, order is more shaped and more threatened by social dynamics than it is by political outputs. This is why the gap between the imagined order and the real one is getting larger and larger and will continue to do so until this understanding is realized and acted on.[141]

Michael Barnett and Martha Finnemore, like the English School, believe that any successful international order must ultimately rest on common values and preferences.[142] Hendrik Spruyt, in his study of historical orders in the Middle

---

[137] See also, Oliver Stuenkel, *Post-Western World: How Emerging Powers are Remaking Global Order* (London: Polity, 2016).

[138] Acharya, *End of American World Order*, pp. 132–61. See also Pabst, *Liberal World Order and Its Critics*, who proposes a radical reconstruction of world order on the basis of cultural commonwealths that build social bonds and cross-border cultural ties that enable international trust and cooperation.

[139] Acharya, *End of American World Order*, pp. 99–131, building on Bjorn Hettne and András Inotai, *The New Regionalism: Implications for Global Development and International Security* (Helsinki: UNU World Institute for Development Economics Research, 1994).

[140] Badie, *Les temps des humiliés*, pp. 223–34.

[141] Badie, *Inter-socialités*.

[142] Michael Barnett and Martha Finnemore, *Rules for the World: International Organizations is Global Politics* (Ithaca, NY: Cornell University Press, 2001).

East and in Southeast and East Asia, finds that collective beliefs were critical to them. They paradoxically allowed for greater heterogeneity than is possible in the modern state system.[143] We should note that these historical orders were regional and largely excluded political units and peoples with radically different beliefs and forms of political organization. The historical record does not bode well for present-day efforts to construct a legitimate order in our deeply divided world, and all the more so because regions can no longer live in relative isolation from one another. There must be some order at the international level in which states and regions feel comfortable about participating.

These circumstances and several critiques of existing orders, most notably of the American-led one, indicate the hazards of top-down orders that are imposed, not negotiated. The liberal order is, of course, both imposed and negotiated. Washington consulted with its major trading partners but more or less dictated its preferred terms on issues of importance. It subsequently sought with much mixed success to draw in other states or impose it on those it deemed powerless to resist. China's nascent order is also a mix of both, with perhaps quite a visible hand of coercion at the outset.

Do bottom-up orders offer more promise? To the extent that they are truly emergent orders based on cooperation and shared cultural values, they are more likely to achieve legitimacy. However, there is no reason to think that regional orders, organized around or by regional powers, would be any less coercive than their top-down counterparts. In present circumstances there seems no way of organizing order without some degree of coercion. Our goal then should be to minimize it as far as possible. Perhaps the best way to achieve this end is to structure orders in which the incentives to use violence and other forms of coercion decline for greater and lesser powers alike. Such an arrangement would combine bottom-up with top-down orders, regional with international, involve extensive negotiation at all levels, and rely more on carrots than sticks. Whatever arrangements come into place would attempt to address the security, material, and status needs of those who are currently most deprived, but also speak to the needs of regional and great powers that feel undervalued.

Progress of this kind would entail a number of bilateral as well as multilateral agreements put in place after the widest possible consultation. Above all, it requires a shift in thinking in many of the world's capitals. This is essential but, alas, the most difficult task of all. It is most needed in the United States, Russia, and China because presumably they would have to take leading roles in this process.

Let us be clear that we are advocating a multilateral process but not the kind of multilateralism traditionally envisaged by liberals. Many liberals believe

---

[143] Spruyt, *World Imagined*.

that the current American-dominated order might be preserved if the United States were to adhere to its rule package and return to multilateralism. It was long considered to be part and parcel of the liberal order; John Ruggie, among others, described it constitutive of that order.[144] John Ikenberry, perhaps the most prominent liberal critic of the existing order, argues that Washington could secure more influence on a range of issues in return for once again embedding its governance in institutions, making it more difficult to exercise its power arbitrarily and at their expense.[145] However, multilateralism in itself is not a solution unless it involves other, less powerful actors in a meaningful way so that they have an important say in shaping order and its institutions. Multilateralism can even be retrograde if it allows Western powers to collaborate more effectively against the rest, as so many Washington-sponsored international institutions do. It must be a more open kind of multilateralism that incorporates other voices and addresses their needs.

Similar voices have been raised in China. In an April 2021 speech, President Xi Jinping affirmed that the world needs to "uphold true multilateralism" and make the global governance system fairer and more equitable by following the principles of extensive consultation, joint contribution, and shared benefits. In a veiled criticism of the United States, he said that we must not let the rules set by one or a few countries be imposed on others, or allow unilateralism pursued by certain countries to set the pace for the whole world. What the world needs today is justice, not hegemony. Big countries should behave in a manner befitting their status and with a greater sense of responsibility.[146] The question for China, however, is the extent to which its action can match its words. Chinese policy announcements are often normatively appealing, as is this one, but they are not always translated into action.

There is no obvious way to convince leaders to recognize that national interests can only be pursued satisfactorily within a community whose members feel some degree of solidarity. The most realistic way to build this recognition is through small steps of successful cooperation that help build community and shared identities. It is a long-term process, but one that is worth embarking upon given the current disorder and its threats to everyone's security and well-being. The remaining chapters of our book explore pathways toward this end.

---

[144] John Ruggie, "Multilateralism: The Anatomy of an Institution," *International Organization* 46, no. 3 (1992), pp. 561–98.

[145] Ikenberry, *Liberal Leviathan*, p. 101. Also Victor Cha, *Power Play: The Origin of the American Alliance System in Asia* (Princeton, NJ: Princeton University Press, 2016).

[146] Xi Jinping, "Pulling Together through Adversity and toward a Shared Future for All," keynote speech at the Boao Forum for Asia Annual Conference, 20 April 2021, https://www.fmprc.gov.cn/mfa_eng/zxxx_662805/t1870296.shtml (accessed 6 May 2021).

7

Justice and Order between America and China

In part I of our book, we argued that justice—and its foundational principles of equality and fairness—is essential to any stable political order. Orders must rest on and partially instantiate accepted principles of justice to have any prospect of building legitimacy, solidarity, and voluntary compliance with their laws, rules, and norms. Bilateral relationships are no exception to this general rule, and all the more so when they are embedded in a larger society. We accordingly build on our earlier discussion of Western and Chinese principles of justice to frame and apply fairness and equality in ways that would be comprehensible and acceptable to leaders and peoples of both China and the United States. We do so with two general goals in mind. We aspire to construct the foundations for Sino-American rapprochement and a more stable and mutually beneficial relationship between these countries. Closer relations between them are also an essential prerequisite for any attempt to reform or change the structure and practices of international order. We take up this even more ambitious project in chapter 8.

Discourses of justice are already central to Sino-American relations, but the two sides deploy them differently, talk past each other, and each feels it is being treated unjustly. Since the Trump administration, the United States has been fixated on fairness, framed rather narrowly as US hegemony and everybody else kowtowing to it. Trump and Biden have dismissed or ignored the principle of equality, to which China strongly appeals. China, for its part, has yet to take the justice in this relationship seriously, despite its professed desire for international justice. It has long demanded equality in the relationship but has neglected fairness and failed to integrate equality and fairness into an overall framework of justice. The Sino-American relationship needs to build on mutually acceptable understandings of justice that incorporate and balance fairness *and* equality. There are obvious trade-offs between the two principles, and they provide some

Justice and International Order: East and West. Richard Ned Lebow and Feng Zhang, Oxford University Press.
© Oxford University Press 2022. DOI: 10.1093/oso/9780197598399.003.0007

room for negotiation as to what is important and how they are to be balanced in different substantive domains.

Rethinking and recalibration is unlikely at the moment. As this book goes to press, the United States is pursuing a strategy of competition toward China, distinct from the engagement strategy of Nixon through Obama. In the words of Biden's secretary of state Antony Blinken, "Our relationship with China will be competitive when it should be, collaborative when it can be, and adversarial when it must be."[1] China blames the United States for worsening the relationship and sees no need for undertaking a critical self-evaluation. It is nevertheless important to lay the foundations for a more positive relationship in the hope that conditions will change and that leaders in both countries will become ready to rethink their relationship.

We offer a framework of justice for Sino-American relations and how policies informed by this framework can contribute to a healthy relationship. We advance a theory of positive competition and reciprocal cooperation between the two countries by drawing on our earlier comparative study of Chinese and Western conceptions of justice. We illustrate the value of our framework by examining some of the pressing disputes in six sectors of Sino-American relations, applying the principles of equality and fairness in each dispute. We show how different understandings or applications of the principles of fairness and equality are at the core of Sino-American conflict, how they lead to exaggerated notions of aggression and intransigence, and how recognition of this problem is a critical first step in improving relations.

Benign Competition

Since the time of the Trump administration, competition has been the watchword of American attitude toward China. In intellectual history the idea of competition has much deeper roots in the West than in China. Liberalism, as we saw in chapter 5, is particularly hospitable to this idea, as it is theorized as the mechanism responsible for economic and intellectual development. Liberals acknowledge that competition will inevitably breed conflict. They welcome the kind of competition and conflict that is effectively constrained by rules and norms, such as those that guarantee the equality of actors, protection of property rights, and enforcement of contracts in the capitalist economy. Competition is thought beneficial when it rewards clever and industrial actors and produces efficiency.

---

[1] Antony J. Blinken, "A Foreign Policy for the American People," Washington, DC, 3 March 2021, https://www.state.gov/a-foreign-policy-for-the-american-people/ (accessed 14 June 2021).

This discourse, which has assumed the status of ideology, suffuses the American economic, political, and intellectual life. Matt Pottinger, a principal architect of the Trump administration's China policy, rightly observed that competition is not a dirty word in America and that freedom and competition lie at the core of America's democracy and market economy. Now that America had brought competition to the forefront of its China policy, he warned, China's failure to acknowledge this fact would lead to misunderstandings and miscalculations.[2] None of this rhetoric appealed to Beijing. Nevertheless, Chinese policymakers seemed resigned to accept competition as a new facet of the relationship, but insisted that it must be benign. Seasoned American observers agreed. Former treasury secretary Henry Paulson, for one, urged keeping Sino-American competition healthy, not pernicious.[3]

Benign competition is China's ostensible preference, but there is a deep current in Chinese thinking that mirrors Washington's penchant for competition and confrontation. Chinese hawks have been screeching for competition since the end of the Cold War, and some have called for Beijing to overtake and displace the United States as the leading power in Asia.[4] Since 2017 a new discourse on struggle against hostile international forces has arisen in response to the change of the US strategy from engagement to competition.[5] Although the policies of the Trump administration were a direct catalyst, this discourse also harks back to the undercurrents of a sort of "struggle philosophy" that is most notable in Mao's thinking.

What makes for benign competition? Is it possible for America and China to realize the liberal ideal of delivering the benefit of competition while keeping conflict within bounds? We contend that liberalism, in its current form, stands in the way of benign competition. The fundamental reason is that modern liberalism is rooted in the assumption of the autonomous and egoistic individual with the slightest concern for other individuals with whom they come

[2] Keegan Elmer, "U.S. Tells China: We Want Competition . . . but Also Cooperation," *Politico*, 1 October 2018, https://www.politico.com/story/2018/10/01/us-china-competition-not-cooperation-854874 (accessed 13 February 2021).

[3] Henry M. Paulson Jr., "Henry M. Paulson, Jr., Proposes Policy of 'Targeted Reciprocity' Toward China," 16 November 2020, https://www.paulsoninstitute.org/press_release/henry-m-paulson-jr-proposes-policy-of-targeted-reciprocity-toward-china/ (accessed 2 March 2021).

[4] See, for example, Liu Mingfu, *Zhongguo meng: zhongguo de mubiao, daolu ji zixinli* [The China Dream: China's Goals, Roads and Self-Confidence] (Beijing: Zhongguo youyi chuban gongsi, 2010).

[5] Xi Jinping, "Juesheng quanmian jiancheng xiaokang shehui, duoqu xinshidai Zhongguo tese shehui zhuyi weida shengli" [Winning a Comprehensive Well-Off Society, Seize the Great Victory of Socialism with Chinese Characteristics in the New Era], Report to the 19th National Congress of the Communist Party of China, 18 October 2017, http://jhsjk.people.cn/article/29613458 (accessed 18 October 2021).

into contact or the relationships and communities of which they form a part. Competition, on this assumption, is geared toward the maximization of one's self-interest; in international relations, the equivalent is states' maximization of their national interest—hardly a recipe for healthy competition. Nor is China's "struggle philosophy," which is a wholly negative doctrine of preserving oneself against external adversaries.

Other traditions in Western and Chinese history offer more relevant insights into the possibility of benign competition. One of the most valuable Western traditions in this regard is tragedy. Developed by Athenian poets in the fifth century BCE, tragedy is one of the West's oldest conceptual and ethical frameworks. Thucydides applied it to international relations in his celebrated account of the Peloponnesian War. A tragic perspective, as we explained in chapter 5, alerts us to four kinds of tragedy in international relations: those of unmerited suffering, the result of character, hard choices, and moral dilemma.

Tragedies of character are most often associated with hubris, a form of excessive self-confidence. Thucydides attributes the catastrophic decisions made by Athens in the Peloponnesian War to hubris. Confucians likewise criticize hubris; Kongzi regards modesty (*sun* 孫), the opposite of hubris, as a key virtue of the exemplary person.[6] Hubris is a fault visible in both Washington and Beijing, albeit in different degrees. Trump, with his impulsiveness, willfulness, and sheer deceit and corruption, epitomized the tragedy of character in recent American politics more glaringly than any other leader.[7] A notable part of China's foreign policy discourse since 2012 has been propagandist, tendentious, and counterproductive. A prime example of this new style is the so-called wolf warrior diplomacy pressed into service in the fight with the United States and other Western countries over the origin and handling of the COVID-19 pandemic.[8]

Tragedies of hard choice arise from scarce resources. Status is an example of such scarce resource and, as we argued in *Taming Sino-American Rivalry*, the quest for status is a principal cause of Sino-American tension.[9] We suggest later an approach based on the principle of fairness for ameliorating Sino-American status competition.

[6] Roger T. Ames and Henry Rosemont Jr., *The Analects of Confucius: A Philosophical Translation* (New York: Ballantine Books, 1998), p. 188.

[7] See John Bolton, *The Room Where It Happened: A White House Memoir* (New York: Simon & Schuster, 2020); Mary L. Trump, *Too Much and Never Enough: How My Family Created the World's Most Dangerous Man* (New York: Simon & Schuster, 2020); James Comey, *A Higher Loyalty: Truth, Lies, and Leadership* (London: Macmillan, 2018).

[8] *Economist*, "China's 'Wolf Warrior' Diplomacy Gamble," 28 May 2020, https://www.economist.com/china/2020/05/28/chinas-wolf-warrior-diplomacy-gamble (accessed 24 February 2021).

[9] Feng Zhang and Richard Ned Lebow, *Taming Sino-American Rivalry* (Oxford: Oxford University Press, 2020).

Tragedies of moral dilemma derived from conflicting values are the most dangerous, for they are apt to generate an unwillingness to compromise. Conflict is inevitable if one side is overcommitted to one's values, attempts to impose one's beliefs and practice on others, and fails to respect their values and practices. America and China must not allow differences over values and political systems to stand in the way of reaching pragmatic compromise over interests. For this they will need to commit themselves to pluralism, as we shall show later.

The larger lesson of tragedy is that people and political units only function effectively as members of communities. Communities constitute individuals and political units by conferring recognition, assigning or confirming roles, and enabling affiliations. Neither people nor states can formulate interests intelligently outside of them. Their first commitment is to uphold their community and its values because they make possible security, wealth, and status. Tragedy also alerts us to the parochial nature of our beliefs, especially of our conceptions of justice. It also makes us aware of the often unpredictable consequences of our actions. These reinforcing insights have the potential to make people more tolerant, cautious, respectful of uncertainty, and humble. America and China need to formulate their interests in the context of the regional and international societies of which they form a part and cock a critical eyebrow at their preconceived beliefs and interests. A foreign policy that is reasonably tolerant of the other side, pragmatically cautious in its execution, and humble in style will serve both sides well.

America's own tradition of exceptionalism, perhaps surprisingly, offers the second intellectual resource for benign competition. American exceptionalism is the idea that, being morally and politically unique, the United States has a destiny and a duty to expand its values and practices around the world—above all freedom, democracy, the rule of law, and capitalism.[10] This notion is often criticized, rightly, for being self-serving, hypocritical, and worse, responsible for a militaristic interventionism that has often plagued American foreign policy. In early US history, however, American exceptionalism primarily took a defensive or passive form, embodied in a tendency to "unfold into an exemplary state separate from the corrupt and fallen world, letting others emulate it as best they can."[11] John Quincy Adams famously declared that America "does not go abroad in search of monsters to destroy."[12]

---

[10] Godfrey Hodgson, *The Myth of American Exceptionalism* (New Haven, CT: Yale University Press, 2009), p. 10.

[11] Anders Stephanson, *Manifest Destiny: American Expansionism and the Empire of Right* (New York: Hill and Wang, 1995), p. xii.

[12] David M. Kennedy, "Editor's Introduction," in George C. Herring, *From Colony to Superpower: U.S. Foreign Relations since 1776* (Oxford: Oxford University Press, 2008), pp. xiii–xvi, at p. xv.

America has long claimed to be a special nation with a special mission. Its presidents have routinely proclaimed that it is a model for the rest of the world and that it leads by example, not by compulsion. President Biden was aware of the promise of exemplification. He announced repeatedly, including in his January 2021 inaugural address, that "We will lead not merely by the example of our power but by the power of our example."[13] This remark was a rebuke of Trump's "America first" doctrine based on naked power and nationalism. It harked back to the tradition of American foreign policy that foregrounds exemplification as a source of influence. Exemplification, in contrast to the blunt instruments of force and power, offers an indirect approach to Sino-American competition, retaining the element of necessary competition while cushioning it against unremitting conflict.

Interestingly, the Chinese tradition also contains a notion of "leading by example" that is very similar to the American tradition. Kongzi remarks that "if those who are distant will not submit, simply refine your culture and virtue in order to attract them."[14] Rejecting forced submission and conquest, he upholds Chinese culture and virtue as a centripetal force that will draw foreign peoples to the Chinese center. This thought has provided an enduring inspiration for the subsequent Chinese claim, repeated up to the present day, that China has historically renounced violent conquest and active transformation of foreign lands as a foreign policy objective.[15] If foreign transformation came about, it was not because of imposition or manipulation but because of China's serving as a model and others' willing emulation of it.[16]

Thus, important traditions in American and Chinese history share the insight that values and ideals are best to be advanced by model emulation, not by imposition or coercion. Foreign policy begins at home, not with entanglements abroad. This is not a difficult precept to follow. At the start of the Biden administration, American officials seemed to be designing a new China policy precisely on this basis. In January 2021, National Security Advisor Jake Sullivan pinpointed refurbishing American democracy and reinvigorating American

---

[13] White House, "Inaugural Address by President Joseph R. Biden, Jr.," 20 January 2021, https://www.whitehouse.gov/briefing-room/speeches-remarks/2021/01/20/inaugural-address-by-presid ent-joseph-r-biden-jr/ (accessed 13 February 2021).

[14] Edward Slingerland, trans., *Confucius Analects: With Selections from Traditional Commentaries* (Indianapolis: Hackett, 2003), p. 192.

[15] Feng Zhang, "The Rise of Chinese Exceptionalism in International Relations," *European Journal of International Relations* 19, no. 2 (2013), pp. 305–28.

[16] Chih-yu Shih, "The West Is Not the West: Identifying the Self in Oriental Modernity," *Cambridge Review of International Affairs* 23, no. 4 (2010), pp. 537–60, at p. 548.

technological innovation as two pillars of this policy.[17] Earlier he had remarked that Biden's foreign policy would focus on revitalizing the United States at home, rehabilitating frayed alliances, and building a team of democracies to solve the world's biggest challenges.[18]

For its part, China has always insisted on the priority of domestic development, as reflected in the slogan "the rejuvenation of the Chinese nation." In July 2020, State Counselor and Foreign Minister Wang Yi declared that China never intends to challenge or replace the United States; what it cares most about is to improve the livelihood of its people. He further asserted that "China does not replicate any model of other countries, nor does it export its own to others."[19] The American and Chinese discourses converge on their focus of exemplification; the test will be in the practice.

In addition to tragedy and exemplification, a third intellectual resource for benign competition is our earlier excavation of theories of fairness developed by Chinese and Western philosophers. Two conceptions of fairness deserve consideration: fairness based on merit, virtue, or status, and fairness based on reciprocal benefits or obligations. In the domestic context, status in the first conception refers to aristocracy or nobility; the international equivalent would be past achievements of great powers. As claims based on nobility have lost its legitimacy in modern politics, so justifications for future status on the basis of past accomplishments are becoming unpersuasive in international relations. What is more compelling is present-day performance and future prospects.

The conception of fairness based on merit or virtue teaches us that in a benign competition, America and China should focus on the merit and virtue of their foreign policies—that is, the benefits their policies can bring to themselves as well as regional and international societies and the ethical grounding of these policies. They may even consider a fair regional and international "division of labor," although they must take care to eschew making invidious comparisons. Both Mengzi and Xunzi, as we saw in chapter 3, expound a conception of fairness on the basis of division of labor. Mengzi holds that the diversity and differences among the myriad things in the world make it possible to attain a harmonizing division of labor that fosters human community. Xunzi believes that division

[17] United States Institute of Peace, "Passing the Baton 2021: Securing America's Future Together," 29 January 2021, https://www.usip.org/sites/default/files/Passing-the-Baton-2021-Transcript-FINAL.pdf (accessed 14 February 2021).

[18] David A. Wemer, "Adviser on Biden's Foreign Policy: Start at Home and Repair Alliances," Atlantic Council, 21 August 2020, https://www.atlanticcouncil.org/blogs/new-atlanticist/adviser-on-bidens-foreign-policy-start-at-home-and-repair-alliances/ (accessed 14 February 2021).

[19] Wang Yi, "Stay on the Right Track and Keep Pace with the Times to Ensure the Right Direction of China-US Relations," Beijing, July 2020, https://www.fmprc.gov.cn/mfa_eng/wjb_663304/wjbz_663308/2461_663310/t1796302.shtml (accessed 10 February 2021).

can achieve harmony as long as it is just. In the West, Plato imagines a division of labor among the three classes of guardians, auxiliaries, and producers as the pathway to justice and harmony.[20] The conception of fairness based on merit or virtue, carried out by policies in a proper division of labor between America and China, holds the promise of at once easing the zero-sum nature of their competition and reinforcing healthy competition through exemplification, as suggested earlier. We shall apply this conception of fairness to the amelioration of Sino-American status competition.

The conception of fairness based on reciprocal benefits or obligations sheds an enlightening light on the relations between great and lesser powers. The Greek concept of *hēgemonia* chimes with the Chinese concept of *wangdao* to offer a vision of legitimate hierarchy in international relations. As we explained in chapter 5, *hēgemonia* describes an honorific status conferred on a leading power by others because of the service it has provided to the community. It represents a clientelist approach to politics: the powerful attain honor by providing benefits to the weak; the latter willingly accept their inferior status in return for economic and security benefits and the constraints such an arrangement imposes on the powerful. *Wangdao*, or humane authority, is the approach whereby the ruler uses his virtue to put humaneness into effect and make others submit; humaneness and morality are expected to bring practical benefits to those who accept the ruler's leadership. The "hegemons" in both cases provided security and material advantages to other members of the community in return for the honor and acceptance of their leadership. This kind of clientelist hierarchy cleverly seeks to construct trade-offs between the needs for security and well-being on the one hand and status on the other. As we will show later, this approach is useful for managing Sino-American competition centered on the American alliance system in Asia.

Reciprocity and Cooperation

In the preceding section we offered tragedy, exemplification, and fairness as three intellectual resources for guiding a positive form of competition between America and China. But positive competition will not by itself suffice to effect a productive relationship; what it can hope to accomplish is to stabilize the relationship and minimize the risk of conflict. A healthy relationship also requires

[20] Aryeh Kosman, "Justice and Virtue: The *Republic*'s Inquiry into Proper Difference," in G. R. F. Ferrari, ed., *The Cambridge Companion to Plato's Republic* (Cambridge: Cambridge University Press, 2007), pp. 116–37.

cooperation. In this section, we develop a conception of Sino-American cooperation that is at odds with much of the conventional scholarship.

Our guiding concept is reciprocity, and we apply it to interest and obligation. Reciprocity has been shown by philosophers, biologists, psychologists, anthropologists, and political scientists to be the driving force of social cooperation. Human societies need cooperation to survive, let alone to thrive. Our earlier discussion of justice framed reciprocity as a bridge between fairness and equality. Many animal groups and human societies are hierarchical, with those at the top receiving more of whatever is valued. It is common for alpha males in animal societies to redistribute what they receive so that everyone gets something. Fairness is acknowledged, but also softened. This practice is central to fairness-based hierarchies where those who receive honor are expected to provide security and material advantages to those who honor them.

Reciprocity in a more general sense is the norm for all human cultures, although its specific expression varies across epochs and cultures. Cooperation may be based on friendship and solidarity but requires a norm of reciprocity to be sustained because it constrains and may even prevent narrow formulations of self-interest. Failure to reciprocate threatens cooperation among individuals and societies.[21]

Reciprocity is the golden rule of cooperation in Confucianism. The Confucian concept for reciprocity is *shu* 恕 (putting oneself in the other's place). As chapter 3 explained, *shu* contains a negative and a positive principle. The negative principle says: "Do not impose upon others what you yourself do not want."[22] The positive principle stipulates: "Humane persons establish others in seeking to establish themselves and promote others in seeking to get there themselves."[23] And further, "Being able to take what is near at hand as an analogy could perhaps be called the method of humaneness."[24]

Confucian reciprocity teaches that humane persons identify themselves with the whole myriad things of the world and harmonize their desires with the desires of the world. They extend their affection from near to far through a continuous gradation, eventually making it permeate the whole world. By caring for others while trying to realize themselves, and by trying to achieve public interests in this way, humane persons overcome their personal desires without eliminating them. *Shu* is not altruism since it starts with oneself, but it

---

[21] David B. Wong, *Natural Moralities: A Defense of Pluralistic Relativism* (Oxford: Oxford University Press, 2006), pp. 47–50.

[22] Ames and Rosemont, *The Analects of Confucius*, p. 153.

[23] Ibid., p. 110.

[24] Ibid.

acquires an other-regarding generosity as it requires taking into consideration the interests of others.[25]

Daniel Bell derives from Confucian thought two forms of reciprocity that might operate in international hierarchy—weak reciprocity whereby hierarchical relations between states are mutually advantageous but fragile and strong reciprocity whereby two states come to think of their relationship from the perspective of both sides, no longer from the perspective of their narrow self-interest.[26] The latter, which imparts more stability to the relationship, is true Confucian reciprocity. It found, in different historical periods, practical expressions in imperial China's tributary relations with its neighbors.[27]

As we noted in chapter 5, Confucian reciprocity finds a close counterpart with the ancient Greek concept of *xenia* (guest friendship). *Xenia* required people to offer food and shelter to visitors, and visitors not to abuse the hospitality they received. These obligations were deemed sufficiently important that hospitality was made one of the epithets of the father of the gods: Zeus Xenios.[28] Equally important was the practice of gift exchange. Featured prominently in Homer, it describes reciprocal gift giving that binds the recipients and their descendants as friends who must cooperate in the future.[29]

Modern liberalism differs dramatically with its presumption of the autonomous individual and transactions among such individuals in a market society. Confucian reciprocity is embodied in the specific roles of people rather than in their transactions. The beneficiary role evokes a set of responses appropriate to that position. They include gratitude, obedience, attentiveness, and so on, whereas the benefactor must demonstrate such attitudes as care, sensitivity, and courage.[30] This is relational reciprocity predicated on obligatory role performance, not individualistic reciprocity based on contract obligations.

---

[25] Roger T. Ames, *Confucian Role Ethics: A Vocabulary* (Honolulu: University of Hawai'i Press, 2011), p. 195.

[26] Daniel A. Bell and Wang Pei, *Just Hierarchy: Why Social Hierarchies Matter in China and the Rest of the World* (Princeton, NJ: Princeton University Press, 2020), ch. 3.

[27] David C. Kang, *East Asia before the West: Five Centuries of Trade and Tribute* (New York: Columbia University Press, 2010); Feng Zhang, *Chinese Hegemony: Grand Strategy and International Institutions in East Asian History* (Stanford, CA: Stanford University Press, 2015).

[28] Moses I. Finley, *The World of Odysseus* (New York: Viking, 1978), pp. 99–101.

[29] Marshall Sahlins, *Stone Age Economics* (Chicago: Aldine-Atherton, 1972); W. Donlan, "Reciprocities in Homer," *Classical World* 75 (1981–82), pp. 137–75; Jonathan M. Parry and Maurice Bloch, eds., *Money and the Morality of Exchange* (Cambridge: Cambridge University Press, 1989), pp. 64–93.

[30] Henry Rosemont Jr., "How to Think about Morality without Moral Agents," in Michael J. Sandel and Paul J. D'Ambrosio, eds., *Encountering China: Michael Sandel and Chinese Philosophy* (Cambridge, MA: Harvard University Press, 2018), pp. 197–227, at p. 217.

Reciprocity in role performance helps to create an order of *li* 禮, or propriety. *Li* is an all-encompassing term referring to rules, norms, and institutions of personal etiquette and social conduct that are the hallmarks of the traditional Chinese society. The ideal Confucian society is family and communally oriented, with customs, traditions, and rituals—that is, *li*—serving as the binding force of and between many relationships and the responsibilities attendant on them.[31] Confucians conceive of *li* as the outward manifestation of justice, while the emotion of *ren* (仁 humaneness) serves as its internal grounding. An order of *li* is one in which cooperation becomes habitual and communal solidarity the norm.

Reciprocity is also the Confucian route to harmony in diversity. Reciprocity presumes the divergence and even conflicts of interests. It proposes to solve the problem of self-interest with the dictum mentioned earlier: "Humane persons establish others in seeking to establish themselves and promote others in seeking to get there themselves." Only by helping others to realize their interests in the process of realizing your own interests will you be able to inaugurate cooperation with that person. This is a reciprocity of both interest and obligation.

In acknowledging the plurality of interests, Confucian reciprocity contains a more profound awareness of the diversity of the world, expressed in the concept of harmony (*he* 和). Harmony presupposes the diversity rather than sameness of things, because diversity produces a lively world while sameness stymies growth. Kongzi famously remarks that "exemplary persons seek harmony not sameness; petty persons seek sameness not harmony."[32] Harmony as a strategy of conflict management is one that applies reciprocity to maximize mutually beneficial cooperation in a world of diversity. In the formulation offered by the contemporary philosopher Zhao Tingyang, it is a strategy by which two parties would each gain greater benefit than if they were to achieve their interests separately.[33] Recently the Confucian insight of harmony in diversity has been carried further by Christian Reus-Smit, who argues that cultural diversity is inherent to all types of order and the central task of order-builders is to construct diversity regimes.[34]

Reciprocity, whether of interest or obligation, can breed trust. This holds major implications for the Sino-American relationship, which is plagued by rampant distrust.[35] During the last decade of the Cold War, President Ronald

---

[31] Henry Rosemont Jr., *Against Individualism: A Confucian Rethinking of the Foundations of Morality, Politics, Family, and Religion* (Lanham, MD: Lexington Books, 2015), p. 101.

[32] Ames and Rosemont, *The Analects of Confucius*, p. 169.

[33] Zhao Tingyang [趙汀陽], *Huashijie yanjiu: zuowei diyi zhexue de zhengzhi zhexue* [壞世界研究 : 作為第一哲學的政治哲學 Investigations of the Bad World: Political Philosophy as First Philosophy] (Beijing: Renmin University Press, 2009), p. 118.

[34] Christian Reus-Smit, *On Cultural Diversity: International Theory in a World of Difference* (Cambridge: Cambridge University Press, 2018).

[35] Zhang and Lebow, *Taming Sino-American Rivalry*, p. 85.

Reagan offered "trust but verify" as a catchword for dealing with the Soviet Union. In the Trump administration, Secretary of State Mike Pompeo played on that catchword with China, pronouncing with contempt "distrust and verify."[36] His distrust of the Chinese leadership was so deep that he wanted to tear down the entire, engagement-centered fabric of US-China relations since the Nixon years.

Trust is the expectation that others will honor their promises. Rational choice approaches contend that trust comes from assessments of the prior performance of the actors under evaluation; cooperation, which builds on trust, is conceived of as a narrow collective action problem and only valued when they serve selfish ends. Consequently, sustained trust and cooperation are made into something of an oxymoron. The great philosophers and sociologists of the past have a different and deeper take. Plato recognizes that trust comes from friendship and the demonstrable willingness to do things for friends that have nothing to do with one's own goals. Treating friends, elites, and countries as ends in themselves, not means to our ends—as Kant would put it—builds trust. It facilitates cooperation, which in turn builds common identities and more trust.[37]

Our theory of justice offers a complementary take. Trust is closely bound up with justice and legitimacy. It rests on both the principles of fairness and equality. Reciprocity is a key mechanism of trust because it can be an expression of both fairness and equality. Greek philosophers and Chinese Confucians conceive of reciprocity in terms of fairness; the Chinese Mohists, as we saw in chapter 4, advocate it for the purpose of equality. We have already spelled out in the previous section how the reciprocity of fairness can guide benign competition. We now add that it can also foster trust and cooperation. The principle of equality is also crucial to trust. In situations where it dominates, trust requires the equal treatment of agents, regardless of other inequalities between them.[38]

It is unrealistic at present to expect America and China to become friends. Even in the best of times, the first two decades following the Nixon rapprochement, for instance, they were not friends to the same degree as between America and its close allies like Britain or Australia. But it is not a stretch to envisage them as partners, especially when confronting a panoply of global challenges including climate change, pandemics, and weapons proliferation. Nevertheless, the ethics

---

[36] Michael R. Pompeo, "Communist China and the Free World's Future," 23 July 2020, https://2017-2021.state.gov/communist-china-and-the-free-worlds-future-2/index.html (accessed 2 February 2021).

[37] Richard Ned Lebow, "Trust and International Relations," in Benedict Wilkinson and James Gow, eds., *The Art of Creating Power: Freedman on Strategy* (Oxford: Oxford University Press, 2017), pp. 243–58, at p. 258.

[38] Ibid., p. 256.

of reciprocity that we have enunciated holds the key to building trust between the two countries. Reciprocity will almost certainly rub against the competitive elements of the relationship discussed in the preceding section. How to balance reciprocity-based cooperation with competition will be the greater test of policy for both countries. Over the long run, if reciprocity pays off, and trust and co-operation build, the two countries have the potential to develop something of a common community embedded in overlapping regional and international societies. As Greek and Chinese philosophers suggest, communities foster co-operation among their members because they see their interests served by the attainment of collective goals.

We now apply our framework of justice and order, and competition and co-operation, to Sino-American relations. We focus on six areas of competition or dispute—status, ideology, security, economy, technology, and society—and show how our approach could improve relations in all these domains. Our proposals are merely illustrative given space limitations. For the same reason, we refrain from considering Sino-American cooperation on global issues such as pandemics and climate change, although we will refer to them en passant in the next chapter. We hope our discussion will convince readers that different future for Sino-American relations is possible from the one of narrow competition and confrontation touted by hawks in both countries.

Status

We argued in *Taming Sino-American Rivalry* that the quest for status is a central source of Sino-American tension, more so than concerns for security and material well-being.[39] Security and wealth aside, any relationship or order must speak to people's needs for self-esteem. In the modern world, this is often projected onto states. People feel good about themselves when their states do well and become powerful or gain the respect of other states and peoples. China and American both claim special status in the world and have encouraged their citizens to define their identities in part in relation to it. People routinely make compromises when their interests clash, but usually dig in their heels when conflict arises over their identities.

Status competition is often masked; the confrontational policies to which it gives rise are often justified to the public in terms of security or material considerations. However, it is not hard to find evidence for status competition

[39] Zhang and Lebow, *Taming Sino-American Rivalry*.

between America and China in the East Asian region. America has long claimed for itself a hegemonic status in East Asia and pursued an ambitious strategy of liberal hegemony.[40]

China's goal in Asia, according to numerous US observers, is dominance by a conscious design to undermine American influence.[41] A more defensible view is that Beijing wants an equal status with Washington. In July 2014, President Xi Jinping declared that "the Pacific Ocean is spacious enough to accommodate both China and America."[42] One may interpret this to imply that the Pacific, which has been dominated by the United States since World War II, must accommodate rising Chinese influence on a par with that of the United States.

A prominent part of the Chinese discourse constructs America as a threat to its self-esteem. When Chinese elites criticize American "hegemony" and accuse it of containing China's rise, they reveal the centrality of the search for status in China's international goals. They believe that it is only natural for China—a country with ancient history, proud traditions, and prior preeminence—to restore its rightful standing in Asia. American efforts to maintain its alleged regional hegemony are seen as attempts to thwart the goal of national rejuvenation—an affront on Chinese self-esteem that justifies competition for honor and standing.

Status can be more competitive than the search for security and wealth because it is relative. Sometimes, security needs of states can be in direct competition, but just as often they are compatible and would be better guaranteed through cooperation. The same is more generally true of economic relations. Since the time of Adam Smith, people have come to realize that wealth is not a finite but an expandable quantity, and that economic cooperation has the potential to increase the wealth of all parties. This is much less true of status, which can be zero-sum if people or states are trying to achieve it in the same way. Hobbes compares it to glory and observes that "if all men have it, no man hath it."[43]

---

[40] See Zhang and Lebow, *Taming Sino-American Rivalry*; Barry R. Posen, *Restraint: A New Foundation for U.S. Grand Strategy* (Ithaca, NY: Cornell University Press, 2014).

[41] See, for example, Michael R. Pompeo, "The China Challenge," 30 October 2019, https://2017-2021.state.gov/the-china-challenge/index.html (accessed 2 February 2021); Oriana Skylar Mastro, "The Stealth Superpower: How China Hid Its Global Ambitions," *Foreign Affairs* 98, no. 1 (2019), pp. 31–39.

[42] Xi Jinping, "Nuli goujian zhongmei xinxing daguo guanxi" [Striving to Build a New Type of Sino-American Major Country Relationship], Beijing, July 2014, http://jhsjk.people.cn/article/25261696 (accessed 14 February 2021).

[43] Thomas Hobbes, *On Citizen*, ed. and trans. Richard Tuck and Michael Silverthorne (Cambridge: Cambridge University Press, 1998 [1651]), 1.1.

The struggle for status has been shown to be the principal cause of international conflict and war, and we maintain that it lies at the core of Sino-American rivalry.[44]

Principles of justice are inseparable from efforts to build security, generate wealth, and gain status. They help determine what actors consider to be appropriate and fair. Conflict is certain to ensure, and be more acute if it already exists, if people or states believe that different principles of justice apply to the issues they confront. Even if they agree, there will be problems if one or both parties violate these principles in the eyes of the other. The former kind of conflict is most likely to occur when one side emphasizes fairness and the other equality. This is frequently the case in many kinds of international interactions, especially between states that differ considerably in their relative power and standing.

We are seeing this dynamic in Sino-American competition for status in East Asia. China and the United States both emphasize fairness: they distinguish themselves from other states and demand more because of their power and culture. The problem arises with the choice of others. For the United States, China is among them. For China, it includes the United States. Thus, for the United States, fairness makes China a lesser state; for China, the United States is an equal one. China is applying equality to relations among superpowers, selected on the principle of fairness.

Is the United States justified in claiming primacy on the basis of fairness? In the modern world, claims to superiority and dominance, especially those that exclude other states' aspirations for status, rub up against the principle of equality and are thus hard to sustain. The United States is in effect making a claim to a future status of supremacy on account of its past status gained through the success of its policies. But that is a false application of the principle of fairness. In competing for status, America and China should dispel the notion that only hegemony or primacy can satisfy their status needs. Status must be disengaged from hegemony, dominance, superiority, or any related concept. There can be multiple pathways to status, with hegemony being only one and a counterproductive one at that. America and China should reject hegemony as the goal of their Asia policy.

Once they free themselves of this illusory goal, they can take advantage of different pathways to status by devoting foreign policy efforts to skills and fields at which they excel. The United States could emphasize rights-based initiatives for the promotion of freedom, human rights, the rule of law, and democracy in places where conditions allow. The best way to promote these American values is, as President Biden has emphasized, by the power of the American example, not, as often in the past, by militaristic interventionism. The United States could highlight traditional security approaches, alliance solidarity, and market economy, and the positive role these can play in fostering development and helping to maintain international strategic and economic stability.

China could do the same by stressing community-based actions for the advancement of economic growth, social harmony, and international peace. Like the United States, it should adopt the method of exemplification by setting itself up as a worthy example rather than exporting or imposing its model on others. China's advantages lie in nontraditional security approaches, development assistance, and large-scale infrastructure building, as manifested in the Belt and Road Initiative. These happen to be areas neglected by the United States.

The American emphasis on rights and China's on community are often framed as a clash of values and politicized as an ideological rivalry. They derive from different intellectual traditions—liberalism for the US case, and Confucianism for China. It is nevertheless possible to reconceive them as different pathways to status. Doing so would transfer the focus from ideology to practice, which would have the salutary effect of transforming the zero-sum nature of Sino-American status competition to one of positive-sum. In the process, both countries could improve their respective performance. America's traditional security policies are too militarized, and the recipe of market economy often results in financial crises without generating sustained economic growth.[45] China's leadership in nontraditional security issues is still incipient and hesitant, and the Belt and Road Initiative has been beset by a host of political, financial, and environmental problems.[46]

The strategy of creating different pathways to status would also require both countries to avoid making invidious comparisons when stressing their comparative advantages and substantive achievements. They need to adhere to the spirit of pluralism, namely, the American and Chinese ways of attaining

---

[45] Robert M. Gates, "The Overmilitarization of American Foreign Policy," *Foreign Affairs* 99, no. 4 (2020), pp. 121–32; Adam Tooze, *Crashed: How a Decade of Financial Crises Changed the World* (London: Allen Lane, 2018).

[46] Suisheng Zhao, "China's Belt-Road Initiative as the Signature of President Xi Jinping Diplomacy: Easier Said than Done," *Journal of Contemporary China* 29, no. 123 (2020), pp. 319–35; Matthew Mingey and Agatha Kratz, "China's Belt and Road: Down but Not Out," Rhodium Group, 4 January 2021, https://rhg.com/research/bri-down-out/ (accessed 16 March 2021).

status may be no worse than each other, each being good through being a good instance of a different pathway. There is no need to claim superiority for the American emphasis on rights or the Chinese emphasis on community. Indeed, the world will benefit if both ways succeed in a complementary fashion.

More generally, the two countries should, as we suggested earlier, engage in fairness-based competition by enhancing the merit or virtue of their policies. That is, they need to develop policies that can bring benefits to themselves as well as regional and international societies, and by grounding those policies in appropriate ethical frameworks. We recommend a fairness-based strategy as an important way of fostering healthy competition between the two countries. The merit and virtue of both countries' policies leave much to be desired, and so this strategy could have a substantial impact. The United States needs to address the pressing problems of political polarization, lack of governance, decaying infrastructure, wealth inequality, and racial tensions; the Chinese list includes political rigidity, ecological degradation, population decline, debt burdens, and social inequality. Climate change is a common challenge facing both countries. If they could devote themselves to developing clean energy technologies and eventually a green economy, that would epitomize a desirable form of positive competition.

China's quest for equality with the United States, paradoxically, may also be accomplished through fairness-centered competition. China has of course attained full formal legal equality with the United States under international law. Both countries are independent, sovereign nations, member states of the United Nations, and more important, permanent members of the UN Security Council. What Beijing desires is not formal legal equality but informal substantive equality in status, security, and wealth, a desire made more acute by its perception that the United States is bent on containing China's rise and entrenching its own superiority.

No international organization can confer on China the sort of substantive equality it craves for with the United States. Only China's own efforts can do so, and the best efforts are those geared toward developing the merit and virtue of its own policies. In other words, the search for equality starts with the practice of fairness. Greater accomplishments in its policies will earn it more respect, and thus higher status, from abroad. This approach of status competition does not require Beijing to train its sights on Washington. Quite the contrary: it urges Beijing to reduce its fixation on Washington as a rival and devote itself to the success of its domestic and foreign policies and the contributions they can make to regional and international societies. The same can be said of Washington. If both sides do so, their competition will be channeled to productive ends.

Ideology

Sino-American ideological competition turned ugly during the Trump administration, with senior American officials calling for regime change in China.[47] Although the Biden administration was not so abrasive, the president also framed the contest between the two countries as one between democracy and autocracy.[48] Conflict over ideology spilled over into other political disputes, especially Hong Kong and Xinjiang. The United States imposed sanctions on account of Chinese crackdown of protests in Hong Kong and accused Beijing of "genocide" against the Uighurs in Xinjiang. Since the time of the Trump administration, the multiple failures of American domestic and foreign policies have afforded Chinese propagandists numerous opportunities to berate American democracy.[49] Chinese leaders usually refrain from open criticism of the US system; in private, however, they have long viewed America as the principal ideological foe.

We address this malaise of ideological rivalry with an appeal to value pluralism. This is the thesis that there are many distinct values, not reducible to one supreme value or way of being good, and that the distinct values may also be incapable of being realized together in the life of a single individual or society.[50] Joseph Raz deploys the concept of "genre" to make the point. We identify something as an instance of one genre, and judge it by the standards of that genre. The thing is good because it is good by the standards of that genre. Thus, one system of criminal justice is good to the extent that it is a good adversarial system; another is good to the extent that it is a good prosecutorial system. "The two systems," Raz says, "may be no worse than each other, each being good through being a good instance of a different, and conflicting, kind."[51]

An important implication of pluralism is that we should see disputes in values or belief systems in terms not of erasure or replacement but of ordering and prioritization. Although there are distinct values within and across peoples and cultures, there is also a significant overlap between these values. The range of true human ethics is limited.[52] There is no one true ethical code established by

---

[47] Pompeo, "Communist China and the Free World's Future."

[48] The White House, "Remarks by President Biden in Address to a Joint Session of Congress," Washington, DC, 29 April 2021, https://www.whitehouse.gov/briefing-room/speeches-remarks/2021/04/29/remarks-by-president-biden-in-address-to-a-joint-session-of-congress/ (accessed 15 October 2021).

[49] For a particularly striking example, see Xin Shiping, "'Chongmei,' 'Guimei' de ruangubing dezhi" [The "Worshiping America" and "Kneeling to America" Soft-Bone Disease Must Be Cured], *Xinhua*, 17 December 2020, https://baijiahao.baidu.com/s?id=16862435809596477498&wfr=spider&for=pc (accessed 16 February 2021).

[50] Joseph Raz, *The Practice of Value* (Oxford: Clarendon Press, 2003), Kindle ed., location 100.

[51] Ibid., location 509.

[52] Wong, *Natural Moralities.*

one group on account of its self-claimed success in some aspects of the human endeavor. It is more useful to see different people in the same or different cultures having different ordering of a limited range of values that virtually every human being holds at some level.[53]

Consider freedom. Freedom is the most prized value in American politics and way of life, at least for Republicans. Pompeo, as noted, brandished it as the central front in the contest between a liberal West and an authoritarian China, framing the goal of the former as securing freedom from the tyranny of the latter. But it is far from the case that the Chinese people, Chinese culture, or the Chinese state as represented by the PRC does not value freedom. Freedom is one of the twelve "socialist core values" propagated by the state, although it ranks far below the top value of "wealth and power." More important, as we explained in earlier chapters, freedom has been a cherished value in Chinese culture from at least the time of the ancient Daoists, and in modern times China's search for freedom against the shackles of its imperial past and foreign domination has been a central theme of its national project. China and America alike value freedom, but they differ notably in their ordering of that value, with the United States placing a much higher priority than China.

Now consider harmony. As we saw in chapter 3, harmony of relationships and community is the supreme ideal of Confucian ethics. Confucians conceive of the family sustained by filial piety as the starting point of harmony, which can then be extended to varying levels of community. In contemporary China, informal negotiation involving interaction and reconciliation between the contending parties is still the traditional way of resolving business disputes in China; Chinese courts encourage mediation between contending parties even after litigation proceedings have begun. The Chinese prefer to eschew legalistic or argumentative victories at the expense of social harmony. The preference for harmony is also discernable in American subcultures including, of course, Chinese American and other Asian American communities, but also Mexican American and other Latino communities. The various European-descended subcultures of American society have in the past demonstrated a stronger preference for family harmony and community cooperation than they do now.[54] And, as we explained in earlier chapters, emphasis on community solidarity has been a prominent part of the Western tradition since Greek times. But it is undeniable that American society as a whole nowhere accords harmony as central a place in the catalogue of moral virtues as Confucianism. What it values much more is individual autonomy unencumbered by community constraints and obligations.

---

[53] Rosemont, *Against Individualism*, p. 21.
[54] Wong, *Natural Moralities*, p. 19.

Between America and China, harmony, like freedom, is a common value differently rank-ordered.

These examples make plain that the value systems of America and China are not diametrically or uniformly opposed to each other. There is diversity, of course, but also overlap; the most productive way to see their difference is in terms of the different rank-ordering of a common core of values. Diversity and commonality are both indispensable for understanding Sino-American relations in the realm of values.

Pluralism has the virtue of reminding us of the intrinsic diversity of the world and making us more tolerant of others. But it does contain a contradiction that must be resolved if it is not to descend down the slippery slope of relativism. The contradiction is that something may be held by one value as good and by another as bad, and yet both values are endorsed by pluralism. There is a risk of affirming contradictory values and losing a critical ability to condemn evaluative beliefs.[55] The consequence may be relativism, sanctioning diversity by conceding that the merit or demerit of something is relative to the society in which it takes place or in which it is judged. In Sino-American relations, the implication of relativism is the position that whatever one country does is right in its own circumstances and the other has no right to criticize those practices that it finds objectionable by its own standards.

But relativism is not a necessary consequence of pluralism. Relativism is itself an untenable doctrine since it cannot answer the question whether the claim that all value is socially relative is itself socially relative.[56] There are conceptually robust ways to resolve evaluative contradictions in pluralism without resorting to relativism. We bring in the Daoist philosopher Zhuangzi for this purpose. Zhuangzi is a pluralist, as we showed in chapter 4. Zhuangzi argues that we should hold our own perspective but not impose it on anything else, so that we can treat everything else from the perspective of the thing being treated. The moral appropriateness of our actions toward others is determined not by our standard as moral agents but by that of our moral patients.[57] This view anticipates Raz, whose conception of genre-based evaluation is essentially a proposal of treating things from the perspective of the things being treated.

Zhuangzi goes beyond resolving evaluative conflicts. His ethics of difference holds that a truly moral person "is one who can naturally, spontaneously, and effortlessly recognize and respect the equal value of diverse ways of life."[58] It

---

[55] Raz, *The Practice of Value*, Kindle ed., location 487.

[56] Ibid., location 201.

[57] Yong Huang, "Respecting Different Ways of Life: A Daoist Ethics of Virtue in the *Zhuangzi*," *Journal of Asian Studies* 69, no. 4 (2020), pp. 1049–69, at p. 1057.

[58] Ibid., at p. 1059.

follows that since this ethic respects different ways of life as having equal worth, it logically cannot respect any ways of life that do not regard other ways of life as having equal worth. This has major implications for moral evaluations. A thoroughgoing relativism cannot condemn Hitler for the Holocaust, but Zhuangzi's ethics of difference can. It can argue that since Hitler did not respect the equal worth of the Jews who had different values from him, we cannot have any respect for Hitler. Zhuangzi enables us to condemn morally repugnant ways of life.[59]

Moreover, Zhuangzi offers a method for overcoming the tendency to impose one's own values and ways of life on others. He attributes this tendency to "the fixed and opinionated mind" (*cheng xin* 成心)—the belief that one's own parochial standard of right and wrong is universal. Plato, of course, made exactly the same claim in his *Republic*. In philosophical fictions for which he is famous, Zhuangzi tells how eels tend to think that damp places are good places to live, not only for eels but all beings; how monkeys tend to think that treetops are good places to live, not only for monkeys but for all beings; and how human beings think that dry places are good places to live, not only for humans but for all beings. They all tend to impose their own standard of right places to live on other beings as a result of their opinionated mind, and this is at the heart of the problem. Zhuangzi consequently urges us to diminish and clear away our opinionated mind by nurturing a natural tendency to respect the natural tendencies of others. We must strive, he says, to sit and forget (*zuo wang* 坐忘), fast the mind (*xin zhai* 心斋), lose oneself (*sang wo* 喪我), and become without self (*wu ji* 無己).[60]

Philosophers East and West have provided intellectual resources for America and China to respect their different values, political systems, and ways of life; evaluate and criticize the other by Zhuangzi's ethics of difference; and overcome the tendency to impose one's values and standards on the other by shrinking "the opinionated mind." Neither America nor China should look the other way if either violates the ethics of difference. America, for example, could criticize China's human rights record in Xinjiang by focusing on the extent to which Beijing has damaged the way of life of the Uighurs as a minority people. If China keeps repressing the Uighurs, it will never be seen as an equal by the United States. China, for its part, may deploy a parallel method to criticize the human rights record of the United States, which is burdened by a depressing history of racism, mass incarceration of young African Americans, and massive rights violations in the penal system.[61]

[59] Ibid.

[60] Ibid., p. 1062.

[61] Katrina Northrop, "Jeffrey Sachs on Not Pointing Fingers," *Wire China*, 24 January 2021, https://www.thewirechina.com/2021/01/24/jeffrey-sachs-on-not-pointing-fingers/ (accessed 9 March 2021).

Most important, the ethics of difference urges both countries to achieve mutual understanding and accommodation by rejecting "the opinionated mind"— that is, by reducing preconceptions and prejudices and focusing instead on the natural or genuine qualities of the other. The Daoist recipe of fasting the mind and losing oneself is perhaps too individualistic and idealistic to be of practical value. But self-cultivation can be extended from the individual to the national foreign policy elite, as Confucians believe. Surely it is possible for the elite to engage in self-reflection and curb "the opinionated mind" as a result.

Security

In *Taming Sino-American Rivalry*, we focused on Taiwan, North Korea, Asian maritime disputes, and the US alliance system in Asia as four major areas of security disputes.[62] The Taiwan dispute is the most dangerous. The Trump and Biden administrations bolstered ties with Taiwan in an incremental but resolute manner, even deploying American troops to train Taiwanese forces on the island.[63] Beijing, for its part, responded by sending fighter jets across the median line of the Taiwan Strait and conducting live combat drills. The nationalistic *Global Times* threatened war, and not just for bluster; Chinese warplanes had begun to simulate attacks on US forces when they flew into Taiwan's air defense zone.[64]

In the South China Sea, the United States rebuked China for creating a "maritime empire."[65] Since 2015 the US Navy has been conducting Freedom of Navigation Operations to challenge China's island building. The Trump and Biden administrations intensified the scale and pace of these operations, all the while buttressing traditional deterrence with large military presence and exercises involving aircraft carriers and allied forces.[66] Neither the United States

[62] Zhang and Lebow, *Taming Sino-American Rivalry* (Oxford: Oxford University Press, 2020).

[63] Gordon Lubold, "U.S. Troops Have Been Deployed in Taiwan for at Least a Year," *Wall Street Journal*, October 7, 2021, https://www.wsj.com/articles/u-s-troops-have-been-deployed-in-taiwan-for-at-least-a-year-11633614043 (accessed 15 October 2021).

[64] Kathrin Hille and Demetri Sevastopulo, "Beijing Lays Down a Marker in South China Sea," *Financial Times*, 3 February 2021, https://www.ft.com/content/858e24a9-1370-4b1e-853f-845ea f7d25c6 (accessed 3 February 2021).

[65] Michael R. Pompeo, "U.S. Position on Maritime Claims in the South China Sea," 13 July 2020, https://2017-2021.state.gov/u-s-position-on-maritime-claims-in-the-south-china-sea/index.html (accessed 4 February 2021).

[66] See Ronald O'Rourke, "U.S.-China Strategic Competition in South and East China Seas: Background and Issues for Congress" (Washington, DC: Congressional Research Service, 2020), p. 34.

nor China wants a war over the South China Sea, but a conflict by accident or miscalculation has become a real possibility.

At the Asian regional level, the United States adopted the so-called Indo-Pacific strategy. This strategy built on the Obama administration's Asia rebalance strategy but prioritized deterrence at the expense of reassurance and diplomacy. In conjunction with the Indo-Pacific strategy, the US military strategy sharpened its focus on deterrence and combat. The Pentagon was investing in both advanced conventional capabilities and game-changing technologies such as hypersonic weapons, 5G communications, integrated air and missile defense, and artificial intelligence. The Indo-Pacific Command called for $20.1 billion in added spending between 2021 and 2026, including funding for offensive weapons and their support systems, distributing forces across the region, and military aid for forces in Southeast Asian countries. Congress introduced the Indo-Pacific Deterrence Initiative, with more than a $6 billion allocation for air and missile defense systems and new military construction in partner countries.[67]

A central pillar of the Indo-Pacific strategy was alliance building through the Quadrilateral Security Dialogue (known informally as the "Quad") among the United States, Japan, Australia, and India. Upgraded to a leader-level summit in March 2021, the Quad was a new mechanism by which the United States hoped to constrain Chinese influence in Asia beyond its traditional hub-and-spokes bilateral alliance system in the region. US officials prized the Quad as a league of democracies and drew a sharp contrast with China's authoritarian system. They held out the prospect of drawing in more countries, inside and outside the region, to work in a common cause on the basis of shared values and interests. In September 2021, the United States, United Kingdom, and Australia formed a new anti-China security pact (nicknamed "AUKUS") centered on military technology collaboration, including supplying Australia with nuclear-powered submarines.[68] Asian military competition intensified, with the real risk of an arms race and devastating consequences should military conflict break out.

We suggest that the American and Chinese security orders in Asia, constructed through alliance or partnership building, can be reconciled by an approach based on the Greek concept of *hēgemonia* and the Chinese concept of

[67] Joe Gould, "Congress Seeks to Confront China with $6 Billion in New Defense Spending," *Foreign Policy*, 16 April 2020, https://foreignpolicy.com/2020/04/16/congress-us-china-competition-6-billion-new-defense-spending/ (accessed 4 February 2021).

[68] David E. Sanger and Zolan Kanno-Youngs, "Biden Announces Defense Deal with Australia in a Bid to Counter China," *New York Times*, 15 September 2021, https://www.nytimes.com/2021/09/15/us/politics/biden-australia-britain-china.html (accessed 15 October 2021).

wangdao, as propounded earlier. These concepts inform a strategy of clientelist but legitimate hierarchy for both countries, with the same spirit but different forms and manifestations. The principle of fairness underlying such a strategy of hierarchy requires rule packages associated with different statuses. The higher the status, the greater the honor and privileges, but also the more demanding the role and more restrictive its rules. Such hierarchy is designed to restrain selfishness and its consequences by embedding actors with resources in a social order that requires them to protect and support those who are less advantaged and feel shame if they do not meet their responsibilities. Robust clientelist hierarchies satisfy the spirit of those with high status and the security and appetites of those with low status.[69]

The American and Chinese orders already exhibit hierarchical qualities. The American order is predominantly security-focused, although economic openness is also a major aspect of it. In the hub-and-spokes bilateral alliance system, Washington is the center, as it is in the new Quad and an emerging network of relationships among the United States and its various allies and partners. The Chinese order is economy-oriented, capitalizing on the success of China's phenomenal growth, but has been acquiring an increasingly strong security component since around 2010. Diplomatically, Beijing has been expanding its influence through partnership diplomacy and institution building, where it is establishing itself as a central actor, although it refrains from talking about its centrality for fear of arousing regional suspicion of a new Sinocentric order mirroring the imperial tribute system.

Such fear stems from domination by a hegemon through the use of force and power rather than persuasion and influence.[70] *Hēgemonia* or *wangdao* would steer clear of this problem by establishing a legitimate hierarchy based on the fairness of reciprocal benefits and obligations. While fairness is the substantive principle, formal equality should also be incorporated given its normative status in modern international relations. A hierarchy like this would be a soft hierarchy embedded in a society that allowed and encouraged multiple hierarchies so that other political units and people could gain status.

Both America and China should reject hegemony as a strategic goal and instead focus on *hēgemonia* or *wangdao*. As long as they share their *hēgemonia* or *wangdao* in Asia and maintain their respective rule packages in relations with regional countries, no conflict should arise between them or their respective hierarchies of alliances and partnerships in the region. For America, it means

---

[69] Richard Ned Lebow, *A Culture Theory of International Relations* (Cambridge: Cambridge University Press, 2008), pp. 64, 84.

[70] On the role of persuasion and influence, see Simon Reich and Richard Ned Lebow, *Good-bye Hegemony! Power and Influence in the Global System* (Princeton, NJ: Princeton University Press, 2014).

discharging its responsibilities to its regional allies and partners while encouraging them to improve relations with China. For China, it means improving relations with neighboring countries without compelling them to choose between Beijing and Washington. Rather than a binary strategy dividing Asia between Chinese-led and US-led spheres of influence or opposing blocks, a common *hēgemonia/wangdao* strategy leads to an intermeshing community of regional countries friendly to both powers.

Moreover, the strategy can be practiced on a global scale, with both countries seeking honor—that is, the respect of others and the influence it confers—in a cooperative, even collaborative manner. Acting this way, America and China would both gain influence and reduce tension between them, while collectively contributing to global governance. Indeed, that would be ideal for the most important bilateral relationship in the twenty-first century.

Economy

The Trump administration's trade war was the opening salvo in a new era of US economic offensive against China. Ostensibly the Biden administration wanted to distance itself from Trump's "America First" approach, but in its China policy, including the tariff-centered trade war, Biden diverged little from his predecessor.

America's dissatisfaction with Chinese trade was widespread. In part this sentiment reflected a mounting disappointment with China's failure to conform to the US free-market economic model. Beijing was said to cling to "its non-market economic structure and state-led, mercantilist approach to trade and investment," and its alleged exploitation of WTO membership for trade advantages without fully embracing the WTO's open market approach is a particular sore point.[71] The Trump administration's "Section 301" investigation report published in March 2018, which technically justified the trade war, described a range of Chinese trade practices deemed unfair, especially forced transfer of technology and theft of intellectual property and trade secrets.[72]

---

[71] President of the United States, "United States Strategic Approach to the People's Republic of China" (Washington, DC: White House, 2020), p. 3.

[72] Office of the United States Trade Representative, "Findings of the Investigation into China's Acts, Policies, and Practices Related to Technology Transfer, Intellectual Property, and Innovation under Section 301 of the Trade Act of 1974," March 2018, https://ustr.gov/sites/default/files/Section%20301%20FINAL.PDF (accessed 4 February 2021).

The stated goal of US economic policy toward China was to rebalance the economic relationship by supporting fair trade and breaking down unjust barriers to US trade and investment.[73] The US frustration also bespoke a worry about the relative decline of America's economic power. US officials charged China with an "economic blitzkrieg" to "seize the commanding heights of the global economy and to surpass the US as the world's preeminent superpower."[74] They singled out Beijing's "Made in China 2025" initiative, a plan for advancing the country's high-tech industries, as "the latest iteration of the PRC's state-led, mercantilist economic model."[75]

The United States correctly diagnosed unfair trade as a key problem in Sino-American economic relations. This unfairness manifested itself at several levels. Most straightforward was the US accusation of nonreciprocal trade policies—China charging higher tariffs on US imports than vice versa. More complicated was concern over China's failure to reform, as its economic evolution had turned away from markets and involved subsidies that drove global overcapacity in old industrial sectors like steel and aluminum. The most complex was a new animosity toward China's economic strategy. American multinational companies alleged that they were forced to transfer their technology to Chinese firms on noncommercial grounds—or, in some cases, even having it stolen in state-sponsored actions—in order to assist Chinese innovation.[76]

Different aspects of perceived unfairness prompted the imposition of different kinds of tariffs. Those on steel, aluminum, and solar panels were a response to the rising importance of State-Owned Enterprises (SOEs), industrial subsidies, and China's failure to reform and become more market-oriented. Others, like those on the $250 billion of Chine imports imposed in 2018 under Section 301 of the Trade Act of 1974, were meant to confront forced technology transfer and intellectual property theft.[77]

America's focus on unfairness may be justified on certain grounds. But its trade war, especially tariffs as crudely applied by Trump, was unnecessarily provocative and destructive. It caused considerable short-run economic losses for the United States itself. The long-run costs were even more damaging: it crippled the international rules-based system that had successfully mediated trade

[73] President of the United States, "United States Strategic Approach to the People's Republic of China," p. 12.

[74] William P. Barr, "Remarks on China Policy at the Gerald R. Ford Presidential Museum," 16 July 2020, https://www.justice.gov/opa/speech/attorney-general-william-p-barr-delivers-remarks-china-policy-gerald-r-ford-presidential (accessed 3 February 2021).

[75] Ibid.

[76] Chad P. Bown, "The 2018 US-China Trade Conflict after Forty Years of Special Protection," *China Economic Journal* 12, no. 2 (2019), pp. 109–36, at pp. 109–10.

[77] Ibid., p. 110.

for nearly seventy years since the establishment of the General Agreement on Tariffs and Trade in 1948.[78]

China's problem was the reverse—a denial of unfairness in its economic relations with the United States and a nonchalance toward trade-generated distributional conflicts inside the United States. In an August 2020 interview, State Councilor and Foreign Minister Wang Yi avowed that Sino-American trade had delivered mutual benefit; no one was being taken advantage of or being ripped off. For evidence he pointed to aggregate gains, including the contributions of trade to job creation and family savings in the United States and to American business investments and profits in China. He showed an awareness of the distributional consequences of trade, but brushed them off by saying that these should be dealt with through internal reform rather than foreign policy.[79]

As it parried the US charge of unfairness, China raised its own demand for equality, as in the disputes over status and ideology. A June 2019 position paper released by the State Council Information Office maintains that trade negotiation, in which the two countries were engaged at the time, must follow the principle of mutual respect, equality, and mutual benefit. Mutual respect is respect for the other side's social institutions, economic system, and development path and rights; one side's gain cannot come at the expense of the other side's rights to development and sovereignty. Equality and mutual benefit mean the equal footing of the two sides in negotiation, the mutual benefit of the outcome of the negotiation, and the win-win nature of the final agreement.[80]

Resolving Sino-American trade disputes requires satisfying both the US demand for fairness and the Chinese appeal to equality. Such a balance was impossible to achieve on the basis of the US and Chinese positions during the Trump administration. The US demands would have required China to undertake significant reforms in its industrial, intellectual property rights, and other economic policies to ensure that the degree of state intervention in the country's economy more or less resembles that of other developed WTO members. This is unrealistic in practice and contradicts the value of pluralism in principle. The Chinese position would have required the United States to content itself with

---

[78] Ibid., p. 131.

[79] Wang Yi, "Interview on Current China-US Relations," *Xinhua News Agency*, 5 August 2020, https://www.fmprc.gov.cn/mfa_eng/wjb_663304/wjbz_663308/2461_663310/t1804328.shtml (accessed 18 February 2021).

[80] The State Council Information Office of the People's Republic of China, "Guanyu zhongmei jingmao cuoshang de zhongfang lichang" [China's Position on the China-US Economic and Trade Consultations], June 2019, https://baijiahao.baidu.com/s?id=1635208022118913214&wfr=spi der&for=pc (accessed 18 February 2021).

the aggregate benefits of trade, which accrue disproportionately to Wall Street investment firms and large multinational corporations rather than the working class, while racing to manage distributional conflicts at home. The trade war has made such a position politically impossible to sustain in the United States. The two countries need to find a balanced expression for both equality and fairness in order to restore a semblance of justice in their trade relationship.

We follow the advice of a distinguished group of American and Chinese economists and legal scholars advanced in an October 2019 joint statement.[81] This advice is threefold. First, America and China, and other countries in general, should be allowed considerable latitude at home to design a wide variety of industrial policies, technological systems, and social standards. This would satisfy the appeal to equality. Second, they should use well-calibrated policies (including tariff and non-tariff trade policies) to protect their industrial, technological, and social policy choices domestically without imposing unnecessary and asymmetric burdens on foreign actors. This would meet the demand for fairness. Third, a set of trade rules should be devised to prevent countries from deploying what economists call "beggar-thy-neighbor" policies—policies that produce benefits to the home country only through the harm they impose on other countries. This is a principle insisted on by China, as we just saw. Since it reflects fairness, it should also be acceptable to the United States.

Overall, this proposal, which the authors call "a regime of peaceful economic coexistence" between the United States and China, is attractive because it sets out to balance the demands for equality and fairness by preserving policy space for both countries—for China to conduct its industrial and growth policies and for the United States to safeguard its labor markets and technological systems. It is a politically sustainable option that can protect the benefits of robust international trade.

Technology

Technology is second only to trade in driving American hostility toward China since the Trump administration. We use the example of US attempts to hobble the Chinese firm Huawei to illustrate how different understandings of the principles of fairness lay at the heart of the conflict. This is an excellent example because rarely, if ever, has the United States used its full power to damage a foreign

---

[81] The US-China Trade Policy Working Group, "US-China Trade Relations: A Way Forward," October 2019, https://rodrik.typepad.com/US-China%20Trade%20Relations%20-%20A%20Way%20Forward%20Booklet%20%28for%20print%29.pdf (accessed 18 February 2021).

company and had such an impact.[82] The US power was in awesome display, but so was its repudiation of justice.

The United States was deeply worried by China's dominance in next generation (5G) telecommunications technology. It trained its sights on Huawei for its challenge to American technological dominance and for its alleged role as the high-tech arm of China's surveillance state. Washington launched an aggressive campaign warning other countries not to use Huawei equipment to build 5G networks, claiming that the Chinese government could use the company to spy and thus undermine the national security of these countries. Semiconductors are central to Huawei's dominance in 5G and China's technological prowess. The battleground in the Sino-US technology war centered on the US attempts to strangle China's access to advanced semiconductors and Chinese efforts to break this stranglehold. Meanwhile, Washington mooted proposals of industrial policy in order to bolster American semiconductor and 5G industries.[83]

Reasonable opinion in both China and the United States is critical of the Trump administration. Despite its unprecedented aggressiveness, the administration produced no compelling evidence of Huawei's spying. Chinese State Counsellor and Foreign Minister Wang Yi accused it of hypocrisy given proven records of the worldwide surveillance, even against allies, by US national intelligence agencies.[84] American scholars warn that a security strategy aimed at eliminating all risks from technological engagement with China is neither necessary nor effective.[85] Still, at a stretch, the United States may build its case around the uncertainty of Huawei's technical capabilities and the company's reported links to the Chinese government.

Nevertheless, it is worth noting that other countries have a taken a different and more cooperative approach. The British government, for example, entered into an arrangement with Huawei under which the company's products in the UK telecoms market undergo an annual security evaluation. Although the 2020

[82] Dan Strumpf, "U.S. Set Out to Hobble China's Huawei, and So It Has," *Wall Street Journal*, 7 October 2021, https://www.wsj.com/articles/u-s-set-out-to-hobble-chinas-huawei-and-so-it-has-11633617478 (accessed 15 October 2021).

[83] Drew FitzGerald and Sarah Krouse, "White House Considers Broad Federal Intervention to Secure 5G Future," *Wall Street Journal*, 25 June 2020, https://www.wsj.com/articles/white-house-federal-intervention-5g-huawei-china-nokia-trump-cisco-11593099054 (accessed 4 February 2021).

[84] Ibid. On US surveillance, see Eli Binder and Katrina Northrop, "The Snowden Effect," 6 December 2020, https://www.thewirechina.com/2020/12/06/the-snowden-effect/ (accessed 26 February 2021).

[85] Peter Cowhey and Susan Shirk, "The Danger of Exaggerating China's Technological Prowess," *Wall Street Journal*, 8 January 2021, https://www.wsj.com/articles/the-danger-of-exaggerating-chinas-technological-prowess-11610117786 (accessed 11 March 2021).

evaluation raised concern, it stopped short of saying that risk mitigation, including remedial actions by Huawei, was impossible.[86] It was not this evaluation, but pressure from the Trump administration, that prompted Britain's decision in July 2020 to ban Huawei from its 5G network.

Even less fair was the US decision to prohibit American companies or companies of any other country using American software or equipment from selling advanced chips and other components to Huawei and its suppliers, regardless of where they operate. As Dani Rodrik and Stephen Walt note, this kind of export ban is far harder to justify on national security grounds than the ban on Huawei's US-based operations. Even if Huawei's operations in third countries pose security risks, it is these countries, not the United States, that is in the best position to evaluate the risks and make corresponding decisions.[87] Beijing appears right to assert, and much of the world agrees, that Washington's intention was to deal a fatal blow to Huawei by starving it of essential inputs and give the United States a breathing space to catch up with China in 5G technology.

How might a fair competition have proceeded differently? We commend the United Kingdom's risk management approach and consider risk mitigation an obligation of Huawei but also a responsibility of the host country. The dispute over the security of Huawei operations reflects the larger and as yet intractable problem of digital trust. As an equipment provider, Huawei bears an essential obligation to satisfy the security requirements of host countries. But the telecoms service providers, professional oversight bodies, and government agencies of these countries must also discharge their responsibilities for enhancing the security of their 5G networks. The US approach of a blanket ban presumes Huawei's extraordinary ability to circumvent the oversight of host countries, or a remarkable impotence of these countries to rein in a single company. It is a presumption that must be subjected to critical scrutiny.

A more fundamental approach of fairness would have involved all countries and international organizations concerned with the issue of digital trust to develop shared norms that could guide legitimate actions and constrain unwarranted provocations. It was not even tried because the Trump administration was hardwired to unilateralism; China, while willing to consider norms of fairness, was averse to offer any for fear of lack of reciprocity from Washington.

---

[86] Huawei Cyber Security Evaluation Centre (HCSEC) Oversight Board Annual Report, September 2020, https://assets.publishing.service.gov.uk/government/uploads/system/uploads/attachment_data/file/923309/Huawei_Cyber_Security_Evaluation_Centre__HCSEC__Over sight_Board-_annual_report_2020.pdf (accessed 19 February 2021).

[87] Dani Rodrik and Stephen Walt, "Constructing a New Global Order: A Project Framing Document," September 2020, https://drodrik.scholar.harvard.edu/files/dani-rodrik/files/new_g lobal_order.pdf (accessed 10 February 2021), p. 18.

Earlier we offered tragedy, exemplification, and fairness as three methods of benign competition. The Trump administration's approach to Huawei was the very antithesis of these methods. Tragedy urges people and states to formulate their interests by taking into account the interests and values of the international society within which they are embedded. The Trump administration's coercion not only damaged the interests of countries where Huawei had already established sizable presence, especially the interests of poor nations overwhelmingly dependent on affordable Huawei equipment, but arguably also damaged the interests of the United States itself by slowing down the rolling out of 5G on US soil. Exemplification would have required the United States to set a shining model on how to resolve the issue of digital trust by taking a measured and rules-based approach to Huawei, rather than using the blunt instruments of prohibition and decimation. Fairness would have urged the United States to focus on the merit and virtue of its policies—competing for 5G by domestic innovation rather than foreign aggression and grounding policies in internationally acceptable ethical frameworks. In all these respects the Trump administration was woefully deficient.

Society

Sino-American ties in other, "soft" areas where no immediate national interest is at stake have also fallen to victim of escalating rivalry. China's Confucius Institutes in the United States, exchange and collaboration in higher education, and media access are the three main bones of contention. Confucius Institutes are a primary vehicle through which China promotes its culture and language abroad. More than 100 Confucius Institutes have opened in the United States, with more than $158 million of funding from the Chinese government.[88] In August 2020, the Trump administration designated the Confucius Institute US Center as a "foreign mission" of the Chinese government, characterizing its role as "an entity advancing Beijing's global propaganda and malign influence campaign on U.S. campuses and K-12 classrooms."[89]

[88] United States Senate Permanent Subcommittee on Investigations, "China's Impact on the U.S. Education System" (Washington, DC: United States Senate, 2019), p. 1.

[89] State Department Office of the Spokesperson, "'Confucius Institute U.S. Center' Designation as a Foreign Mission," 13 August 2020, https://2017-2021.state.gov/confucius-institute-u-s-cen ter-designation-as-a-foreign-mission//index.html (accessed 31 January 2021); State Department Special Briefing, "Briefing with Assistant Secretary for East Asian and Pacific Affairs David R. Stilwell and Acting Director of the Office of Foreign Missions Clifton C. Seagroves on Actions Taken to Counter PRC Influence Operations," 13 August 2020, https://2017-2021.state.gov/briefing-with-assistant-secretary-for-east-asian-and-pacific-affairs-david-r-stilwell-and-acting-director-of-the-off

America is suspicious of Confucius Institutes for four reasons. First, the Chinese government controls nearly every aspect of Confucius Institutes at US schools, providing little transparency into the selection of directors and teacher positions. Second, Chinese funding compromises academic freedom. Controversial topics such as Taiwan, Tibet, and Xinjiang are off limits, and speakers and activists with "anti-China" views are unwelcome.[90] Third, there is lack of reciprocity in Beijing's attitude toward American cultural programs in China. A case in point is its obstructionist approach toward the American Cultural Centers in China, a program created by the State Department in 2010 to partner US schools with Chinese schools, much like Confucius Institutes. Finally, the United States suspects that Confucius Institutes are part of China's soft power strategy to win influence abroad and cannot be seen as a purely cultural initiative. As such, it falls within the scope of American countermeasures against Chinese influence operations.[91]

The American side focuses on the imbalance in the two countries' cultural exchange programs and its underlying unfairness. US schools from kindergarten to college have provided a level of access to the Chinese government that the Chinese government has refused to provide to the United States. That level of access may stifle academic freedom and spread China's political influence that runs counter to US interests at home and abroad. A 2019 Senate subcommittee report recommends that "[a]bsent full transparency regarding how Confucius Institutes operate and full reciprocity for U.S. cultural outreach efforts on college campuses in China, Confucius Institutes should not continue in the United States."[92] The report urges the State Department to demand reciprocal and fair treatment of its diplomats and employees in China.[93] By February 2021, more than forty-five Confucius Institutes had closed down.[94]

The United States also sought to restrict scientific and educational collaboration with China, setting its sights on the Thousand Talents Program, a plan by Beijing to lure foreign talent and advance Chinese innovation. As the program

---

ice-of-foreign-missions-clifton-c-seagroves-on-actions-taken-to-counter-prc-i/index.html (accessed 1 February 2021).

[90] Naima Green-Riley, "The State Department Labeled China's Confucius Programs a Bad Influence on U.S. Students. What's the Story?" *Washington Post*, 25 August 2020, https://www.washingtonpost.com/politics/2020/08/24/state-department-labeled-chinas-confucius-programs-bad-influence-us-students-whats-story/ (accessed 31 January 2021).

[91] United States Senate Permanent Subcommittee on Investigations, "China's Impact on the U.S. Education System," pp. 1–3.

[92] Ibid., p. 4.

[93] Ibid., p. 10.

[94] Green-Riley, "The State Department Labeled China's Confucius Programs a Bad Influence on U.S. Students."

targeted not only Chinese researchers but also American scientists, it fed American concern over Chinese economic espionage and intellectual property theft. The United States believed that China was exploiting America's openness to advance its own interests.[95]

Related, Washington alleged that some Chinese students and researchers, especially those with links to the Chinese military, were being used by Beijing to acquire sensitive US technologies and intellectual property and thus must be restricted entry to the United States. In May 2020, President Trump issued a proclamation to this effect.[96] Four months later, his administration revoked more than 1,000 visas of Chinese nationals affected by the proclamation.[97] Most provocative of all, the Trump administration considered a sweeping ban on travel to the United States by CCP members and their families.[98] The CCP membership stands at around 90 million; including family members, this number could reach 270 million people and cover leaders from every corner of Chinese life. The ban would have completely severed meaningful bilateral ties from diplomatic communication to societal exchange. Not even during the height of the US-Soviet Cold War did such politicization of diplomacy come to pass.

Conflict over media access flared up in a series of tit-for-tat retaliations. In February 2020, China expelled three *Wall Street Journal* reporters based in Beijing over an opinion piece from the *Journal* that referred to China as the "real sick man of Asia."[99] One month later, the Trump administration retaliated by limiting to 100 the number of Chinese citizens who may work in the United States for five state-controlled Chinese news organizations, forcing about sixty Chinese reporters to leave the country. China responded by expelling American journalists working for the *New York Times, Wall Street Journal,* and *Washington Post.* Meanwhile, in February and again in June 2020, the United States

---

[95] United States Senate Permanent Subcommittee on Investigations, "Threats to the U.S. Research Enterprise: China's Talent Recruitment Plans" (Washington, DC: United States Senate, 2019), p. 1.

[96] White House, "Proclamation on the Suspension of Entry as Nonimmigrants of Certain Students and Researchers from the People's Republic of China," 29 May 2020, https://trumpwhitehouse.archives.gov/presidential-actions/proclamation-suspension-entry-nonimmigrants-certain-students-researchers-peoples-republic-china/ (accessed 1 February 2021).

[97] Humeyra Pamuk, "U.S. Revokes More than 1,000 Visas of Chinese Nationals, Citing Military Links," *Reuters,* 10 September 2020, https://www.reuters.com/article/us-usa-china-visas-students-idUSKBN26039D (accessed 1 February 2021).

[98] Paul Mozur and Edward Wong, "U.S. Weighs Sweeping Travel Ban on Chinese Communist Party Members," *New York Times,* 3 December 2020, https://www.nytimes.com/2020/07/15/us/politics/china-travel-ban.html (accessed 21 February 2021).

[99] *Wall Street Journal,* "China Expels Three Wall Street Journal Reporters," 19 February 2020, https://www.wsj.com/articles/china-expels-three-wall-street-journal-reporters-11582100355?mod=hp_lead_pos4 (accessed 1 February 2021).

designated nine Chinese news organizations as "foreign missions," including the *People's Daily*, the newspaper of the Central Committee of the Chinese Communist Party, and Xinhua News Agency, China's official press agency. The State Department contended that "while Western media are beholden to the truth, PRC media are beholden to the Chinese Communist Party."[100] The US goal, according to Secretary of State Pompeo, was reciprocity and the establishment of a level playing field.[101]

We agree that the United States has a strong case for fairness and reciprocity in Sino-American societal relations, although many of its policies in limiting, downgrading, and in extreme cases cutting ties are counterproductive. The onus is on China to acknowledge America's legitimate demand for reciprocity and reach an agreement on the appropriate degree of reciprocity in present circumstances. Looking back, it is clear that the United States has tolerated a high degree of asymmetry in the past because it accepted the Chinese argument for special treatment based on China's developmental stage and the nature of its political system. As a late developer, China had more to learn from America in educational and scientific matters, so it was fair for the United States to be more open to China than vice versa. Moreover, the United States wanted to shape China's political and economic evolution in a more liberal direction; its strategy of engagement, with this hope in mind, built in asymmetrical toleration as an inherent feature. But as China increasingly claims great power status and equality with the United States, and as China has turned away from liberalism, the US toleration for asymmetry has plummeted. The demand for reciprocity is a consequence of this historical process—and one that China needs to accept.

Reciprocity, as we have argued, is the principal mechanism of trust and cooperation. A carefully crafted strategy of reciprocity from both sides holds the promise of advancing Sino-American trust and cooperation. Reciprocity can be of various shades and degrees; not all cooperation requires full reciprocity. Full reciprocity in the political sphere will be hard for China to offer given the constraints imposed by its political system. The Trump administration, contrasting America's justly celebrated openness with China's opacity, gave the impression of demanding complete reciprocity from Beijing or closing the United States down to it. Such a dichotomous strategy was doomed from the start.

---

[100] Morgan Ortagus, "Designation of Additional Chinese Media Entities as Foreign Missions," State Department Press Statement, 22 June 2020, https://china.usembassy-china.org.cn/designation-of-additional-chinese-media-entities-as-foreign-missions/ (accessed 1 February 2021).

[101] Lara Jakes and Marc Tracy, "U.S. Limits Chinese Staff at News Agencies Controlled by Beijing," *New York Times*, 2 March 2020, https://www.nytimes.com/2020/03/02/world/asia/china-journalists-diplomats-expulsion.html (accessed 1 February 2021).

What degree of reciprocity in Sino-American societal relations is appropriate? In the Confucius Institutes dispute, it is important that China reciprocate with a more open mind toward the American Cultural Centers or other cultural outreach initiatives, granting the same, or at least a substantial, number of such initiatives in China that the United States has granted to Confucius Institutes in America. As China can never guarantee the same degree of academic freedom as the United States, the US call for more academic freedom is likely to be disappointed. A method to sidestep this issue is to limit Confucius Institutes' programs strictly to the teaching and promotion of Chinese language and culture. In this way the Confucius Institutes would stay true to their stated mission, which would have the salutary effect of defusing the US criticism of its waging political influence operations, and the issue of reciprocity in academic freedom would not arise.

In the dispute over educational and scientific exchanges, the United States needs a new risk management approach.[102] It must uphold openness as the foremost principle but also develop safeguard measures against illegal or nefarious ways of knowledge transfer. In particular, it should come up with a more nuanced, transparent, and precise way of evaluating cases of Chinese espionage and intellectual property theft. The Trump administration's sledgehammer approach was based on fear, contrary to the American spirit of fair competition. While serving to capture some genuine perpetrators, it would implicate innocent victims, cast a pall over attitudes of Chinese students and scholars toward the United States, and damage societal ties between the two countries. In fact, cases of abuse have been widely reported.[103] China, for its part, needs to win back the trust of the US government by offering more transparency to its recruitment and exchange programs and encouraging its researchers to follow the internationally accepted norms of scientific research.[104]

[102] David Barboza, "Huang Yasheng on De-Risking University Collaboration with China," *Wire China*, 10 January 2021, https://www.thewirechina.com/2021/01/10/huang-yasheng-on-de-risking-university-collaboration-with-china/ (accessed 4 March 2021).

[103] Ellen Nakashima and David Nakamura, "China Initiative Aims to Stop Economic Espionage. Is Targeting Academics over Grant Fraud 'Overkill'?" *Washington Post*, 15 September 2021, https://www.washingtonpost.com/national-security/china-initiative-questions-dismissals/2021/09/15/530ef936-f482-11eb-9738-8395ec2a44e7_story.html (accessed October 15, 2021); Ellen Barry, "A Scientist Is Arrested, and Academics Push Back," *New York Times*, 26 January 2021, https://www.nytimes.com/2021/01/26/us/mit-scientist-charges.html (accessed 21 February 2021).

[104] David Zweig and Siqin Kang, "America Challenges China's National Talent Programs," Center for Strategic and International Studies, May 2020, https://csis-website-prod.s3.amazonaws.com/s3fs-public/publication/20505_zweig_AmericaChallenges_v6_FINAL.pdf?bTLm4WdtG93lA VmxLdlWsgkgeNQDQUAv (accessed 21 February 2021), pp. 14–15.

Media access is one issue where reciprocity in the number of reporters each country posts to the other could help improve relations. The confrontation in 2020 started with a dispute over a *Wall Street Journal* editorial, a minor incident. To negotiate a new agreement of media access, Beijing needs to show political courage by not only restoring the access of the *New York Times, Washington Post,* and *Wall Street Journal,* but also accepting more journalists from American news organizations than before 2020. A truly bold, and fully reciprocal, initiative would be accepting an equal number of American journalists in China and Chinese journalists in America. China's traditional fear of foreign journalists is that they may expose the countries' deficiencies, reduce the appeal of its governance model, and undermine CCP leadership. Yet if China insists on only telling other people about how great it is, it will simply turn them off.[105] Beijing needs to appreciate that truthful reporting of China, even of its failings, may buttress China's international image if the leadership is seen to be committed to openness and progress. Again, we point to the importance of the method of exemplification discussed earlier as a strategy of positive competition. As long as China sets itself up as a positive model, there is nothing to fear from foreign media.

Full reciprocity in media relations will be hard to achieve owing to China's Internet restrictions and censorship known as the Great Firewall. This firewall blocks US outlets from disseminating their content inside China. Chinese outlets, in contrast, are free to disseminate their content in the United States, especially via US social media platforms such as Twitter, Facebook, and YouTube. This problem is unlikely to be resolved any time soon, since censorship is an inherent part of Chinese governance. But at least, the issue of reporter access does not impinge so deeply on the Chinese model.

Conclusion

In this chapter we have offered an alternative explanation of Sino-American conflict. Instead of focusing on conflicts of interests and aggressive intent, we stress commitments to fairness and equality and how each side sees the other as standing in the way of their achievement. By harmonizing, even if only in part, their understandings and making them aware of the other's framing, we can move the relationship forward.

---

[105] Zhengxu Wang and Daniel A. Bell, "To Improve China's Image Globally, Welcome Foreigners and Let Them Be Bridges to the West," *South China Morning Post,* 1 April 2021, https://www.scmp.com/comment/opinion/article/3127609/improve-chinas-image-globally-welcome-foreigners-and-let-them-be (accessed 2 April 2021).

None of the disputes in the six sectors we examined are so intractable as to prevent amelioration. The Sino-American conflict over status is one between the American preference for fairness-based hegemony and the Chinese appeal to equality. The two countries can take advantage of different pathways to status to ease this conflict, with the United States emphasizing rights-based initiatives and China community-based ones. Their conflict over ideology, framed by the United States as one between democracy and autocracy, can be finessed by adhering to value pluralism and the ethics of difference. Conflict over security is normally impervious to moral appeals such as justice. We nevertheless suggest that the parallel Greek concept of *hēgemonia* and the Chinese concept of *wangdao*, both underpinned by the principle of fairness, offers a way out. To do this, America and China need to share their *hēgemonia/wangdao* in Asia and maintain their respective rule packages in relations with regional countries.

In economic conflict, the United States again appeals to fairness in waging its trade war against China, while China insists on equality. The two countries can balance their different demands for fairness and equality by adjustments in their bilateral trade policies and by reforms in global trade rules. In technology competition, the US argument of fairness on national security grounds betrays a fear of its technological decline; it also rests on flimsy factual grounds. Here, a risk management approach based on a faithful application of the fairness principle should serve to assuage US fears. A more fundamental approach of fairness would involve all countries and relevant international institutions to collectively address the issue of digital trust. In societal relations, the United States has a strong case for fairness and reciprocity, but the two countries need to work out the appropriate degree of reciprocity across different issue areas. Full reciprocity is probably impossible given the unbridgeable differences between their political systems, but neither is it essential to a stable relationship.

In the next chapter we expand our discussion from the Sino-American bilateral relationship to world order. Our conceptual approach will be the same. We start from the premise that justice—and its principles of equality and fairness—is essential to any stable political order. Neither bilateral relations nor the multifaceted relations in world order are exception to this rule. With world order the issues to be considered are much more complex than those in a bilateral relationship. We offer our thoughts on possible changes in two kinds of order—not-so-distant worlds and distant worlds—and how understandings and applications of the principles of justice might affect changes of order.

8

Reimagining World Order

In this chapter we expand our discussion of order to include all the world's political units and peoples. Our analysis is based on the premise that the principles
of justice we elaborated earlier in the book and then used to offer pathways for
restructuring Sino-American relations are with some modification universally
applicable. We start from the same assumption that we used in thinking about
China and the United States: that common understandings of justice must undergird any order and for that order to succeed in practice, behavior must to a
great extent be consistent with these principles.

We recognize that expanding our scope from two countries to almost 200 is
a challenging task in a double sense. These countries represent greater diversity
in values, interests, and relative power. Any successful order must, by definition,
be the product of negotiation, and success with such a large number of agents
is far harder than reaching a bilateral agreement. With multiple countries, the
bottom-up and top-down distinction also works differently. In bilateral relations
involving great powers it is entirely internal. Each of the two leaderships must
work out arrangements with important domestic institutions and constituencies.
They can impose new rules and procedures on them that enable or follow on
their rapprochement. They can also reach an accommodation in part because
of domestic pressures, or those pressures can shape or determine its outline
or particular form. With multilateral arrangements, the top-down, bottom-up
distinction assumes a double meaning: it can apply to negotiations within the
participating states or between them and non-state actors.

Process is always important in negotiations, and how they are structured can
shape their outcomes.[1] It is especially important in a multilateral context where

---

[1] Harald Müller and Daniel Druckman, eds., "Justice in Security Negotiations," special issue,
International Negotiation 19, no. 3 (2014); Harald Müller, *The 2005 NPT Review Conference: Reasons
and Consequences of Failure and Options for Repair*, Study of the Weapons of Mass Destruction
Commission, Number r. 31, Stockholm 2005.

Justice and International Order: East and West. Richard Ned Lebow and Feng Zhang, Oxford University Press.

less powerful political units, especially those of the Global South, must feel like valued participants whose concerns are listened to and addressed in any restructuring of order. It is much easier to conduct bilateral negotiations in accordance with the principle of equality. Historically, multilateral negotiations, even when involving only a small number of parties, have usually been organized around the principle of fairness, with the more powerful actors making the most important decisions—and generally behind closed doors. Process and substance are accordingly related. Success requires addressing the interests and needs for recognition and self-esteem of large numbers of actors, and this can only be done through a process that is largely egalitarian. It must accordingly have a significant bottom-up component.

Working within these guidelines, we explore several kinds of orders and pathways to them. None of the orders and pathways are mutually exclusive. All orders share key features, although they may put a different emphasis on them. The same pathways, or combinations of them, can be used to realize different orders. We treat orders and pathways separately and sequentially. If any significant change ever comes about, we recognize that it is almost certain to be partial rather than total and to be realized over a long time span. Our orders accordingly represent something akin to ideal types.

We recognize that some of our orders are visionary. Even those closest to today's world represent meaningful changes in the current state of affairs. Any of these orders must, by definition, be acceptable to the leading powers—the United States, China, the European Union—and they are divided on numerous issues. In the absence of some prior rapprochement between China and the West, any larger shift in global arrangements is unrealistic. This is why we focused on China and the United States in the previous chapter, written, alas, at a moment when relations between these countries were becoming more, not less, antagonistic. Russia is, of course, another important power, but it is only the eleventh largest economy, smaller than Brazil, Italy, and Canada. It is only a great power by virtue of its military might. Under Putin, it has played the role of spoiler in any efforts to bring about negotiated changes to international order. Perhaps a post-Putin Russia will frame its interests differently.

Why engage in our exercise if far-reaching international change is unlikely? We do so to encourage people to think about the possibility and the kinds of orders from which they and others would benefit. We offer models of better worlds, and describe ways of getting to them. Throughout Western history, utopias have inspired efforts to improve the world, and it is difficult to imagine that as much directed change would have occurred in their absence.

Some of our worlds are undeniably utopian, but others no more than extensions of the present that incorporate incremental improvements. These kinds of worlds are less difficult to achieve and their consequences are easier to foresee. More visionary transformations are, of course, less likely to be realized even when they are demonstrably in almost everyone's interest. We propose our far-reaching transformations with considerable caution, and not only because of the difficulty of achieving them. In literature, philosophy, and later, in politics, utopias spawned dystopias. Utopias are perfect worlds without conflict in which diverse interests are somehow harmonized. Such visions are unrealistic, and some are downright dangerous, as was the Soviet experiment.[2] The orders we moot are far from utopian; they acknowledge ongoing conflicts and some degree of dissatisfaction and disenchantment by participant states and peoples.

We design our institutions and practices on the basis of a close study of the history of international relations. We nevertheless acknowledge the "Oedipus problem": the possibility that human actions, policies, and institutions will produce the opposite effects of that which is intended.[3] This is a frequent occurrence in international relations. Consider, for example, the Anglo-American invasion of Iraq or NATO's intervention in Libya. The future is inherently unpredictable so we need to tread carefully. The best way to do this is through incremental changes that allow time to assess their consequences and to build support for further change.

Several additional caveats are in order before proceeding. Many contemporary international relations scholars equate order and peace. They are related but different. A regional or international society can be highly ordered but also violent, as were ancient Greece, many Meso-American societies, and those of the Plains Indians. For the Greeks, order structured cooperation and conflict in high stylized ways that allowed competition, even war, among city states but reduced the violence associated with it. Something similar developed in eighteenth-century Europe. As noted, utopias err in conceiving of worlds without conflicts. No kind of order, except the most brutal, oppressive kind, can do away with conflict, and such orders merely repress it at enormous costs. Successful orders must accept conflict and do their best to channel and regulate it. Postwar Western European states have been noticeably successful in this regard. Conflicts among them are frequent, but the parties involved pursue their interests by peaceful means. As we write, British and French tempers are rising over their respective post-Brexit fishing rights.[4] Both national leaders are under great pressure to

---

[2] Richard Ned Lebow, *The Politics and Ethics of Identity: In Search of Ourselves* (Cambridge: Cambridge University Press, 2012), ch. 2, for a discussion of utopias and dystopias.

[3] Richard Ned Lebow, *Reason and Cause: Social Science in a Social World* (Cambridge: Cambridge University Press, 2020), ch. 2.

[4] Fatoumata Sillah, "Tensions à Jersey: la pêche dans la Manche, un sujet encore conflictuel après l'accord post-Brexit," *Le Monde*, 7 May 2021, https://www.lemonde.fr/international/article/2021/05/07/tensions-a-jersey-la-peche-dans-la-manche-un-sujet-encore-conflictuel-apres-l-accord-post-brexit_6079535_3210.html; *Economist*, "A Fish Fight between Britain and France," 7 May 2021, https://www.economist.com/britain/2021/05/08/a-fish-fight-between-britain-and-france; Mark

demonstrate their support for their respective fishing industries. In May 2021 this led to a marine standoff in the Channel Islands involving fishing boats and military vessels. The event was dramatic but entirely peaceful and diplomacy is now at work. The confrontation is an indication of post-Brexit tensions and insecure leaders anxious to assuage important constituencies, but also of the recognition in both countries that any use of force between them is simply out of the question.

All reasonably consensual orders embrace principles of justice and instantiate them to a reasonable degree. All invent discourses to paper over the differences between theory and practice in the hope of gaining or retaining legitimacy. All foster and depend on some degree of solidarity, and here too principles of justice are foundational. In all of our imaginary and better worlds we incorporate the principles of equality and fairness. We recognize that they are frequently at odds and that differences must be negotiated or finessed. Most compromises split differences, involve trade-offs across issues, or present concessions in the expectation of future rewards. For this reason among others, such worlds—whether historical or the kind we envisage—do not resemble anything that would qualify as rational in their design. They are messier still in that they build on what is already in place and are therefore highly path-dependent. Although we start with justice, our ultimate goal is workable worlds that instantiate its principles as far as it is feasible.

Not-So-Distant Worlds

Our strategy for improving Sino-American relations sought a situation not all that far from its present state. The principal improvement is the reduction of the likelihood of war between these two superpowers. Given the current parlous state of their relations, this would be a big step forward and much of the world would breathe a sigh of relief. Accommodation, which involves close economic relations and friendship between peoples, goes a giant step beyond reducing the threat of war and is accordingly a more distant world.[5] The two stages are nevertheless related because accommodation cannot take place in the shadow of a possible war. There must be a minimum degree of rapprochement and trust on which to build cooperation through

Landler and Stephen Castle, "U.K. and France Call In the Navy, Sort of, in Channel Islands Fishing Dispute," *New York Times*, 7 May 2021, https://www.nytimes.com/2021/05/06/world/europe/uk-france-jersey-fishing.html; (all accessed 7 May 2021).

[5] For this distinction, Richard Ned Lebow, "Transitions and Transformations: Building International Cooperation," *Security Studies* 6 (Spring 1997), pp. 154–79.

reciprocity in multiple domains. This opens the door to a more far-reaching accommodation.

When we shift our focus from bilateral relations to global order, the limitation of violence is only one important goal. Even more than in Sino-American relations, it is closely connected to and dependent on other goals. Most notable in this regard is self-esteem, and with it the belief that one's country and people are not treated as inferior or inconsequential by those at the apex of the hierarchy. As noted in chapter 6, much of the Global South harbors resentment of this kind and it needs to be addressed if any progress toward a consensual order is to be made.

Equality is also an issue in Sino-American relations. China insists on being treated as an equal, and the United States is committed to maintaining its self-proclaimed hegemony. The differential in military power or wealth between the two countries and other states is considerable. The conflict between the principles of fairness and equality is more pronounced because of Chinese sensitivities left over from the era of colonialism and overt racist discrimination by the West against Asians. Improvements in substantive issues would be made much easier by first addressing the emotional ones. It is necessary to overcome the hostility that stands in the way of cooperation and to provide positive incentives toward this goal. Western leaders have consistently ignored the psychological aspect of the problem, thinking only in narrowly rationalist and materialist terms, convinced that economic rewards should provide sufficient incentives for meaningful cooperation. As we saw in chapter 6, such a strategy can backfire by intensifying the sense of humiliation felt by leaders and elites in the Global South. The Washington Consensus and its heavy-handed application by Western governments and international organization is a striking case in point.

Overcoming humiliation depends at least as much on process as it does on substance. So let us reverse the normal order of design and begin with the former. We suggest a largely bottom-up process. The initial input, in the form of expressions of great power interest in reforming the existing order and openness to proposals to do so, would be top-down. In lieu of working out proposals among themselves and then presenting them to the rest of the world, the great powers, individually or collectively, should encourage a global discussion about what could be done to improve regional and international orders. Suggestions and proposals should emerge from discussions among multiple actors, some of them states now more or less marginalized, or if admired (i.e., Norway, Costa Rica, New Zealand, South Korea), not normally consulted, and certainly not treated as equals by the great powers in matters of "high politics."

This bottom-up process could be organized in a variety of ways. The choice would depend in the first instance among the extent of agreement among the great powers to solicit and consider proposals for restructuring the international order. If China and the United States were willing to collaborate toward this end, the prospects for some change would be high, but in their absence correspondingly low, but not impossible. So let us consider how such willingness might come about.

China and the United States have traditionally seen themselves at the center of the political universe and are dismissive of others on cultural and political grounds. For Chinese, this has been the mindset for over a millennium. Relations with "civilized" neighbors as opposed to "cultural inferiors" were hierarchical and based on the principle of fairness. Koreans, Japanese, Ryukyu islanders, Taiwanese, and Vietnamese paid homage to the emperor, offered symbolic tribute, accepted the Chinese calendar, and in return received trade and security advantages.[6] Post-1949 China pursued a different policy toward its neighbors, one based more on equality. Mao Zedong and Zhou Enlai understood that a weak and externally threatened China needed to counter American encirclement and made a series of agreements with many of its neighbors in which it settled territorial disputes in their favor in return for recognition and agreement on their part not to tolerate anti-Chinese Communist forces on their territory.[7] China also sought to mobilize what were then called Third World countries for a radical, revolutionary transformation of the world order.[8] In recent years, under the leadership of Xi Jinping, China has become increasingly assertive toward its neighbors and in its foreign policy more generally.[9]

The United States has always seen itself as superior to Europeans for political reasons and to everyone else on racial grounds. It has cooperated with

---

[6] John K. Fairbank, ed, *The Chinse World Order: Traditional China's Foreign Relations* (Cambridge, MA: Harvard University Press, 1968); David Kang, *East Asia before the West: Five Centuries of Trade and Tribute* (New York: Columbia University Press, 2010); Feng Zhang, *Chinese Hegemony: Grand Strategy and International Institutions in East Asian History* (Stanford, CA: Stanford University Press, 2015).

[7] M. Taylor Fravel, *Strong Borders, Secure Nation: Cooperation and Conflict in China's Territorial Disputes* (Princeton, NJ: Princeton University Press, 2008; Chien-Peng Chung, *Domestic Politics: International Bargaining, and China's Territorial Disputes* (London: Routledge, 2004); Nie Hongyi, "Explaining Chinese Solutions to Territorial Disputes with Neighbor States," *Chinese Journal of International Politics* 2, no. 4 (2009), pp. 487–523; Zhang Yungling, "China and Its Neighbourhood: Transformation, Challenges and Grand Strategy," *International Affairs* 92, no. 4 (2016), pp. 835–48; Zhihua Shena and Julia Lovell, "Undesired Outcomes: China's Approach to Border Disputes during the Early Cold War," *Cold War History* 15, no. 1 (2015), pp. 89–111; Richard Ned Lebow, *Ethics and International Relations: A Tragic Perspective* (Cambridge: Cambridge University Press, 2020), ch. 4.

[8] Chen Jian, *Mao's China and the Cold War* (Chapel Hill: University of North Carolina Press, 2001).

[9] Alastair Iain Johnston, "How New and Assertive Is China's New Assertiveness?" *International Security* 37, no. 4 (2013), pp. 7–48; Liu Feng, "The Recalibration of Chinese Assertiveness: China's Responses to the Indo-Pacific Challenge," *International Affairs* 96, no. 1 (2020), pp. 9–27.

other states when its leaders believed it to be in their interests but has generally more focused in establishing a hegemony in the Western Hemisphere and, following World War II, extending it on a more global scale. US leaders and many academics describe their country as "the indispensable nation" and claim that its hegemony is essential to maintain international security and economic intercourse. Providing public goods is a justification of special privileges.[10] For the United States to seek guidance from others rather than telling them what to do, take the back seat rather than the lead in any negotiations where its interests are involved, and accept norms, rules, or laws that restrict its freedom of action would require a new way of thinking. This seems unlikely. The Biden administration has done its best to distance itself from Donald Trump but only to reassert all the traditional beliefs and policies of the national security establishment.[11]

Are there incentives for great power cooperation? And if so, are there reasons why China, the United States, and the European Union would encourage proposals for change from the less powerful? As things now stand, we could argue until we are blue in the face that reforms reached by consensus have the potential to make everyone more secure and are essential to addressing climate change. Logic has rarely, if ever, convinced leaders not only to change course, but to do business—that is to pursue their interests—in a radically different way. So there is no reason at the moment to think that these powers will agree to open what their leaders and their advisors will unquestionably regard as a Pandora's box, and even less so to think they will do so collectively.

Should more enlightened leadership emerge in even one of these units, our process might get under way. It needs only one great power to get the ball rolling. To the extent that a request for reform proposals is launched—say, by the European Union—and receives a positive response from a number of countries, China and the United States will begin to feel nervous. If further diplomacy gives more salience and structure to these proposals and support for them grows, the United States, and possibly China, will see incentives for getting involved. If not, they will have no say in shaping any outcome and will incur considerable wrath

---

[10] Ian Clark, *Hegemony in International Society* (Oxford: Oxford University Press, 2011), pp. 23–28; Stephen G. Brooks and William C. Wohlforth, *World out of Balance: International Relations and the Challenge of American Primacy* (Princeton, NJ: Princeton University Press, 2008); John G. Ikenberry and Charles A. Kupchan, "Socialization and Hegemonic Power," *International Organization* 44, no. 3 (1990), pp. 283–315; Fareed Zakaria, *The Post-American World* (New York: W. W. Norton, 2008). For critiques, Simon Reich and Richard Ned Lebow, *Good-Bye Hegemony! Power and Influence in the Global System* (Princeton, NJ: Princeton University Press, 2014), ch. 2; Christopher Fettweis, "Unipolarity, Hegemony, and the New World Peace," *Security Studies* 26, no. 3 (2017), pp. 423–51.

[11] Richard N. Haass, "Biden's First Hundred Days," *Project Syndicate*, April 30, 2021, https://www.project-syndicate.org/commentary/biden-hundred-days-foreign-policy-continuity-with-trump-by-richard-haass-2021-04?barrier=accesspaylog (accessed 4 June 2021).

if they try to veto or undermine it, and all the more so if considerable effort by diverse parties imparts momentum to these proposals and raises expectations of their success. The most relevant precedents here are the treaty to ban landmines and the norm of "responsibility to protect" (R2P).

The modern landmine eradication initiative began in the 1970s with the efforts of the Swiss-based International Committee (ICRC) of the Red Cross. They influenced Protocol II of the Convention on Conventional Weapons in 1980.[12] In 1993, Handicap International convinced President François Mitterrand to declare that France would voluntarily abstain from the export of landmines.[13] Other NGOs sought similar declarations from other European governments. In 1994, the Canadian government tabled the issue of an anti-landmine initiative at the G-7 meeting in Naples.[14] The Swedish government expressed its support.[15] In 1995, Belgium became the first country to ban the production, use, trading, or stockpiling of landmines. Norway and Switzerland soon followed. In 1996, the United Nations Review Conference for the Convention on Certain Conventional Weapons (CCW), called at France's request, adopted the Amended Mines Protocol. In May 1997 a Joint Statement issued by the German, French, and British foreign ministers helped to push other European Union states toward support of a landmine ban.[16]

Foreign Minister Lloyd Axworthy of Canada took the next step. The "Ottawa Process" brought together prominent individuals, NGOs, and representatives of fifty governments to "fast-track" initiatives to ban landmines. Austria submitted the original and revised drafts that became the basis for the Prohibition of the Use, Stockpiling, Production and Transfer of Anti-Personnel Mines and on their Destruction.[17] By 1999, 122 states had signed the Convention, and it entered into force in March of that year.[18] Signatories were required to destroy all

---

[12] International Committee of the Red Cross, http://www.icrc.org/ihl.nsf/FULL/510?OpenDocument (accessed 10 May 2022).

[13] Maxwell A. Cameron, Robert J. Lawson, and Brian W. Tomlin, "To Walk without Fear," in Cameron, Lawson and Tomlin, eds., *To Walk without Fear: The Global Movement to Ban Landmines* (Oxford: Oxford University Press, 1998), pp. 1–28.

[14] John English, "The Ottawa Process: Paths Followed, Paths Ahead," *Australian Journal of International Affairs* 52, no. 2 (1998), pp. 121–32.

[15] Cameron, Lawson, and Tomlin, "To Walk without Fear."

[16] Ibid.; Ann Peters, *International Partnerships on the Road to Ban Anti-Personnel Landmines* (Washington, DC: Open Society Institute), p. 15.

[17] David Long, "The European Union and the Ottawa Process to Ban Landmines," *Journal of European Public Policy* 9, no. 3 (2002), pp. 429–446, at p. 434; Stuart Casey-Maslen, "The Context of the Adoption of the Convention on the Prohibition of the Use, Stockpiling, Production and Transfer of Anti-Personnel Mines and Their Destruction (Anti-Personnel Mine Ban Convention)," Audiovisual Library of International Law, 18 September 1997, http://untreaty.un.org/cod/avl/ha/cpusptam/cpusptam.html (accessed 10 May 2021).

[18] Ibid.

anti-personnel mine stockpiles under its jurisdiction or control in no more than four years, and they had ten years to clear all anti-personnel mines in areas they controlled.[19]

The Americans were incredulous and sought to derail the process by developing a different venue for discussion, the Conference on Disarmament.[20] The Clinton administration opposed the eradication of landmines because the US military insisted that they were necessary to protect South Korean against an attack from the North. Clinton sought to derail the Ottawa process by drawing in the major producers, exporters, and users of landmines to an alternative forum.[21] Clinton's proposal and his attempt to assert leadership found little support.[22] The Europeans and Canadians pressed ahead with their efforts.[23] Success compelled the Americans to support a treaty they had strenuously opposed.[24] In collaboration with the major proponents of the Ottawa Convention, the United States reluctantly set up the Geneva International Center for Humanitarian Demining and provided critical matching funds for the International Trust Fund for removing mines and assisting victims.[25] The American domestic Mine Action Assistance budget grew by over 150 percent between 1999 and 2010, to $129.6 million, representing as much as one-quarter of all global expenditures.[26]

The problem of civilian protection offers another telling example of agenda-setting by non-great powers. In the 1990s, the Norwegian government awarded funds to the Peace Research Institute of Oslo to think through the problem of protecting civilians in civil and international conflicts and what would be required to make it a reality.[27] Norway subsequently made serious efforts to

[19] Ibid.

[20] Cameron, Lawson, and Tomlin, "To Walk without Fear."

[21] "Transcript: Clinton Remarks on Landmines," 17 September 1997, http://www.usembassy-israel.org.il/publish/press/whouse/archive/1997/september/wh4918.htm (accessed 10 May 2021).

[22] Cameron, Lawson, and Tomlin, "To Walk without Fear."

[23] For the text of The Convention on the Prohibition of the Use, Stockpiling, Production and Transfer of Anti-Personnel Mines and on Their Destruction, see International Campaign to Ban Landmines, "Treaty in Detail," http://www.icbl.org/en-gb/the-treaty/treaty-in-detail/treaty-text.aspx (accessed 10 May 2021).

[24] Julian Davis, "The Campaign to Ban Landmines: Public Diplomacy, Middle Power Leadership and an Unconventional Negotiating Process," *Journal of Humanitarian Assistance*, 15 May 2004, http://sites.tufts.edu/jha/archives/836 (accessed 10 May 2021)

[25] Mines Action Canada, *Landmine Monitor Report, 2011* (Ottawa: International Campaign to Ban Landmines, 2011), p. 52.

[26] *Landmine Monitor Report*, for 2002, 2003, 2006, and 2011, http://www.the-monitor.org/. See also US State Department, "The United States Is a World Leader in Humanitarian Mine Action," 30 November 2009, http://www.state.gov/r/pa/prs/ps/2009/nov/132591.htm (accessed 10 May 2021).

[27] Steven Radelet, "A Primer on Foreign Aid," Working Paper no. 92, Center for Global Development, July 2006.

promote the R2P doctrine in collaboration with other states and NGOs, including the Brussels-based International Crisis Group. R2P inverts the traditional realist focus on sovereignty and the rights of states by stressing their responsibility to protect civilians or be subject to the prospect of multilateral intervention.[28] By 2001, the R2P initiative had gained significant momentum and won the unstinting support of then UN Secretary-General Kofi Annan.[29] In 2005, the language of the R2P doctrine was embraced by the UN as consistent with Chapters VI and VIII of the UN Charter. By then, more than 150 world leaders had adopted R2P, legitimating the use of force through multilateral intervention initiatives sanctioned by the UN Security Council.[30] The Obama administration, like the Bush administration before it, strongly opposed R2P. In the face of widespread international support for the treaty initiative, Washington had to grit its teeth and incorporate it in its 2010 *National Security Strategy*.[31] Clever diplomacy by lesser powers, occupation by them of the moral high ground, and widespread backing from countries around the world compelled the United States to accede.

Security has traditionally been the preserve of the great powers, yet as these examples indicate, meaningful change can originate as a bottom-up process. It can succeed in the face of great power opposition and is most likely to do so when leaders of great powers conclude that they cannot stop the initiative or will lose influence and standing if they do. It also helps if they convince themselves—rightly or wrongly—that by supporting the initiative they can help shape it or possibly gain control over it. These considerations were determining

---

[28] Simon Reich, "The Evolution of a Doctrine: The Curious Case of Kofi Annan, George Bush and the Doctrines of Preventative and Preemptive Intervention," in William Keller and Gordon Mitchell, eds., *Hitting First: Preventive Force in US Security Strategy* (Pittsburgh: University of Pittsburgh Press, 2006), pp. 45–69.

[29] "Secretary-General Reflects on 'Intervention' in Thirty-Fifth Annual Ditchley Foundation Lecture," UN Press Release, SG/SM/6613, 26 June 1998, http://www.un.org/News/Press/docs/1998/19980626.sgsm6613.html; Gareth Evans and Mohamed Sahnoun, *The Responsibility to Protect: A Report by the International Commission of Intervention and State Sovereignty* (Ottawa: International Development Research Center, December 2001), http://www.dfait-maeci.gc.ca/iciss-ciise/pdf/Commission-Report.pdf; Simon Reich, "Power, Institutions and Moral Entrepreneurs," ZEF-Discussion Papers on Development Policy No. 65, Center for Development Research (ZEF), Bonn, March 2003, http://www.zef.de/publications.html; (all accessed 10 May 2021); Bruce W. Jentleson, "Coercive Prevention: Normative, Political and Policy Dilemmas," *Peaceworks*, no. 35 (Washington, DC: United States Institute of Peace, October 2000).

[30] United Nations General Assembly, "2005 World Summit Outcome," Articles 138 and 139, A/60/L.1, 15 September 2005.

[31] *National Security Strategy, May 2010*, p. 48, and also cited on the website of "The International Coalition for the Responsibility to Protect," 28 May 2010, http://www.responsibilitytoprotect.org/index.php/component/content/article/35-r2pcs-topics/2785-white-house-releases-may-2010-national-security-strategy-with-reference-to-rtop (accessed 10 May 2021).

for the Clinton administration with regard to the landmine treaty and for the Bush and Obama administrations for R2P.

Such a strategy is also feasible for bringing about more substantial changes in the international order. Here, too, there are essential preconditions. Those seeking change must make a strong ethical case so that their opponents appear unethical and open to criticism abroad, but even more importantly at home. The changes being called for cannot be directly inimical to major interests of the great powers. Great power leaders may initially think that they are, as the Americans did with the landmines treaty and R2P, and before that with arms control. They must be educated to the benefits of the proposals for themselves and the global community. Those responsible for initiatives must cobble together a large and diverse coalition of states, NGOs, and other actors. They must find or create appropriate fora in which to make their case, invite participation and support, and gain as much publicity as possible. In this regard, it helps to have some leader or state take the lead in transforming altogether diverse strands of opinion and proposal into a treaty or other formal statement which others can sign. Organizing lobbies and domestic pressure groups within the great powers can also be helpful. This was done successfully during the Cold War by Europeans anxious to advance arms control and restrain Ronald Reagan during his first term.[32]

It is therefore possible for less powerful, even peripheral, states and NGOs to start the ball rolling when it comes to structural reforms of international society. It is more likely to happen if one great power, or a coalition of them, encourages others to think about meaningful change. As noted, neither the United States nor China is likely to do this at the present time. They are also likely to resist, at least at the outset, any collective effort by other actors to float proposals for change. The hurdle in this regard is probably less in the realm of substantive interests than the challenge it constitutes to deep-seated great power beliefs in the legitimacy—even the world's need—of their status and authority.

The landmines treaty and R2P challenged great power authority by abrogating the role of sponsorship. Their advocates sought to mute the challenge to great powers by making them the principal agents for enforcement. This has traditionally been a privilege of great powers, and both treaties were rooted in this tradition, although other states were also required to perform certain tasks by the treaties. The principle of fairness was challenged by this initiative but also reinforced by the landmine treaty. The United States contributed money to clear landmines and compensate victims, and, by performing these tasks, saved face and possibly enhanced its status.

---

[32] Thomas Risse-Kappen, *Cooperation among Democracies* (Princeton, NJ: Princeton University Press, 1997); Matthew Evangelista, *Unarmed Forces: The Transnational Movement to End the Cold War* (Ithaca, NY: Cornell University Press, 2002).

More problematic would be bottom-up initiatives that seek to redistribute authority or wealth or end practices that those at the bottom of both hierarchies consider against their interests or even demeaning. Such initiatives are likely to pit more directly the principle of equality against that of fairness. They may do so, moreover, in ways that make it difficult to finesse trade-offs between the two. A case in point is the dispute that arose over the mining of metal modules on the ocean floor. Developed countries insisted that they receive the lion's share of the economic rewards because they had developed the requisite technology. Poorer countries demanded a significant share on the grounds that the ocean floor was a common human heritage. The United Nations Convention on the Law of the Sea (UNCLOS), which took effect in 1994, reflects a compromise. One of its distinguishing features is recognition of international seabed and its mineral resources as "the common heritage of mankind" and that mining operations and other activities there should be conducted "for the benefit of all mankind." There are still disputes over sharing of proceeds between African countries and the corporations that mine the seabed.[33]

Some initiatives are problematic because they involve different interpretations of one of our two principles of justice, interpretations that are likely to unite the great and developed powers against the rest. Consider various proposals for cutting carbon emissions. Developed countries want all states to cut back on their carbon emission by roughly the same percentages. Many states in the Global South argue that equality is an inappropriate criterion. Developed countries are responsible for most of the world's pollution and should make a disproportionate effort to reduce it. Developing states in turn should be given some leeway with pollutants, as they are poorer countries. The same dispute exists with respect to cutting methane emission. This fairness-based appeal has led to the principle of "common but differentiated responsibility" enshrined in the United Nations Framework Convention on Climate Change.[34]

One way to address these conflicts is through bundling. If multiple initiatives are on the table in multiple domains there is more room for trade-offs than there is any single initiative. Simultaneous pursuit of too many initiatives will lead to confusion and disagreements about which ones should be prioritized. Some careful strategizing is accordingly necessary by those hoping to foster

---

[33] Robert J. Payne, "Mining the Seabed: The Political, Economic and Legal Struggle," *Journal of Politics* 40, no. 4 (1978), pp. 933–55; Axel Hallgren and Anders Hanssen, "Conflicting Narratives of Deep Sea Mining," MDPI, *Sustainability*, 13 (2021), https://www.mdpi.com/2071-1050/13/9/5261/pdf (accessed 14 June 2012).

[34] Steve Vanderheiden, "Climate Equity in the Real World," in Chris Brown and Robyn Eckersley, eds, *The Oxford Handbook of International Political Theory* (Oxford: Oxford University Press, 2018), pp. 533–45.

change. They need to focus on no more than a few at most at a time; build as large and diverse a coalition as possible behind them; formulate workable, carefully formulated, proposals that ultimately take the form of treaties or contracts; convince the great powers that the initiatives are in their best interest; and cater to their needs to display leadership and affirm that status.

On many issues it will be difficult to cobble together a sufficiently compelling coalition of sponsors, given the cleavages and deep divisions within the world community. There is no question that developed powers construct their interests differently than do developing ones, and that there are great divisions among developing powers. The latter are prevented from coming together by ideology, regime type, regional rivalries, and degrees of development. There are also sharp differences about sovereignty, with the more authoritarian and least legitimate regimes generally its strongest supporters. Efforts to build support for some kinds of initiatives are almost certain to expose these differences and heighten divisions among developing countries. The greater the divisions and dissensus, the easier it is for the great powers to maintain their advantages and authority.

As noted, gaining the support of the great powers is probably the most difficult step. The weaker the coalition among other states, the less pressure great powers will feel to reach an accommodation. The larger the coalition and the more significant the initiative the more threatened they are likely to be. Escaping this catch-22 may require lining up the prior support of as many states as possible and at least one of the three dominant powers or power blocs in the world. Toward this end, serious efforts must be made to win over support of public opinion and political parties, something which is feasible in the United States and European Union.

Another key to success is the support of middle powers with aspirations to become great powers. They are commonly referred to as BRICS, an acronym that describes five major emerging economies: Brazil, Russia, India, China, and South Africa.[35] China is, of course, now a great power, if not a superpower. The relevant actors for our purpose are Brazil, India, and South Africa since as noted, Russia in Putin's grip is unlikely to participate in any of the initiatives we have in mind. Brazil under Jair Bolsonaro has lost influence for many reasons, including his response to the COVID pandemic. All three countries exercise some degree of regional leadership, or have the potential to, so are critical states to enlist.

---

[35] Pádraig Carmody, *The Rise of BRICS in Africa: The Geopolitics of South-South Relations* (London: Zed Books, 2013); Kwang Chun, *The BRICs Superpower Challenge: Foreign and Security Policy Analysis* (Farnham: Ashgate, 2013); Oliver Stuenkel, *Post-Western World: How Emerging Powers Are Remaking Global Order* (London: Polity, 2016), and *The BRICS and the Future of Global Order* (New York: Lexington Books, 2020).

Let us now try to imagine some of the initiatives that might emerge in a bottom-up process. Building on our analysis in the previous chapter, we think it likely, and more effective, if initial proposals are sector-specific. They must also be anchored in shared conceptions of justice, or at least of what is wrong and prohibited, permissible, and well within the envelope of accepted practice. All initiatives must advance national substantive and psychological interests without escalating conflict or threatening to beggar neighbors. Our suggestions for Sino-American rapprochement in chapter 7 emphasize reciprocity, equally central to Confucianism and Western conceptions of justice. Reciprocity not only makes agreement more likely, when successful it has the potential to build trust. In Sino-American relations we have focused on six areas of competition or dispute: status, ideology, security, economy, technology, and society. We will do the same here.

Status

The great powers are unwilling to grant higher status to others if it results in a corresponding lowering of their own. This is evident in their stonewalling efforts to expand the number of permanent seats on the Security Council. However, the number of "G" states participating in high-level international summits has increased over the years.[36] There is an important difference between the two kinds of organization. Status, as noted, is relational, but wealth is absolute. The fact that another person or state gains wealth does not make you less well off. It only matters if wealth becomes a marker of status, as both Rousseau and Smith observed it had to a greater degree in the modern world.[37] We suspect another consideration mattered with respect to "G" organizations. They are a club, and a high-status one. Clubs retain their status by being restrictive in their membership but lose it if they do not admit new members. They must strike a fine balance between elitism and openness,

[36] Peter M. Haas, "Introduction: Epistemic Communities and International Policy Coordination," *International Organization* 46, no. 1 (1992), pp. 1–35; Peter I. Hajnal, *The G8 System and the G20: Evolution, Role and Documentation* (Aldershot: Ashgate, 2007); John J. Kirton, *G20 Governance for a Globalized World* (Abingdon: Routledge, 2013).

[37] Jean-Jacques Rousseau, *Discourse on the Origin and Foundations of Inequality* (Second Discourse), in Roger D. Masters, ed., Roger D. Masters and Judith R. Masters, trans., *The First and Second Discourses* (New York: St. Martin's, 1964), pp. 115–16, 147–60; Adam Smith, *The Theory of Moral Sentiments* (Cambridge: Cambridge University Press, 2002 [1759]), I.iii.2, p. 71; IV.1, pp. 257–68; VI.1, pp. 310–12.

and the best way to do this is to admit from time to time a few outstanding candidates.

The great powers—like people in general—are more willing to grant status to others when it is not in the same domain as they claim theirs. Championship League footballers do not feel threatened by those who achieve recognition as outstanding chefs. So it is in international relations. States have sought to expand the number of ways in which status can be achieved and to raise the level of prestige associated with existing statuses. Switzerland, and to a lesser extent, Sweden and Austria, transformed the once lowly status of neutrality into a high-status one by virtue of their hosting international organizations and acting as disinterested third parties in conflicts.[38] In the postwar world, wealth became as much a source of status as military might. Germany and Japan gained standing by virtue of their miraculous economic recoveries. So did the Four Asian Tigers of South Korea, Taiwan, Singapore, and Hong Kong, and now China, which underwent rapid economic development and with it a significant rise in the living standards of the populations. The Netherlands, Scandinavian countries, and more recently South Korea gained prestige by virtue of their foreign aid programs, to which they devote a higher percentage of the GDP than do other developed countries. Norway and Canada have enhanced status because of their efforts at sponsorship, mediation, and peacekeeping, although in Canada's case some claim it is now more than a myth than a practice.[39] The United States, the former Soviet Union, and Germany did the same through scientific achievements. Saudi Arabia and Iran have sought prestige and influence through their support respectively of Sunni and Shia branches of Islam.

Most of these niches were developed by wealthy countries, or countries in the process of becoming wealthy. Fewer options are open to less-developed countries, although it is still possible for them to improve their standing.

---

[38] Johanna Rainio-Niemi, *The Ideological Cold War: The Politics of Neutrality in Austria and Finland* (London: Routledge, 1914); Herbert R. Reginbogin, *Faces of Neutrality: A Comparative Analysis of Switzerland and Other Neutral Nations during World War II* (Berlin: Lit Verlag, 2009); Mikael Malmborg, *Neutrality and State-Building in Sweden* (Houndmills: Palgrave, 2001); Richard Ned Lebow, *National Identities and International Relations* (Cambridge: Cambridge University Press, 2016), pp. 92–93.

[39] Elin Marthinussen Gustavsen and Andreas Forø Tollefsen, "What Became of the Norwegian Peacekeeping Forces?" *Peace Research Institute Oslo*, 8 August 2018, https://blogs.prio.org/2018/08/what-became-of-the-norwegian-peacekeeping-forces/; Michael K. Carroll, "Peacekeeping: Canada's Past, but Not Its Present and Future?" *International Journal* 71, no. 1 (2016), pp. 167–76; Corbett Hancey, "The International Myth of Canada as a Peacekeeping Nation," *Walrus*, 6 July 2019, https://thewalrus.ca/the-international-myth-of-canada-as-a-peacekeeping-nation/ (both accessed 31 May 2021).

Bhutan attracted considerable attention for its leadership's commitment to the overall well-being of its still relatively poor population. It also lost prestige, however, for its persecution of its Hindu minority.[40] Costa Rica achieved respect for its democratic institutions and disbanding of its armed forces.[41] Botswana has gained standing for possessing the most robust democracy in Africa.[42] New Zealand, Taiwan, and South Korea were greatly admired for their effective responses to COVID, but so too were poor countries like Mauritius, Nigeria, Kenya, Peru, and Vietnam.[43] Nigeria has gained regional standing through the size of its economy, appeal of its music, and its active role in peacekeeping.[44]

Less-developed states and those with more resources must become entrepreneurs in pioneering new pathways to status or exploiting existing ones. With the shift in appeal from fairness to equality, new possibilities have opened up. Many of the above examples could not have happened in a fairness-dominated world. The countries involved would not have had the freedom to act as they did or gained prestige from doing so. There are many ways equality, public goods and services, and accomplishments in all kinds of realms can be exploited for purposes of status. Success here requires those seeking higher status to develop strategies appropriate to their diverse resources but also openness on the part of the great powers and more developed states to conferring status on them. China, Russia, and India all sought prestige through the export of their anti-COVID vaccines. The United States and the European Union, by contrast, gave priority to internal needs and only belatedly committed themselves to dropping barriers

[40] William J. Long, *Tantric State: A Buddhist Approach to Democracy and Development in Bhutan* (New York: Oxford University Press, 2019); Bill Frelick, "Bhutan's Ethnic Cleansing," *Human Rights Watch*, 1 February 2008, https://www.hrw.org/news/2008/02/01/bhutans-ethnic-cleansing# (accessed 31 May 2012).

[41] Judith Eve Lipton and David P. Barash, *Strength through Peace* (Oxford: Oxford University Press, 2018).

[42] Kenneth Good and Ian Taylor, "Botswana: A Minimalist Democracy," *Democratization* 15, no. 4 (2008), pp. 750–65. Kebapeste Lotshwao, Robert Imre, and Jim Jose, "Democracy Assistance for Botswana: Maintaining the Status Quo in a Peripheral Capitalist Country," *Journal of Developing Societies* 35, no. 2 (2019), pp. 205–29.

[43] Amy Maxmen, "How Poorer Countries Are Scrambling to Prevent a Coronavirus Disaster," *Nature*, 2 April 2020, https://www.nature.com/articles/d41586-020-00983-9; Maru Mormina and Ifeanyi Nosfor, "What Developing Countries Can Teach Rich Countries about How to Respond to a Pandemic," *Conversation*, 15 October 2020, https://theconversation.com/what-developing-countries-can-teach-rich-countries-about-how-to-respond-to-a-pandemic-146784 (both accessed 8 April 2021).

[44] Suleiman Hamman, Ibrahim Khalid Mustafa, and Kayode Omojuwa, "The Role of Nigeria in Peacekeeping Operations from 1960 to 2013," *International Affairs and Global Strategy* 21 (2014), https://core.ac.uk/download/pdf/234670591.pdf (accessed 31 May 2021).

to the transfer of technology necessary to manufacture vaccines and then to the export of millions of vaccines.[45]

In traditional societies, status was a function more of birth than of achievement, and war and athletic prowess were the principal achievements that were respected. One of the features of modernity is the opening up of multiple and diverse pathways to status. This allows anyone who excels at something to gain the respect of their peers, or even society at large, and feel better about themselves. International society, by contrast, has been slow to follow suit, and is only now doing so.[46] China, the United States, the European Union, and other developed countries must do their best to recognize new pathways and reward states that exploit them successfully. This reciprocal process can increase prestige and status throughout the international community without lowering that of states who already rank high in status.

Ideology

Ideology has historically been a means for an elite to justify its rule and privileges, and for counter-elites to challenge them. It has functioned in a similar way in international relations. The concept of Christendom was used to exclude the Ottoman Empire for some centuries and to marginalize other "heathen" political units. So too did Western countries invoke the concept of the state as a sign of civilization, providing the justification for war and colonization of other kinds of political units.[47] In the postwar era, democracy was mobilized by the West, and Marxism by the East, to claim the high ground, acquire prestige and influence, and justify behavior unambiguously at odds with the principles each bloc

---

[45] Simon Frankel Pratt and Jamie Levin, "Vaccines Will Shape the New Geopolitical Order," *Foreign Policy*, 29 April 2021, https://foreignpolicy.com/2021/04/29/vaccine-geopolitics-diplomacy-israel-russia-china/ (accessed 4 June 2021); Francesco Guarascio and Robin Emmott, "EU, U.S. to Agree Reduction of Vaccine Export Barriers, Summit Draft Says," *Reuters*, 9 June 2021, https://www.reuters.com/business/healthcare-pharmaceuticals/eu-us-reduce-vaccine-export-barriers-summit-draft-says-2021-06-09/; White House, "FACT SHEET: Biden-Harris Administration Is Providing at Least 80 Million COVID-19 Vaccines for Global Use, Commits to Leading a Multilateral Effort toward Ending the Pandemic," 17 May 2021, https://www.whitehouse.gov/briefing-room/statements-releases/2021/05/17/fact-sheet-biden-harris-administration-is-providing-at-least-80-million-covid-19-vaccines-for-global-use-commits-to-leading-a-multilateral-effort-toward-ending-the-pandemic/ (both accessed 14 June 2021).

[46] Lebow, *National Identifications and International*, ch. 4.

[47] Anthony Pagden, *Lords of All the World: Ideologies of Empire in Spain, Britain, and France, c. 1500–c. 1800* (New Haven, CT: Yale University Press, 1995); David Armitage, *The Ideological Origins of the British Empire* (Cambridge: Cambridge University Press, 2000); Sankar Muthu, *Enlightenment against Empire* (Princeton, NJ: Princeton University Press, 2003).

insisted it was encouraging and upholding. Ideology was mobilized to gain prestige, and some allege it is one of the bases of soft power.[48]

Ideology was used by other countries to gain status and influence. Nationalism and anti-colonialism were mobilized to this end by China, India, Egypt, and Indonesia in the 1950s and 1960s. They found collective expression in the Bandung Conference of 1955.[49] In 1961, the Non-Aligned Movement was founded in Belgrade. By 2012, it had 120 members.[50] Gamal Abdel Nasser's nationalization of the Suez Canal in 1956 and challenge of Israel in 1967 brought him and Egypt prestige in the "Third World" even though it provoked two wars in which Egypt was defeated.[51] Saudi Arabia's control of Mecca and management of the Haj confers prestige throughout the Muslim world.[52] The United Kingdom punched above its weight for much of the Cold War due to its "special relationship" with the United States.[53] Both the United Kingdom and the United States gain status from the usage of English as a lingua franca. Castro's Cuba, the Sandinistas in Nicaragua, Bolivia's Evo Morales, and Hugo Chávez in Venezuela have used ideologies to their regional advantage. Right-wing dictators in Turkey and Hungary aspired to do the same.[54]

---

[48] Burcu Baykurt and Victoria de Grazia, eds., *Soft-Power Internationalism: Competing for Cultural Influence in the 21st-Century Global Order* (Cambridge: Cambridge University Press, 2021).

[49] George McTurnan Kahin, *The Asian-African Conference: Bandung, Indonesia, April 1955* (Ithaca, NY: Cornell University Press, 1956); Amitav Acharya, "Studying the Bandung Conference from a Global IR perspective," *Australian Journal of International Affairs* 70, no. 4 (2016), pp. 342–57.

[50] Sally Morphet, "Multilateralism and the Non-Aligned Movement: What Is the Global South Doing and Where Is It Going?" *Global Governance* 10 (2004), pp. 517–37; William C. Potter and Gaukar Mukhatzanova, *Nuclear Politics and the Non-Aligned Movement: Principles vs. Pragmatism* (New York: Routledge, 2012).

[51] Fawaz A. Gerges, *Making the Arab World: Nasser, Qutb, and the Clash That Shaped the Middle East* (Princeton, NJ: Princeton University Press, 2018).

[52] Menno Preuschaft, "Islam and Identity in Foreign Policy," in Neil Partrick, ed., *Saudi Arabian Foreign Policy: Conflict and Cooperation*, Library of International Relations (London: Tauris, 2016), ch. 2; Fred Dews, Peter Mandaville, Shadi Hamid, and William Frey, "How Saudi Arabia and Iran Use Islam in Foreign Policy," *Brookings Institution*, podcast, 11 January 2019. Text available at https://www.brookings.edu/wp-content/uploads/2019/01/190111_BrookingsCafeteria_HamidMandaville1.pdf (accessed 31 May 2021).

[53] William Roger Louis and Hedley Bull, eds., *The "Special Relationship": Anglo-American Relations since 1945*, 2nd ed. (Oxford: Oxford University Press, 1987); Christopher John Bartlett, *The Special Relationship: A Political History of Anglo-American Relations since 1945* (London: Longman, 1992).

[54] Ross Douthat, "Why Hungary Inspires So Much Fear and Fascination," *New York Times*, 7 August 2021, https://www.nytimes.com/2021/08/07/opinion/sunday/hungary-orban-conservatives-free-speech.html; Kenneth P. Vogel and Benjamin Novak, " Hungary's Leader Fights Criticism in U.S. via Vast Influence Campaign," *New York Times*, 4 October 2021, https://www.nytimes.com/2021/10/04/us/politics/hungary-orban-lobbying.html; Benjamin Wallace-Wells, "What Rod Dreher Sees in Viktor Orbán," *New Yorker*, 13 September 2021, https://www.newyorker.com/news/annals-of-inquiry/what-rod-dreher-sees-in-viktor-orban (both accessed 10 October 2021).

The so-called Washington Consensus was a tool of neoliberals and the United States to advance Western economic and financial interests at the expense of poorer, indebted countries.[55] Within the European Union, Germany, France, and the Netherlands did something similar with respect to the poorer countries of southern Europe.[56] As noted in chapter 6, neoliberals proclaimed the end of ideology following the end of the Cold War and of communism in Europe.[57] Democracy and globalization together were to unify the world, promote prosperity, and do away with regional and international conflict. Neoliberalism and democracy promotion, like communism before it, were efforts to impose an ideology and its associated institutions and way of life on other countries. These efforts badly backfired, first for the Soviet Union, and more recently, although less dramatically, for the United States.

Ideological pluralism would be a positive step toward regional and world order. It rests on the acceptance that all understandings of justice, political order, and economic organizations are subjective. Leaders and peoples should be free to make their own choices without being labeled as "rogue states" and made into pariahs. US efforts to isolate a series of states for largely ideological reasons have not been welcome or particularly effective, beginning with attempts to isolate Cuba and assassinate its leader. Fidel Castro was not initially a communist, but US efforts to overthrow his regime pushed him into the arms of the Soviet Union.[58] The United States sought unsuccessfully to isolate China and keep it out of the United Nations.[59] China tried to squeeze the international space of Taiwan by similar means, and still holds open the possibility of invasion. Taiwan has prospered despite Chinese attempts to isolate it by denying recognition to

[55] Adam Tooze, "Everything You Know about Global Order Is Wrong," *Foreign Policy*, January 2019, https://foreignpolicy.com/2019/01/30/everything-you-know-about-global-order-is-wrong/ (accessed 6 January 2021); Philip Mirowski, "Neoliberalism: The Movement That Dare Not Speak Its Name," *American Affairs* 2, no. 1 (2018), pp. 1–20.

[56] Mirowski, "Neoliberalism"; Tooze, "Everything You Know About Global Order Is Wrong."

[57] Francis Fukuyama, *The End of History and the Last Man* (New York: Free Press, 1992); Thomas Friedman, *The Lexus and the Olive Tree* (New York: Farrar, Straus & Giroux, 1999); Alexander L. Wendt, "Why a World State Is Inevitable," *European Journal of International Relations* 9, no. 4 (2003), pp. 491–542.

[58] Piero Gleijeses, *Conflicting Missions: Havana, Washington, and Africa, 1959–1976* (Chapel Hill: University of North Carolina Press, 2002); Emily J. Kirk, Anna Clayfield, and Isabel Story, eds., *Cuba's Forgotten Decade: How the 1970s Shaped the Revolution* (Lanham, MD: Lexington Books, 2018); James G. Hershberg, "New Russian Evidence on Soviet-Cuban Relations, 1960–61: When Nikita Met Fidel, the Bay of Pigs, and Assassination Plotting," *Cold War History Project*, Working Paper #90, February 2019, https://www.wilsoncenter.org/publication/new-russian-evidence-soviet-cuban-relations-1960-61-when-nikita-met-fidel-the-bay-pigs (accessed 31 May 2021).

[59] See John Pomfret, *The Beautiful Country and the Middle Kingdom: America and China, 1776 to the Present* (New York: Henry Holt, 2016); Henry A. Kissinger, *On China* (New York: Penguin, 2011).

any country that recognizes it. The future of Beijing-Taipei relations remains uncertain, and the possibility of war cannot be ruled out.

Superpower restraint would pay off in other ways, most notably by easing, or at least not increasing, the sense of powerlessness and humiliation felt by peoples in much of the Global South. There are nevertheless important trade-offs to consider here. Total political laissez-faire would mean voicing no protest in response to human rights violations made by other states. This would be politically difficult for some leaders and could make silent states appear to be tacit accomplices in oppression and genocide. We will return to this problem.

Security

Security is a universal concern, and realists insist should be the primary concern of states. Traditionally, the search for security prompted states to maintain armies and navies and make alliances with one another. There is a time-honored Latin saying that the best way to prevent war is to prepare for it: *si vis pacem, para bellum*. Modern history offers much evidence that such preparations are a major cause of war. Collective security developed as an alternative, based on the idea that the community as a whole would band together to punish aggressors and that its overwhelming might would deter them.[60]

Collective security was made a principal responsibility of the United Nations Security Council. Aggression is, of course, a freighted concept; different states have quite opposed understandings of the use of force in many circumstances. For much of its existence, the Security Council has been hamstrung by division. States have accordingly continued to rely on their own armed forces and alliances like NATO. As in the Cold War, they continue to be major sources of contention and are more likely to be causes of war than its prevention. Nuclear proliferation by India, Pakistan, and North Korea, attempts at it by Iran, and naval competition between China and the United States are cases in point.

Another problem of collective security is that there is nobody to police the policemen. The great powers, the superpowers during the Cold War, and the United States in its aftermath, have been the principal initiators of military action, along with India and Israel. They used force for diverse reasons, but all

[60] Robert Osgood, "Woodrow Wilson, Collective Security, and the Lessons of History," *Confluence* 5, no. 4 (Winter 1957), pp. 341–54; Richard K. Betts, "Systems for Peace or Causes of War? Collective Security, Arms Control and the New Europe," *International Security* 17, no. 1 (1992), pp. 5–43; George Downs, ed., *Collective Security beyond the Cold War* (Ann Arbor: University of Michigan Press, 1994).

claimed to be acting in the name of security, if not collective security. Britain and France, and other European colonial powers, sought to maintain their empires or their interests in former colonies. The Soviet Union used force to maintain its hegemony in Eastern Europe and fought a losing war in Afghanistan. Russia under Putin has been an expansionist power, initiating several wars in its near abroad. The United States acted in defense of the status quo in Korea and the Persian Gulf, but it is difficult to justify most of its other interventions with reference to common interest—or its own national interest. China used force more sparingly, and like the other powers, for perceived defensive purposes. It nevertheless waged an unnecessary and costly war against Vietnam and holds out the threat of using it against Taiwan if it declares de jure independence. The United States continues to carry out airstrikes, usually by drones, against terrorists in multiple countries.

The great powers are by no means the only threats to peace. Israel waged defensive wars, but there was no legitimate excuse for its ill-conceived 1982 invasion and temporary occupation of Lebanon. Other regional powers like India, Iran, Iraq, and Argentina have waged expansionist wars. North Korea invaded South Korea in 1950 and has used force on a smaller scale against the South ever since. North Korea, Pakistan, Libya, Iran, and the Palestinians have used or sponsored terrorism against their opponents, sometimes provoking military reprisals. Many states have used violence against their own citizens, sometimes leading to extremely destructive civil wars, as in Sri Lanka, Syria, and several African countries.

Global security is thus a multifaceted problem. Collective security will not work in the absence of a fundamental consensus among the great powers, and there seems little likelihood that China, Russia, the United States, France, and the United Kingdom will see eye to eye in the near future. They are more likely to support client states in their wars, as Russia has done with Syria, than to cooperate to prevent or end third-party wars. Territorial disputes and pretensions of regional dominance among lesser powers show no sign of abating. Non-state actors, like al-Qaeda and ISIS, have played an increasingly prominent role in starting or fighting wars.

For all these reasons, we are not optimistic about the prospects of reducing international violence. Some degree of Sino-American rapprochement could lessen the chance of war in the Taiwan Strait and perhaps the use of force in conflicting claims to the islands and islets in the Pacific Rim. A Western accommodation with Putin's successor would reduce the likelihood of violence in Eastern Europe and possibly make disputes in the Caucasus more amenable to negotiation. So too would any kind of accommodation among the leading powers reduce the chances of wars by regional powers, or if not, keep them more limited in scope and duration.

Traditional great power accommodations frequently involved delineating spheres of influence. They could advance the interests of peace by resolving, finessing, or avoiding territorial conflicts, which were usually a principal cause of war. They are out of the question today, in a world in which nationalism is rife and equality has replaced fairness as the dominant principle of justice. Territories and countries can no longer be occupied, swapped, or arbitrarily assigned to one or another power's sphere of influence. At best, great powers acting in concert can intervene to mediate or, in some circumstances, impose and enforce ceasefires, and help negotiate settlements. In the absence of some kind of great power accommodation, this is unlikely to happen. We can only hope that progress in the other domains we discuss will create more incentives for such a rapprochement and make it easier to achieve.

Economy

Economy, especially the capitalist mode of growth, is a central pillar of the modern world order. It is also a source of international rivalry and global instability. In the twenty-first century, the two central issues of the global economic order are economic inequality between the North and South and the Sino-American trade conflict and its unsettling impact on the international trade system.

Global inequality between the rich and poor has reached unconscionable levels in the twentieth century. In 1989 the two richest countries—the United States and Japan—accounted for 45 percent of the global GNP, while the forty-four least-developed countries had a share of world income of less than 0.6 percent. In 1996 the combined GDP of the poorest 180 countries was less than the GDP of one country—the United States.[61] In the first two decades of the present century, inequality between the West and the developing world declined somewhat, largely owing to the rapid growth of China and other emerging economies.[62] Nevertheless, income inequality among the world's population continued to rise. In 2016 the richest 1 percent's share of wealth was over 50 percent, greater than the combined wealth of the remaining 99 percent, whereas in 2009 it was about 44 percent.[63]

---

[61] Debra Satz, "International Economic Justice," in Hugh LaFollette, ed., *The Oxford Handbook of Practical Ethics* (Oxford: Oxford University Press, 2005), pp. 620–42, at p. 620.

[62] Branko Milanovic, *Global Inequality: A New Approach for the Age of Globalization* (Cambridge, MA: Harvard University Press, 2016), p. 123.

[63] Darrel Moellendorf, "Real World Global Egalitarianism," in Chris Brown and Robyn Eckersley, eds., *The Oxford Handbook of International Political Theory* (Oxford: Oxford University Press, 2018), pp. 119–29, at p. 119.

The global wealth gap of this magnitude was in the first instance a consequence of the highly unequal modern world order created—by force when necessary—by the European colonial powers and their North Atlantic offshoots. With Western industrialization and colonialism in the nineteenth century came a gulf between rich and poor nations, powerful and powerless nations, that was unprecedented in world history.

Once again, the principles of fairness and equality are sharply at odds. Rich nations justify their wealth on the basis of the education, skills, and other qualities of their populations. Following liberal ideology, their spokesmen frequently assert that the rest of the world benefits enormously from their wealth. Those favoring some redistribution insist that growing inequality across nations is inexcusable in today's world and that a more significant contribution from rich to poor nations would not significantly affect the former's standard of living.

Some philosophers argue that in the pursuit of global justice, rich nations in the developed West bear a moral responsibility to transfer part of their wealth to poor countries in the Global South. Martha C. Nussbaum, for example, proposes that the governments of rich nations ought to give a minimum of 2 percent of GDP to poor nations.[64] Other scholars counter that global wealth transfer conflicts with the right of national self-determination. Those who are poorer cannot have any claim on the wealth of the richer. Such claim would generate a moral hazard problem, where some people would expend less effort or make irresponsible collective choices and then ask to share income acquired by those who were more hard-working and prudent or made better decisions. But these objections have their own problems. The right of national self-determination can be interrogated in an inquiry into global justice; it is certainly not an absolute right, as the debates on humanitarian intervention and the norm of the R2P attest. The moral hazard objection would apply equally in a domestic setting; yet domestically most people think wealth transfer justified.[65] There must be an additional argument against international redistribution of wealth.

Ultimately, global wealth transfer is more a problem of feasibility than of principle. At present no government of rich nations is willing—or is able—to persuade its public to engage in outright wealth transfer to the Global South. Branko Milanovic plumps for a less demanding option: an orderly migration from poor to rich countries, with quotas at the level of both the sending and the recipient countries.[66] Migration, even if tainted by discriminatory treatment of

---

[64] Martha C. Nussbaum, *Creating Capabilities: The Human Development Approach* (Cambridge, MA: Harvard University Press, 2011), p. 117.

[65] Milanovic, *Global Inequality*, p. 141.

[66] Ibid., p. 231.

migrants in rich countries, could contribute to the reduction in world poverty and inequality. He notes that this might require a redefinition of citizenship in rich countries whereby mild differences in the treatment of local and foreign labor can be legalized. This in turn would have the salutary effect of overcoming the current anti-immigrant, and in some cases xenophobic, public opinion in these countries.[67]

Even so, migration is no panacea. A more lasting solution to global economic inequality is the sustainable development of the Global South. Economic growth is the most powerful tool for reducing global poverty and inequality.[68] It is therefore extremely important for the rich and powerful nations to create a favorable international economic environment for the growth of the developing world. China in the reform era is the quintessential success story of a country determined on economic development and able to exploit a facilitating international environment. But the success of China is hardly enough. In fact, after reducing global inequality for three decades the continued growth of China might widen inequality by increasing the gap between itself and other developing countries. In the coming decades, growth in the Global South beyond China will be essential.

That growth will depend to a significant extent on the international trading system, and yet this system is now under assault by the Sino-American trade conflict. We examined the bilateral dimension of this conflict in the previous chapter; now is the time to consider its global ramifications. The postwar international trading regime as embodied by the General Agreement on Tariffs and Trade (GATT, 1947–1994) and the World Trade Organization (WTO, 1995–present) was a creation of the United States and its allies. Washington constructed liberal rules and institutions of global economic governance to project its power and influence. The accession of China to the WTO in 2001 and the continued growth of the Chinese economy, however, have severely weakened Washington's ability to dominate the rules and institutions of global trade. As the United States has adjusted its China strategy from engagement to competition since the Trump years, the two countries are engaged in a struggle over the rules of global trade, with each seeking to shape the rules to reflect and advance its interests. China is no longer willing to be a rule-taker, or to accept rules demanded by the United States. As Kristen Hopewell shows, the Sino-American confrontation has paralyzed global trade governance and led to a breakdown in rulemaking. This undermines the institutions that are essential to ensuring stability and order in the international trading system. It also adversely affects a

---

[67] Ibid., p. 154.
[68] Ibid., p. 232.

broad set of issues, including efforts to promote global development and protect the environment.[69]

Some kind of cessation or resolution to the Sino-American trade war is necessary to advance international trade. In the previous chapter we endorse a three-fold solution. First, both America and China should be allowed considerable latitude at home to design a wide variety of industrial policies, technological systems, and social standards. Second, they should use well-calibrated policies (including tariff and non-tariff trade policies) to protect their industrial, technological, and social policy choices domestically without imposing unnecessary and asymmetric burdens on foreign actors. Third, they should cooperate to devise a set of trade rules to prevent countries from deploying "beggar-thy-neighbor" policies—those that produce benefits to the home country only through the harm they impose on other countries.

The WTO is the venue for the third step of crafting new trade rules. This is difficult because consensus is lacking over how China should be classified and treated under multilateral trade rules. China is now the world's largest trading nation and the second largest economy; yet when it comes to per capita income, which at the 2021 level of $11,000 is only 16 percent of the US figure of $68,000, it may be seen as a developing country. Naturally, China demands certain exemptions from global trade disciplines—especially those concerning market access and subsidies—in light of its developing country status, but the United States refuses to extend such special treatment to its chief economic and strategic competitor. Instead, it demands the application of universal rules of reciprocity and fairness. The confrontation underscores the challenge of negotiating trade rules between two dominant powers at different levels of development and reflects the tension between two core principles of the multilateral trading system: reciprocity versus special and differential treatment.[70] Hopewell observes:

> At the heart of this conflict are competing interests, as well as ideas of fairness. From the perspective of the US, fairness means a level playing field, based on universal rules applying equally to all, and the reciprocal exchange of concessions. But from China's perspective, what the US perceives as a level playing field is, in fact, one that serves to perpetuate its industrial and economic supremacy.[71]

---

[69] Kristen Hopewell, *Clash of Powers: US-China Rivalry in Global Trade Governance* (Cambridge: Cambridge University Press, 2020), p. 12.

[70] Ibid., p. 34.

[71] Ibid., p. 37.

We argue that China must resolve to untangle its conflicted identities. It cannot have it both ways—leadership in global economic governance and developing country status. If it clings to the latter, it should abandon some of its leadership ambitions that come into conflict with the United States. China must realize, however, that even if its developing country status may be justified on per capita grounds, it is unlike any other developing country given the enormous aggregate size of its economy and its outsized effect on the global economy. It will be in a rank of its own, and that implies special obligations for global economic governance, with which Beijing has yet to come to grips.

If China wants to strive for global leadership, it should no longer fight a defensive battle for its self-identification as a developing country. There is nothing wrong with great powers longing for global leadership, as long as that leadership is commensurate with its power and is exercised wisely. At present this cannot be said of China. Despite setting itself up as a champion of developing countries, its massive subsidies and export credit for its own industries and companies are damaging the development of poor countries in addition to creating frictions with the West. If China does not change course, it will follow the footsteps of the United States and other Western countries whose trade policies have harmed the Global South. This will run counter to Beijing's stated objective of achieving a fair and just international order that accommodates the needs of the Global South for development.

In WTO reform, no serious observer is under the illusion that China will transform itself into a liberal market economy by virtue of Western pressure. But it is possible to resolve the two biggest irritants in Sino-Western trade relations—the role of state-owned enterprises (SOEs) and forced transfer of technology—by engaging in a new round of multilateral negotiations. As scholars of international trade point out, new multilateral agreements such as the Comprehensive and Progressive Trans-Pacific Partnership and the US-Mexico-Canada Agreement already contain detailed clauses regarding the discipling of SOEs and forced technology transfers. A renegotiated WTO agreement should make it clear that all SOEs are presumptively "public bodies" and must act in accordance with "commercial considerations." And, to address the issue of forced technology transfer, WTO signatories should be constrained not to enforce contracts between domestic and foreign firms that oblige the foreign investor to transfer technology to its domestic partner against its wishes.[72] This kind of reform will meet the US and Western demands for fairness and is not unfair to China. To take advantage of the global trading regime centered on the WTO, which has an

---

[72] Petros C. Mavroidis and Andre Sapir, "China and the WTO: How Can They Work Together Better?" *Vox EU*, 30 April 2021, https://voxeu.org/article/china-and-wto-how-can-they-work-toget her-better (accessed 12 June 2021).

implicit liberal underpinning, it is proper for Beijing to offer concessions on the illiberal aspects of its economic practices.

This does not mean that the United States commands the moral high ground. Historically, Washington relied on state intervention and employed a range of protectionist policies during its own process of economic development. Alexander Hamilton famously used the infant industry argument for applying tariffs and subsidies to foster early industrialization. Throughout the nineteenth century the United States aggressively adopted and not infrequently stole the latest technology from Britain, the most advanced country at the time.[73] In the postwar period, when Washington claims to be the hegemon of the liberal international order, it has deviated from the principles of free trade and made use of protectionism when doing so served its interests. Under the four years of Trump, the United States actively sabotaged the global trade order by blatantly violating its rules and principles through the raw use of power. Neither the United States nor China has lived up to their leadership roles in global economic governance.

Technology

Technology has increasingly become a source of wealth, status, and well-being. It has also become more diffuse. A century ago, scientific and technological advances were the preserve of a small number of European powers and the United States. Today, Japan, China, South Korea, Taiwan, and Israel are increasingly major players, as is India in biotechnology. As we write, China has landed a space probe with a rover on Mars, becoming the second nation to do so.[74] The spread of technology, we contend, is in everyone's interest.

The diffusion of technology encourages interdependence. Liberals have long contended that interdependence more generally reduces the likelihood of war between countries by raising its costs. International relations theorists have explored this question in some detail, with much debate centered on the seeming failure of interdependence to prevent World War I.[75] Specifically

---

[73] Clyde Prestowitz, *The World Turned Upside Down: America, China, and the Struggle for Global Leadership* (New Haven, CT: Yale University Press, 2021), ch. 5.

[74] Steven Lee Myers and Kenneth Chang, "China's Mars Rover Mission Lands on the Red Planet," *New York Times*, 19 May 2021, https://www.nytimes.com/2021/05/14/science/china-mars.html (accessed 30 May 2021).

[75] Patrick McDonald, *The Invisible Hand of Peace: Capitalism, the War Machine, and International Relations Theory* (Cambridge: Cambridge University Press, 2012); Edward D. Mansfield and Brian Pollins, eds., *Economic Interdependence and International Conflict* (Ann Arbor: University of Michigan Press, 2003); David M. Rowe, "The Tragedy of Liberalism: How Globalization Caused the First World War," *Security Studies* 14, no. 3 (2005), pp. 407–47; Erik Gartzke and Yonatan Lupu,

addressing the question of technology, Stephen Brooks argues the kind of interdependence that exists in Western Europe makes war among these states unthinkable, in part because their weapons production has become so interdependent.[76] The rest of the world has not come anything close to developing this kind of interdependence.

As we argue in chapter 6, interdependence is a double-edged sword. More or less equally beneficial economic relationships between countries probably promote peace, but one-sided ones are more likely to breed resentment. For this reason, enthusiasm for globalization among liberals has given way to a more cautious or even jaundiced view of its consequences.[77] Even countries that benefit from interdependence may be wary of it for strategic reasons. China has identified the sectors where the United States or others could cut off access to crucial technologies and has allocated tens of billions of dollars to its tech industry to develop these capabilities. They have made clear their ambitions to become an innovation superpower beholden to none.[78]

We nevertheless believe that technology transfer is the longer-term interest of all parties. It can be accomplished by locating high-tech businesses and research institutes in developing countries and the large-scale education of students from these countries in developed ones. Funds could also be made available for start-ups and other businesses that would help transform their economies and move them away from suppling raw materials for finished goods. Some of this research and technology could be focused on combating climate change.[79] Developing countries will always be behind the economic curve until they develop a

"Trading on Preconceptions: Why World War I Was Not a Failure of Economic Interdependence," *International Security* 36, no. 4 (2012), pp. 115–50.

[76] Stephen G. Brooks, *Producing Security: Multinational Corporations, Globalization, and the Changing Calculus of Conflict* (Princeton, NJ: Princeton University Press, 2005).

[77] John Gray, *False Dawn: The Delusions of Global Capitalism* (New York: Free Press, 2000); Joseph Stiglitz, *Globalization and Its Discontents* (New York: W. W. Norton, 2002), and *Globalization and Its Discontents Revisited: Anti-Globalization in the Era of Trump* (New York: W. W. Norton, 2020); Dani Rodrik, *The Globalization Paradox: Democracy and the Future of the World Economy* (New York: W. W. Norton, 2012); Andrew Hurrell, *On Global Order: Power, Values, and the Constitution of International Society* (Oxford: Oxford University Press, 2007), ch. 8; Klaus Schwab. "We Need a New Narrative for Globalization," *World Economic Forum*, 17 March 2017, https://www.weforum.org/agenda/2017/03/klaus-schwab-new-narrative-for-globalization/ (accessed 1 January 2021); Patrick Porter, *The False Promise of the Liberal Order* (London: Polity, 2020), pp. 148–49; Randall D. Germain, ed., *Globalization and Its Critics: Perspectives from Political Economy* (Houndmills: Macmillan, 2000).

[78] Paul Mozur and Steven Lee Myers, "Xi's Gambit: China Plans for a World without American Technology," 13 April 2021, https://www.nytimes.com/2021/03/10/business/china-us-tech-rivalry.html (accessed 30 June 2021).

[79] Steven Bernstein, "The Absence of Great Power Responsibility in Global Environmental Politics," *European Journal of International Relations* 26, no. 1 (2020), pp. 8–32, for a thoughtful account of why great powers have not done more to address the problem of climate change.

modern, high-tech economy, as China, South Korea, Taiwan, Singapore, and Israel have. Progress is a two-way street. In return for technology, student support, and business grants, loans, and investment, the countries in question would have to demonstrate the ability to profit from these opportunities. The quid pro quo would be significant movement toward stable, democratic regimes, the rule of law, and tolerance and respect for diverse opinion and criticism. Only a few governments are likely to be willing to move in this direction. Their success might encourage others in the longer term.

Breakthrough digital technologies present a more long-term, and perhaps revolutionary, challenge to global order and human civilization. Some predict that in the next few decades we will develop computing systems of astonishing capability. They may rival or surpass humans across a wide range of functions. They will capture, record, sort, store, and process information about human beings as digital data. In the long run, the distinctions between human and machine, online and offline, virtual and real, will no longer be a sharp binary.[80] Such revolutionary transformations will call forth new paradigms of politics and society, of which few have been offered yet.[81]

Technology is a primary cause of climate change and is equally central to coping with its consequences. There can be no doubt that climate change is real, that the earth is warming and water levels rising, and that the consequences of these developments will be felt everywhere. Richer countries will be better able to cope than poor ones but will still be seriously threatened. In the worst case, civilization could be threatened. Some studies suggest that in response to warming and the release of desalinated, cold, meltwater into the Atlantic the Gulf Stream will change its course and not cross the Atlantic and continue to warm Europe. If so, North America will become considerably hotter and have to cope with rising sea levels. Europe will cool and could be subjected to another ice age, and much of it would be covered by glaciers in relatively short order.[82]

---

[80] Jamie Susskind, *Future Politics: Living Together in a World Transformed by Tech* (Oxford: Oxford University Press, 2018), p. 2.

[81] Some deep questions are posed in Henry A. Kissinger, "How the Enlightenment Ends," *The Atlantic*, June 2018, https://www.theatlantic.com/magazine/archive/2018/06/henry-kissinger-ai-could-mean-the-end-of-human-history/559124/ (accessed 12 June 2021).

[82] Brandon Spektor, "The Gulf Stream Is Slowing to a 'Tipping Point' and Could Disappear," *Live Science*, February 2021, https://www.livescience.com/gulf-stream-slowing-climate-change. html; David Fleshler, "The Gulf Stream Is Slowing Down. That Could Mean Rising Seas and a Hotter Florida," *PHYSORG*, 9 August 2019, https://phys.org/news/2019-08-gulf-stream-seas-hotter-flor ida.html; Potsdam Institute for Climate Impact Research, "Gulf Stream System at Its Weakest in over a Millennium," *Science Daily*, 25 February 2021, https://www.sciencedaily.com/releases/2021/02/ 210225113357.htm; Fiona Harvey, "Atlantic Ocean Circulation at Weakest in a Millennium, Say Scientists," *Guardian*, 26 February 2021, https://www.theguardian.com/environment/2021/feb/ 25/atlantic-ocean-circulation-at-weakest-in-a-millennium-say-scientists (all accessed 1 June 2021).

Preventing what may be irreversible and catastrophic change in the biosphere depends on political will and technology. The former is necessary to impose the short-term sacrifices necessary for longer-term gains, and the latter, to help make those gains. The most obvious, and perhaps most important, step is curtailing carbon and methane emissions, and here, new technologies are critical both for developing substitute forms of energy and finding ways of storing carbon dioxide that had already been produced. Slowing or reversing climate change also entails major shifts in food production and consumption. Here, too, political will and technology need to be reinforcing.

This is not a chapter about climate change, so we will not address it in any substantive way. Our focus is on the ways in which any successful response must be a global effort, not national ones, that such efforts are predicated not only on taking the threat seriously but also on changes in international cooperation and governance. There are three obstacles to effective global collective action: free-riding, asymmetric interests between poorer and richer countries, and enforcement problems. Reducing emissions or avoiding more emissions is costly, and countries, especially poorer ones, will try to free-ride on the efforts of others. This task is doubly challenging in that it partakes of the prisoner's dilemma while also being exacerbated by the tragedy-of-the-commons logic. International cooperation is further hampered by strong asymmetry in benefits and costs of problem solving, mainly across richer and poorer countries. Rich countries have to contribute most to problem solving, but they also have a high capacity for adaptation. Poor countries, on the other hand, prefer to grow first and "clean up" later.[83] Enforcement is always an issue in multilateral agreements, and it is perhaps not surprising that the 2015 Paris Agreement takes the form not of a binding treaty but a statement of non-binding country-specific commitments.

Coping with climate change requires different kinds of sacrifices from different countries. The poorer and less developed the country, the more difficult it is to make these sacrifices. In rich countries, changes are deterred by powerful coalitions of polluters and politicians afraid to challenge them. The periodic global summits to address climate change have been unsuccessful for these reasons. Reports about the run-up to the next climate summit in Glasgow, Scotland, offer little hope of a breakthrough. The looming disaster offers China and the United States, and also the European Union, the opportunity to gain prestige, status, and authority by saving the world through the exercise of effective leadership.

[83] Thomas Bernauer, "Climate Change Politics," *Annual Review of Political Science* 16 (2013), pp. 421–48.

To be credible, their leadership must begin at home. They must take unilateral action to cut carbon emissions and other forms of pollution and put major resources into alternative forms of energy production. President Biden has taken some important steps in this direction. China has advanced more ambitious emission-cutting goals. In 2020, President Xi announced that China will strive to peak carbon dioxide emissions before 2030 and achieve carbon neutrality before 2060. In 2021 he further pledged to strictly control coal-fired power generation projects and phase down coal consumption in the next decade.[84] The next step is negotiating with other countries to introduce their own measures to address the problem. The United States, China, and the European Union should make major funds available toward this end where they are necessary.

There is an analogy here to non-proliferation. The 1968 Non-Proliferation Treaty (NPT) calls upon signatories to not begin or terminate any programs to develop nuclear weapons, and for the five nuclear-weapon states at the time—the United States, Soviet Union, United Kingdom, France, and China—to share the benefits of peaceful nuclear technology and pursue nuclear disarmament aimed at the ultimate elimination of their arsenals.[85] The NPT failed in its goals because of the desire of other states to acquire nuclear weapons (i.e., Israel, India, Pakistan, and North Korea) but also because the five nuclear powers failed to live up to their end of the bargain. This deprived their only marginal efforts at non-proliferation of any legitimacy.[86] The United States and the Soviet Union (succeeded by Russia) did not begin any serious build-down of their arsenals until the end of the Cold War. They have reduced their inventories by almost 90 percent, but only after most of the countries noted above had acquired nuclear weapons. Efforts to address climate change must avoid the hypocrisy of non-proliferation. The leading powers must also be prepared to use both carrots and sticks to bring about a serious and successful global effort to reduce carbon emissions.

The proliferation problem foundered on a perceived injustice. The nuclear powers were offering a deal to non-nuclear powers based on the principle of equality. However, the restraint of the signatories was not matched by a rapid builddown by the nuclear powers. They deemed their weapons essential for

[84] Xi Jinping, "For Man and Nature: Building a Community of Life Together," remarks at the Leaders' Summit on Climate, 22 April 2021, https://www.fmprc.gov.cn/mfa_eng/zxxx_662805/t1870852.shtml (accessed 12 June 2021).

[85] United Nations, Office for Disarmament Affairs, "Treaty on the Non-Proliferation of Nuclear Weapons (NPT)," https://www.un.org/disarmament/wmd/nuclear/npt/ (accessed 1 June 2021).

[86] Daniel H. Joyner, *Interpreting the Nuclear Non-Proliferation Treaty* (Oxford: Oxford University Press, 2011); Olav Njølstad, *Nuclear Proliferation and International Order: Challenges to the Non-Proliferation Treaty* (London: Routledge, 2010); Sverre Lodgaard, *Nuclear Disarmament and Non-Proliferation: Towards a Nuclear-Weapon-Free World?* (London: Routledge, 2010).

security or as a defining marker of their great power status. They preached equality but practiced a particular kind of fairness at the expense of the signatories.

Any environmental agreement that goes beyond the Paris Agreement must avoid this error. It must blend equality and fairness in a manner that is acceptable to all signatories. How can this be done? Fairness is represented by hierarchy, and usually by one that privileges those at the top at the expense of those at the bottom. International relations has functioned this way in the modern era. Great powers have higher status and special privileges. In theory, both status and privileges are justified by the services they perform for the community of states. In practice, the advantages have flowed upward, not downward. The United States, China, and the European Union must reverse this pattern in taking the lead in addressing climate change. They must give more than they take, make sacrifices in the interest of the community, and by doing so lend an aura of legitimacy to their proposals and make them more acceptable to others. These parties can afford to do this because of their far greater relative affluence. They can justify it to their populations as sacrifice for the common good from which they will gain the most in the long term.

Equality finds expression in the expectation that all states, or at least most, will participate in the resulting agreement. They will be treated as equal units in the agreement, and any revisions will require a majority vote. They will be asked to contribute on the basis of fairness, that is, in proportion to their ability to make relevant sacrifices. Fairness framed in this way supports equality and vice versa. The two principles can be made reinforcing, not cross-cutting, as they are in the NPT.

The negotiation of the 2015 Paris Agreement offers an early example of such a process. Fairness continued to underpin the negotiation, and the prior agreement between the United States and China was essential to its success. Yet, the Paris process was also a significant manifestation of the principle of equality. As Anne-Marie Slaughter notes, 195 countries participated in the negotiation and hammered out a non-binding agreement for raising their individual obligations every five years. As negotiators eschewed top-down obligations, fully aware of the impossibility of imposing them on such a diverse array of countries, the process manifested the bottom-up approach we emphasized earlier. Moreover, business, philanthropy, civil society, academia, and ordinary people all played a role in the process. The final agreement "is a sprawling, rolling, overlapping set of national commitments brought about by a broad conglomeration of parties and stakeholders."[87] If future climate summits draw on and improve the Paris process, humanity may have a chance of collectively tackling the climate challenge.

[87] Anne-Marie Slaughter, "The Paris Approach to Global Governance," *Project Syndicate*, 28 December 2015, https://www.project-syndicate.org/commentary/paris-agreement-model-for-global-governance-by-anne-marie-slaughter-2015-12 (accessed 12 June 2021).

Society

Society, both civic and global, is a salient feature of modernity. Most political theorists think it has had a beneficial effect. It has created a space relatively free of government control in many countries where people can encounter one another, exchange ideas, and develop businesses, educational, cultural, and other institutions. For this reason, dictatorships and authoritarian regimes do their best to restrict and control civil society. Governments that encourage civil society and civil liberties are deeply suspicious of those who repress them, and vice versa. These differences are apparent in all regions of the world and in relations between the West on the one hand and China and Russia on the other.

This kind of conflict has become more acute in the last decade. Western expectations that China would liberalize with trade and be a fully willing participant in the US-led political and economic order have not been realized. Rather, the country has become more closed and authoritarian under the leadership of Xi Jinping. Chinese policies toward Muslims and the suppression of protest in Hong Kong have fueled Western hostility and strengthened the hand of those who portray China as an enemy. Western labeling of Chinese treatment of Uighurs as "genocide"; their criticisms of Chinese policies toward Hong Kong and Taiwan, which Beijing regards as its own domestic affairs; and their diplomatic and military challenges to Chinese claims to islands in the East and South China Seas have intensified Chinese suspicions of the United States and other Western countries.

Rapprochements between countries with different political systems usually require those involved to accept the other's domestic structure and practices, or at least to soften their criticism of it. Leaders on both sides must be willing to adopt a live-and-let-live policy in return for the very real advantages they expect to derive from accommodation. This approach characterized Sino-American accommodation in the 1970s. Zhou Enlai and Henry Kissinger found wording that would allow each country to interpret the accords in terms with its proclaimed principles and policies. This is much harder to do today for many reasons. Most important, not only does the United States no longer expect to derive benefits from accommodation, but it perceives mounting threats from China. In theory, global challenges like climate change, by posing a greater threat to US well-being than does China, should prompt the two countries to cooperate for joint solutions. In practice, they carry far less urgency than the Soviet threat did during the Cold War. The US national security elite is still hardwired to a traditional military security mindset; to reorient them from that frame of mind to one attuned to a non-traditional security agenda will require a generational undertaking.

For the West, rapprochement with China would at first glance require remaining silent at the official level about Beijing's treatment of its Muslim population, suppression of democracy in Hong Kong, and an array of other human rights abuses. This would not have troubled Nixon and Kissinger, but it is much less palatable to Biden and his advisors, and the American foreign policy elite more generally. In the previous chapter we offered a philosophical method derived from Zhuangzi's ethics of difference for America and China to respect each other's way of life while reserving the right to criticism. Neither America nor China should look the other way if either violates the ethics of difference. America could criticize China's human rights record in Xinjiang by focusing on the extent to which Beijing has damaged the way of life of the Uighurs as a minority people.

Karl W. Deutsch famously coined the concept of a "pluralistic security community" to describe states between whom war was unthinkable.[88] They have good state-to-state relations, but more important, there is a high degree of empathy among their citizens. There is what Deutsch called a degree of "we feeling." People in these countries regard the citizens of the others as different in some ways but still very much like themselves. In 1957, Deutsch identified only two pluralistic security communities: the US-Canada, and the Scandinavian countries. Today, much of Western Europe, the South Pacific, and some of the Pacific Rim arguably qualify.[89]

There is little evidence of a pluralistic security community developing between China and its neighbors, and even less so between it and the United States. Deutsch theorizes that such communities are the result of top-down and bottom-up processes. They rely on close relations and cooperation between or among governments in a range of domains, but also a thick web of interpersonal relations among their citizens. These face-to-face encounters, some of them sustained, built friendships and trust, and were critical preconditions for the US-Canada and Scandinavian pluralistic security communities. They were equally important for France and Germany.[90] People-to-people encounters do not always create incentives for improving state-to-state relationships. There is some evidence that many Chinese

---

[88] Karl W. Deutsch et al., *Political Community and the North Atlantic Area* (Princeton, NJ: Princeton University Press, 1957).

[89] Emanuel Adler and Michael Barnett, eds., *Security Communities* (Cambridge: Cambridge University Press, 1998); Alex J. Bellamy, *Security Communities and Their Neighbours* (New York: Springer, 2004).

[90] Andreas Hasenclever, "Frankreich und Deutschland: Von der Rivalität zur organisierten Freundschaft," *Die internationale Organisation des Demokratischen Friedens* (Frankfurt am Main: Nomos Verlagsgesellschaft, 2010).

students who attend US universities struggle with cultural, linguistic, and mental health problems, intensified by growing American hostility toward their country.[91] The Chicago Council on Public Affairs found that Americans favor having foreign students, but the percentage of those who want to limit Chinese students has risen considerably.[92] This may reflect the findings of a Pew survey that nine in ten Americans said they view China as a competitor or enemy, not as a partner.[93]

Society is also a barrier to multilateral accommodation and cooperation of the kind we envisage in this chapter. Freedom House estimates that democracy is in decline in 75 percent of the countries it ranks as democratic.[94] The majority of the world's countries are dictatorships or authoritarian regimes where civil society is severely restricted and public opinion carries little, if any, weight with political leaders. There is little chance of bringing about the bottom-up or top-down conditions necessary for pluralistic security communities. More troubling for international reform is that many leaders or authoritarian elites in such societies are corrupt and self-serving. They have little interest in doing what will benefit their society, let alone the world community, if it involves personal political or economic costs.[95] Many of the reforms we explored, and especially action to address climate change, involve up-front costs. Such leaders cannot easily be convinced to assume them or take any of the risks that might be involved. Their compliance can only be gained by some combination of carrots and sticks. However, the use of coercion violates the premises of our approach to world order.

[91] Helen Gao, "Chinese, Studying in America, and Struggling," *New York Times*, 12 December 2017, https://www.nytimes.com/2017/12/12/opinion/chinese-students-mental-health.html; Karin Fischer, "Is This the End of the Romance between Chinese Students and American Colleges?" *Chronicle of Higher Education*, 11 March 2021, https://www.chronicle.com/article/is-this-the-end-of-the-romance-between-chinese-students-and-u-s-colleges (both accessed 14 June 2021).

[92] Karin Fischer, "Americans' Negative Views of Chinese Students," *Open Campus*, 8 March 2021, https://www.opencampusmedia.org/2021/03/08/americans-negative-views-of-chinese-students/ (accessed 14 June 2021).

[93] Pew Research, "Most Americans Support Tough Stance toward China on Human Rights, Economic Issues," 4 March 2021, https://www.pewresearch.org/global/2021/03/04/most-americans-support-tough-stance-toward-china-on-human-rights-economic-issues/ (accessed 3 June 2021).

[94] Sarah Repucci and Amy Slipowitz, "Democracy under Siege," *Freedom House*, https://freedomhouse.org/report/freedom-world/2021/democracy-under-siege (accessed 3 June 2021).

[95] Brett L. Carter, "The Rise of Kleptocracy: Autocrats versus Activists in Africa," *Journal of Democracy* 29, no. 1 (2018), pp. 54–68; Christopher Walker and Melissa Aten, "The Rise of Kleptocracy: A Challenge for Democracy," *Journal of Democracy* 29, no. 1 (2018), pp. 20–24.

Distant Worlds

A true transformation of international relations is a very unlikely prospect, especially in the short term. It would require a revolution or the arrival of aliens with the power to impose order from above. Neither strikes us as terribly likely or necessarily beneficial. But then prior domestic and international transformations were also thought highly unlikely before they happened. Who in 1945 would have given any credence to predictions that France and Germany would not only bury the hatchet but become the closest of friends, that China would become an economic superpower, or that the United States would consistently be considered the greatest threat to world peace by public opinion in multiple countries?

None of these events was determined, so it was not a matter of blindness that they were not predicted at the time. With the benefit of hindsight, we can build plausible accounts of why they happened and why they might have been seen as possible at the time. Europe's developed countries were becoming increasingly integrated prior to 1914 and long-standing rivalries largely resolved, as in the case of France and Britain, or becoming less acute, as was true of France and Germany. The two world wars put an end to interdependence and rapprochement, but it resumed again in their aftermath. The United States had long exercised a quasi-hegemony in Latin America, where it had regularly intervened with money and military forces in support of its political and economic interests.[96] There was little reason to think it would be more restrained when more powerful. As for China, a longer perspective is required. From the beginning of history until the late eighteenth century, China had led the world in economic development, longevity, science, and public health. Once it was reunified it could be expected to flourish again.

Human beings fear change on the whole and across cultures make conservative predictions. People expect the future to be more like the past and are surprised when it is not. They also make the mistake of thinking that the world has turned upside down when something unexpected has happened. Consider the overreaction of Americans to the 9/11 terrorist attacks. Even professional forecasters and intelligence experts give evidence of these biases. One of us participated in an inter-agency forecasting exercise run by the National Security Council with the goal of briefing the incoming Trump administration about the foreign threats they were likely to face. We were broken into groups to consider five existing kinds of threats. To nobody's surprise, each group came back with

---

[96] Walter Lafeber, *Inevitable Revolutions: The United States in Central America*, 2nd ed. (New York: W. W. Norton, 1993).

a straight-line projection—which they judged most likely—and slightly lower and higher projections. Nobody was allowed to suggest novel threats. Nor did the group overall examine possible synergies and non-linear interactions among the kinds of threats we considered. It is no surprise that intelligence agencies are blindsided on a regular basis.

We live in a world of uncertainty, not of risk. In the former we have no base rates and cannot put numbers of the likelihood that this or that kind of social or political event will occur. Unexpected developments take place regularly, are usually only explicable in retrospect, and can have dramatic consequences. World War I, antibiotics, the information revolution, and the collapse of the Soviet Union are all cases in point. Two of them were transformative for international relations. We accordingly cannot dismiss the possibility that some combination of events and process will do the same in the next decade or two and bring about changes in international relations that were largely, if not entirely, unexpected. We offer two examples, not in the expectation that they are likely, but in the way of illustration. We hope they encourage readers to invent possibilities of their own. The first is a scenario of the peaceful resolution of the Taiwan problem leading to accommodation between China and the United States. As we write this in the autumn of 2021, the press is full of speculations about a mainland Chinese invasion of Taiwan in the next decade or sooner. American pundits have been prodding Washington to abandon strategic ambiguity in favor of a new clarity of American commitments to defend Taiwan against Chinese attack.[97] Yet a war across the Taiwan Strait would be a catastrophe for the Chinese nation, and people on both sides across the Strait understand this.

If Beijing decides to wait for a few more decades, new and more favorable conditions for reunification might well emerge, especially if the mainland continues to prosper and Taiwan becomes all but an appendage to the mainland in terms of prosperity and security. By that time the de facto independence currently enjoyed by Taiwan may be transmuted into de facto reunification by virtue of its economic and security dependence on the mainland. A flexible confederation of the Chinese nation in lieu of the old framework of "one country, two systems" might then become a viable solution. If that comes to pass, the United States will face a transformed political and security landscape in East Asia and a historic opportunity to reach accommodation with China.

Our second example is a future in which the West shares wealth, power, and cultural and political authority with the rest of the world in a more or less equal

---

[97] Richard Haass and David Sacks, "American Support for Taiwan Must Be Unambiguous," *Foreign Affairs*, 2 September 2020, https://www.foreignaffairs.com/articles/united-states/american-support-taiwan-must-be-unambiguous (accessed 12 June 2021).

manner. Amitav Acharya and Barry Buzan argue that such a process, which they call "deep pluralism," is already underway. Moreover, it is ushering in a new epoch of non-Western modernity distinct from the first round of Western modernity unleashed by European powers after the sixteenth century.[98] Milanovic forecasts that economic convergence between Asia and the West might well occur in the present century. He doubts whether African growth can accelerate, but it is too early to write Africa off given its unique demographic advantages.[99]

In a world where the West and the rest share a rough equality, global order in the six domains we have examined will manifest a new set of dynamics. Status competition will be less intense, as the United States will in all likelihood lose its superpower status and need to share great power status with a range of other powers or intergovernmental organizations, principally the European Union, China, Russia, Japan, and India. Ideological pluralism will become a matter of fact, and liberalism, the hitherto dominant ideology of the modern world, will recede into one of several contending ideologies. This will temper its universalizing impulse and constrain the interventionist policies of the liberal powers. Security competition will acquire a more prominent regional dimension and, with the return of balance-of-power politics, it will probably intensify in some regions, especially the Middle East and East Asia. Many in the West will lament the decline of the American hegemon and attribute new instabilities to the disappearance of American security guarantee. But the stabilizing function of the United States has been proved highly suspect in the postwar period, and it is by no means obvious that a more regionalized security order will necessarily be more unstable. Technology will be more diffuse, although the most advanced kinds are likely to be possessed by a handful of great powers or regional groupings such as the United States, China, Russia, the European Union, and Japan. In a more equal world, societies will develop more respect for one another, a major progress in world politics where for more than 200 years a sense of superiority toward the rest of the world was firmly entrenched in the West. There is no guarantee, however, that pluralistic security communities will develop beyond the North Atlantic region. A more equal world may be an equally competitive world.

Conclusions

Changes in the overall pattern of international relations are more difficult to imagine and bring about than those in bilateral relations. We have done our

---

[98] Amitav Acharya and Barry Buzan, *The Making of Global International Relations: Origins and Evolution of IR at Its Centenary* (Cambridge: Cambridge University Press, 2019).

[99] Milanovic, *Global Inequality*, p. 213.

best to consider the kinds of changes that political will and clever diplomacy might bring about, changes from which most states and peoples might benefit. Most can be effects in isolation, although success on several fronts might create synergism, energy, and commitment to go further.

We have not considered negative possibilities, and they are legion. Escalating tensions between China and the United States could lead to another Cold War or worse, especially if China uses force against Taiwan. Russian-Western relations could continue to deteriorate. Any kind of stand-off or increased competition among these powers and the European Union would rule out the kind of great power cooperation that is necessary to bring about most of the changes we have mooted. Soo too could escalation of regional conflicts, like those between Israel and Iran or India and Pakistan.

Also to be considered are the effects of climate change. When we are only experiencing them in mild, if still impressive, form, as we are now, they provide an incentive for cooperation. When—probably not if—they become more pronounced different countries will feel their effects in widely divergent ways. This will be true with respect to the kind of disruption and its extent. This will generate very different and increasingly incompatible demands for compensation and measures to keep things from getting worse. Climate change will divide, not unite, the world's peoples. For this and other reasons we need to act quickly. What appears visionary is also necessary. It requires political will and that in turn depends on public opinion and the pressures it can exert.

CONCLUSION

9

Smart Power and Great Learning

Our concluding chapter speaks to three substantive issues or problems. First is the relationship between Sino-American accommodation and efforts to construct a global order. How much does the latter depend on the former? And in what ways might the former hinder the latter? How might changes in bilateral and global relationships be made more synergistic than antagonistic? Any meaningful accommodation depends upon changes in mindsets: leaders must realize that their most important goals are best, or perhaps only, achieved through rapprochement. Our second question is in how this might come about. Is there any reason to think that Chinese and American leaders, and those elsewhere, can be encouraged to reframe their interests? Our third focus is on how a Sino-American accommodation might be nested in a global one. Toward this end, we suggest the possibility of a new form of clientelist relationship.

We began our inquiry with a discussion of justice and its relevance to accommodation and global order. In part I of this book we examined Eastern and Western ethical traditions looking for similarities and differences with the aim of finding mutually acceptable principles that could provide the basis for Sino-American accommodation and perhaps a reordering of global relationships. This prompts us to consider the problem of global versus national justice. Just how do the principles of fairness and equality relate and contribute to the existing literature on global justice? There are three fault lines in modern theorizing about global justice: the goods of distributive justice (rights vs. needs), claimants/holders of justice (cosmopolitan vs. communitarian), and scope of justice principles (particularism vs. universalism). We have something to say about each of them and offer a novel perspective based on Chinese conceptions derived from the classic *Great Learning*.

Justice and International Order: East and West. Richard Ned Lebow and Feng Zhang, Oxford University Press.
© Oxford University Press 2022. DOI: 10.1093/oso/9780197598399.003.0009

Bilateral vs. Multilateral Ordering

Sino-American accommodation can take many forms. In its minimalist version it constitutes an effort to do nothing more than reduce the risk of war between the two countries. Such an effort, if successful, is almost certainly in the interest of all Pacific Rim countries and the world more generally. The only exception might be Taiwan, at whose expense such an accommodation might be reached. This, of course, would depend very much on the particulars. There are many variants of accommodations that reduce the prospect of a cross-straits war from which Taiwan would gain.

Accommodation could stop here. The 1978 Camp David Accords produced an uneasy peace between Egypt and Israel. Their relations have not significantly improved since then but did significantly reduce the threat of war. It is now more than forty years since these countries engaged in any kind of combat and there is good reason to believe that this state of affairs will continue into the foreseeable future. Egyptian-Israeli relations offer a sharp contrast to Anglo-French relations, where the 1904 Entente not only removed the threat of war—which had been very real up through the 1898 Fashoda crisis—but paved the way for a full accommodation. A similar story can be told about post-1945 Franco-German relations. Russo-American relations is a more sobering tale. Gorbachev and Bush reached an accommodation in the last days of the Soviet Union that transformed a confrontational relationship into a cooperative one, but in the last decade it has become increasingly confrontational.

Sino-American relations resembles Russo-American in its reversal, although economic relations remain robust. They have nevertheless become more politicized and securitized, resulting in mutual recriminations and denunciations, tariffs, and temporary embargos. From the American perspective, Chinese politics under President Xi Jinping has become more authoritarian and repressive, snuffing out any hope of liberalization in the near term. Chinese foreign policy has also become more assertive and even aggressive, especially in its coercive handling of its sovereignty and maritime disputes with its neighbors. From the Chinese perspective, post–Cold War America has never relented in its attempts to contain China's rise, and the shift to an overt strategy of competition since the Trump years simply vindicates this long-held suspicion.

One way of looking at Sino-American relations is to see it as stalled and in need of jump-starting. The initial détente between the two countries was begun in this manner, through secret diplomacy between Zhou Enlai and Henry Kissinger. The incentive was mutual concern for a powerful and aggressive Soviet Union. Both diplomats and the leaders of the two countries found ways of overcoming their opposition—which was more symbolic than substantive—and a formula for finessing their differences over Taiwan. Reassurance was a more effective strategy than deterrence because what had poisoned Sino-American relations since 1949 was largely unfounded fears on both sides.[1]

We think it would be difficult to repeat the success of the 1970s because today's conditions differ. There is no Soviet Union to push the two countries toward cooperation on the principle that my enemy's enemy is, or should be, my friend. The closest substitute is climate change, which arguably constitutes an even greater and more certain threat than did the USSR. The military threat posed by Moscow was more visible, its consequences easier to imagine, and the effects of any war more immediate. Climate change is more diffuse, longer-term, more difficult to envisage, and perhaps most important, an issue of global rather than a bilateral concern—as is its solution. China and America, the two greatest contributors to climate change, could nevertheless take the lead in addressing the problem. However, this will almost certainly require a prior improvement in their relations, and that depends, as we have noted, on a major shift in thinking in both countries. As matters now stand, climate change cannot serve as a catalyst for accommodation but it certainly could become a focus of an emerging or ongoing rapprochement. At the very least, climate change could incentivize limited cooperation and put a brake on runaway competition.

The principal barrier in the way of such an accommodation is the deep-seated emotional commitment to superiority that characterizes American and Chinese culture. It prompts leaders, elites, and much of the public to view the other as a rival and their relationship as something close to a zero-sum game. The United States will not admit it publicly, but what really threatens it has nothing to do with security, economics, or human rights. It is China's meteoric rise to power and the challenge this constitutes to American claims to hegemony. Since its victory in World War II, American presidents have mobilized support for a large military and interventionist foreign policy on the grounds that as a hegemon their country has special responsibilities. Americans have been told repeatedly that others around the world look up to their way of life, admire their democracy and economy, and want them to lead the "Free World." All of this played into a long history of American exceptionalism that had its roots in the radical Protestantism of many of the country's white settlers. The end of the Cold War, the collapse of the Soviet Union and communism in Europe, the claim of "unipolarity" and even of the end of history, further fueled this sense of pride. America's standing in the world was not only a source of pride but of self-esteem. This euphoria was deflated by 9/11 and other threatening events, including the

---

[1] See our discussion of reassurance in Feng Zhang and Richard Ned Lebow, *Taming Sino-American Rivalry* (Oxford: Oxford University Press, 2020), ch. 6.

rise of China. Americans nevertheless still yearn for the restoration of what they imagine is their justified and valued hegemony and leadership.

China has its own imaginary. It is anchored in the long-standing belief that China and its civilization are at the center of the world, surrounded by cultural inferiors or other societies that acknowledge its primacy, assimilate its values, honor it, and receive practical rewards in return. Up to the nineteenth century it led the world in scientific development, public health, aggregate wealth, and longevity. Being surpassed by the West, forced to concede territory to colonial powers, and having its capital occupied and ransacked by its armies constituted a national humiliation and severe blow to Chinese self-esteem. Chinese continue to believe in their superiority, and many are convinced that they are in the process of re-establishing it. Judging the United States to be a declining power, they expect to pull even with, if not ahead of it in wealth, technology, and military power. Since the 2008 global financial crisis, which they saw as a harbinger of the decay of US economic and political institutions, they are unwilling to defer to it on any level and regard doing so as an affront.

The two countries are further divided by their very different political systems. America's political and economic liberalism confronts China's hybrid system, which the West labels "authoritarian" but Beijing prefers to call "socialism with Chinese characteristics." Each superpower is convinced that their form of ordering is superior and the appropriate response to the challenges of modernity. Each behaves in ways that appear to challenge the other's core values. Some of these differences, we suggest, can be designed around and others finessed. This requires self-restraint in policy and rhetoric, and a commitment to a live-and-let-live attitude. It does not, however, entail America's silence, and thus tacit acceptance, of China's crushing democracy in Hong Kong and its treatment of its Muslim minorities, which some in the West have labeled as "genocide." We have offered Zhuangzi's ethics of difference as a method for evaluative criticism. The United States should not look the other way if China violates the ethics of difference in its treatment of the Uighurs. It could criticize China by focusing on the extent to which Beijing has damaged the way of life of the Uighurs as a minority people.

Ironically, the mutual sense of superiority could in theory be the basis for cooperation based on the idea of a condominium. This might ease Sino-American tensions, though at the expense of heightening them with everyone else. A more constructive way of securing status would be for both countries to take the lead in ordering the world in ways more beneficial to third parties, including middle powers and the presently disadvantaged countries of the Global South. The model here is the kind of clientelist relationship theorized and practiced by the ancient Greeks and premodern China. It needs some reformulation as it foregrounds fairness over equality. It is nevertheless a useful starting point for our inquiry.

In *Taming Sino-American Rivalry* we describe a surprising parallel between ancient Greek and traditional Chinese conceptions of ordering relations between great and lesser political units.[2] Drawing on Homeric portrayals of honor, Greeks developed the concept of *hēgemonia*, from which our contemporary but different idea of hegemony derives. *Hēgemonia* described an honorific status conferred on a leading power because of the services it had provided to the community. It conferred a right to lead, based on the expectation that this leadership will continue to benefit the community as a whole. *Hēgemonia* represents a clientelist approach to politics: the powerful gain honor in return for providing practical benefits to the weak. The latter willingly accept their inferior status in return for economic and security benefits and the constraints such an arrangement imposes on the powerful.

Imperial China drew on Confucian ethics to develop a similar concept of clientelist relations. Such relations were hierarchically centered on the centrality and superiority of the Chinese emperor as the authority of world politics. Their purpose was to promote a universal ethical world order based on Confucian propriety and underpinned by China's relational authority. Imperial Chinese elites believed that such ethically based relationships would cultivate the moral excellence of all peoples while bringing security, peace, and order to the world, thus fulfilling the moral purpose of Chinese authority in the world. The Chinese used the concept of *li* (禮 propriety) to describe a set of reciprocal obligations between China and lesser powers in their hierarchical relationships. Foreign rulers were required to observe loyalty and trustworthiness to the Chinese emperor; the Chinese emperor, in return, would treat them with humaneness and bring prosperity and security to their mutual benefit.[3]

Such humane statecraft is captured by the traditional Chinese concept of *wangdao*. *Wangdao*'s literal meaning is "the kingly way," but it should be more meaningfully translated as "humane authority." It describes a form of Confucian statecraft that prescribes an ethically based clientelist approach to asymmetrical relationship that should provide benefit to all parties involved.[4] Like *hēgemonia*, *wangdao* confers the right to lead, but only if the powerful leads by providing benefits to the wider community. *Wangdao* was not just a Confucian ideal; it was close to reality in various periods of Chinese history. During the early years of the Ming dynasty (1368–1644), for example, the founding emperor Hongwu tried to establish an affective relationship of hierarchical but mutual affection

---

[2] Ibid.

[3] Feng Zhang, *Chinese Hegemony: Grand Strategy and International Institutions in East Asian History* (Stanford, CA: Stanford University Press, 2015).

[4] For a relevant discussion, Yan Xuetong, *Ancient Chinese Thought, Modern Chinese Power*, Daniel Bell and Sun Zhe, eds., trans. Edmund Ryden (Princeton, NJ: Princeton University Press, 2011).

and obligation between himself and the king of Korea. He expected Korean obligations of loyalty and integrity, and he tried to fulfill his own obligations of humaneness and care by advising the Korean king on domestic governance. He apparently assumed that a relationship based on such reciprocal affective obligations was the most appropriate outcome in Sino-Korean relations.[5]

In recent years, *wangdao* has gained some traction in China, emerging as a possible template for Chinese leaders, officials, and intellectuals. It differs from both hegemony and a balance of power in fundamental ways. In fact, the Chinese government has adamantly rejected both hegemony and the balance of power, which it sees as Western ideas of international politics, as possible strategies for China in the Asia Pacific. But Beijing realizes that the rise of Chinese power calls for a greater Chinese role in the region—a kind of leadership, though no one has been able to describe it in detail. Influential scholars are increasingly relying on traditional Chinese thought for guidance.[6] The ethically based hierarchical foreign relations of imperial China provide just such a source. Thus, amid tensions in China's relationship with Singapore in 2016, for example, a scholar uses Mengzi's dictum of "the small serves the big with wisdom; the big serves the small with humaneness," which we noted in chapter 5, to analyze the causes of tension.[7]

Hēgemonia and *wangdao* are parallel concepts. They both denote legitimate leadership based on clientelist relationships. As long as the United States and China share their *hēgemonia* or *wangdao* in Asia and maintain their respective "rule packages" with regional countries, there should be no conflict between the two countries or their respective networks of alliances and partnerships in the region.

Unlike hegemony, *hēgemonia* can be shared, as it was between Athens and Sparta in the decades prior to the Archidamian and Peloponnesian War, which broke out in 431 BCE. There is no contradiction in China and the United States framing and doing the same in their relations with Pacific Rim states. *Hēgemonia* or *wangdao* can also be practiced on a global scale, with both countries seeking honor—that is, the respect of others and the influence it confers. This can be done in a cooperative, even collaborative manner, but does not have to be. It seems more likely, at least at the outset, that China and the United States would

---

[5] Zhang, *Chinese Hegemony*, p. 56.

[6] Yan, *Ancient Chinese Thought, Modern Chinese Power*; Yan Xuetong, *Shijie quanli de zhuanyi: zhengzhi lingdao yu zhanlue jingzheng* [The Transition of World Power: Political Leadership and Strategic Competition] (Beijing: Peking University Press, 2015).

[7] Xue Li, "Zhongxin guanxi jinru fansi yu tiaoshi qi" [Sino-Singaporean Relationship Enters a Period of Reflection and Adjustment], *FT Chinese*, 24 January 2017, http://www.ftchinese.com/story/001071132?full=y (accessed 5 April 2017).

do so as rivals. We write two years into the COVID-19 pandemic, when developed countries have vaccinated most of their populations but many countries of the Global South are finding it difficult to get access to vaccines. China and the United States, and the European Union, could make vaccines available free of charge or at minimal cost. Such an initiative would be in everyone's interest and gain respect for the donors. In 2021 the United States made an initial offer of eighty million vaccines to COVAX to distribute in poorer countries.[8] China pledged to provide two billion doses of vaccines by the end of the year, including donation of 100 million doses to developing countries.[9] This is only one example of the ways in which *hēgemonia* or *wangdao* is achieved and sustained and can be channeled down acceptable and productive pathways. Acting this way, China and the United States would both gain influence and reduce tensions between them.

Athens and Sparta offer a sobering counterexample. Their shared *hēgemonia* lasted some forty-plus years and was characterized by growing tensions between them. Thucydides tells us Sparta was initially willing to accept Athens as a co-hegemon and that Athens was initially pleased by its upgrade in status. Mutual satisfaction did not last long. Modern-day power transition theorists elevate a particular passage of Thucydides—which is misleadingly translated in English—into a universal principle of inter-state relations, conveniently ignoring that Thucydides uses this passage to set up tensions and contrasts, not to offer a definitive account of the causes of the war between Sparta and Athens.

Thucydides offers a nuanced account in book 1, which elaborates the context and meaning of his famous statement in 1.23.6 "that the rise to power of Athens made war with Sparta highly likely."[10] The core issue was not security but wealth and status. Hegemons were expected to exercise self-restraint and to act in support of the common interests of the community. As their wealth and naval power grew, Athenians felt unreasonably constrained by its rule package. They pursued self-interest at the expense of the community, increasingly relied on force rather than persuasion, and transformed their alliance into an empire. Key Spartan allies felt threatened and pleaded with their hegemon to come to their support.

---

[8] The White House, "Statement by President Joe Biden on Global Vaccine Distribution," 5 June 2021, https://www.whitehouse.gov/briefing-room/statements-releases/2021/06/03/statement-by-president-joe-biden-on-global-vaccine-distribution/; Zeke Miller, "Biden Doubles US Global Donation of COVID-19 Vaccine Shots," *Associated Press*, 22 September 2012, https://apnews.com/article/united-nations-general-assembly-joe-biden-pandemics-business-united-nations-e7c09c1f8 96d83c0ed80513082787bd3 (both accessed 8 October 2022).

[9] Xi Jinping, "Full Speech at the UN's 76th General Assembly," September 21, 2021, https://asia.nikkei.com/Politics/International-relations/Xi-Jinping-s-full-speech-at-the-U.N.-s-76th-General-Assembly2 (accessed 13 October 2021).

[10] Thucydides, *History of the Peloponnesian War*, 1.23.6. Ned Lebow's translation.

Their appeals fell on receptive ears. Athens' commercial, cultural, and political successes had begun to marginalize Sparta. It could not compete with Athens, which had become a role model for many other Greeks, while Sparta was widely regarded as old-fashioned. Spartiates derived their self-esteem from their military prowess and the respect this engendered for their polis throughout Hellas. Urged by their allies to draw their swords in defense of their allegedly common interests, they did not hesitate to vote for war. Interestingly, those who had good appreciation of Athenian military power, as did King Archidamus, urged caution. Those wanting to retain the esteem of their allies and reassert their primacy in Greece made light of Athenian power. Sparta went to war in defense of its identity, not out of fear for its security.[11]

Power transition theories are badly formulated, have no historical evidence in support, and have never been subjected to counterfactual evaluation by the proponents.[12] They have nevertheless become the conventional wisdom in the United States as they were useful for those who wanted to portray China as a military threat. Graham Allison's version of it, based on the assumption that history suggested that war between China and the United States was highly likely, became a national best-seller.[13] And this despite every serious critics excoriating it for its gross historical inaccuracies and conceptual flimflam.[14]

Thucydides' account of the Peloponnesian War nevertheless holds important lessons for the present day. It suggests that appetite and *thumos* are fundamental causes of human conflict and war. Appetites readily become insatiable unless constrained by reason, custom, and social obligations. *Thumos* for the Greeks described the human drive to excel in activities valued by people's peer group or society, to win their approbation, and for people in turn to feel good about themselves. Athens succumbed to its appetites and kept expanding in the expectation of becoming ever more powerful and wealthy. The two were closely related, as wealth bought the ships and crews necessary for expansion. Athenians did not hesitate to trespass on Sparta's allies, discounted the likelihood of war arising from their actions, and were confident of their ability to fight it if it nevertheless

---

[11] For elaboration, Richard Ned Lebow, *The Tragic Vision of Politics: Ethics, Interests, and Orders* (Cambridge: Cambridge University Press, 2003), ch. 3.

[12] Steve Chan, *China, the US and Power-Transition Theory* (New York: Routledge, 2007); Richard Ned Lebow and Benjamin Valentino, "Lost in Transition: A Critique of Power Transition Theories," *International Relations* 23, no. 3 (September 2009), pp. 389–410.

[13] Graham Allison, *Destined for War: Can America and China Escape Thucydides's Trap?* (New York: Barnes & Noble, 2017).

[14] For example, Richard Ned Lebow and Daniel Tompkins, "The Thucydides Claptrap," *Washington Monthly*, 28 June 2016, https://washingtonmonthly.com/thucydides-claptrap (accessed 27 May 2021); Steve Chan, *Thucydides's Trap? Historical Interpretation, Logic of Inquiry, and the Future of Sino-American Relations* (Ann Arbor: University of Michigan Press, 2020).

broke out. Spartiates allowed themselves to be stampeded by their allies and went to war. In the run-up to the war, neither hegemon formulated its interests intelligently, nor could it when reason lost control over *appetite* and *thumos*.

China and the United States are not Sparta and Athens. Neither country is turning an alliance into an empire and expanding it through force. Nor is either country in a sharp decline relative to the other and dependent for its status on skills that are becoming less valued. But there are worrying similarities. Like Sparta and Athens, both have difficulty in controlling their appetites and *thumos*. The United States greatly overextended itself economically and strategically. It arrogated responsibility for political and economic order; demanded special privileges; treated other states as second-class citizens of world society; intervened regularly in the political, economic, and military means in the affairs of others; and exploited the order it helped to create and was allegedly committed to preserving it for selfish economic ends. All these actions undermine American influence and account for the paradox that the United States is the greatest power the world has ever seen but is less and less able to persuade others to do what it wants. Rather, it increasingly relies on bribes and coercion, and without notable success. This process found its most extreme manifestation to date under the presidency of Donald Trump, but it is an outgrowth of a trend long under way and intensified after the end of the Cold War under Democratic and Republican administrations alike. President Joe Biden is a far cry from Trump, but his secretary of state and national security advisor routinely assert that the "America is back" and expects to resume its leadership role.

China's global ambition hardly approaches the scale of that of the United States, but it has its own problems of appetite and *thumos* to address. Chinese *thumos* underlies desires for their country to be recognized as a power equal to the United States, and many Chinese consequently seethe at the US attempt to maintain primacy in Asia. Appetite drives its quest for advantages commensurate with its rising power, especially the fulfillment of its claims to sovereignty and maritime interests. Since 2010 its relations with an array of its neighbors have deteriorated, partly owing to its adoption of a more coercive approach to sovereignty disputes, especially with respect to Taiwan and the South China Sea. It has even fallen out with countries with which it had no prior disputes, among them Australia and Canada. China's assertive security policy prompted a widespread Western criticism of coercion and rising fear of its power by its neighbors.[15]

---

[15] Feng Liu, "The Recalibration of Chinese Assertiveness: China's Responses to the Indo-Pacific Challenge," *International Affairs* 96, no. 1 (2020), pp. 9–27; Fergus Hanson, Emilia Currey, and Tracy Beattie, "The Chinese Communist Party's Coercive Diplomacy" (Canberra: Australia Strategic Policy Institute, 2020).

Smart Power

To achieve *hēgemonia* or *wangdao*, the two superpowers must each internalize and practice its values. They must recognize their responsibilities to the world community in return for being honored by it. For a start, American leaders, talking heads, and academics must give up the quest for hegemony. It is an illusion.[16] Hegemony does not exist, is unobtainable, and would be counterproductive to American interests and world order even if it was feasible. It is time for Americans to recognize this truth and reframe their relationship with the world in more realistic and productive ways. As for China, PRC leaders from Mao to Xi have uniformly renounced Western-style hegemony as an international goal.[17] They recognize, better than American leaders, that hegemony was a morally reprehensible and practically impossible goal. What they want is equality with the United States, not hegemony of the international system.

The historical practices *hēgemonia* and *wangdao* were rooted in the principle of fairness. Ming Empire practice of *wangdao* foregrounded the inequality of China's relationship with neighboring political units through the requirements of tributes and kowtow.[18] Such practices are unthinkable today in a world where equality has replaced fairness as the dominant principle of justice. *Hēgemonia* and *wangdao* have to be reformulated to balance fairness against equality in a manner acceptable to all participants.

The principle of fairness has always been central to international affairs. Great powers—a status that achieved something of legal recognition at the 1815 Congress of Vienna—receive honor and special privileges in return for assuming the responsibility of maintaining international society and its ordering principles.[19] The United Nations, established in 1945, enshrined this principle in its Charter with the creation of the Security Council. Its permanent members, five states deemed to be great powers, were given responsibility for the security

---

[16] Simon Reich and Richard Ned Lebow, *Good-Bye Hegemony! Power and Influence in the Global System* (Princeton, NJ: Princeton University Press, 2014), ch. 2. See also Christopher Fettweis, "Unipolarity, Hegemony, and the New World Peace," *Security Studies* 26, no. 3 (2017), pp. 423–51.

[17] See, for example, Xi Jinping, "Pulling Together through Adversity and toward a Shared Future for All," speech delivered at the Boao Forum for Asia Annual Conference, 20 April 2021, https://www.fmprc.gov.cn/mfa_eng/zxxx_662805/t1870296.shtml (accessed 31 May 2021).

[18] Zhang, *Chinese Hegemony.*

[19] Leopold von Ranke, "The Great Powers," in Georg C. Iggers and Konrad von Moltke, eds., *The Theory and Practice of History* (Indianapolis: Bobbs-Merrill, 1973), pp. 65–110; Clark, *Hegemony in International Society*; Georges-Henri Soutou, "L'ordre Européen de Versailles à Locarno," in C. Carlier and G-H Soutou, eds., *1918–1925: Comment faire la paix?* (Paris: Institut de Stratégie Comparée, 2001); Richard Ned Lebow, *National Identifications and International Relations* (Cambridge: Cambridge University Press, 2016), ch. 4.

of the world. Many subsequent international organizations like the Group of Five, established in 1970, continue this principle. The Group of Five was later expanded to Seven and Eight, to include the largest economies of the world, countries that assumed responsibility for the maintenance of economic order.[20] Equality has also become increasingly important in international relations. The General Assembly of the United Nations includes all member states, and each has one vote. Some nations want the Security Council to be enlarged to include developing nations and nations of the Southern Hemisphere. In the current century a new version of the Group of Five has evolved, now called the BRICS to describe the five largest emerging economies of the world: Brazil, Russia, India, China, and South Africa.[21]

In practice, hierarchy, and even more so, the imposition of a more rigid hierarchy with the United States or China—or both—at the top has become increasingly indefensible. International hierarchy is widely regarded as an atavism: an attitude and structure from the past that is long past its use-by date. Even those countries like Brazil, Japan, India, and Germany, who seek permanent seats on the Security Council, use the language of equality to advance their claims for superior status and privileges vis-à-vis their neighbors.[22] The United States needs to follow suit in lieu of its until now blatant use of the language of hierarchy. American proponents of hegemony claim that it is widely valued and welcomed by others. This is another self-propagated myth. Others put up with, work around, attempt to finesse American power, or attempt to exploit it for their parochial ends. The people who are happiest with American claims of hegemony are dictators who receive billions of US aid and do little to nothing in return.

The focus on power and hegemony in international relations theory obscures the ways in which international society has been evolving. There is a general reluctance to recognize that regional and international governance must be based more on equality than on fairness. *Hēgemonia* and *wangdao*, if suitably reformulated, can be anchored in equality and to some degree legitimize hierarchy. Before elaborating our claim, we want to disassociate ourselves from the efforts of neo-liberals to do this. They understand hierarchy to be legitimate if all actors have had an equal opportunity to compete for whatever is at stake. In practice, they never do, as the wealthy, well-educated, and well-connected start out with innumerable advantages. The neo-liberal model assumes that everyone

---

[20] Bob Reinalda and Bertjan Verbeek, *Autonomous Policy Making by International Organizations* (London: Routledge, 1998); Nicholas Bayne and Robert D. Putnam, *Hanging in There: The G7 and G8 Summit in Maturity and Renewal* (Aldershot: Ashgate, 2000).

[21] Lebow, *National Identities and International Relations*, pp. 67, 85–88, 192, 198.

[22] Ibid., pp. 192–97.

wants to compete, which misrepresents the diversity of personality types and, worse, assumes that the liberal model of society based on competition among autonomous, egoistic individuals is the only appropriate one. John Rawls offers a slightly more sophisticated defense of hierarchy. He is willing to give more financial rewards to people whose labor produces more for the society in general, such as physicians and entrepreneurs—in effect reproducing the kinds of distribution of income that currently prevails.[23]

We have no survey data about international hierarchies, but lots about domestic ones, especially American society. It suggests that people's decisions about distributing rewards are more cognitive than ethical.[24] Sidney Verba and his colleagues documented this in Sweden, Japan, and the United States, where people expressing distributional preferences take their cue from existing distributions.[25] In Sweden, where variation in incomes is relatively low, they make the smallest adjustments to reach an ideal. In Japan, where it is higher, they make greater adjustments, and in the United States, where it is the most pronounced, they make the greatest adjustments.[26] The same pattern prevails in the three countries with respect to preferred differentials between worker and executive compensation.[27] Other studies show that Americans—and presumably others—consistently underestimate the extent of inequality in their society.[28] After being shown charts of the wealth distribution in the United States and Sweden, 92 percent of participants chose the Swedish model.[29]

Most research to date is focused on the use of fairness or equality as a seeming decision rule.[30] It evaluates choices by different kinds of people in different situations. Since the 1970s, surveys and experiments have been carried out in diverse domains (e.g., business, pensions, health care), with individuals and small groups, and with people of different genders, ages, classes, and nationalities. They indicate that the triumph of the principle of equality is far from total. Americans

[23] John Rawls, *A Theory of Justice*, rev. ed. (Cambridge, MA: Harvard University Press, 1999), *The Law of Peoples* (Cambridge, MA: Harvard University Press, 1999), and *Justice as Fairness*, ed. Erin Kelly (Cambridge, MA: Harvard University Press, 2001).

[24] David Miller, *Principles of Social Justice* (Cambridge, MA: Harvard University Press, 1999), p. 75.

[25] Sidney Verba, Steven Kelman, Gary R. Orren, Ichiro Miyake, Johi Watanuki, Ikuo Kabashima, and G. Donald Ferree Jr., *Elites and the Idea of Equality: A Comparison of Japan, Sweden, and the United States* (Cambridge, MA: Harvard University Press, 1987), pp. 127–28, 133.

[26] Ibid.

[27] Ibid., pp. 139–40.

[28] M. I. Norton and D. Airely, "Building a Better America—One Wealth Quintile at a Time," *Perspectives on Psychological Science* 6 (2011), pp. 9–12.

[29] Ibid.

[30] G. C. Homans, *Social Behavior: Its Elementary Forms*, rev. ed. (New York: Harcourt, Brace, Jovanovich, 1974 [1961]).

opt for equality in making certain kinds of distributions but for fairness (generally called equity by experimenters) in making others.[31] Depending on what is at stake, they may go with a different principle. An everyday example is a group of friends paying the bill in restaurants. They generally opt for tab splitting, but less often if there is big variation in what people have consumed.

Other studies have people to make society-wide rather than individual distributions. They tend to support Brickman's claim that moving to higher levels of social aggregation affects how people frame distributional questions. When asked if "the fairest way of distributing wealth and income would be to give everyone an equal share," about one-third of Americans concur. This percentage drops markedly when people are presented with a statement to the effect that "under a fair economic system people with more ability would earn higher salaries."[32] Swift, Marshall, and Burgoyne asked people to decide if those working in different professions of different gender and marital statuses were over- or underpaid. Their findings support other studies that indicate that Americans consider fairness the most applicable principle to income distribution. However, they also think equality germane because they favor income distributions less unequal than they are in practice.[33] Occupation turns out to be the single most important variable, with participants favoring more rewards for those in high-status professions.[34] However, a 2016 Gallup poll found that 63 percent of Americans think that rich Americans pay too little in taxes, down from a high of 77 percent in the 1990s.[35] British distributional

---

[31] For discussion, Jerald Greenberg and Ronald L. Cohen, *Equality and Justice in Social Behavior* (New York: Academic Press, 1982); Morton Deutsch, *Distributive Justice* (New Haven, CT: Yale University Press, 1985), evaluated the two principles and "winner takes all" under different conditions. Also, Melvin J. Lerner and Susan Clayton, *Justice and Self-Interest; Two Fundamental Motives* (New York: Cambridge University Press, 2011). pp. 40–58.

[32] Hebert McCloskey and John Zaller, *The American Ethos: Public Attitudes toward Capitalism and Democracy* (Cambridge, MA: Harvard University Press, 1984), pp. 154–56.

[33] Adam G. Swift, Gordon Marshall, and Carole Burgoyne, "Which Road to Social Justice?" *Sociology Review* 2, no. 2 (1992), pp. 28–31.

[34] G. Jasso and P. H. Rossi, "Distributive Justice and Earned Income," *American Sociological Review* 42, no. 4 (1977), pp. 639–51; W. M. Alves, "Modeling Distributive Justice Judgments," in Peter H. Rossi and Steven L. Nock, eds., *Measuring Social Judgments* (Beverley Hills, CA: Sage, 1982), pp. 205–34; W. M. Alves and P. H. Rossi, "Who Should Get What? Fairness Judgments of the Distribution of Earnings," *American Journal of Sociology* 84, no. 3 (1978), pp. 541–64; Sidney Verba and Gary R. Orren, *Equality in America: The View from the Top* (Cambridge, MA: Harvard University Press, 1985).

[35] Frank Newport, "Americans Still Say Upper-Income Pay Too Little in Taxes," *Gallup*, 15 April 2016, http://www.gallup.com/poll/190775/americans-say-upper-income-pay-little-taxes.aspx (accessed 27 May 2021).

preferences are roughly similar, although they reveal a greater commitment to equality.[36]

Presumably, this pattern, if not universal, is widespread, and would apply just as much to states as to individuals within them. The studies focus on the distribution of wealth, but the preferences they reveal are likely to carry over to the distribution of power as well. Equality paved the way for and legitimized democracy, which is based on the principle that all citizens are equal and should share power. This is feasible in communes, kibbutzim, and New England town meetings, where the number of people involved is small enough to allow for the direct democracy. Elsewhere, representative democracy is the norm, and elected officials wield power. However, they are responsible to an electorate and can be recalled or defeated when up for re-election.

Great powers and superpowers have wielded considerable authority without the legitimation provided by elections. They must accordingly find other ways to legitimize their authority and the status that accompanies it. Charles Kindleberger, who first theorized hegemonic stability theory, expects a hegemon to perform three functions: agenda setting, economic management, and sponsorship.[37] Simon Reich and Ned Lebow argue that in the post–Cold War era the United States no longer performs any of these functions. It has exploited its position as the world's leading economy to become the world's biggest borrower. It often uses its leadership to maintain the status quo in face of widespread demands for change; it has consistently opposed progressive international measures of all kinds, from the International Court of Justice to the treaty banning landmines to the responsibility to protect civilians in conflict zones. The United States is widely regarded as a principal threat to world peace, especially in the aftermath of its invasions of Afghanistan and Iraq.[38]

Hēgemonia and *wangdao* can be achieved and maintained by performing these three functions in a collaborative way and in the interests of the community as a whole. This is a very different conception from hegemony, although it incorporates the three functions imputed to it.

Agenda setting can function in a top-down or bottom-up fashion. China or the United States can author initiatives that others will see in their interest, or back those mooted by other actors. Successful agenda setting requires

---

[36] James R. Kluegel and Eliot R. Smith, *Beliefs about Inequality: Americans' View of What Is and What Ought to Be* (New York: Aldine, 1986); Joanna Mack and Stuart Lansley, *Poor Britain* (London: Allen & Unwin, 1985); Tom W. Smith, "Inequality and Welfare," in Roger Jowell, Sharon Witherspoon, and Lindsay Brook, eds., *British Social Attitudes: Special International Report* (Aldershot: Gower, 1989), pp. 59–77.

[37] Charles P. Kindleberger, *The World in Depression, 1929–1939* (Berkeley: University of California Press, 1973).

[38] Reich and Lebow, *Good-Bye Hegemony!*

knowledge and manipulation of appropriate discourses.[39] It demands insight into how other actors define their interests, what problems they consider critical, and what responses they consider appropriate. In contrast to the realist emphasis on material power, agenda setting emphasizes cultural and political sensitivity and values persuasion over coercion. It brings about collective action through effective appeals to shared values and norms. Power is important but understood as embedded in institutional and normative structures. Normative influence is heavily dependent on political skill, and all the more so in a world in which so many, if not most, important initiatives are multilateral.

The problem of civilian protection offers a telling example of how the United States stood in the way of agenda setting. As noted in chapter 8, Norway, far from being a great power, nevertheless played an important role in the promotion of the concept of civilian protection. In the 1990s, the Norwegian government awarded funds to the Peace Research Institute of Oslo to think through the concept and what would be required to implement it.[40] In the UN, Norway worked with middle powers like Canada to promote human security. The Norwegians focused much of their efforts on promoting the "responsibility to protect" (R2P) doctrine in collaboration with other states and NGOs, including the Brussels-based International Crisis Group. R2P inverts the traditional realist focus on sovereignty and the rights of states by stressing their responsibility to protect civilians or be subject to the prospect of multilateral intervention.[41] By 2001, the R2P initiative had gained significant momentum and won the unstinting support of then UN Secretary-General Kofi Annan.[42] By 2005, the language of the R2P doctrine was embraced by the UN as consistent with chapters VI and VIII of the

[39] Michael Barnett and Raymond Duvall, "Power in International Politics," *International Organization* 59, no. 1 (2005), pp. 39–75; Ian Manners, "Normative Power Europe: A Contradiction in Terms?" *Journal of Common Market Studies* 40, no. 2 (2002), pp. 235–58.

[40] Steven Radelet, "A Primer on Foreign Aid," Working Paper no. 92, Center for Global Development, July 2006, p. 5.

[41] Simon Reich, "The Evolution of a Doctrine: The Curious Case of Kofi Annan, George Bush and the Doctrines of Preventative and Preemptive Intervention," in William Keller and Gordon Mitchell, eds., *Hitting First: Preventive Force in US Security Strategy* (Pittsburgh: University of Pittsburgh Press, 2006), pp. 45–69.

[42] "Secretary-General Reflects on 'Intervention' in Thirty-Fifth Annual Ditchley Foundation Lecture," UN Press Release, SG/SM/6613, 26 June 1998, http://www.un.org/News/Press/docs/1998/19980626.sgsm6613.html; Gareth Evans and Mohamed Sahnoun, *The Responsibility to Protect: A Report by the International Commission of Intervention and State Sovereignty* (Ottawa: International Development Research Center, December 2001), http://www.dfait-maeci. gc.ca/iciss-ciise/pdf/Commission-Report.pdf; Simon Reich, "Power, Institutions and Moral Entrepreneurs," ZEF-Discussion Papers on Development Policy No. 65, Center for Development Research (ZEF), Bonn, March 2003, http://www.zef.de/publications.html; (all accessed 27 May 2021); Bruce W. Jentleson, "Coercive Prevention: Normative, Political and Policy Dilemmas," *Peaceworks*, no. 35 (Washington, DC: United States Institute of Peace, October 2000), p. 20.

UN Charter. At that time, over 150 world leaders adopted R2P, legitimating the use of force through multilateral intervention initiatives sanctioned by the UN Security Council.[43] Good diplomacy and legitimacy trumped power.

The second constituent of hegemony is economic management. In the post-hegemonic era this function is primarily *custodial*. Custodianship entails the management of risk through market signaling (information passed, intentionally or not, among market participants) and intergovernmental negotiations in a variety of venues. The intent, according to Kindleberger, is to stabilize and undergird the functions of the global economic system.[44] His formulation became foundational for his realist and liberal successors as they seek to justify the global need for continued American hegemony.[45] However, America has either willingly contravened, or is increasingly incapable of performing, these functions.

The United States routinely transgresses the principle of free trade. President Trump has been the most egregious offender, rejecting the North American Free Trade Agreement (NAFTA), coercing Canada and Mexico into renegotiating the treaty, and, far more threatening to international stability, waging an escalating trade war with China. American unilateralism and abuses go back to 1973 and the Nixon administration's closing of the "gold window." It shook the foundations of the global economic order by unilaterally ending the convertibility of the dollar. The United States subsequently exploited its dominant economic position by borrowing vast sums of money and at times running high rates of inflation that it would not have been possible for any other country to do without encountering sanctions.[46] Chinese and Japanese investors subsidize American consumers. The United States has been a regular exploiter, rather than provider, of public goods. It was responsible for the 2008 Great Recession through lax financial regulation. During the Vietnam War and the Great Recession, Washington's exploitation of its position destabilized existing patterns of global finance.[47] The image of American "hegemony" as characterized by a broader, enlightened conception

[43] United Nations General Assembly, "2005 World Summit Outcome," Articles 138 and 139, A/60/L.1, 15 September 2005.

[44] In more formal terms, these economic functions consist of maintaining an open market for distress goods; providing countercyclical lending; policing a stable system of exchange rates; ensuring the coordination of macroeconomic policies; and acting as a lender of last resort. Kindleberger, *The World in Depression*, p. 305.

[45] G. John Ikenberry, *A World Safe for Democracy: Liberal Internationalism and the Crises of Global Order* (New Haven, CT: Yale University Press, 2020).

[46] Joanne Gowa, *Closing the Gold Window: Domestic Politics and the End of Bretton Woods* (Ithaca, NY: Cornell University Press, 1983); Fred Block, *The Origins of International Economic Disorder: A Study of United States International Monetary Policy from World War II to the Present* (Berkeley: University of California Press, 1977), pp. 182–98.

[47] Block, *Origins of International Economic Disorder*, pp. 182–98.

of self-interest is sharply contradicted by short-sighted, self-serving, unilateral American behavior.

Like America, China portrays itself as a contributor to the global economy. In many respects it undoubtedly is. In the ten years through 2019, China, on average, accounted for about one third of global economic growth, larger than the combined share of global growth from the United States, Europe, and Japan.[48] It has lifted 800 million people out of poverty, a tremendous contribution to global development and stability. But it has also sparked criticisms of "predatory economics," especially from Western governments and commentators. The Trump and Biden administrations accused China of unfair trade practices, especially forced transfer of technology and theft of intellectual property and trade secrets. Some of these accusations have merits, although it is unfair to blame trade with China for the woes of American manufacturing.[49] China is yet to fulfill all the terms of its accession to the World Trade Organization in 2001, even though it has met most of them.[50] Beijing has also been accused of "predatory liberalism," the practice of leveraging the vulnerabilities of market interdependence to exert power over others in pursuit of political goals, whether over non-governmental entities such as the National Basketball Association or states such as Australia.[51] More broadly, China is deficient in its attention to the massive effects—negative as well as positive—of its phenomenal economic rise on the rest of the world. It is remarkable that it still clings to the identity of a developing country despite having become world's second largest economy and claiming leadership status in global governance.

For the time being the global economic system functions, for better and worse, without a responsible leader. Leadership, economic management, and security provisions are no longer interrelated. Key management functions— providing market liquidity, reinforcing open trading patterns, market and currency stability, and reinforcing patterns of economic development—take place without a hegemon. Divorced from the concept of hegemony, these functions are best described as "custodianship."

The third element of hegemony is *sponsorship*. It encompasses enforcement of rules, norms, agreements, and decision-making processes as well

---

[48] Andy Rothman, "The Benefits of Engagement," *Wire China*, 28 March 2021, https://www.thewirechina.com/2021/03/28/the-benefits-of-engagement/ (accessed 31 May 2021).

[49] Ibid. The American government is more guilty of failing to help American workers who have suffered the negative consequences of change, whether due to imports or to technology (especially automation).

[50] Yeling Tan, "How the WTO Changed China: The Mixed Legacy of Economic Engagement," *Foreign Affairs* 100, no. 2 (2021), pp. 90–102.

[51] Victor Cha and Andy Lim, "Flagrant Foul: China's Predatory Liberalism and the NBA," *Washington Quarterly* 42, no. 4 (2020), pp. 23–42.

as the maintenance of security to enhance trade and finance.[52] Liberals and realists consistently maintain that only hegemons can provide such enforcement because of their preponderance of material power. They assume that American hegemony is legitimate in the eyes of other important actors who welcome its leadership and enforcement as beneficial to global stability and their national interests. When empirical support is mustered for these claims, the foreign voices invariably cited are conservative politicians in allied states or authoritarian leaders who benefit personally from US backing. During the Cold War, German conservatives welcomed US leadership as a means of offsetting Soviet power and of constraining Social Democratic opponents. Leaders of South Korea, Taiwan, South Vietnam, the Philippines, Iran, Egypt, and various Latin American states were, to varying degrees, dependent on US military and foreign aid and happy to say in public what Washington wanted to hear to keep these dollars flowing. Their opponents regarded US influence as regressive as it supported regimes opposed to democracy and human rights.

There has been a noticeable decline in pleas for US leadership since the end of the Cold War, and as noted earlier, a corresponding increase in opposition to US military and economic initiatives. Since the Iraq War, the United States has undergone a shift in its profile from a status quo to a revisionist power. A BBC World Service poll dated 3 July 2017 revealed increasingly negative views of the United States, rising to majorities, as are now found in several of its NATO allies, including the United Kingdom (up from 42% to 64%), Spain (44% to 67%), France (41% to 56%), and Turkey (36% to 64%). Negative opinion has also sharply risen in the Latin American nations of Mexico (up from 41% to 59%) and Peru (29% to 49%). In Russia, negative views of the United States have risen from 55 percent to 64 percent.[53] By September 2020, views of the United States reached an all-time low across thirteen countries, with only 34 percent having confidence in the country or its president.[54] This and other surveys indicate that the United States is not perceived as acting in the interests of the international community. Whatever legitimacy its leadership once had has significantly eroded as publics around the world are particularly worried about the way in

---

[52] Simon Reich, *Global Norms, American Sponsorship and the Emerging Patterns of World Politics* (New York: Palgrave-Macmillan, 2010), pp. 62–63.

[53] BBC World Service, Media Centre, "Sharp Drop in World Views of US, UK: Global Poll for BBC World Service," 4 July 2017, https://www.statista.com/statistics/246420/major-foreign-holders-of-us-treasury-debt/ (accessed 26 May 2021).

[54] BBC World Service, Media Centre, "Global Perception of US Falls to Two-Decade Low," 15 September 2020, https://www.bbc.com/news/world-us-canada-54169732 (accessed 26 May 2021).

which the United States uses its military power.[55] Not surprisingly, respect for the United States took a big dip during the Trump presidency, with Europeans and others appalled by the administration's response to the COVID pandemic.[56]

Leadership and legitimacy are closely connected, and enforcement clearly depends on the latter. In situations where US efforts at enforcement have been seen as legitimate (e.g., Korea, the First Gulf War), international support has been forthcoming, and with it, backing by relevant regional and international organizations, notably the UN Security Council. Key to the legitimacy of enforcement has been a common perception of threat but also a commitment on Washington's part to limit its military action in pursuit of a consensus. It often requires collaborative decisions concerning processes of implementation as well. The Truman administration won support for the liberation of South Korea, but not the invasion of the North, and George H. W. Bush for the liberation of Kuwait, but not the overthrow of Saddam Hussein. When George W. Bush insisted on the invasion of Iraq with the goal of removing Saddam, he was unable to gain support from NATO or the UN. When the administration went to war in the absence of international institutional support, it had to cobble together a coalition based largely on bribes and threats. Its subsequent decline in standing was precipitous, and this began before the insurgency in Iraq.

China has set its gaze on international leadership since President Xi came to power in 2012. Announcing that China is moving closer to the center stage of world affairs, Xi has been actively pushing for Chinese leadership in global governance. This leadership is most manifest on the economic front. China is investing heavily in all forms of technology from clean energy to artificial intelligence and has made notable strides. It has set out a grand vision for global connectivity, the Belt and Road Initiative (BRI), which, if suitably devised and implemented, could transform the international landscape. But the BRI is also self-serving; one of its initial impetuses was to offload Chinese overcapacity in heavily polluting industries such as steel and glass by building infrastructure elsewhere. By offering financial and technical assistance to other, usually developing, countries, China also hopes to gain political influence and economic clout in

---

[55] Pew Research Center, "Obama More Popular Abroad Than at Home, Global Image of US Continues to Benefit," 17 June 2011, http://www.pewglobal.org/2010/06/17/obama-more-popular-abroad-than-at-home/ (accessed 26 September 2011); Pew Research Global Attitudes Project, "Global Opinion of Obama Slips, International Policies Faulted," 13 June 2012, http://www.pewglobal.org/2012/06/13/global-opinion-of-obama-slips-international-policies-faulted/ (accessed 28 January 2013).

[56] Pew Research Center, "U.S. Image Plummets Internationally as Most Say Country Has Handled Coronavirus Badly," 15 September 2020, https://www.pewresearch.org/global/2020/09/15/us-image-plummets-internationally-as-most-say-country-has-handled-coronavirus-badly/ (accessed 28 May 2021).

these countries. And, as noted, the sharp edge of China's economic strategy does not inspire confidence in its leadership. It has wielded its economic leverage not to advance global goods such as containing nuclear proliferation but instead to punish other countries for perceived political transgressions. Unless and until China is willing and able to bring others to the table to forge consensus, and to align and, if necessary, subordinate its own narrow interests to those of the larger international community, global leadership will prove elusive.[57]

The theoretical and policy lessons of these experiences are straightforward. Material power is a necessary but insufficient condition for enforcement. The latter depends on legitimacy, which is the most important component of influence. In its absence, even successful enforcement—as defined by Washington or Beijing—will not be perceived as such by other states, and possibly as aggrandizement as the Iraq invasion was by public opinion in France, Germany, Canada, and Japan. China's BRI is sometimes interpreted as a ploy to weaken target countries' political and economic sovereignty in the service of China's mercantilist interests. Such perceptions undermine legitimacy and make future enforcement more difficult.

The functions of agenda setting, custodianship, and sponsorship overlap in part. All confer advantages to states that perform them and to the community at large. They require consultation, bargaining, and consensus, but also reflect competition and jockeying for influence among powerful states. We suggest neither that there is, nor that there should be, a division of labor in the global system. Decisions to perform these functions are driven by cultural conceptions, domestic politics, and consideration of national self-interest. Within limits, powerful actors generally attempt to exert what degrees of influence they can. This will depend in part on the nature of their resources but also the priorities they establish and their legitimacy in the eyes of other actors. They are also affected by domestic and international constraints and opportunities.

All three functions of hegemony require contingent forms of influence rather than the blunt exercise of power. Their application is becoming increasingly diffused among states, rather than concentrated in the hands of a hegemon. These functions are performed by multiple states, sometimes in collaboration with non-state actors. Global governance practices are sharply at odds with the formulations of realists and liberals alike. Western Europeans have made consistent efforts to extend their normative influence by promoting agendas well beyond those with which they are traditionally associated. These include environmental and human rights initiatives, but also security issues and corporate

---

[57] Elizabeth Economy, "China: Pretender to the Throne," Council on Foreign Relations, 8 January 2018, https://www.cfr.org/blog/china-pretender-throne (accessed 31 May 2021).

regulation. Asian states, most notably China, have increasingly assumed a custodial role, as reflected in the China-centered BRI and the Asian Infrastructure
Investment Bank.

It is time for the United States and China to adjust their goals and methods
to a world in which hegemony is impossible and counterproductive if it could
be achieved, in which power must be masked to be used effectively and can only
be so in pursuit of objectives accepted as legitimate by other actors. American
leaders need to lead in different ways than they have in the past but also be prepared to follow. This approach to the world is more sophisticated and more appropriate to contemporary conditions and ultimately will gain more respect and
influence than crude assertions of power.

Joseph Nye Jr. has attracted a lot of attention with his concept of soft power.
It is said to derive from the worldwide appeal of American culture and its way
of life. [58] Consumption of Coca-Cola, the sporting of blue jeans, and interest
in American TV and movies are assumed, in unspecified ways, to make foreign publics more receptive and supportive of US foreign policy goals.[59] Nye
concedes that soft power, like material power, is diffuse, reliant on both local
interpreters and a willing audience. Governments accordingly find it difficult
to exploit soft power or anticipate its outcomes. Senior American policymakers
nevertheless routinely invoke "soft power" as another mechanism for enhancing
US influence.[60]

The logic that leads from attraction to American culture and its products to
support for American foreign policy is unclear. It is also questionable. The appeal of Japanese electronics, Chinese clothes, and Cuban cigars has not made
Americans any more pro-Japanese, Chinese, or Cuban. Quite the reverse is the
case in response to the "invasion" of Chinese products in European and American
markets.[61] There has been an equally negative reaction to some American
exports, like McDonald's and other fast-food chains, and computer and Internet
giants like Microsoft, Facebook, and Amazon. They have aroused anti-American
feeling in Europe and some have become the target of attacks and demonstrations.
Most consumers seem capable of distinguishing between a country's products
and its policies. Every anti-American demonstration in Europe and Asia features

---

[58] Joseph Nye Jr., *Soft Power: The Means to Success in World Politics* (New York: Public Affairs,
2004), pp. 5–11.

[59] Joseph S. Nye Jr., "The Future of American Power," *Foreign Affairs* 89, no. 6 (2010), pp. 2–14;
G. John Ikenberry, *Liberal Order and Imperial Ambition* (Cambridge: Polity, 2006), pp. 1–18, and
America Unrivaled: The Future of the Balance of Power (Ithaca, NY: Cornell University Press, 2002).

[60] Hillary Rodham Clinton, "Leading through Civilian Power: Redefining American Diplomacy
and Development," *Foreign Affairs* 89, no. 6 (2010), pp. 13–24.

[61] Globescan/PIPA poll, "Global Views of United States Improves While Others Decline," BBC
Views, 18 April 2010, p. 7.

protesters clad in jeans. Those few American products—often movies or TV shows—that are distinctly opposed to the American imperial project are extremely popular abroad. They may build respect for American democracy and toleration of dissent, but certainly not for its foreign policies.

Smart power should not be confused with soft power. It has nothing to do with the alleged appeal of a country's culture, political system, or way of life to others. It is not directed in the first instance at influencing public opinion in other countries, although this may be a positive side effect. It is a foreign policy anchored in an astute understanding of what is good for the country in the longer term. Its starting point is the recognition, to paraphrase John Donne, that no country is an island unto itself. All live check-to-jowl in an increasingly dependent world. Each state accordingly must assume certain responsibilities with respect to the other, and more so the richer and more powerful they are. Donne's poem starts from the recognition that individuals can only lead fulfilling lives as members of communities and must pursue their interests within them, not in opposition to them. The stronger and more robust the community, the more secure the individual and the greater the possibility of fulfilling their substantive, emotional, and intellectual needs and desires. The same is true for states. Smart leaders recognize this reality and make the preservation and prospering of the international community one of the core concerns. Policies that foster its well-being often take the form of agenda setting, economic management, and sponsorship. Other forms of public service include peacekeeping, foreign aid and technical assistance, and the welcoming of immigrants and refugees.

Smart foreign policy recognizes the relationship between respect and influence. In past centuries, status was achieved by military prowess. In was the sine qua non for recognition as a great power. Today, conquest is illegal and unacceptable, and countries who use force without the prior approval of relevant regional and international organizations lose status. This was evident in the aftermath of the American invasions of Afghanistan and Iraq and subsequent use of drones in multiple countries to attack suspected terrorists. We have no doubt that public opinion polls will show an even steeper drop in Russia's evaluation after its invasion of Ukraine. China in turn declined in status by economic coercion and threats to use force to make good its claims to island and islets disputed with its neighbors. Partly as a result, in the first two decades of the present century positive evaluations of China plummeted in Asia and the West. According to a 2019 Pew survey, in the Philippines positive attitudes toward China declined from 63 percent in 2002 to 42 percent in 2019, in Australia from 52 to 36 percent, in Indonesia from 73 percent to 36 percent, in South Korea from 66 percent to 34 percent, in India from 35 percent to 23 percent, and in Japan from 55 percent to 14 percent.[62]

---

[62] Pew Research Center, "China's Economic Growth Mostly Welcomed in Emerging Markets, but Neighbors Wary of Its Influence," December 2019, https://www.pewresearch.org/global/2019/

Today, status is achieved and maintained in different ways. Its principal markers are the wealth and well-being of one's citizens, cultural, scientific, and other achievements; the sharing of these benefits with other countries; and the kinds of contributions to the international community represented by agenda setting, economic management, and sponsorship. The quest for *hēgemonia* and *wangdao* is a time-honored strategy but is achieved in different ways today than it was in ancient Greece or imperial China. The overall relationship has not changed; great powers gain recognition, and the leadership is welcomed to the extent they are perceived to act in the general interest. This requires the kind of positive initiatives we have discussed but also self-restraint. Great powers must not abuse their power to achieve wealth or other goals at the expense of others. *Hēgemonia* and *wangdao* also require some degree political restraint that includes allowing or encouraging others to voice their views and needs and to assume their share of responsibility for proposing and helping to implement common initiatives.

This is where Sino-American rapprochement and global order converge. Both superpowers have legitimate security and economic concerns. They can be pursued in collaboration with other powers or in competition with them. Competition between the two superpowers is inevitable, but China and America will gain more through cooperative relationships with each other and with other countries. Toward this end, they must listen more than they speak, and respond to the needs, and better yet, the initiatives of others. By benefiting the world community, they will gain respect and legitimacy for their leadership.

Great Learning

We close this book by returning to where we started: with principles of justice. But we want to advance the global justice agenda by offering a new vision based on our comparative study of Chinese and Western conceptions of justice. In chapter 5 we posed the question of how to expand the circles of justice from the smallest unit of society (usually the individual) to the largest social aggregations (usually some conceptions of the world) and derived some initial answers.

Chinese and Western thinkers adopt overlapping but distinct approaches to this question. Jews initially focused on the family and later extended ethics to embrace other members of their community, and in the rabbinic era, people more generally. Greeks scaled up from individuals to families, to cities, and to

12/05/chinas-economic-growth-mostly-welcomed-in-emerging-markets-but-neighbors-wary-of-its-influence/ (accessed 31 May 2021).

relations among them, but the scope of the Greek conception was limited to the Hellas; barbarians were kept out of the Hellenic world, to whom the rules that regulate relations among the Greeks did not apply. Christians developed a more universalist understanding of community and ethics, but in practice made sharp distinctions between themselves and others. The dissonance created by such contradictions had to be reduced by perceptual sleights of hand. In the colonial era, colonists everywhere devised stereotypes of the colonized to reconcile their Christian beliefs with the barbaric treatment of those they colonized.

Like Jews and Greeks, Chinese Confucians also sought to expand the circles of justice through the mechanism of extension, but in a distinct way. They started with personal cultivation and love of family, and sought to extend this sentiment out to community, nation, and eventually the whole world. No other work represents this conception of the ever expanding circles of justice better than the Confucian classic *Great Learning* (daxue 大學):

> The ancients who sought to demonstrate real excellence to the whole world first brought proper order to their states; in seeking to bring proper order to their states, they first set their families right; in seeking to set their families right, they first cultivated their own persons; in seeking to cultivate their persons, they first knew what is proper in their own heart-and-minds; in seeking to know what is proper in their heart-and-minds, they first became sincere in their purposes; in seeking to become sincere in their purposes, they first become comprehensive in their wisdom. And the highest wisdom lies in seeing how things fit together most productively.
>
> Once they saw how things fit together most productively, their wisdom reached its heights; once their wisdom reached its heights, their thoughts were sincere; once their thoughts were sincere, their heart-and-minds knew what is proper; once their heart-and-minds knew what is proper, their persons were cultivated; once their persons were cultivated, their families were set right; once their families were set right, their state was properly ordered; and once their states were properly ordered, there was peace in the world.[63]

The central message of these passages, as Roger Ames observes, is that "personal, familial, social, political, and indeed cosmic cultivation is ultimately coterminous and mutually entailing."[64] And yet the Confucian priority is always

---

[63] Zhu Xi [朱熹], *Sishu zhangju jizhu* [四書章句集註 Commentaries on the Four Books] (Beijing: Zhonghua shuju, 2016), pp. 3–4. Translation, with minor modifications, is taken from Roger T. Ames, *Confucian Role Ethics: A Vocabulary* (Honolulu: University of Hawai'i Press, 2011), p. 93.

[64] Ames, *Confucian Role Ethics*, p. 92.

personal cultivation. As the *Great Learning* again says: "From the emperor down to the common folk, everything is rooted in personal cultivation."[65]

We can draw from these insights a Confucian theory of global justice that might be called "cultivationist extensionism." It is cultivationist because it holds that justice, of whatever kind and scope, depends ultimately on personal cultivation. It is tempting to see this emphasis on personal cultivation as a sort of learning-centered Confucian individualism, distinct from rights-based liberal individualism. The theory is extensionist because it conceives of a concentric circle of justice and extends those circles from the individual to the family to the community to the state and finally to the world, potentially leaving no one and nothing outside. Justice ripples out, as it were, in concentric circles from personal cultivation within the family to different kinds of communities and then return again to nourish the person in the family.

This mutually entailing, concentric-circle conception of justice transcends the cosmopolitanism vs. communitarianism and particularism vs. universalism divides in current theories of global justice. Cosmopolitanism privileges individual human freedom above all else, for the universal realization of which it is willing to batter down cultural, ethnic, and national barriers; communitarians emphasize the community-bound nature of the individual and argue that ethics are embedded in local cultures and practices and cannot be imposed from outside.[66] Cosmopolitanism gives rise to a universalism of applying a single set of ethical standards—individual liberty and human rights—to the whole of humanity, while communitarianism leans toward a particularism of emphasizing local conditions, although the universalism-particularism divide is a general moral controversy not confined to the cosmopolitan-communitarian debate.[67]

As we have seen in earlier chapters, Confucianism, like cosmopolitanism, recognizes equal human worth everywhere in the world, but this recognition is not coupled with a universalism of imposing Confucian principles. Broad principles exist, such as *shu* (恕 putting oneself in the other's place), but their applications always depend on local contexts. In this sense the Confucian perspective may be called particularistic cosmopolitanism. On the other hand, although like communitarianism it emphasizes local culture and community, it promotes with equal force a mechanism of extending humaneness from the local to the universal, for it regards humaneness as the common core of humanity. In

---

[65] Zhu, *Sishu zhangju jizhu*, p. 4; Ames, *Confucian Role Ethics*, p. 93.

[66] Gillian Brock, "Cosmopolitanism," in William Edelglass and Jay L. Garfield, eds., *The Oxford Handbook of World Philosophy* (Oxford: Oxford University Press, 2011), pp. 582–95.

[67] Chandran Kukathas, "Moral Universalism and Cultural Difference," in John S. Dryzek, Bonnie Honig, and Anne Phillips, eds., *The Oxford Handbook of Political Theory* (Oxford: Oxford University Press, 2008), pp. 581–98.

this sense it can be called universalistic communitarianism.[68] It can hold these apparently paradoxical positions because it believes, as the *Great Learning* teaches, that personal cultivation, and by extension the cultivation of communities of various scope, can help to put particularism generated out of the local context to a universal application.

Perhaps most important, the cultivationist theory offers a new foundation for global ethics and justice. Western philosophers from Socrates onward have tried to discover the foundations of ethics. In modern times this search has boiled down to the tension between reason and emotion. The utilitarians and contract theorists uphold reason, while sentimentalists such as David Hume and the later Romantics emphasize emotion. Surveying a range of ethical theories, Simon Blackburn concludes that the foundations of moral motivations are not the procedural rules derivable from Kantian or utilitarian reason, but the feelings to which we can rise. He observes that Kongzi saw the human emotion of humaneness (*ren* 仁) as the indispensable root of ethics.[69]

Humaneness, the *Great Learning* tells us, is the foundation of ethical life upon which personal cultivation and family living are based. By the logic of extension, it is also the foundation of global justice. Perhaps Hume, with his emphasis on sentiment, would agree. We began this book by discovering that equality and fairness are common principles of justice across the East and West, albeit with different forms and manifestations. We close this book by pointing to another, and deeper, common ground between Eastern and Western thought—that humaneness or compassion is the foundation of our moral life. In the emerging world where the West will need to share wealth, power, and cultural and political authority with the East, these two common grounds—the principles and foundation of justice—suggest ample room for East-West accommodation, if not harmony.

---

[68] For an interesting discussion along these lines, see A. T. Nuyen, "Confucianism, Globalization and the Idea of Universalism," *Asian Philosophy* 13, no. 2-3 (2003), pp. 75–86.

[69] Simon Blackburn, *Ethics: A Very Short Introduction* (Oxford: Oxford University Press, 2001), p. 114.

INDEX